AF739104

OXFORD STUDIES IN EUROPEAN LAW

Series Editors

PAUL CRAIG

Professor of English Law at St John's College, Oxford

GRÁINNE DE BÚRCA

Professor of Law at the European University Institute, and Florence Ellinwood Allen Professor of Law at New York University

The Eurosceptic Mobilization of Constitutional Law

OXFORD STUDIES IN EUROPEAN LAW

Series Editors:

Paul Craig, Professor of English Law at St John's College, Oxford, and
Gráinne de Búrca, Professor of Law at the European University Institute, and
Florence Ellinwood Allen Professor of Law at New York University

The aim of this series is to publish important and original research on EU law. The focus is on scholarly monographs, with a particular emphasis on those which are interdisciplinary in nature. Edited collections of essays will also be included where they are appropriate. The series is wide in scope and aims to cover studies of particular areas of substantive and of institutional law, historical works, theoretical studies, and analyses of current debates, as well as questions of perennial interest such as the relationship between national and EU law and the novel forms of governance emerging in and beyond Europe. The fact that many of the works are interdisciplinary will make the series of interest to all those concerned with the governance and operation of the EU.

OTHER TITLES IN THIS SERIES

The Competence Question in the (Con)Federal European Union
Sacha Garben

The Law of EU Border Controls
Constitutional Compliance and Conditions for an Area without Internal Frontiers
Leandro Mancano

Protecting EU Consumers in Internet of Things Ecosystems
The Intersection between Consumer, Competition, and Data
Christof Koolen

When Deportation Fails
Non-Removable Migrants in the European Union
Diego Ginés Martín

EU Values in Investment Law and Policy
Promises of Democracy and Rule of Law?
Maria Laura Marceddu

Legal Mobilization for Migrant Rights
Opportunities and Barriers at the European Court of Justice
Virginia Passalacqua

Saving the European Union from its Illiberal Member States
András Jakab and Lando Kirchmair

Constitutional Disintegration and Disruption
Withdrawal and Opt-Outs from the European Union
Oliver Garner

Business Freedoms and Fundamental Rights in European Union Law
Niall O'Connor

Compliance with European Consumer Law
The Case of E-Commerce
Felix Pflücke

Legislative Authority and Interpretation in the European Union
Martijn van den Brink

Secession and European Union Law
The Deferential Attitude
Núria González Campañá

Fiscal State Aid Law and Harmful Tax Competition in the European Union
Dimitrios Kyriazis

The Abuse of Constitutional Identity in the European Union
Julian Scholtes

Judging European Democracy
The Role and Legitimacy of National Constitutional Courts in the EU
Nik de Boer

EU Values Before the Court of Justice
Foundations, Potential, Risks
Luke Dimitrios Spieker

Postnational Constitutionalism
Europe and the Time of Law
Paul Linden-Retek

The Legislative Priority Rule and the EU Internal Market for Goods
A Constitutional Approach
Eadaoin Ní Chaoimh

The Jurisprudence of Constitutional Conflict in the European Union
Ana Bobić

Reflexive Governance in EU Equality Law
Emma Lantschner

Enhanced Cooperation and European Tax Law
Caroline Heber

The Eurosceptic Mobilization of Constitutional Law

PABLO CASTILLO-ORTIZ
Senior Lecturer, School of Law, University of Sheffield, UK

GIUSEPPE MARTINICO
Full Professor of Comparative Public Law,
Scuola Superiore Sant'Anna, Pisa, Italy

OXFORD
UNIVERSITY PRESS

OXFORD
UNIVERSITY PRESS

Great Clarendon Street, Oxford, OX2 6DP,
United Kingdom

Oxford University Press is a department of the University of Oxford.
It furthers the University's objective of excellence in research, scholarship,
and education by publishing worldwide. Oxford is a registered trade mark of
Oxford University Press in the UK and in certain other countries.

© Pablo Castillo-Ortiz and Giuseppe Martinico 2026

The moral rights of the authors have been asserted.

All rights reserved. No part of this publication may be reproduced, stored in a retrieval system, transmitted, used for text and data mining, or used for training artificial intelligence, in any form or by any means, without the prior permission in writing of Oxford University Press, or as expressly permitted by law, by licence or under terms agreed with the appropriate reprographics rights organization. Enquiries concerning reproduction outside the scope of the above should be sent to the Rights Department, Oxford University Press, at the address above.

You must not circulate this work in any other form
and you must impose this same condition on any acquirer.

Public sector information reproduced under Open Government Licence v3.0
(https://www.nationalarchives.gov.uk/doc/open-government-licence/)

Published in the United States of America by Oxford University Press
198 Madison Avenue, New York, NY 10016, United States of America.

British Library Cataloguing in Publication Data

Data available

Library of Congress Control Number: 2025950530

ISBN 9780198959175

DOI: 10.1093/9780198959205.001.0001

The manufacturer's authorised representative in the EU for product safety is
Oxford University Press España S.A. of El Parque Empresarial San Fernando
de Henares, Avenida de Castilla, 2 – 28830 Madrid (www.oup.es/en or
product.safety@oup.com). OUP España S.A. also acts as importer into Spain
of products made by the manufacturer.

To our families, whose love and patience made this possible

Series Editors Preface

There is, as is well known, a Eurosceptic element within the EU. It is also generally acknowledged that Eurosceptic actors use various strategies to attain their goals, including recourse to national constitutional law and constitutional courts to effectuate their desired ends. However, there has hitherto not been an in-depth study of the ways in which constitutional law has been deployed to realize this end. The present book by Pablo Castillo-Ortiz and Giuseppe Martinico fills this gap.

It explores Eurosceptic constitutional counter-narratives from theoretical, doctrinal, and empirical angles. The theoretical dimension captures the different meanings of Euroscepticism, informed by thoroughgoing examination of the Eurosceptic mobilization of constitutional law. In doctrinal terms, there is analysis of national case law, especially that of constitutional courts, coupled with academic scholarship that seeks to analyse the national legal system and clarify the meaning of its rules. The empirical analysis includes study as to why Eurosceptic parties choose to mobilize constitutional law, and how they do so. There is discussion of the ways in which the mobilization of Eurosceptic constitutional counter-narratives is linked to the contestation of aspects of European integration, such as the role of courts or EU policies.

The book is informed by four case studies—UK, Italy, Spain, and Poland—which facilitate understanding of the ways in which Eurosceptic parties mobilize constitutional law against European integration. The case studies provide an admixture of countries that subscribe to legal constitutionalism (Spain, Italy, and Poland), with the UK providing a case study of how the Eurosceptic mobilization of constitutional law arguments operated in an environment of parliamentary sovereignty. The four case studies are geographically diverse, with one Northern European country, the UK, two Southern European countries, Spain and Italy, and one Eastern European Member State, Poland. The case studies explain the country's constitutional system; explore the position of Eurosceptic political actors when using constitutionalism against European integration; and provide a theoretical and doctrinal analysis of the ways in which the Eurosceptic counter-narratives clash with approaches to the interpretation of national constitutions that are open to supranational law.

This book explores a topic that is important in itself, with broader implications for the future of the European project. It will be of interest to all those who study EU law.

Paul Craig and Gráinne de Búrca

Preface and Acknowledgements

As political scientists have pointed out, a new wave of Euroscepticism is hitting the EU, following the political crisis due to Brexit and the pandemic.[1]

We feel that it is right to make it clear from the outset that this is not a self-defence manual for Europeanists.[2] It is worth clarifying this, since those who argue for the existence of a body of European constitutional law have recently been accused of offering bad faith representations of the allegedly technocratic (and, according to some, even autocratic) and neo-liberal tendencies of the European integration process. It is no coincidence that, for some years now, scholars have accused colleagues interested in European constitutional law of constructing a dangerous mythology and have also boldly suggested that 'it is simply impossible to claim that acknowledging to European law the condition of "constitutional order" is either a neutral way of referring to the object of study of a legal-dogmatic discipline, or a means of promoting the transformation of European law in the semblance of democratic and social constitutionalism'.[3] In works like these, the EU today is depicted as a dangerous and undemocratic entity, the rejection of everything constitutionalism stands for.

Other authors have used the formula 'authoritarian constitutionalism'[4] to define the EU. We believe that this theorizing risks 'stretching' the concept of constitutionalism too far, and applying it to dynamics to which it is alien.[5] We

[1] Vít Hloušek and Vratislav Havlík, 'Eurosceptic Narratives in the Age of COVID-19: The Central European States in Focus' (2024) 40 *East European Politics* 154.

[2] Sergio Fabbrini, *Manuale di autodifesa europeista. Come rispondere alla sfida del sovranismo* (LUISS University Press 2019).

[3] Marco Dani and Agustín J Menéndez, 'European Constitutional Imagination: A Whig Interpretation of the Process of European Integration?' (2020) iCourts Working Paper Series No 243, 42 <https://papers.ssrn.com/sol3/papers.cfm?abstract_id=3807102>.

[4] Michael Wilkinson, 'Authoritarian Liberalism as Authoritarian Constitutionalism' in Helena Alviar Garcia and Günter Frankenberg (eds), *Authoritarian Constitutionalism: Comparative Analysis and Critique* (Edward Elgar 2019) 317.

[5] It is true that authoritarian regimes can be endowed with documents called constitutions, but in these cases they are constitutions without constitutionalism and these fundamental laws will only be instruments of government. See Tom Ginsburg and Alberto Simpser (eds), *Constitutions in Authoritarian Regimes* (Cambridge University Press 2014). The constitutions forged by constitutionalism are much more than this, as they tend not only to protect the power of the contingent majority to govern but also to preserve minorities. This is after all the essence of democracy. Hans Kelsen, *Vom Wesen und Wert der Demokratie* (JBC Mohr 1929) 61.

also believe that calling the EU an 'authoritarian' project misrepresents the nature of the process of European integration.

These readings start from the premise that the EU is something other than national democracies, which are the true homelands of constitutionalism, and that EU law consists of a set of external constraints that limit and condition (conditionality is a key word) national democracies, neutralizing physiological, political, and social conflicts. The image of the EU as an external constraint to democracies has, over the years, become a mantra of the Eurosceptic narrative:

> With the Maastricht Treaty, this constraint was transformed into a key element of the public narrative about 'Europe'. The emphasis placed on budgetary discipline that must be respected to join the Eurozone promoted an identification between tool and objective: the constraint was Europe. The recent economic-financial crises paved the way for a reversal of the meaning of the constraint, which turned into a negative paradigm. This reversal implies a form of 'othering': 'Europe' is opposed to the Italian people. Eurosceptic parties have promoted and taken advantage of this reversal. The alleged otherness of 'Europe' has given them the chance to call for a return to full national sovereignty.[6]

In these works, the EU is seen not only as other than our democracies but also as a threat to democratic political life. This theme is very much present in the arguments used by the opponents of the constitutional interpretation of the EU, according to which the constitutionalization of the EU would automatically lead to the replacement of national constitutions. This idea is related to what we have elsewhere tried to define as the argument of constitutional exhaustiveness[7] and probably finds its roots in the case law of the German Constitutional Court.[8]

According to this argument, the EU could only truly become an entity of constitutional law if it succeeded in replacing national constitutions, centralizing all the constitutional dynamics of the multilevel system and thus exhausting the functions of state constitutions.

[6] Daniele Pasquinucci, 'From Narrative to Counter-narrative: The European Constraint and the Rise of Italian Populist Euroscepticism' (2020) 30 Journal of Contemporary European Studies 39, 39–40. See also Daniele Pasquinucci, *Il frutto avvelenato. Il vincolo europeo e la critica all'Europa* (Mondadori 2022).

[7] Giuseppe Martinico, *Lo spirito polemico del diritto europeo: studio sulle ambizioni costituzionali dell'Unione* (Aracne 2011).

[8] See for instance *BVerfGE 123, 267*, para 216.
2 BvR 2661/06, www.bundesverfassungsgericht.de/entscheidungen/rs20100706_2bvr266106.html.

However, this reasoning overlooks the fact that even in mature federal systems the existence of federal constitutional law does not imply the disappearance of state constitutional laws. The US scholarly debate on subnational constitutionalism[9] and the events in the aftermath of the *Dobbs* ruling[10] seem to confirm this.

Of course, the EU, like any political organization, makes mistakes and errors. However, we believe that many of the failures that are attributed to the EU stem instead from the national level. In this sense, the EU should not be seen as solely responsible for the crisis of national democracies and politics (the EU is often portrayed as a depoliticizing factor[11]); what are described as technocratic degeneracies are actually the product of the paucity of national politics due to the crisis of liberal democracies (and constitutionalism).

What does this book add to the debate? First of all, it brings the perspective of two academics who are interested not only in EU law in the narrow sense but also in comparative constitutional law and politics. This is important because, as we said before, we conceive of the EU as a product of national democracies, not as something external to them. Consequently, we think of the EU as a complex order, based on the nexus between domestic and supranational laws.[12]

In particular, we are interested in how Eurosceptic forces use, and sometimes even manipulate, national constitutional law. Eurosceptic forces try to create an opposition that does not exist between national constitutional law (with all its principles of sovereignty and democracy) and the European legal order. We argue that this is a false opposition, which does not take into account the fact that the EU is the direct product of the constitutional openness that characterizes the particular historical experience that is post-World War II (WWII) constitutionalism. This is why we have decided to begin this contribution with a detailed analysis of the principle of constitutional openness, which is the main antidote to the constitutional counter-narrative of Eurosceptic movements that rely, for example, on a notion of sovereignty that does not correspond to the contents of post-WWII constitutionalism. Of course, such continuity between international and domestic constitutional law does not exclude possible conflicts between national and European courts, and this brings

[9] Robert F Williams and G Alan Tarr, 'Subnational Constitutional Space: A View from the States, Provinces, Regions, Lander, and Cantons' in G Alan Tarr, Robert F Williams, and Joseph Marko (eds), *Federalism, Subnational Constitutions, and Minority Rights* (Praeger 2004) 3; James A Gardner, 'In Search of Sub-National Constitutionalism' (2008) 4 European Constitutional Law Review 325.

[10] *Dobbs v Jackson Women's Health Organization* 597 US (2022).

[11] Alessandro Somma, *Quando l'Europa tradì sé stessa. E come continua a tradirsi nonostante la pandemia* (Laterza 2021) IX.

[12] Giuseppe Martinico, *The Tangled Complexity of the EU Constitutional Process: The Frustrating Knot of Europe* (2nd edn, Routledge 2022).

us to another important point in our book, the need to distinguish between constructive criticism and Euroscepticism.

On this, we have in fact always maintained that European law is polemical in nature,[13] being founded on constitutional conflicts[14] that are much more than juridical: they also have a symbolic scope and dimension because they often touch on the theme of the national identities of member states 'inherent in their fundamental, political and constitutional structure'.[15] However, we also believe that political conflicts exist not only at the national level but also at the supranational level; just think of those that produced the Next Generation EU[16] and those between the European Parliament and the Commission on various political issues, from immigration to the protection of the rule of law.

As said, we do not think that the EU is infallible or unassailable; after all, in our academic works, we have extensively studied the role of national forms of resistance to EU law (or to the European Convention on Human Rights, the ECHR). In this regard, we have put forward the distinction between functional disobedience (to the development of European law) and non-functional disobedience.[17] We also defend the rationale of article 4(2) Treaty on European Union (TEU), suggesting how the European Court of Justice (ECJ) should interpret it, instead of renouncing this provision, which has sometimes been abused by some national constitutional and supreme courts.[18] This is not a mere detail in a historical phase in which articles and blogs have been written

[13] Martinico (n 7).

[14] Constitutional conflicts can be defined as conflicts between the primacy of EU law and national constitutional supremacy, to quote the Spanish Constitutional Court. Tribunal Constitucional, Declaración 1/2004.

[15] Art 4.2 TEU. On article 4.2 TEU, see Barbara Guastaferro, 'Beyond the Exceptionalism of Constitutional Conflict: The Ordinary Functions of the Identity Clause' (2012) 31 Yearbook of European Law 263; Monica Claes, 'National Identity: Trump Card or Up for Negotiation?' in Alejandro Saiz Arnaiz and Carina Alcoberro Llivina (eds), *National Constitutional Identity and European Integration* (Intersentia 2013); Elke Cloots, *National Identity in EU Law* (Hart 2015); Giacomo Di Federico, *L'identità nazionale degli stati membri nel diritto dell'Unione europea. Natura e portata dell'art. 4, par. 2, TUE* (Editoriale Scientifica 2017).

[16] 'We identify three main dimensions of conflict underlying the political negotiations: the fiscal dimension, the rule-of-law dimension and the policy dimension, especially the climate and digitalization agendas', Caroline de la Porte, Mads Dagnis Jensen, 'The Next Generation EU: An Analysis of the Dimensions of Conflict Behind the Deal' (2021) 55 Social Policy & Administration 388, 388.

[17] Giuseppe Martinico, 'The "Polemical" Spirit of European Constitutional Law: On the Importance of Conflicts in EU Law' (2015) 16 German Law Journal 1343; Giuseppe Martinico, 'National Courts and Judicial Disobedience to the ECHR: A Comparative Overview' in Oddný Mjöll Arnardóttir and Antoine Buyse (eds), *Shifting Centres of Gravity in Human Rights Protection. Rethinking Relations between the ECHR, EU, and National Legal Orders* (Routledge 2016) 59; Giuseppe Martinico, 'Functional Disobedience, National Courts and the ECtHR' in András Sajó and Renáta Uitz (eds), *Critical Essays on Human Rights Criticism* (Eleven 2020) 247.

[18] On the abuse of national constitutional identity, see Julian Scholtes, *The Abuse of Constitutional Identity in the European Union* (Oxford University Press 2023).

against the concept of constitutional national identity and the related theory of constitutional pluralism.[19]

However, we think that EU law participates in many of the functions performed by constitutionalism and that the process of European integration is part of what we call open constitutionalism. How? For instance, EU law, through its direct effect,[20] has enriched the set of fundamental rights enjoyed by individuals in the multilevel legal space. This has also been admitted by constitutional courts that have traditionally been 'competitors' to the ECJ, such as the Italian Constitutional Court, which has defined the Charter of Fundamental Rights as a source of an exquisitely constitutional nature.[21] Secondly, EU law helps protect national constitutions in the absence of the possibility of judicial review of legislation.[22] Third, EU law contributes to the functions of constitutionalism by governing new powers, especially those of global tech corporations that are difficult for state law to govern.[23] Finally, EU law, through the procedures designed to defend the values of the Union in article 2 TEU, contributes to creating a system of checks and balances against the hyper-majoritarian approach of populisms in some Member States. For all these reasons, we consider the EU to be an important piece of constitutionalism[24] and are therefore interested in how national constitutional law is mobilized against the primacy of EU law. This does not exclude the fact that national actors can sometimes be right to challenge the work of supranational institutions and can thus exercise a critical function, inducing systemic changes.[25]

[19] Roger Daniel Kelemen and Laurent Pech, 'Why Autocrats Love Constitutional Identity and Constitutional Pluralism. Lessons from Hungary and Poland', Reconnect Working Paper no 2 (2018) <http://icedd.luiss.it/files/2019/02/Why-autocrats-love-constitutional.pdf>; Federico Fabbrini and András Sajó, 'The Dangers of Constitutional Identity' (2019) 25 European Law Journal 457.

[20] ECJ, Case 26/62 *NV Algemene Transport- en Expeditie Onderneming Van Gend en Loos v Netherlands Inland Revenue Administration* ECLI:EU:C:1963:1.

[21] Corte costituzionale, sentenza 269/2017 < www.cortecostituzionale.it>.

[22] As was the case in the United Kingdom according to the well-known Bogdanor's thesis or in the Netherlands where the judicial review of legislation is even prohibited by article 140 of the Grondwet ('Existing Acts of Parliament and other regulations and decrees which are in conflict with an amendment to the Constitution shall remain in force until provisions are made in accordance with the Constitution'). Vernon Bogdanor, *Beyond Brexit: Towards a British Constitution* (IB Tauris 2019); 'The European Union Withdrawal Bill, currently before Parliament, seeks to do something quite unprecedented in the constitutional history of the modern world by withdrawing Britain from a protected constitution into an unprotected one', Vernon Bogdanor, *Brexit and Our Unprotected Constitution* (2018) <https://consoc.org.uk/wp-content/uploads/2018/02/Brexit-and-our-unprotected-constitution-web.pdf>.

[23] ECJ, Case C-131/12 *Google Spain SL v Agencia Española de Protección de Datos (AEPD)* ECLI:EU:C:2014:317.ECJ, Case C-18/18 *Glawischnig-Piesczek v Facebook Ireland Limited* ECLI:EU:C:2019:821.ECJ, Case C-362/14 *Maximillian Schrems v Data Protection Commissioner* ECLI:EU:C:2015:650; Case C-311/18 *Facebook Ireland v Schrems* ECLI:EU:C:2020:559.

[24] Miguel Poiares Maduro, 'Passion and Reason in European Integration' (2010) <https://papers.ssrn.com/sol3/papers.cfm?abstract_id=1709950>.

[25] As happened with the *Frontini* doctrine or the *Solange* doctrine in the 1970s. Corte costituzionale, sentenza 183/1973; BVerfGE 37, 271 2 BvL 52/71 *Solange I*-Beschluß. On the importance of conflicts in

After all, we have also written about the role of constitutional conflicts as an important component in the development of European constitutional law. Clearly, there are elements which, if taken into account, help us distinguish whether national courts are operating in good faith: the level of commitment with which national courts come to terms with the argumentation of the Court of Justice and EU law, the use of the preliminary reference, and, generally, the respect for sincere cooperation.

In this sense, it is possible to identify functional (positive) forms of resistance, insofar as they contribute to the development of supranational case law.[26] There are, of course, instances of 'bad' (non-functional) resistance, such as the Hungarian and Polish cases that were triggered without prior activation of the preliminary mechanism governed by art 267 of the Treaty on the Functioning of the European Union TFEU, as we will see.

Therefore, we believe that it is not true that all resistance to EU law is bad or is based on purely parochial reasons.

* * *

The idea for this book came to us during a wonderful conference organized by our mutual friends Nicoletta Perlo and Aurélie Duffy in Aix-en-Provence in 2023, and devoted to 'La justice constitutionnelle illibérale'. We happened to end up at the same table at dinner and spent a couple of hours catching up on our personal lives (we have been friends for almost ten years, but we had lost touch a little during the pandemic) and talking about future projects. From there, the idea of writing something together was born, and within a few months, that idea turned into a book proposal that we submitted to the editors of the series. Writing a book is an enriching process, but it also takes time away from those who love us, which is why we would like to thank our families for supporting (and putting up with) us over the years. We would also like to thank Oxford University Press and the editors of this prestigious series, Professor

European constitutional law, see Martinico (n 12) and Ana Bobić, *The Jurisprudence of Constitutional Conflict in the European Union* (Oxford University Press 2022).

[26] See those who also read the BVG's reaction to the ECJ judgment in *Weiss* as if it were a call for transparency; on this debate, see Mattias Wendel, 'Constructive Misunderstandings—How the PSPP Conflict was Eventually Settled and How it Reflects Constitutional Pluralism', in Matej Avbelj (ed), *The Future of EU Constitutionalism* (Hart 2023) 53–70. Another example of a functional constitutional conflict is the *Taricco* case; Daniel Sarmiento, 'Adults in the (Deliberation) Room. A comment on M.A.S.' (2018) 37 Quaderni Costituzionali 228. The *Taricco* saga comprises the following decisions: ECJ, Case C-105/14 *Ivo Taricco et al.* ECLI:EU:C:2015:555; Corte costituzionale, ordinanza 24/2017; ECJ, Case C-42/17 *M.A.S. and M.B.* ECLI:EU:C:2017:936; Corte costituzionale, sentenza 115/2018.

Paul Craig and Professor Gráinne De Búrca, for giving us the opportunity to work on this project. This research was funded by the EXPRESS2 ('Specify and Protect the EU Social Contract') project of the European Union (Horizon Europe research and innovation programme under Grant Agreement N° 101132426).[27]

We are grateful to our academic institutions, Scuola Superiore Sant'Anna (Sant'Anna School of Advanced Studies) in Pisa and the University of Sheffield, for their continuous support and encouragement during the preparation of this research. In closing, we would like to thank our friends who provided feedback on the drafts of our chapters. Without their support, we would not have been able to produce a work of such high quality: Antoni Abat i Ninet, Nicola Abate, Pasquale Annicchino, Agnieszka Bień-Kacała, Enrico Bonadio, Edoardo Bressanelli, Josep Maria Castellà Andreu, Pablo Cruz Mantilla de los Ríos, Giacomo Delledonne, Elaine Fahey, Cristina Fasone, Silvia Filippi, Oliver Garner, Katarzyna Granat, Barbara Grabowska-Moroz, Gisela Hernández, David Mier Galera, Jock Gardiner, Matteo Monti, Rachele Marconi, Alberto Nicotina, Leonardo Pierdominici, Paolo Sandro, Orlando Scarcello, Marta Simoncini, Nikos Skoutaris, Oana-Stefan, John Stanton, Francesca Strumia, and Silvia Talavera Lodos.

[27] Whose website is available at: <https://express2project.eu/en>. In this book, all websites were last consulted on 9 June 2025, unless otherwise stated.

Brief Contents

Detailed Contents

1

Constitutionalism and Euroscepticism

1.1. Introduction

Scholars in the field of European politics and law are starting to devote more attention to the use of legal rhetoric and institutions against European integration.[1] The phenomenon itself is not new. There has been a decades-long discussion about the capacity of the European Union to sustain a constitutional democracy.[2] National higher courts have frequently been mobilized against the ratification of European Union Treaties[3] or even against EU law outside the processes of treaty ratification.[4] In academia, however, these phenomena have not been sufficiently studied from a holistic and comprehensive perspective, especially not as a political strategy with far-reaching constitutional implications.

This is surprising, because several political parties have systematically mobilized the law and legal institutions against European integration, whether that has been against the European Union or against other continental organizations such as the Council of Europe.[5] Very frequently, supranational courts have been the preferred object of attack. This is sometimes done very explicitly. For instance, the British Conservatives not only promised an 'in/out of the EU' referendum in their 2015 election manifesto, but the party also pledged

[1] See R Daniel Kelemen and Laurent Pech, 'The Uses and Abuses of Constitutional Pluralism: Undermining the Rule of Law in the Name of Constitutional Identity in Hungary and Poland' (2019) 21 Cambridge Yearbook of European Legal Studies 59; Marlene Wind, 'The Backlash to European Constitutionalism: Why We Should Not Embrace the Identitarian Counter Wave' (2021) 2 Revue Européenne du Droit 48; Petra Bárd and Adam Bodnar, 'The End of an Era. The Polish Constitutional Court's Judgment on the Primacy of EU Law and Its Effects on Mutual Trust' (2021) CEPS Policy Insights No 2021-15.

[2] Julio Baquero Cruz, 'The Legacy of the Maastricht-Urteil and the Pluralist Movement' (2007) European University Institute RSCAS Working Paper 2007/13; Dieter Grimm, 'Does Europe Need a Constitution?' (1995) 1 European Law Journal 282; Neil MacCormick, 'The Maastricht-Urteil: Sovereignty Now' (1995) 1 European Law Journal 259.

[3] Carlos Closa, 'National Higher Courts and the Ratification of EU Treaties' (2013) 36 West European Politics 97; Pablo Castillo-Ortiz, *EU Treaties and the Judicial Politics of National Courts. A Law and Politics Approach* (Routledge 2017).

[4] Bárd and Bodnar (n 1).

[5] Pablo Castillo-Ortiz, 'Right-Wing Eurosceptic Parties and the Strategic Use of Law' (2023) 61 Journal of Common Market Studies 1125.

The Eurosceptic Mobilization of Constitutional Law. Pablo Castillo-Ortiz and Giuseppe Martinico, Oxford University Press. © Pablo Castillo-Ortiz and Giuseppe Martinico 2026. DOI: 10.1093/9780198959205.003.0001

to 'break the formal link between British courts and the European Court of Human Rights, and make our own Supreme Court the ultimate arbiter of human rights matters in the UK'.[6] At other times, the threat is implicit. For example, Vox, in the two 2019 Spanish elections, claimed in its manifesto that it would 'recover national sovereignty in the application of rulings of our courts'.[7]

This book is about political pledges of this type. For a long time, Eurosceptic actors have not only promised to leave European organizations, even if this is their most visible strategy, but have also committed themselves to actions that have great potential to undermine the process of European integration from within. To make these arguments, constitutional law is turned against the EU or the Council of Europe. In this book, we will scrutinize this strategy in detail, analysing its implications for national constitutional law and its potential effect on the EU integration process.

The book, thus, answers an important question: how do Eurosceptic parties mobilize constitutional law, ideas, and institutions against European integration? In answering this question, we will also have the opportunity to shed light on the effects of this approach on the process of European integration, on the causes behind the use of this strategy, on the different varieties of this practice used by Eurosceptic parties, and on the potential for a pro-European response that is coherent with the post-World War II (WWII) tradition of open constitutionalism.

This chapter, in particular, seeks to set the scene for our discussions throughout the book. After this introduction, we give a brief, initial discussion on the relationship between Euroscepticism, European integration, and constitutional law. We then present some of the literature on Euroscepticism, focusing on the social science definitions of the concept and linking them to constitutional phenomena. Sections 1.4 to 1.6 focus on constitutional matters and explain the nature of European post-WWII constitutionalism, the role of constitutional openness in this type of constitutionalism, and the way in which European constitutions integrated this openness. These discussions are particularly relevant because with them we justify one of our central claims: that Eurosceptic constitutional counter-narratives fail to grasp the nature of the constitutions that they seek to turn against European integration. The final section concludes the chapter by summarizing the remainder of this book and by presenting and justifying our main research choices.

6 Conservative Party, 'Strong Leadership, a Clear Economic Plan and a Brighter, More Secure Future' (2015) 60.

7 Vox, '100 medidas para la España viva' (2018) 21. Our translation.

1.2. Constitutionalism and the Politics of the Eurosceptic Backlash against European Integration

In the liberal tradition, a constitution is defined as a set of rules that limit political power through arrangements such as catalogues of rights and checks and balances.[8] However, in addition to this substantive content, constitutions are characterized, from a formal perspective, as the higher law of a certain jurisdiction.[9] In most contemporary European political systems, constitutions are codified documents that can be judicially enforced, even against the decisions of state authorities, usually by a constitutional court.[10] Democracies which, like the United Kingdom, rely on the notion of parliamentary sovereignty have become an oddity;[11] nevertheless, in these countries the idea of constitutionalism—albeit used in a more political sense—remains hegemonic.[12]

National constitutionalism has a complex relationship with European integration. The supremacy of the national constitution in the internal legal system has not been an obstacle to the integration of countries into the European Union. In fact, several national constitutions have 'integration clauses'[13] that facilitate, precisely, membership in the EU. At the same time, however, some national courts with powers of constitutional review (judicial review of legislation) have developed a line of case law in which the primacy of EU law is not accepted unconditionally.[14] Furthermore, some of those courts have started to act on their threats to make exceptions to the application of the principle of the primacy of EU law.[15]

The questioning of the primacy of EU law is, however, not a monopoly of the courts. In fact, several Eurosceptic parties have started to mobilize national constitutional law against European integration, arguing that there is an inherent tension between the two that has to be resolved in favour of national

[8] Giovanni Sartori, 'Constitutionalism: A Preliminary Discussion' (1962) 56 The American Political Science Review 853.

[9] Hans Kelsen, 'Judicial Review of Legislation: A Comparative Study of the Austrian and the American Constitution' (1942) 4 The Journal of Politics 183.

[10] András Sajó and Renáta Uitz, *The Constitution of Freedom: An Introduction to Legal Constitutionalism* (Oxford University Press 2017).

[11] Alec Stone Sweet, 'Constitutional Courts and Parliamentary Democracy' (2002) 25 West European Politics 77.

[12] John A Griffith, 'The Political Constitution' (1979) 42 Modern Law Review 1; Sartori (n 8).

[13] Monica Claes, 'The "European Clauses" in the National Constitutions: Evolution and Typology' (2005) 24 Yearbook of European Law 81.

[14] Ana Bobić, *The Jurisprudence of Constitutional Conflict in the European Union* (Oxford University Press 2022).

[15] Bárd and Bodnar (n 1).

constitutional supremacy.[16] This phenomenon, the questioning of the law of the EU on constitutional grounds, can be conceptualized as belonging in the framework of the literature on backlash politics.[17] As part of this backlash, Eurosceptic parties react against the case law of the European Court of Human Rights (ECtHR), or even the primacy principle developed by the European Court of Justice (ECJ), and seek to undermine these institutions and the regional organizations to which they belong. For the purposes of this book, we will focus on the case of the European Union, which is characterized by a special legal order due to the existence of structural principles such as primacy and direct effect.

1.3. Literature on Euroscepticism: A Weak Connection to Constitutional Studies?

It has been argued that the term 'Eurosceptic' can be traced back to the 1980s in the UK.[18] With this background, there is nowadays an abundant body of general literature on Euroscepticism in the social sciences, ranging from general definitional works to case studies on party politics or electoral behaviour.[19]

Legal literature on Euroscepticism is, however, scarcer. In his meta-analysis of 444 pieces of research on Euroscepticism in the period from 1995 to 2020, Marzi identified only seven as belonging to the area of law,[20] although there are works that have, for instance, put this phenomenon in dialogue with

[16] Castillo-Ortiz, 'Right-Wing Eurosceptic Parties and the Strategic Use of Law' (n 5).

[17] Karen J Alter, James T Gathii, and Laurence R Helfer, 'Backlash against International Courts in West, East and Southern Africa: Causes and Consequences' (2016) 27 European Journal of International Law 293; Karen J Alter and Michael Zürn, 'Theorising Backlash Politics: Conclusion to a Special Issue on Backlash Politics in Comparison' (2020) 22 The British Journal of Politics and International Relations 739.

[18] Nathalie Brack and Nicholas Startin, 'Introduction: Euroscepticism, From the Margins to the Mainstream' (2015) 36 International Political Science Review 239, 239.

[19] See, among the extensive list of works in this area, Paul Taggart and Aleks Szczerbiak, 'The Party Politics of Euroscepticism in EU Member and Candidate States' Sussex European Institute Working Paper 51 (2002); Tobias Theiler, 'The Origins of Euroscepticism in German-Speaking Switzerland' (2004) 43 European Journal of Political Research 635; Catherine E De Vries and Erica E Edwards, 'Taking Europe to Its Extremes: Extremist Parties and Public Euroscepticism' (2009) 15 Party Politics 5; Sofia Vasilopoulou, 'The Party Politics of Euroscepticism in Times of Crisis: The Case of Greece' (2018) 38 Politics 311; Paul Taggart and Aleks Szczerbiak, 'Contemporary Euroscepticism in the Party Systems of the European Union Candidate States of Central and Eastern Europe' (2004) 43 European Journal of Political Research 1; Tim Bale, 'Who Leads and Who Follows? The Symbiotic Relationship between UKIP and the Conservatives—and Populism and Euroscepticism' (2018) 38 Politics 263; Beatriz Carrasco, Elena González, and Jean-Baptiste Harguindéguy, 'Euroscepticism in Spain: A Phenomenon of Extremes?' in Xavier Coller and Leonardo Sánchez-Ferrer (eds), *Politicians in Hard Times: Spanish and South European MPs Facing Citizens after the Great Recession* (Springer International Publishing 2021).

[20] Paolo Marzi, 'Euroscepticism: A Meta-Analysis' (2025) 60 Acta Politica 704.

constitutional studies and considered aspects such as the so-called 'EU democratic deficit'.[21] Nevertheless, we believe that there is a paucity of research on the way in which Eurosceptics mobilize constitutional law, ideas, and institutions against the process of European integration, despite the importance of this phenomenon.[22]

With regard, in particular, to definitions of Euroscepticism, these generally come from works in disciplines such as political science and sociology. It may be because of that that their implications for the areas of constitutional law or even European law have been less comprehensively analysed. Throughout this book, however, we will demonstrate that there is an important intersection between Euroscepticism and constitutional law.

In their definition of this phenomenon, Taggart and Szczerbiak differentiated between hard and soft Euroscepticism. For them, hard Euroscepticism relates to a principled opposition to EU and European integration which includes a preference for withdrawing from European organizations and for policies that are 'tantamount to being opposed to the whole project of European integration as it is currently conceived'.[23] Even if this definition has been questioned in some works,[24] it has become a central distinction in studies in the field.[25] For instance, the most recent literature still applies this distinction to post-Brexit Eurosceptic discourse, showing that in the present period, 'long-term principled opposition to the European Union can hide behind equivocal rhetoric'.[26] Thus, grounded on this classical definition, we believe that the Eurosceptic mobilization of constitutional law can be considered as a form of hard Euroscepticism: when Eurosceptic parties mobilize the national constitution to reject principles such as the primacy of EU law, they are de facto 'opposed to the whole project of European integration as it is currently conceived', to borrow again the wording of Taggart and Szczerbiak.[27] This is because the

[21] Grimm (n 2); Andreas Follesdal and Simon Hix, 'Why There Is a Democratic Deficit in the EU: A Response to Majone and Moravcsik' (2006) 44 Journal of Common Market Studies 533; R Daniel Kelemen, 'Europe's Other Democratic Deficit: National Authoritarianism in Europe's Democratic Union' (2017) 52 Government and Opposition 211.

[22] But see, inter alia, Kelemen and Pech (n 1); Wind (n 1).

[23] Paul Taggart and Aleks Szczerbiak, 'The Party Politics of Euroscepticism' (n 19) 7.

[24] See, for instance, José M Magone, 'Divided Europe? Euroscepticism in Central, Eastern and Southern Europe' in Kyriakos N Demetriou (ed), *The European Union in Crisis: Explorations in Representation and Democratic Legitimacy* (Springer International Publishing 2015) 33.

[25] Sofia Vasilopoulou, 'Continuity and Change in the Study of Euroscepticism: Plus Ça Change?' (2013) 51 Journal of Common Market Studies 153, 155.

[26] Vratislav Havlík and Vít Hloušek, 'Where Have All the "Exiters" Gone? Contextualising the Concept of Hard Euroscepticism' (2025) 63 Journal of Common Market Studies 351, 351. See also on this Sergio Fabbrini and Tiziano Zgaga, 'Right-Wing Sovereignism in the European Union: Definition, Features and Implications' (2024) 62 Journal of Common Market Studies 341.

[27] Castillo-Ortiz, 'Right-Wing Eurosceptic Parties and the Strategic Use of Law' (n 5).

principle of primacy is structural to the EU legal system, to the point that the status quo of European integration cannot be conceived without it.[28]

We also argue that the Eurosceptic mobilization of constitutional law fits, at least to a large extent, the 'rejecting type' of Euroscepticism in Vasilopoulou's definition: these are parties that reject the idea, practice, and future of European Union cooperation.[29] When a party argues that the national constitution should have precedence over EU law, or when it seeks to mobilize the national constitution against decisions of the ECJ, it is rejecting European cooperation, as this is structured around the ideas of integration through law and the efficacy of decisions of supranational European courts.

De Vries has also classified Eurosceptic strategies, although she does so in connection with the core ideas that structure them. For this author:

> Party Euroskepticism evolves around two dimensions: economics and cultural opposition to integration. Parties may oppose European integration with the defense of national sovereignty and national community and/or reject the European project on the basis of its neoliberal character, which undermines the national welfare state (De Vries & Edwards, 2009). These Euroskeptic extremist parties play an important part in the mobilization of public sentiment against the EU. They rally opposition to the European project, but the raison d'être to do so varies between left-wing and right-wing parties. Extremist parties on the right tap into feelings of cultural insecurity to reject further integration and to defend national sovereignty from control from Brussels. These parties mobilize national identity considerations against the EU.[30]

Again, we believe that a connection between these ideas and the field of constitutional studies can be traced. For Eurosceptic parties on the right, the mobilization of constitutional rules, ideas, and institutions can be a way 'to reject further integration and to defend national sovereignty', as De Vries puts it. For parties that reject the European project on the basis of its alleged neo-liberal

[28] Mattias Kumm and Victor Ferreres Comella, 'The Primacy Clause of the Constitutional Treaty and the Future of Constitutional Conflict in the European Union' (2005) 3 International Journal of Constitutional Law 473; Matej Avbelj, 'Supremacy or Primacy of EU Law—(Why) Does It Matter?' (2011) 17 European Law Journal 744.

[29] Sofia Vasilopoulou, 'Varieties of Euroscepticism: The Case of the European Extreme Right' (2009) 5 Journal of Contemporary European Research 3; see also on this Castillo-Ortiz, 'Right-Wing Eurosceptic Parties and the Strategic Use of Law' (n 5).

[30] Catherine E De Vries, 'Public Opinion in European Union Politics', *Oxford Research Encyclopedia of Politics* (2020) 10 <https://oxfordre.com/politics/view/10.1093/acrefore/9780190228637.001.0001/acrefore-9780190228637-e-1049>.

character, the link to constitutional ideas might, in principle, appear weaker. This is not always the case, however. The response of left-wing parties to the management of the Euro-crisis demonstrates this. For instance, in Spain, the Izquierda Unida party argued that the policies used to deal with the Euro-crisis were a 'de-constituent process' in which 'national sovereignty is displaced from the national constitution to (. . .) the Troika'.[31] Constitutional rhetoric is thus very often the language into which Eurosceptic parties on the right and the left translate their Eurosceptic views when it comes to presenting those views to the public. As we explain later in this book, we believe that this has to do with the prestige of constitutionalism, which is here strategically mobilized against European integration.

The discussion above shows the links between Euroscepticism and constitutional studies. So far, we have mostly presented these links at the theoretical level, but we will illustrate them comprehensively throughout this book with examples. There is still one more aspect to consider in relation to the definition of Euroscepticism: its connection to other concepts such as populism and illiberalism. With regard to populism, the many definitions gravitate around the idea of a strategy that constructs an opposition between the people and the elite, with a particular political actor claiming to be the embodiment of the people.[32] Illiberalism, in turn, is often defined with reference to the undermining of checks on power and executive control and the instrumentalization of counter-majoritarian institutions.[33]

These three phenomena—Euroscepticism, illiberalism, and populism—are conceptually different, but we believe that they are nonetheless connected.[34] Furthermore, we argue that the strategic mobilization and potential abuse of

[31] Izquierda Unida, 'Programa para las elecciones europeas 2014' (2014) 6–7. Our translation. See more on this later in this book in the case study chapter on Spain.

[32] Cas Mudde, 'Three Decades of Populist Radical Right Parties in Western Europe: So What?' (2013) 52 European Journal of Political Research 1; Sonia Alonso and Cristóbal Rovira-Kaltwasser, 'Spain: No Country for the Populist Radical Right?' (2015) 20 South European Society and Politics 21; Luis Ramiro and Raul Gomez, 'Radical-Left Populism during the Great Recession: Podemos and Its Competition with the Established Radical Left' (2017) 65 Political Studies 108.

[33] Laurent Pech and Kim Lane Scheppele, 'Illiberalism within: Rule of Law Backsliding in the EU' (2017) 19 Cambridge Yearbook of European Legal Studies 3; Pablo Castillo-Ortiz, 'The Illiberal Abuse of Constitutional Courts in Europe' (2019) 15 European Constitutional Law Review 48.

[34] See, on these connections, Robert Harmsen, 'Concluding Comment: On Understanding the Relationship between Populism and Euroscepticism' (2010) 11 Perspectives on European Politics and Society 333; Cas Mudde, *Are Populists Friends or Foes of Constitutionalism?* (The Foundation for Law, Justice and Society 2013); Tímea Drinóczi and Agnieszka Bień-Kacała, 'Illiberal Constitutionalism: The Case of Hungary and Poland' (2019) 20 German Law Journal 1140; Pech and Scheppele (n 33); Wojciech Sadurski, *Poland's Constitutional Breakdown* (Oxford University Press 2019); Yaniv Roznai and Tamar Hostovsky Brandes, 'Democratic Erosion, Populist Constitutionalism, and the Unconstitutional Constitutional Amendments Doctrine' (2020) 14 Law & Ethics of Human Rights 19.

constitutional ideas and institutions have an important explanatory capacity when it comes to shedding light on the connections between the triad. For instance, in our case study about the UK (Chapter 4), we will shed light on how populist Eurosceptic actors resort to constitutional law arguments to varnish Eurosceptic positions and portray them as a mere defence of democratic constitutionalism. Our case study on Poland (see Chapter 7) shows that illiberal parties seek to mobilize the national constitution against European integration to undermine the efforts of the EU to protect the rule of law in member countries.

More than ten years ago, Vasilopoulou urged scholars to examine Euroscepticism 'beyond the study of party politics and public opinion'.[35] In this book, we seek to contribute to that endeavour by bridging the general literature on Euroscepticism across to the fields of constitutional and European law. The literature on Euroscepticism is vast and predominantly rooted in political science. What, then, can this book contribute? While previous research has largely focused on Euroscepticism as a political strategy, our aim is to examine the instrumentalization of a seemingly technical and neutral tool: constitutional law.

1.4. Setting the Scene: The Importance of Post-WWII Constitutionalism

In the aftermath of WWII, a new historical tradition of constitutionalism developed in continental Europe and beyond which we shall, for convenience, call post-WWII constitutionalism.[36] In this sense, post-WWII constitutionalism should be understood as a particular historical tradition, because there are not only different forms of Euroscepticism[37] but also different forms of constitutionalism.[38]

Although scholars often interpret constitutionalism and constitutions as efforts to rationalize power, this perspective should not imply the exclusion

[35] Vasilopoulou, 'Continuity and Change in the Study of Euroscepticism' (n 25) 153.

[36] Cesare Pinelli, 'The Formation of a Constitutional Tradition in Continental Europe since World War II' (2016) 22 European Public Law 257, 257.

[37] On the different forms of Euroscepticism, see Paul Taggart, 'A Touchstone of Dissent: Euroscepticism in Contemporary Western European Party Systems' (1998) 33 European Journal of Political Research 363; Vasilopoulou, 'Continuity and Change in the Study of Euroscepticism' (n 25) 153.

[38] Robert Schütze, 'Constitutionalism(s)' in Roger Masterman and Robert Schütze (eds), *Cambridge Companion to Comparative Constitutional Law* (Cambridge University Press 2019) 40; Signe Rehling Larsen, 'Varieties of Constitutionalism in the European Union' (2021) 84 Modern Law Review 477.

of emotions from constitutional law. In fact, emotions, particularly fear, have played a significant role.[39] In identifying the emotions that influence the content of a national constitution, the history of the particular legal system plays a crucial role. Horrors, conflicts, and past experiences that led to a break with the previous legal regime and the establishment of a new system of norms are particularly influential. Post-WWII constitutions, for instance, are shaped by a belief in democratic systems in which temporary majorities are restricted from making decisions over certain fundamental goods, as evidenced by the inclusion of devices such as eternity clauses,[40] entrenchment clauses,[41] and strong forms of judicial review of legislation.[42]

Indeed, the post-WWII experience in constitutional design is marked by a fascinating blend of majoritarian and counter-majoritarian elements.[43] The majoritarian components of the constitution are those that govern the formation and functioning of the government—the quintessential majoritarian actor—in its interactions with parliament and other constitutional bodies. On the other hand, counter-majoritarian elements are designed to protect minority rights. It is important to clarify that, in this context, 'counter-majoritarian' should not be interpreted as anti-democratic or opposed to democracy. This distinction is crucial to avoid reducing democracy to mere majority rule. Democracy is a more complex concept, in which the majority has the right to govern, but this right is contingent upon safeguarding the equality of citizens and the pluralism of ideas. Therefore, concrete protections for minorities are essential to the functioning of a true liberal

[39] Jon Elster, 'Constitution-making and Violence' (2012) 41 Journal of Legal Analysis 7; András Sajó, 'Emotions in Constitutional Design' (2010) 8 International Journal of Constitutional Law 354.

[40] 'Perhaps the most famous example of constitutional unamendability is Article 79(3) of the German Basic Law (Grundgesetz) of 1949. Written against the background of the experience of the Weimar Constitution and the Holocaust, Article 79(3) prohibits constitutional amendments affecting the division of the Federation into states (Länder), human dignity, the constitutional order, and basic institutional principles describing Germany as a democratic and social federal state. This provision is commonly referred to as "the Eternity Clause" (die Ewigkeitsklausel), and following the German jargon, the terminology of "eternity" to describe such protected provisions spread in the constitutional literature', Yaniv Roznai, 'Negotiating the Eternal: The Paradox of Entrenching Secularism in Constitutions' (2017) 86 Michigan State Law Review 253, 255–256; article 79(3) of the German Basic Law states: 'Amendments to this Basic Law affecting the division of the Federation into Länder, their participation in principle in the legislative process, or the principles laid down in Articles 1 and 20 shall be inadmissible'. See also Pietro Faraguna, 'Unamendability and Constitutional Identity in the Italian Constitutional Experience' (2019) 21 European Journal of Law Reform 329 and, more generally, Silvia Suteu, *Eternity Clauses in Democratic Constitutionalism* (Oxford University Press 2021).

[41] Michael Hein, 'Do Constitutional Entrenchment Clauses Matter? Constitutional Review of Constitutional Amendments in Europe' (2020) 18 International Journal of Constitutional Law 88.

[42] On this and other related concepts see Mark Tushnet, 'Alternative Forms of Judicial Review' (2003) 101 Michigan Law Review 2781.

[43] To cite the terminology used by Alexander Bickel, *The Least Dangerous Branch* (Yale University Press 1986).

democracy. This means that counter-majoritarian actors are not an exception to democracy; rather, they are essential democratic actors[44] to preserve pluralism.

Against this background, post-WWII constitutionalism is certainly a 'thick' version of constitutionalism, which has galvanized its counter-majoritarian component. However, this does not exclude the fact that different types of constitutionalism exist elsewhere, where experiences are marked by different historical events. Besides, it is possible to mention other provisions that make sense from a legal point of view only if contextualized in the particular atmosphere characterizing that period. We can start with the Preamble to the German Basic Law, which opens by referring to 'responsibility before God and man'. Article 1 of the same text is devoted to dignity, defined as 'inviolable'. Dignity is indeed a keyword in the text of the Basic Law adopted after WWII. Further evidence of this political atmosphere is the Preamble to the 1948 Universal Declaration of Human Rights, which begins with the following words: 'Whereas disregard and contempt for human rights have resulted in barbarous acts which have outraged the conscience of mankind, and the advent of a world in which human beings shall enjoy freedom of speech and belief and freedom from fear and want has been proclaimed as the highest aspiration of the common people'.[45]

This leads us to the most important element in post-WWII constitutionalism: the principle of openness. It also recalls a crucial point from the Preface: we do not share the widespread notion that the EU is something external to state democracies and that it is designed to condition state political processes, acting as a device of depoliticization.[46] In our view, on the contrary, the EU is so strongly connected to state democracies as to be their direct product. This is not to say that the EU is without flaws: our point is that many of the problems from which the EU currently suffers are due to a more general crisis of constitutionalism at the national level.

[44] As Rawls put it: 'A supreme court fits into this idea of dualist constitutional democracy as one of the institutional devices to protect the higher law. By applying public reason the court is to prevent that law from being eroded by the legislation of transient majorities, or more likely, by organised and well situated narrow interests skilled at getting their way. If the court assumes this role and effectively carries it out, it is incorrect to say that it is straight-forwardly antidemocratic', John Rawls, *Political Liberalism* (Columbia University Press 2005) 233–234.

[45] Universal Declaration of Human Rights, Preamble.

[46] Alessandro Somma, *Quando l'Europa tradì sé stessa. E come continua a tradirsi nonostante la pandemia* (Laterza 2021) IX.

1.5. What Do We Mean by Constitutional Openness?

The background to European post-WWII constitutionalism takes us to the principle of openness. In order to achieve the goals of constitutionalism and to avoid the absolute and omnipotent power of states, international systems for the protection of human rights were consolidated, and countries became committed to processes of integration as a means to secure peace. These goals, with the approval of opening clauses, became an integral part of constitutions. Contrary to the assertions of many populist forces (which tend to reduce democracy to majority rule), the institutions of international law not only do not undermine popular sovereignty but also strengthen the state, their work being decisive in guaranteeing democratic integration.[47] In our view, this also explains the emergence of EU law, given that many of these clauses designed to open domestic law to international law have been used by constitutional courts to justify, in the light of their internal parameters, the direct effect and primacy of Community law. As we will show in this book, Eurosceptic constitutional counter-narratives clash with one central principle of post-WWII constitutionalism, that of constitutional openness.

By openness, in this book, we mean the constitutionally established friendliness (*Freundlichkeit*) towards legal sources that are, from a formal point of view, external to those governed by the national system, or, in other words, that are not produced by the national actors in charge of the lawmaking functions according to the constitution (and, as such, are not traceable to the general traditional understanding of 'the will of the people'). The German literature has emphasized the relationship between openness and friendliness towards international law, conceiving them as synonyms, as distinct concepts, or interpreting openness as broader than *Freundlichkeit*.[48] As we shall see, there are differences even within constitutional openness. In other words, the openness defined here is not an undifferentiated monolith, but a constantly developing phenomenon that has gone through different phases.

[47] Chris Thornhill, 'Constitutionalism and Populism: National Political Integration and Global Legal Integration' (2020) 12 International Theory 1, 24.

[48] On this debate, see Christian Tomuschat, 'Staatsrechtliche Entscheidung für die internationale Offenheit' in Josef Isensee and Paul Kirchhof (eds), *Handbuch des Staatsrechts*, vol XI (CF Müller 2013) § 226 para 9. See also Berenike Schriewer, *Zur Theorie der internationalen Offenheit und der Völkerrechtsfreundlichkeit einer Rechtsordnung und ihrer Erprobung am Beispiel der EU-Rechtsordnung* (Duncker & Humblot 2017) 61; Albert Bleckmann, 'Die Völkerrechtsfreundlichkeit der deutschen Rechtsordnung' (1979) 32(9) Die Öffentliche Verwaltung 309, 317.

In 2008, Carrozza[49] described constitutional openness as one of the characteristics of constitutions 'born out of the Resistance',[50] a formula used to refer to a series of constitutions that were created with the explicit aim of rejecting and overcoming the values—or, rather, the anti-values—that characterized the totalitarian era. This category comprised the Italian Constitution and other documents, such as the French Constitution (of the Fourth Republic) and the German Basic Law. As Carrozza[51] observed, one could extend this group to include the Greek, Portuguese, and Spanish Constitutions, which were drafted in the 1970s.

A common feature of many of these post-WWII constitutions, born out of the Resistance, is that they emerged from a political compromise among diverse democratic forces. Very frequently, these forces were united solely by their shared rejection of totalitarianism and authoritarianism.

This explains why these constitutions are grounded in a genuine rejection of the previous regime's characteristics and a desire for an entirely different society. Some of them, including the Italian one, express a strong commitment to new societal models and are rich in declarations of principle, reflecting a clear intention to break with the past. However, in some cases, these so-called 'announced revolutions'[52] just remained on paper, as one of the most influential members of the Italian Constituent Assembly, Calamandrei, lamented a few years after the Italian Constitution came into effect.[53]

The programmatic nature of these constitutions required a significant shift in how values and the foundations of social life were conceived within national boundaries. Moreover, this shift often led the framers of these constitutions, born out of the Resistance, to take the bold step of codifying the values that should guide their nations' roles and contributions in the international arena and the global community, embodying the principle of constitutional openness.

Although constitutional openness is precisely one of the most evident features of post-WWII constitutionalism, it is possible to find the roots of this

[49] Paolo Carrozza, 'Constitutionalism's Post-modern Opening', in Martin Loughlin and Neil Walker (eds), *The Paradox of Constitutionalism: Constituent Power and Constitutional Form* (Oxford University Press 2008) 169.

[50] Costantino Mortati, *Lezioni sulle forme di governo* (CEDAM 1973) 222.

[51] Carrozza (n 49) 180.

[52] Calamandrei wrote about a 'promised revolution' in exchange for the failed revolution that had been sought by the leftist forces, or a rupture with the past that had to be even more radical than it was at that time. Piero Calamandrei, 'Cenni introduttivi sulla Costituente e i suoi lavori', in Piero Calamandrei and Alessandro Levi (eds), *Commentario sistematico alla Costituzione italiana* (G Barbèra 1950), now in Piero Calamandrei, *Scritti e discorsi politici*, vol II (La Nuova Italia 1966) 421.

[53] Piero Calamandrei, 'La Costituzione e le leggi per attuarla', in Piero Calamandrei, *Opere giuridiche*, vol III (Morano 1965) 553.

phenomenon even earlier, looking back to what, in the 1930s, Mirkine-Guetzévitch called the 'internationalization of constitutional law',[54] when describing the '*nouvelles tendances du droit constitutionnel*'.[55] The seeds of this trend can be found in the Weimar Constitution of 1919, in its preamble (which referred to the need 'to preserve peace at home and abroad and to foster social progress') and in article 4, for example, which stated that: 'The generally accepted rules of international law are to be considered as binding integral parts of the German Reich'.

This type of openness can take various forms: it may be confined to what we refer to as general public law, such as international customary law, or it may extend to international treaties. Among the latter type, some constitutions exhibit a broader openness, particularly concerning human rights treaties, due to the alignment between their core values and the principles embodied in these treaties. Spain and Portugal, as we will explore, are prime examples of this broader openness. This type of openness, scholars explain,[56] can serve a dual function of constitutional significance. It can reinforce the original pact codified in the constitution by offering new instruments to protect the fundamental rights enshrined in the constitutional text. The Dutch case is emblematic from this point of view: article 94[57] of the *Grondwet* empowers national judges to disapply national laws that conflict with international treaties, particularly the European Convention on Human Rights (ECHR). This is an example of how constitutional openness can provide new instruments to safeguard constitutional rights. Additionally, constitutional openness can serve a transformative function by revitalizing the constitutional text—updating the list of rights included in the original document and making it more adaptable to the evolving needs of society. The Dutch example is again particularly illustrative here, as the openness of the *Grondwet* has often been cited to argue against the need for new amendments to its first part.[58]

[54] Boris Mirkine-Guetzévitch, *Les Nouvelles tendances du droit constitutionnel* (Giard 1936) 72.

[55] Mirkine-Guetzévitch (n 54).

[56] Anne Peters, 'Compensatory Constitutionalism: The Function and Potential of Fundamental International Norms and Structures' (2006) 19 Leiden Journal of International Law 579.

[57] 'Statutory regulations in force within the Kingdom shall not be applicable if such application is in conflict with provisions of treaties that are binding on all persons or of resolutions by international institutions'. On constitutional openness in the Netherlands, see Barbara Oomen, 'Strengthening Constitutional Identity Where There Is None: The Case of the Netherlands' (2016) 77 Revue interdisciplinaire d'études juridiques 235; Gerrit Betlem and André Nollkaemper, 'Giving Effect to Public International Law and European Community Law before Domestic Courts. A Comparative Analysis of the Practice of Consistent Interpretation' (2003) 14 European Journal of International Law 569.

[58] See Oomen (n 57) 245; Janneke Gerards, 'The Irrelevance of the Netherlands Constitution, and the Impossibility of Changing It' (2016) 77 Revue interdisciplinaire d'études juridiques 207. A similar

This elasticity in the original constitutional texts has its limitations, as many of these constitutions also include a set of core principles that must remain intact. Violating these principles would undermine the fundamental values on which their legal systems are based. As mentioned earlier, at the national level, constitutional law scholars describe this set of principles in various ways. For example, in Italy, it is referred to as the 'republican form' ('*forma repubblicana*'[59]), while in Germany, it is known as the 'eternity clause' ('*Ewigkeitsklausel*'[60]).

This openness is embodied in certain constitutional provisions that address not only the impact of external norms within the national territory but also the country's role and contributions to the international community. These provisions are grounded in the idea of axiological continuity, which links the principles and values governing a polity within its own borders to those that should define the international community. In other words, these constitutions have not confined the promotion of their values within their domestic boundaries. Even when their provisions refer specifically to 'citizens', constitutional courts have often extended the reach of these norms to non-citizens, particularly in the realm of fundamental rights.[61] These constitutions also aim to regulate the actions of their domestic actors beyond the national borders, promoting their values even in the postnational arena. The Italian experience is particularly emblematic of this approach, yet it also reflects a broader trend observed in various constitutional systems.[62]

Indeed, nowadays national constitutions do not provide a closed list of fundamental rights, reflecting their inherent openness. According to Saiz Arnaiz, this openness leads constitutions to make reference to international and supranational law to safeguard certain constitutional values.[63] In the case of Italy, for example, the general clause for the protection of fundamental rights in article 2 of the Constitution is considered an 'open' norm. This interpretation has enabled the Italian Constitutional Court to recognize and protect emerging

dynamic can be found in Belgium: the ECHR and the Charter of Fundamental Rights are used to integrate and update the old liberal bill of rights (1831).

[59] Article 139 of the Italian Constitution.

[60] Article 79 para 3 of the Basic Law (Grundgesetz-GG) of the Federal Republic of Germany.

[61] This is the case in Italy; for instance, see sentenza 432/2005 (available at: www.cortecostituzionale.it).

[62] See Antonio Cassese, 'Modern Constitutions and International Law' (1985) 192 Recueil des Cours 331.

[63] Alejandro Saiz Arnaiz, *La apertura constitucional al derecho internacional y europeo de los derechos humanos. El artículo 10.2 de la Constitución Española* (Centro de Estudios Políticos y Constitucionales 1999).

rights, such as the right to know, the right to privacy, and environmental rights, thereby keeping the Constitution aligned with the evolving need to protect the person, that is, the individual understood as contextualized in social relations ('*principio personalista*').

1.6. Constitutional Openness in the Waves of European Constitutionalism

European contemporary constitutionalism has been created in successive stages, strongly linked to the waves of democratization. Constitutional openness, as a core principle of post-WWII constitutionalism, was present in these different phases of constitutionalization.

In the 1990s, when discussing certain provisions of Central-Eastern European constitutions, Eric Stein highlighted the emergence of a 'paradigm of progressive internationalization of constitutions'.[64] However, these provisions represented only the fifth stage of this process,[65] which, in that context, was linked to a broader phenomenon of mixed or partially guided domestic constituent processes influenced by the international community.[66] This influence laid the groundwork for what Cope now refers to as 'intermestic constitutionalism'.[67]

[64] Eric Stein, 'International Law in Internal Law: Toward Internationalization of Central-Eastern European Constitutions?' (1994) 88 American Journal of International Law 427, 429.

[65] Stein recalls how Cassese ('Modern Constitutions' (n 62) 351) had identified four previous stages in this process of the internationalization of constitutions: 'Writing in 1985, he perceived four historic stages: the first extending from 1787 to World War I; the second, from the Weimar Constitution of 1919 to World War II; the third, from the French Constitution of 1946 to the late 1950s; and the fourth starting in the early 1960s. The United States Constitution of 1789, written after a revolutionary war against a monarchy, was the first milestone on this historic continuum (. . .). After more than a century, and another war and revolution against a monarchy the short-lived democratic Weimar Constitution of 1919 made "generally recognized rules of international law" a part of federal law. This formula was extended (after still another war) in the 1949 Basic Law of the Federal Republic of Germany so as to make general international law superior to legislation and directly invocable by individuals (. . .). The 1931 Constitution of the democratic, socialist Spanish Republic took the lead by establishing for the first time in history the precedence of treaties over ordinary legislation, enforceable by a Constitutional Court—a solution embraced in substance after almost half a century of war and dictatorship by the new Spanish Constitution of 1978. The Constitutions of 1946 and 1958 restructuring post-World War II democratic France carried on the idea of treaties' superiority over legislation, subject, however, to the perplexing new requirement of reciprocity—a pattern followed by the Francophone countries of Africa', Stein (n 64) 427–429.

[66] Andrea Lollini and Francesco Palermo, 'Comparative Law and the "Proceduralization" of Constitution-Building Processes' in Julia Raue and Patrick Sutter (eds), *Facets and Practices of State-building* (Brill/Martinus Nijhoff, 2009) 301.

[67] 'Intermestic constitutionalism demonstrates how international and domestic constitutionalism can exist side-by-side, that is, how a single constitution can be at once transnational and indigenous (. . .). More important, intermestic constitutionalism shows that under certain conditions, these dual influences will methodically impact the two main components of constitutions—human rights

The Central-Eastern European constitutions share a spirit of openness with the German and Italian constitutions, a connection noted by scholars such as Cassese.[68] In this process of the internationalization of modern constitutions, the Republic of Weimar represented an important starting point. That the Weimar Constitution originated from the acknowledgement of the atrocities of World War I can be inferred by looking at its Preamble and at article 227 of the Treaty of Versailles, which condemned Germany's actions as 'a supreme offence against international morality and the sanctity of treaties'.[69]

This combination of factors led to the establishment of norms that integrated both internal and external dimensions within the constitutional framework. Another relevant provision is article 162 of the Weimar Constitution, which stated that 'the Reich advocates an international regulation of the rights of the workers, which strives to safeguard a minimum of social rights for humanity's working class'. In this, article 162 created a parallelism of values between the domestic and the international spheres.

Another important innovation, later revived by the Spanish Constitution of 1931, was the progressive involvement of parliament in foreign affairs.[70] The Spanish Constitution of 1931 included several noteworthy provisions, beginning with article 7 ('The Spanish State shall abide by the universal norms of international law, including them in its positive law'[71]) and, above all, article 65, which considered 'all international conventions ratified by Spain and registered in the League of Nations and in the nature of international law' as 'a constitutive part of Spanish legislation'.[72] In this way, the 1931 Spanish Constitution established a clear obligation for the national legislature to act in accordance with international law, and this resulted, as Cassese noted,[73] in the transformation of a possible violation of international law into a breach

provisions and structural/institutional framework; transnational forces tend to affect human rights, and indigenous influence tends to dominate structural arrangements', Kevin L Cope, 'The Intermestic Constitution: Lessons from the World's Newest Nation' (2013) 53 Virginia Journal of International Law 667, 670.

[68] Cassese, 'Modern Constitutions' (n 62) 351.

[69] The Versailles Treaty, 28 June, 1919, Part VII, article 227 <https://avalon.law.yale.edu/subject_menus/versailles_menu.asp>. The translations of the Weimar Constitution provisions used in this chapter are taken from the following websites: <https://germanhistorydocs.ghi-dc.org/pdf/eng/ghi_wr_weimarconstitution_Eng.pdf> and <https://en.wikisource.org/wiki/Weimar_constitution>.

[70] See also article 35 of the Weimar Constitution. Antonio Cassese, 'Politica estera e relazioni internazionali nel disegno emerso alla Assemblea Costituente' in Ugo de Siervo (ed), *Scelte della Costituente e cultura giuridica. I: Costituzione italiana e modelli stranieri* (Il Mulino 1980) 505, 519.

[71] Article 7, Spanish Constitution of 1931.

[72] Article 65, Spanish Constitution of 1931.

[73] Cassese, 'Modern Constitutions' (n 62) 510–511.

of the constitution (a constitution guaranteed by the Tribunal de Garantías Constitucionales).

Another example of the external openness of modern constitutions is clearly illustrated by the German Basic Law. Its Preamble begins by acknowledging the responsibility of the German people 'before God and man' and affirms 'the determination to promote world peace as an equal partner in a united Europe'.[74] Article 25 establishes the primacy of general rules of international law over national norms. In practice, the German legal system has demonstrated a strong openness to international law, notably through techniques such as the famous '*Völkerrechtsfreundliche Auslegung*'.[75]

Another wave of constitutional internationalization is represented by the current Spanish and Portuguese Constitutions. These constitutions introduced a crucial distinction between the general category of international treaties and the specific group of treaties focused on human rights. For Portugal, the key provision is article 16 of the Constitution,[76] which recognizes that international human rights treaties have a complementary role to the Constitution. This provision grants an interpretative role to the Universal Declaration of Human Rights, seemingly excluding other conventions such as the ECHR. However, the Portuguese Constitutional Court frequently employs the ECHR and other human rights treaties as significant auxiliary tools for interpreting the Constitution.[77] The most significant confirmation of the special status of human rights treaties in Spain is article 10(2),[78] which acknowledges that these treaties offer interpretive guidance for applying constitutional clauses related to human rights. However, the Constitutional Court has clarified that this does not mean that human rights treaties have constitutional status.[79]

[74] German Basic Law, Preamble.

[75] 'According to this technique, any German law should be construed as far as possible in conformity with international law, parallel to the established method of interpretation to comply with EU law ("Europarechts konforme Auslegung"). This mode concerns any norm in national law, since any norm must be in conformity with the international law obligations of Germany', Philipp Dann and Marie von Engelhardt, 'The Global Administrative Order Through a German Lens: Perception and Influence of Legal Structures of Global Governance in Germany' (2011) 12 German Law Journal 1371, 1386.

[76] Article 16 of the Portuguese Constitution: '1. The fundamental rights enshrined in this Constitution shall not exclude such other rights as may be laid down by law and in the applicable rules of international law. 2. The provisions of this Constitution and of laws concerning fundamental rights shall be interpreted and construed in accordance with the Universal Declaration of Human Rights'.

[77] Portuguese Constitutional Court, Acórdão 345/99 <https://www.tribunalconstitucional.pt/tc/en/acordaos/rulings.html>.

[78] Article 10(2) Constitution: 'The norms relative to basic rights and liberties which are recognized by the Constitution shall be interpreted in conformity with the Universal Declaration of Human Rights and the international treaties and agreements on those matters ratified by Spain'.

[79] Tribunal Constitucional, Judgment 30/1991.

A similar provision can be found in Article 20, paragraph 1 of the Romanian Constitution: 'Constitutional provisions concerning the citizens' rights and liberties shall be interpreted and enforced in conformity with the Universal Declaration of Human Rights, with the covenants and other treaties Romania is a party to'.

Finally, a particularly interesting case for studying the openness of constitutions to international human rights treaties is that of the Czech Republic.

Before the Czech Euro amendment, articles 10 and 87 of the Constitution[80] distinguished between international treaties in general and international human rights treaties, assigning the latter a super-primary status. However, the Constitution did not address the question of whether international human rights treaties were considered part of the constitutional block. At the same time, article 87, paragraph 1,[81] of the Constitution empowered the Constitutional Court to declare laws unconstitutional if they conflicted with either the Constitution or international human rights treaties. With the Czech Euro amendment,[82] the new article 10 of the Constitution abandoned this distinction, granting all international treaties a super-primary rank, although they were still formally sub-constitutional.[83] However, the Czech Constitutional Court has adopted a broad interpretation of the ECHR and other human rights treaties, treating them as distinct from and superior to other international treaties.[84]

In fact, the Czech Constitutional Court has adopted a highly creative interpretation of the new constitutional provisions, effectively rewriting them. The Court considers itself empowered to review national legislation in the light of the ECHR,[85] despite the new text of the Constitution. In a 2002 ruling, the Czech Constitutional Court stated that 'the inadmissibility of changing the substantive requirements of a democratic state based on the rule of law also

[80] Article 10 (previous version) of the Czech Constitution: 'Ratified and promulgated international accords on human rights and fundamental freedoms, to which the Czech Republic has committed itself, are immediately binding and are superior to law'.

[81] Article 87, para 1 (previous version) of the Czech Constitution: '(1) The Constitutional Court resolves: (a) the nullification of laws or their individual provisions if they are in contradiction with a constitutional law or an international agreement under Article 10 [international human rights treaties]'. On this, see Oreste Pollicino, *L'allargamento ad est dell'Europa e rapporti tra Corti costituzionali e Corti europee. Verso una teoria generale dell'impatto interordinamentale del diritto sovranazionale?* (Giuffrè 2010) 104.

[82] Constitutional Act 395/2001 Coll.

[83] See Michal Bobek and David Kosař, 'Report on the Czech Republic and Slovakia', in Giuseppe Martinico and Oreste Pollicino (eds), *The National Judicial Treatment of the ECHR and EU Laws: A Comparative Constitutional Perspective* (Europa Law Publishing 2010) 133.

[84] Judgment of 15 April 2003 (I ÚS 752/02).

[85] Judgment of the Czech Constitutional Court of 30 November 2004, Pl ÚS 15/04; Judgment of the Czech Constitutional Court of 22 March 2005, Pl ÚS 45/04.

contains an instruction to the Constitutional Court, that no amendment to the Constitution can be interpreted in such a way that it would result in limiting an already achieved procedural level of protection for fundamental rights and freedoms'.[86] Thus, the Constitutional Court concluded that 'the international human rights treaties have retained their constitutional status'.[87]

The constitutional openness described in this chapter, which has been amplified by post-WWII constitutionalism, has marked a turning point in the way in which general principles are understood within these legal systems. In comparative law, the concept of general principles is often linked with the idea of openness, as general principles function as open norms. First of all, principles are characterized by what Betti defined as a 'surplus of axiological meaning',[88] and this means that they are often broad and flexible, allowing for a range of interpretations. Second, principles are open because they bridge domestic and international legal systems, particularly in the post-WWII era. Although general principles have for many years been associated with the idea of openness, comparative law reveals that this was not always the case.[89] The debate on codifications in continental Europe reveals that there was a time when general principles were linked to the closedness of a legal system. This was especially evident in systems in which civil codes were seen as expressions of legal nationalism, reflecting a more insular and self-contained approach to law.[90] If once they were seen as the moment a legal system became closed (nothing outside the Code, and no reference to natural law allowed), principles are today perceived as the moment of the opening of a legal order that connects domestic and international law, with systematic interpretation (often combined with consistent interpretation[91]) no longer being seen as the last resort for the interpreter. If this is true, constitutionalism has favoured the emergence of a kind of 'osmotic law'.[92]

This transformation of general principles is linked to the notion of openness, as described by Carrozza.[93] The process should be read in the light of the axiological (desired) continuity between the domestic and international levels,

[86] Judgment of the Czech Constitutional Court of 25 June 2002, Pl ÚS 36/01.
[87] Bobek and Kosař (n 83) 135.
[88] Emilio Betti, *Teoria generale della interpretazione*, vol II (Giuffrè 1955), 850.
[89] Giorgio Del Vecchio, 'Les bases du droit comparé et les principes généraux du droit' (1960) 12 Revue internationale de droit comparé 493.
[90] Paolo Grossi, *A History of European Law* (Blackwell 2010) 154.
[91] Roberto Bin, 'L'interpretazione conforme. Due o tre cose che so di lei' (2015) 5 Rivista AIC 1.
[92] Antonio Ruggeri, 'Dimensione europea della tutela dei diritti fondamentali e tecniche interpretative' (2009) 6 Federalismi.it. Rivista di diritto pubblico italiano, comunitario e comparato 1.
[93] Carrozza (n 49) 182.

which supports the effort to extend the values of constitutionalism beyond national borders.

1.7. Structure and Content of this Book

This book investigates Eurosceptic constitutional counter-narratives from theoretical, doctrinal, and empirical angles. For the purposes of this book, we give two meanings to the term doctrinal. On the one hand, 'doctrinal' refers to the doctrine of judicial case law, as we will explore judicial decisions—especially those of constitutional courts—related to the areas of inquiry addressed in this book. On the other hand, we use 'doctrinal' to denote a form of academic work that seeks to understand the legal system and clarify the meaning of its rules. After this introduction (Chapter 1), we provide, in Chapter 2, a comprehensive theoretical definition of the Eurosceptic mobilization of constitutional law. Chapter 3 seeks to understand *why* Eurosceptic parties either opt or do not opt to mobilize constitutional law. Chapters 4 to 7, in turn, shed light on *how* parties carry out this mobilization. Chapter 8 revisits the key stages of our research journey, underscoring both the added value of our book and the originality of its findings. This concludes the volume.

Some clarifications of our method and research design are thus relevant at this point. Chapter 3 turns to empirical causal analysis to understand why Eurosceptic parties do or do not resort to the mobilization of constitutional law against European integration. Our analysis uses a subsample of the possible cases: the stances of right-wing Eurosceptic parties in Western European general elections. The findings of this chapter are illustrative of the way in which the mobilization of Eurosceptic constitutional counter-narratives is linked to the contestation of aspects of European integration such as the role of courts, or policies such as those followed in the management of the Euro-crisis. Furthermore, these findings are tested beyond the subsample by considering left-wing Eurosceptic parties and Eurosceptic parties in Central and Eastern Europe.

Chapters 4 to 7 are in-depth case studies shedding light on the ways that Eurosceptic parties mobilize constitutional law against European integration. For the four case studies, we have selected the UK, Italy, Spain, and Poland. These countries have been selected because, given the variation in many important aspects, they can help us test the Eurosceptic constitutional counter-narratives.

At the chronological level, these countries joined the European project at different stages: Italy as a founding member, the United Kingdom in 1973 (before leaving in 2020), Spain in 1986, and Poland during the 2004 enlargement to Central and Eastern Europe.

At the constitutional level, while most of these four countries are originally based on a model of legal constitutionalism (Spain, Italy, and Poland), the UK is an interesting case study of how the Eurosceptic mobilization of constitutional law arguments operates in an environment of predominantly political constitutionalism.

At the geographical level, the sample covers a Northern European country (the UK), two Southern European countries (Spain and Italy), and one Eastern European Member State (Poland). While openness is certainly a defining feature of continental European constitutionalism, some doubts may arise in the case of the United Kingdom, which has largely remained immune to the introduction of strongly counter-majoritarian elements and continues to be inspired by forms of political constitutionalism (see Chapter 4). However, two factors, in our view, justify the inclusion of the British case in this discussion.

First, the constitutionalism of the United Kingdom has undergone a profound transformation since WWII. Although the UK did not adopt a new written constitution in the post-WWII period, it nevertheless experienced a significant evolution in constitutional thinking that aligns with key elements of post-WWII constitutionalism. This transformation includes a stronger commitment to liberal democracy and the protection of fundamental rights, notably with the incorporation of international human rights norms—particularly following the adoption of the Human Rights Act in 1998. It also involves an evolving role for the courts, especially in the fields of public law and administrative review, which reflects a growing sense of constitutional adjudication even in the absence of a codified constitution. Moreover, one can observe a deepening of democratic discourse, exemplified by institutional reforms and sustained debates around devolution and the nature of parliamentary sovereignty.

Some of these changes have been driven by the United Kingdom's openness to the international community, and indeed, as we will see, several of these innovations were introduced in response to international and supranational obligations.

Secondly, the case of the United Kingdom has always been a testing ground for Eurosceptic techniques, so we felt it was necessary to address it in a study such as this, despite all the peculiarities of this case. In this chapter, unlike the others, we will devote some attention to the debate on the ECHR. We do so because the UK's discussion on the ECHR largely draws on arguments and methods first developed around EU law. Thus, the legal Euroscepticism explored in this book appears in the British context in distinct yet comparable forms, sustaining a debate that remains unmatched elsewhere in Europe.

At the political level, the role of Eurosceptic parties has been very different in each of these countries. In Spain, Eurosceptic parties have generally been the opposition, and all governments have systematically declared themselves to be pro-European. Spain could be deemed to provide an example of Euroscepticism as the 'politics of opposition'.[94] An exception to this is the recent Partido Socialista Obrero Español (PSOE)-led governments under Sánchez: these governments—and especially the senior coalition partner, the PSOE—were clearly Europhile, but junior coalition members such as Podemos and Izquierda Unida occasionally defended certain Eurosceptic positions. In Italy, Eurosceptic parties of differing ideologies have been both in government and in opposition at different times after 1994. In the UK, the Brexit referendum took place under a government led by the Conservative Party, at the time a member of the soft Eurosceptic group of European Conservatives and Reformists. While Prime Minister David Cameron called the referendum, he supported the option of remaining in the EU. After that option was rejected, the country was led by different prime ministers, including Boris Johnson, who, during the referendum campaign, had argued in favour of leaving the EU. Finally, in Poland (until 2023), the government of Law and Justice clearly fostered Eurosceptic constitutional counter-narratives, even if they did not propose an exit from the EU. Furthermore, under this government, Poland underwent a process of rule of law backsliding, as acknowledged by a large body of literature.[95]

These four case studies, however, all follow the same structure. They all do three things: (i) they explain the country's constitutional system and, in particular, its relationship to European integration; (ii) they empirically explore the positions of Eurosceptic political actors when it comes to using constitutional law against European integration; and (iii) they provide a theoretical and doctrinal analysis of these forms of Euroscepticism by explaining how the Eurosceptic counter-narratives clash with approaches to the interpretation of national constitutions that are open to supranational law.

[94] Nick Sitter, 'The Politics of Opposition and European Integration in Scandinavia: Is Euroscepticism a Government-opposition Dynamic?' (2001) 24 West European Politics 22.

[95] Sadurski (n 34); Drinóczi and Bień-Kacała (n 34); Kriszta Kovács and Kim Lane Scheppele, 'The Fragility of an Independent Judiciary: Lessons from Hungary and Poland—and the European Union' (2018) 51 Communist and Post-Communist Studies 189.

For each of the chapters, our analysis generally goes back in time to approximately 2004, the year in which the Treaty Establishing a Constitution for Europe was signed. The reason for the choice of date is that this Treaty was drafted in explicit constitutional language for the EU, and it codified in its body the principle of the primacy of EU law. While the debate on constitutionalism and EU law predates the Constitutional Treaty, we consider the treaty to be a likely catalyst for the growth in the debate.

In these chapters, we exhaustively analyse the national election manifestos of the Eurosceptic parties.[96]

Chapter 8 concludes the book. In addition to taking stock of our findings, we provide a more comprehensive critique in this final chapter of Eurosceptic, closed approaches to constitutional law. Finally, we argue in favour of an open interpretation of constitutionalism that is both compatible with European integration and capable of addressing its many challenges.

[96] Available at the Manifesto Project Database: Volkens, Andrea, Burst, Tobias, Krause, Werner, Lehmann, Pola, Matthieß, Theres, Regel, Sven, Weßels, Bernhard, Zehnter, Lisa, 'The Manifesto Data Collection. Manifesto Project (MRG/CMP/MARPOR). Version 2021a' (2021) Wissenschaftszentrum Berlin Für Sozialforschung (WZB) <https://doi.org/10.25522/manifesto.mpds.2021a>.

2
Mobilizing National Constitutional Law for Eurosceptic Purposes

2.1. Introduction

The intuition behind this book is that Euroscepticisms (in the plural) have evolved, so to speak, to the point of constructing constitutional counter-narratives. By constitutional counter-narratives we mean the mobilization of constitutional law arguments in order to use constitutional provisions in a way that is consistent with Eurosceptic political goals.

Obviously, the concept of counter-narratives implies the existence of narratives to which they are opposed. In this respect, we concur with those who argue that constitutions are not merely legal texts or political documents but also embody narratives and are presented as collective stories. In other words, constitutions have 'an interesting story to tell'.[1]

In Eurosceptic counter-narratives, interpretations often deviate from, and even contradict, traditional post-WWII premises characterized by constitutional openness, especially when they result in the subversion of the core values shared by national constitutional orders and EU Treaties and represented by article 2 of the Treaty on European Union (TEU). Indeed, in some cases, Eurosceptic forces have not failed to attack even their own constitutional texts, questioning this or that provision or making proposals for amendments that would revise the constitutional text profoundly.[2] More generally, however, the Eurosceptic approach to constitutions is more subtle, not necessarily resulting in the production of amendments or a purely confrontational attitude. Often, as we will see in the book, Eurosceptic movements seek to make technical arguments about constitutional law part of their political playbook.

[1] As was emphasized, for example, by Günter Frankenberg, *Comparative Constitutional Studies: Between Magic and Deceit* (Edward Elgar 2018) ix.

[2] Sometimes even by supporting unconstitutional constitutional amendments. On this concept, see Yaniv Roznai, *Unconstitutional Constitutional Amendments: The Limits of Amendment Powers* (Oxford University Press 2019).

The Eurosceptic Mobilization of Constitutional Law. Pablo Castillo-Ortiz and Giuseppe Martinico, Oxford University Press. © Pablo Castillo-Ortiz and Giuseppe Martinico 2026. DOI: 10.1093/9780198959205.003.0002

Mobilization has been defined in the following terms: 'The law is mobilized when a desire or want is translated into a demand as an assertion of one's rights'.[3] Traditionally, mobilization is associated with progressive movements that have fought for the affirmation of rights in different parts of the world through various techniques that often include forms of strategic litigation. In this volume, 'mobilization' will denote a more neutral concept. As the literature has emphasized, rights are tools that can be used as weapons,[4] and conservative arguments can also be mobilized with regressive aims. This insight can be applied to other tools of liberal constitutionalism, as Blokker emphasized, since 'various actors involved in lawfare put forward claims that they deem incontestable because of their "natural, universalistic, and depoliticized nature".[5] In this, Bob helpfully reminds us that both liberal movements/activists and conservative and religious counter-movements may promote such universalistic and depoliticized understandings of rights'.[6] Against this background, by 'mobilizing constitutional law', we will then refer to the use of constitutional law arguments that, in our case, aim to challenge, inter alia, the primacy of EU law, which is one of the pillars of the case law of the Court of Justice and a structural principle that distinguishes EU law from classic international law.

This Eurosceptic use of constitutional law is a multifaceted phenomenon, and the use of constitutional law against European integration varies from country to country, across political parties and over time. Its target is often the EU, but it can also be linked to criticisms of the Council of Europe. On occasions, it targets both.[7] In some instances, it will be coupled with proposals to withdraw from European organizations, while in other instances these latter proposals will be absent.

[3] Frances Kahn Zemans, 'Legal Mobilization: The Neglected Role of the Law in the Political System' (1983) 77 American Political Science Review 690, 699. On this concept, see also Lisa Vanhala, *Making Rights a Reality? Disability Rights Activists and Legal Mobilization* (Cambridge University Press 2010) 1.

[4] Clifford Bob, *Rights as Weapons: Instruments of Conflict, Tools of Power* (Princeton University Press 2019). 'Given that populism has also acquired a legal character in addition to its political dimension, such mobilization can be considered primarily legal. As populism "mimics" or "parasitizes" liberal democracy, the right-wing mobilization it unleashes employs the instrumentality of liberal legal mobilization. Populism in power opens new windows of opportunity for existing and facilitates new waves of right-wing legal mobilization', Karolina Kocemba and Michał Stambulski, 'Populism, Non-State Actors and Right-Wing Legal Mobilization in Europe' (2024) 20 International Journal of Law in Context 297, 299.

[5] In this passage, Blokker cited Bob (n 4) 14.

[6] Paul Blokker, 'Using Liberal–Legal Tools for Illiberal Gains: The European Court of Human Rights and Legal Mobilisation by Conservative Right-wing Actors' (2024) 20 International Journal of Law in Context 401, 408.

[7] In this chapter and throughout this book, we often refer to examples about the EU, as this is the main target of Eurosceptics. However, we understand that Euroscepticism argues against not only the EU but European organizations in general, thus also covering, for instance, the Council of Europe.

Despite these cross-case differences, we show in this book that there are some traits that tend to be present in most of these Eurosceptic constitutional counter-narratives. In this chapter, we present these traits systematically. To do so, we rely on existing theoretical and empirical literature, and on our own knowledge of the different constitutional counter-narratives of Eurosceptic parties. Later in this book (in Chapters 4 to 7), we detail how this Eurosceptic mobilization of constitutional law works in four specific case studies.

In particular, this chapter sets out theories about the Eurosceptic instrumentalization of constitutional law at three levels. First, at the theoretical-constitutional level, it is argued that this phenomenon relies on a nationalist, exclusionary constitutional counter-narrative. In this approach, only the national demos is presented as real, the national constitution is closed to supranational integration, and only the national constitution can be supreme. Second, at the level of judicial politics, the Eurosceptic constitutional counter-narrative attacks the ECJ, seeking to mobilize national political and judicial actors against the Luxembourg Court. Third, at the level of party politics, the Eurosceptic mobilization of constitutional law can be deemed to be a political strategy. On the one hand, Eurosceptic parties borrow the prestige of constitutional terminology, and use it against European integration. On the other hand, the Eurosceptic use of constitutional law becomes an alternative to the traditional Eurosceptic strategy of simply exiting European organizations.

2.2. Eurosceptic Mobilization of Constitutional law as Constitutional Counter-Narrative

In modern constitutional theory, constitutions are frequently conceptualized as the democratic expression of the will of the people. The basis of this idea can be found in Sieyès' 1789 pamphlet *Qu'est-ce que le Tiers-État?*. According to Sieyès, the constitution is the product of the constituent power, which pre-exists state institutions. In fact, in traditional constitutional theory, state institutions, and public authorities in general, are created and legitimized by the *pouvoir constituent*, which only the nation holds.[8]

For Sieyès, the constituent power did not act in a vacuum. The widespread misconception of constituent power as pure power operating in a legally empty space is probably due to Carl Schmitt,[9] who famously distorted and

[8] Emmanuel-Joseph Sieyès, *Qu'est-ce que le Tiers-État?*, 1789, available at: <http://www.leboucher.com/pdf/sieyes/tiers.pdf>.

[9] Carl Schmitt, *Constitutional Theory* (Duke University Press 2008) 126.

manipulated Sieyès' thought.[10] This view does not correspond to Sieyès' idea, according to which natural law was 'prior to the nation and above the nation',[11] understood as the bearer of constituent power. In this context, natural law ideally represented a constraint (or an external limit) on the will of the nation.

Sieyès' view, which attributed the constitution to the *pouvoir constituent* of the nation, can help us understand the contemporary view of a constitution as the source of the legitimacy of state bodies. Because constitutional law is the expression of the constituent power of the nation, there is a democratic link between the constitution and the people. Since the nation, through its constituent power, constitutes the state authorities via the constitution, it is obvious that those state authorities ought to remain constrained by the constitution that produced them. However, in order to constrain these *pouvoirs constitués*, the constitution needs to be enforced one way or another. After WWII, the usual way to achieve this in most contemporary European countries has been through judicial review of legislation—usually (with important exceptions) carried out by a Kelsenian-style constitutional court holding the monopoly on the review of constitutionality.[12]

We thus identify three core ideas underlying what could be called the stereotypical version of modern constitutional theory. First, the nation as the bearer of the *pouvoir constituent*. Second, the constitution as a fruit and expression of the sovereignty of the people. Third, the supremacy of the constitution. These three ideas, which are complementary, are re-interpreted in the Eurosceptic constitutional counter-narratives. We will explore them one by one.

2.2.1. *An exclusionary version of the demos*

The first aspect concerns the people. In the traditional approach to constitutionalism, the nation is regarded as the bearer of constituent power—but who is considered part of the nation? It is important to note that, in contemporary Eurosceptic counter-narratives, the terms nation and people are often used interchangeably—sometimes erroneously—blurring the distinction between the source of constitutional authority and the political community it governs.

[10] Lucia Rubinelli, *Constituent Power: A History* (Oxford University Press 2020) 23.

[11] Sieyès (n 8).

[12] See, inter alia, Hans Kelsen, 'Judicial Review of Legislation: A Comparative Study of the Austrian and the American Constitution' (1942) 4 The Journal of Politics 183; Hans Kelsen, *The Guardian of the Constitution: Hans Kelsen and Carl Schmitt on the Limits of Constitutional Law* (Lars Vinx ed and tr, Cambridge University Press 2015).

Reflecting on the manipulation of the concept of the nation, Halikiopoulou, Nanou, and Vasilopoulou argue in their work that nationalism is, in fact, a common denominator of both radical right and radical left Euroscepticism:

> The argument we put forward contests this idea that radical right- and left-wing parties are so dissimilar that they take positions at opposite ends of the political spectrum across a range of issues. Instead, we argue that radical parties share elements of nationalist ideology leading to a common eurosceptic stance. Radical left-wing opposition to EU integration is grounded in the very nationalist narratives to which in theory it is fundamentally opposed. Paradoxically, nationalism is the underlying feature that unites the radical right and the radical left, cross-cutting traditional alignments and mobilising support across the political spectrum.[13]

If nationalism is thus a common thread within Eurosceptic parties of the left and the right, then we can expect a nationalist approach to constitutional law in Eurosceptic parties of either ideology. Let us go back to Sieyès and the idea of constituent power. Today, constituent power can be conceptualized as a legal-historical fiction behind which there is a normative claim.[14] Indeed, behind the correspondence between 'constitution' and 'constituent power', there is the need to conceive of the constitution as the product of the will of a pre-existing political entity (the people) which 'serves' as a source of legitimacy for the constitution, helping us conceive of the constitution—as the product and then the limit of the constituent power—as 'democratic'.[15]

[13] Daphne Halikiopoulou, Kyriaki Nanou, and Sofia Vasilopoulou, 'The Paradox of Nationalism: The Common Denominator of Radical Right and Radical Left Euroscepticism' (2012) 51 European Journal of Political Research 504, 505.

[14] To confirm the fact that we are describing a historical-legal fiction, just think about a historical argument: usually, constitutions and the revolutions behind them—understood in a technical sense, as a break in the chain of validity à la Kelsen—have been a product of the action of the elite. The obsession with the constituent power and a constitutional moment has led to the description of the United Kingdom as the only example of an evolutionary (ie non-revolutionary) constitutionalism in Europe, but actually many other countries, provided with written constitutions, are in a problematic relationship with the 'constituent power': the German and the French cases (1958) are two other examples of this problematic trend. Many other EU Member States, then, do not have a document formally termed a constitution (Sweden, the Netherlands). Another example is represented by the Eastern European countries characterized by constituent processes that are atypical because they were influenced by the international community.

[15] 'When the discourse moves from the descriptive to the normative, it changes and becomes the claim that the constituent power in modern societies should be the people, for democracy is tied to the people and the legitimacy of legal authority depends on a democratic foundation', Denis J Galligan, 'The Paradox of Constitutionalism or the Potential of Constitutional Theory?' (2008) 28 Oxford Journal of Legal Studies 343, 353.

Comparative law shows that many constitutional experiences are not the product of constituent power and that nowadays constituent power rarely appears in its revolutionary forms; in this, it has been argued, constituent power has been replaced by the constituent process, a set of procedures that guarantee a gradual, incremental, and inclusive transition to a new constitution.[16] The classic example is provided by the 1996 South African Constitution. Indeed, the South African case demonstrates that constituent authority can then operate within a framework of legality.

The fiction of the constituent power is necessary in order to justify and legitimate the rupture with the past and the new constitutional design present in the fundamental charter:

> We attribute this power to the people. We behave as if the constitution is a product of the popular will. The fiction helps to bring the act in line with the requirements of democratic legitimacy. However, the term 'fiction' should not be misunderstood as a mere imagination. It makes a difference whether the constituent power is or is not attributed to the people. If the fiction is taken seriously it establishes a relationship of accountability between the government and the people which in spite of its fictitious basis has real consequences.[17]

The Eurosceptic mobilization of constitutional law uses a very peculiar version of this theoretical construction, interpreting its core concepts in a nationalist fashion. The people or the nation are, in the Eurosceptic constitutional counter-narrative, interpreted in an exclusionary manner, bringing us back to the confusion between these two terms, which we have already noted. For Eurosceptic readings of constitutional law, the only legitimate demos is the national one; any alternative approach to this core concept is regarded as a distortion. In particular, the idea of making decisions jointly with other European citizens within the framework of a democratic European Union is rejected. This rejection is grounded in the claim that a European demos does not exist, cannot exist, or should not exist—depending on the specific version of the argument.

Scepticism of the European Union demos is not new. In his work on this topic in the 1990s (in the post-Maastricht Treaty scenario), Dieter Grimm put

[16] See, among others, Peter Häberle, 'Die verfassunggebende Gewalt des Volkes im Verfassungsstaat – eine vergleichende Textstufenanalyse' (1987) 112 Archiv des öffentlichen Rechts 54; Andrew Arato, *Post Sovereign Constitution Making: Learning and Legitimacy* (Oxford University Press 2016).

[17] Dieter Grimm, 'Constituent Power and Limits of Constitutional Amendments' (2016) 2 Nomos 1.

forward the idea that Europe does not have a demos, among other reasons because of the absence of a true European media system and a common language, to mention some elements.[18] Because of his concerns about the non-existence of a true, viable European demos, Grimm firmly opposed what he saw as the process of 'converting the European Union into a federal state'.[19] Whether he was right or wrong in his assessment, Grimm's concerns were, we believe, truly linked to democratic considerations. Paradoxically, however, certain traits of this approach have subsequently been used by Eurosceptic parties too, many of which have questionable democratic credentials, as we will see.

2.2.2. Constitution, sovereignty, and identity

The second, connected, aspect of Eurosceptic constitutional counter-narratives is the way in which they understand the relationship between constitutions and sovereignty. This, again, connects with the claim that Eurosceptic parties of both radical left and radical right ideologies share a nationalist approach.[20] Above, we explained that this nationalism is often expressed in the way the demos is delimited, but it can also be found in the way the constitutional document is interpreted.

Examples of this can be found in the way constitutional clauses on the limitation of sovereignty are interpreted in connection with participation in international or, where there are specific clauses, supranational organizations. In these cases, sovereignty is interpreted as if it were only a shield unilaterally activated to protect the national interest (whatever that means[21]), forgetting that, in post-WWII constitutionalism, sovereignty is not only a shield but also, and above all, a key that allows participation in multilateral organizations. In other words, while sovereignty in post-WWII constitutionalism is open, in the reconstructions supported by Eurosceptic forces it is presented as if it were a closed and monolithic concept.

Linked to this, Eurosceptic constitutional counter-narratives use the argument of constitutional identity, based on the textual reference to the duty to respect countries' national identities 'inherent in their fundamental structures, political and constitutional'.[22]

[18] Dieter Grimm, 'Does Europe Need a Constitution?' (1995) 1 European Law Journal 282.
[19] Grimm, 'Does Europe Need a Constitution?' (n 18) 297.
[20] Halikiopoulou, Nanou, and Vasilopoulou (n 13).
[21] On the ambiguity of national interest, see Serena Giusti, *The Fall and Rise of National Interest: A Contemporary Approach* (Palgrave 2022).
[22] Article 4.2 TEU.

Sometimes these two concepts (sovereignty and constitutional identity) are used in conjunction, as if they were twin notions. An emblematic example of this is the famous ruling delivered by the Hungarian Constitutional Court in 2016. In this case, the constitutional judges were asked to interpret the constitutional text with reference to Council Decision (EU) 2015/1601 of 22 September 2015.[23] In the words of the Court:

> According to Article 4 (2) TEU, 'the Union shall respect the equality of Member States before the Treaties as well as their national identities, inherent in their fundamental structures, political and constitutional, inclusive of regional and local self-government.'
>
> The protection of constitutional identity should be granted in the framework of an informal cooperation with EUC based on the principles of equality and collegiality, with mutual respect to each other, similarly to the present practice followed by several other Member States' constitutional courts and supreme judicial bodies performing similar functions.
>
> The Constitutional Court of Hungary interprets the concept of constitutional identity as Hungary's self-identity and it unfolds the content of this concept from case to case, on the basis of the whole Fundamental Law and certain provisions thereof, in accordance with the National Avowal and the achievements of our historical constitution—as required by Article R) (3) of the Fundamental Law. The Constitutional Court establishes that the constitutional self-identity of Hungary is a fundamental value not created by the Fundamental Law—it is merely acknowledged by the Fundamental Law. Consequently, constitutional identity cannot be waived by way of an international treaty—Hungary can only be deprived of its constitutional identity through the final termination of its sovereignty, its independent statehood. *Therefore the protection of constitutional identity shall remain the duty of the Constitutional Court as long as Hungary is a sovereign State. Accordingly, sovereignty and constitutional identity have several common points, thus their control should be performed with due regard to each other in specific cases.*[24] *(emphasis added)*

In this passage, the Hungarian Constitutional Court takes article 4(2) TEU (which mentions the concept of 'national identity') as its starting point and

[23] Decision 2015/1601 (EU) establishing provisional measures in the area of international protection for the benefit of Italy and Greece.

[24] Hungarian Constitutional Court, Decision 22/2016 <https://public.mkab.hu/dev/dontesek.nsf/0/1361afa3cea26b84c1257f10005dd958/$FILE/EN_22_2016.pdf, paras 62–66>.

then, however, uses the concept of 'constitutional identity', coupling it with the need to preserve national sovereignty (a term not employed in the wording of article 4 TEU). Finally, the Hungarian Constitutional Court reads the concept of constitutional identity in the light of article R(3) of the Hungarian Constitution, thereby offering an alternative reading of the same term. In doing so, the Hungarian Constitutional Court knowingly ignores the fact that respect for national identity must necessarily be read in conjunction with article 4(3) TEU, which codifies the principle of sincere cooperation.

Constitutional identity and the very notion of sovereignty are thus used in the Eurosceptic counter-narratives in a very specific way: as core aspects of a closed approach to the interpretation of national constitutions. These counter-narratives signal a political rejection of the commitment to supranational integration and international cooperation.

2.2.3. Constitutional supremacy against European integration

As we saw at the beginning, the concept of mobilization is much more neutral than it might initially appear. It has, in fact, rightly been decoupled from the idea of a progressive interpretation and application of human rights law. This understanding can also be extended to constitutional provisions not specifically devoted to rights, forming the basis for the analysis of the case studies discussed in this book. We argue that the Eurosceptic use of constitutional law is a paradigmatic example of the political mobilization of the law against European integration.

The Eurosceptic use of constitutional law is, in a way, a new and somewhat unexpected turn in one of the most long-standing controversies in European law. We know that post-WWII European constitutionalism is, generally,[25] based on the idea of a rigid and entrenched constitution, whose provisions are judicially enforced.[26] The premise behind post-WWII European constitutionalism is thus that legislators are no longer sovereign but, rather, are constrained by the legal system itself.[27]

The primacy of EU law had to be built against the background of the traditional supremacy of national constitutional law. This led to fascinating

[25] Cesare Pinelli, 'The Formation of a Constitutional Tradition in Continental Europe since World War II' (2016) 22 European Public Law 257.

[26] Luigi Ferrajoli, *Iura Paria. Los Fundamentos de La Democracia Constitucional* (Trotta 2020) 19–51.

[27] Paolo Sandro, *The Making of Constitutional Democracy: From Creation to Application of Law* (Hart Publishing 2022).

academic and judicial debates. One of the most prominent approaches to this question tried to understand the interaction between European and national law in terms of constitutional pluralism: a model in which the relationship between legal systems would be heterarchical, not hierarchical.[28] In fact, for a long time, constitutional pluralism seemed to be a good description of the European status quo. However, in recent times, this approach has become the object of strong criticism, on the grounds that it has given illiberal governments in EU Member States a constitutional law basis to justify their attacks on the fundamental values of the European Union, most notably respect for the rule of law.[29]

The Eurosceptic use of constitutional law is associated with this debate. However, we believe that there is a strong discontinuity between pluralist approaches to European constitutionalism and Eurosceptic constitutional counter-narratives. Constitutional Eurosceptics do not conceive of the European legal arena as one in which different legal systems coexist in a co-operative and pluralist manner. Rather, they argue that coexistence between national constitutions and the EU Treaties is impossible, as EU law is considered to be in conflict with national constitutional law, and they take the side of the latter. This is evident in the Italian context, where many supporters of sovereignism have claimed that, in particular, the post-Maastricht EU is radically inconsistent with the fundamental choices made in the Constitution.[30]

Ultimately, Eurosceptics justify the supremacy of the national constitution—seen as incompatible with European Treaties—on the basis of popular sovereignty. Since, for Eurosceptics, only the national demos is a real demos, only the national constitution can be supreme, as it is consistent with the democratic principle. The idea of EU law having primacy even over constitutional law, as was articulated by the ECJ, is thus, from their viewpoint, a constitutional aberration.

These arguments frequently borrow from noble scholarly debates, going further and instrumentalizing them. Again, in Grimm's work we can already find some discussion of this:

[28] Neil MacCormick, 'The Maastricht-Urteil: Sovereignty Now' (1995) 1 European Law Journal 259; Neil MacCormick, 'Democracy, Subsidiarity, and Citizenship in the "European Commonwealth"' (1997) 16 Law and Philosophy 331.

[29] R Daniel Kelemen and Laurent Pech, 'The Uses and Abuses of Constitutional Pluralism: Undermining the Rule of Law in the Name of Constitutional Identity in Hungary and Poland' (2019) 21 Cambridge Yearbook of European Legal Studies 59.

[30] Luciano Barra Caracciolo, *Euro e (o?) democrazia costituzionale. La convivenza impossibile tra costituzione e trattati europei* (Dike Giuridica, 2022).

> With a constitution in the full sense of the term, the Union would acquire competence to decide about competences (Kompetenzkompetenz). Similarly, the primacy of Community law over national law would no longer be the consequence of the Member States' order issued in the Treaties, but of the constitutional precept in the Community constitution. The Community would in principle also have the power in the constitution to decide itself on its endowment with resources, including taxation, instead of being dependent on transfers from Member States. These features are not those of an association of States. They typify the State. Since this State would not however have the mediatory structures from which the democratic process lives, the Community would after its full constitutionalisation be a largely self-supporting institution, farther from its base than ever (...). A European Constitution would not be able to bridge the existing gap and would consequently disappoint the expectations associated with it. The legitimation it would mediate would be a fictitious one. Accordingly, when it comes down to it constitutions are still something to do with States, and anyone calling for one for Europe should be aware what movement he is thereby setting going.[31]

It is worth repeating that we believe that the underlying concern in Grimm's approach was respect for democracy, even if we might disagree with how this is interpreted. Moreover, as clarified earlier, the roots of his approach must be contextualized in the post-Maastricht Treaty debate. Interestingly enough, Eurosceptic parties that often show a strong disregard for liberal-democratic values mobilize constitutional counter-narratives against European organizations. Furthermore, cases like Poland under PiS (the Law and Justice party) show how these constitutional counter-narratives about national supremacy can have, as their main purpose, the undermining of liberal-democratic checks on power, rather than the protection of democracy.

2.3. The Eurosceptic Use of Constitutional Law as a Stance in European Judicial Politics

A corollary of the previous point leads directly towards the interaction between the courts in the European legal arena. Such interaction is doomed to

[31] Grimm, 'Does Europe Need a Constitution?' (n 18) 298–299.

be complex, with the ECJ in charge of enforcing the EU legal system and the national higher courts in charge of enforcing the national constitutions. The relationship between the ECJ and the national higher courts is, with this background, marked by elements of both cooperation and conflict.[32]

Lawyers often understood the European judicial landscape as one marked by complexity, yet characterized by techniques developed by national higher courts and supranational courts to communicate and avoid confrontation.[33] In parallel, however, several approaches emerged—particularly in political science—highlighting the conflictual aspects of this relationship.[34] The intricacies of these complex relationships have been explained by, among others, Ana Bobić.[35] According to this author:

> The penetration of Union law and its peculiarities into national constitutional orders has created a relationship of unease between the Court of Justice and national courts with constitutional jurisdiction. The Court of Justice, on the one hand, is convinced in the utmost value of effectiveness of Union law and is expecting all national courts to share its zeal. On the other hand, national courts performing constitutional review tend to prioritize their respective constitutions. Consequently, they have employed different methods of adhering to the requirements of EU law while at the same time fulfilling their original role of safeguarding the supremacy of the national constitution. Some rejected particular findings of the Court of Justice by declaring them ultra vires, whereas others joined ordinary national courts in submitting preliminary questions to the Court of Justice.[36]

What is interesting, for the purposes of this book, is that Eurosceptics seem to have understood the potential of this complex European judicial landscape when pursuing their agenda. Taking a stance in the debates about European judicial integration, Eurosceptics seek to undermine the process of European integration by amplifying the tensions and antagonisms between national courts and the European Court of Justice.

[32] See, for a detailed review, Ana Bobić, *The Jurisprudence of Constitutional Conflict in the European Union* (Oxford University Press 2022).

[33] Andreas Voβkuhle, 'Multilevel Cooperation of the European Constitutional Courts: Der Europäische Verfassungsgerichtsverbund' (2010) 6 European Constitutional Law Review 175.

[34] Karen J Alter, 'The European Court's Political Power' (1996) 19 West European Politics 458.

[35] Bobić (n 32).

[36] Bobić (n 32) 7.

2.3.1. Rejecting the European courts and their authority

As has already been suggested, constitutional Eurosceptics take a purely conflictual approach to the relationship between courts. Against this background, the rejection of the authority of the ECJ *va de soi.*

In fact, in their opposition to the authority of the ECJ, constitutional Eurosceptics found an interesting set of tools in the case law of European national constitutional courts. This is not to say that European constitutional courts have traditionally taken Eurosceptic positions—addressing that question would require a full monograph. What we mean is simply that Eurosceptics have often been able to borrow constitutional law arguments and incorporate them into their political strategies, sometimes even citing constitutional case law in their election manifestos.[37]

The fact is that many national constitutional courts had traditionally been reluctant to accept an unconditional version of the principle of primacy. Examples include the Italian constitutional doctrine of *contro-limiti*,[38] and the decisions of the German Federal Constitutional Court in cases such as *Solange*,[39] *Maastricht-Urteil*,[40] or *Lisbon*,[41] but also the positions of other courts such as the Czech Constitutional Court in its *Lisbon I* ruling,[42] or the subtle caveats of the Spanish Constitutional Court in its Declaration 1/2004 on the Constitutional Treaty.[43] The literature on all these decisions is extensive, showing their importance in the history of European integration.[44]

The common denominator of most of these cases consists of two ideas. First, national constitutional courts accept the principle of primacy, but, rather than basing it on the EU Treaties, they find the ultimate source of the legitimacy of the principle in their national constitutions. Second, because of this, the primacy of EU law is not always unconditional,[45] and the constitutional courts

[37] Pablo Castillo-Ortiz, 'Right-Wing Eurosceptic Parties and the Strategic Use of Law' (2023) 61 Journal of Common Market Studies 1125.

[38] Corte costituzionale, sentenza 183/1973 <https://www.cortecostituzionale.it/default.do>.

[39] German Federal Constitutional Court, case 2 BvL 52/71, *Solange I*, 29 May 1974.

[40] German Federal Constitutional Court, case 2 BvR 2134 et al. *Treaty of Maastricht*, 12 October 1993.

[41] German Federal Constitutional Court, case 2 BvE 2/08 et al. *Treaty of Lisbon*, 30 June 2009.

[42] Czech Constitutional Court, Case No Pl. ÚS 19/08, *Treaty of Lisbon I*, 30 September 2008.

[43] Declaration 1/2004 of the Spanish Constitutional Court, 13 December 2004.

[44] See, inter alia, Neil MacCormick, 'The Maastricht-Urteil' (n 28); Julio Baquero Cruz, 'The Legacy of the Maastricht-Urteil and the Pluralist Movement' (2007) European University Institute RSCAS Working Paper 2007/13; Mattias Wendel, 'Lisbon before the Courts: Comparative Perspectives' (2011) 7 European Constitutional Law Review 96; Pablo Castillo-Ortiz, *EU Treaties and the Judicial Politics of National Courts: A Law and Politics Approach* (Routledge 2017); Ana Bobić and Mark Dawson, 'Making Sense of the "Incomprehensible": The PSPP Judgment of the German Federal Constitutional Court', (2020) 57(6) Common Market Law Review 1953.

[45] Miguel Poiares Maduro, 'Interpreting European Law: Judicial Adjudication in a Context of Constitutional Pluralism' (2007) 1 European Journal of Legal Studies 137.

tend to claim the ultimate say in order to protect their constitutional core, by relying on different techniques, such as ultra vires review or identity review, among others.[46]

As we will see in Chapter 4, Eurosceptics also frequently seek to undermine the authority of the European Court of Human Rights. The political attacks against this court by some Eurosceptic parties are particularly illuminating when it comes to showing how it is also an important target for these actors. To mention one example, the Conservative Party pledged, in its 2015 manifesto, to 'scrap the Human Rights Act, and introduce a British Bill of Rights. This will break the formal link between British courts and the European Court of Human Rights, and make our own Supreme Court the ultimate arbiter of human rights matters in the UK'.[47] After Brexit, attacks on the European Court of Human Rights by British Eurosceptics are still frequent in the political debate in this country.

2.3.2. Instrumentalizing national constitutional institutions

With this background, a very interesting development takes place when Eurosceptics manage to gain leverage over the national constitutional courts. The most visible case is probably that of Poland. In this country, the previous PiS government managed to take control of the Constitutional Court.[48] The consequences of this takeover for the rule of law and liberal democracy in Poland have been well documented by a large body of academic literature,[49] and its explanation goes beyond the remit of this book. What matters for the purposes of this research is, however, that the Polish Constitutional Court issued decisions that question the primacy of EU law and the authority of the ECJ.[50] This development is actually the materialization of the core menace of Eurosceptics. It shows that beyond rhetorical threats, the intersection of

[46] On these techniques as devised and developed by the German Constitutional Court's case law, see, for instance, Mattias Wendel, 'The Fog of Identity and Judicial Contestation: Preventive and Defensive Constitutional Identity Review in Germany' (2021) 27 European Public Law 474.

[47] Conservative Party, 'Strong leadership, a clear economic plan and a brighter, more secure future' (2015).

[48] Bojan Bugarič and Tom Ginsburg, 'The Assault on Postcommunist Courts' (2016) 27 The Journal of Democracy 69.

[49] Bugarič and Ginsburg (n 48); Pablo Castillo-Ortiz, 'The Illiberal Abuse of Constitutional Courts in Europe', (2019) 15 European Constitutional Law Review 48; Wojciech Sadurski, *Poland's Constitutional Breakdown* (Oxford University Press 2019).

[50] Petra Bárd and Adam Bodnar, 'The End of an Era: The Polish Constitutional Court's Judgment on the Primacy of EU Law and Its Effects on Mutual Trust' (2021) CEPS Policy Insights No 2021-15.

illiberalism and the Eurosceptic mobilization of constitutional law can lead to actual decisions that undermine a core aspect of the process of European integration.

In this context, the synergy between illiberalism and the Eurosceptic abuse of constitutional law is, in fact, absolute. Illiberalism is, to a large extent, a strategy followed by certain governments to take over the constitutional courts and other constitutional institutions, in order to weaken the checks on their power. In these cases, the Eurosceptic use of constitutional law allows such governments to challenge the European Union, in order to protect their illiberal takeover of national constitutional institutions, advancing, in this way, a subversive counter-narrative that can affect the hard nucleus of EU integration. In this game, the European Union is concerned about the illiberal control of national institutions such as the constitutional court, but, once it has been taken over, the national constitutional court becomes a tool of the illiberal government against precisely the European Union.

One might ask what distinguishes these cases from those of other constitutional courts—such as the Italian and German courts—which, as early as the 1970s, employed domestic legal arguments to challenge the case law of the Court of Justice, particularly the decision in *Internationale Handelsgesellschaft*.[51]

As discussed elsewhere,[52] what has changed is the context: constitutional courts once focused on the functionalization and adaptation of constitutional texts in an attempt to explain primacy and direct effect, operating on the assumption that two distinct criteria applied—one governing the relationship between domestic law and Community law (the principle of the separation of competences), and the other governing the relationship between domestic constitutional law and national legislation (the principle of hierarchy). This interpretation was partially called into question by the emergence of fundamental rights in the supranational sphere, because constitutionalization through general principles has created an area of overlap and because, as always, fundamental rights question an interpretation based on the mere principle of competence. This constitutionalization is the result of the reaction of constitutional courts to the monist case law of the European Court of Justice. In 1992,[53] this area of overlap was confirmed by reference to common constitutional

[51] ECJ, Case 11/70 *Internationale Handelsgesellschaft mbH v Einfuhr- und Vorratsstelle für Getreide und Futtermittel* ECLI:EU:C:1970:114.

[52] Giuseppe Martinico, *The Tangled Complexity of the EU Constitutional Process: The Frustrating Knot of Europe* (2nd edn, Routledge 2022).

[53] Anthony Arnull, 'What Is a General Principle of EU Law?' in Stefan Vogenauer (ed), *Prohibition of Abuse of Law: A New General Principle of EU Law?* (Hart Publishing 2017) 7.

traditions, and then progressively in the codification of clauses such as article 2 TEU and article 6 TEU (as well as in the provisions of the Charter of Fundamental Rights of the European Union). This has been recognized even in 'polemical' rulings such as judgments of the Italian Constitutional Court, for instance no 269/2017.[54]

Today, lawyers use the same techniques that were invented by the constitutional courts in the 1970s (the counter-limits and Solange doctrines[55]) for different types of conflict, which are no longer due to the absence of an equivalent norm at the supranational level (*Solange I*[56]) but are the result of the need to have the final say on norms that belong to both legal systems.[57]

In particular, the codification of article 2 TEU confirms this gradual and partial convergence between domestic and supranational legal systems, and establishes a presumption of 'structural compatibility'[58] between the domestic and the supranational levels. This presumption of structural compatibility is undermined by Eurosceptics when they attack this core value, violating both the hard nucleus of the European Union legal order and national constitutions. This is where we see the abusive nature of the mobilization of domestic constitutional law arguments. They end up not only questioning the special nature of EU law but also legitimizing an attack on the core of post-WWII European constitutionalism. When, on the other hand, this core is not contested, we might be dealing with the non-abusive mobilization of national constitutional law arguments. This mobilization is always problematic from the viewpoint of EU law, as it implies a clash in the European legal arena which questions the primacy of EU law and creates legal uncertainty, but at the same time it might have positive aspects, contributing to the development of supranational law. This was the case in the 1970s, when the absolute understanding of primacy was challenged on the basis that Community law had to acknowledge a form of protection for fundamental rights, conceived of as constitutional goods at the national level. This gave rise to the above-mentioned partial convergence, as confirmed today by the language of the EU Treaties.

[54] Corte costituzionale, sentenza 269/2017 <https://www.cortecostituzionale.it/default.do>.

[55] Corte costituzionale, sentenza 183/1973; BVerfGE 37, case 271 2 BvL 52/71 *Solange I-Beschluß*.

[56] BVerfGE 37, 271 2 BvL 52/71 *Solange I-Beschluß*.

[57] These could be defined as multi-sourced equivalent norms. For this concept, see Tomer Broude and Yuval Shany (eds), *Multi-Sourced Equivalent Norms in International Law* (Hart Publishing 2011).

[58] Armin von Bogdandy, 'Founding Principles' in Armin von Bogdandy and Jürgen Bast (eds), *Principles of European Constitutional Law* (Hart Publishing 2009) 11, 22. Giacomo Delledonne and Luke Spieker explicitly discuss the possibility of comparing article 2 TEU to the federal clauses of constitutional homogeneity: Giacomo Delledonne, *L'omogeneità costituzionale negli ordinamenti composti* (Editoriale Scientifica 2017) 215; Luke Dimitrios Spieker, *EU Values before the Court of Justice: Foundations, Potential, Risks* (Oxford 2023) 165.

Obviously, not all uses of constitutional law arguments by Eurosceptic movements can be defined as abusive. The abusive nature of constitutional law arguments can take different forms, and it is not the aim of our book to offer an abstract classification of the phenomenon, which has already been the subject of important academic contributions.[59] Possible examples, as we shall see, of the abusive nature of the invocation of constitutional law arguments include the decontextualization or selective use of provisions that lead to a distortion of the rationale of the constitutional law arguments invoked. In certain cases, abuse also takes the form of the cosmetic use of constitutional law, when the real aim is to support an interpretation of the law itself that distorts the core of post-WWII constitutionalism, as explained in Chapter 1.

This should serve as a warning if another Eurosceptic party in Europe were to incorporate constitutional courts into its political strategy, which is not uncommon.[60] The Polish example shows how this question has implications not only for the process of European integration but also for national constitutional law. The Polish case, in fact, is marked by a paradox. As we explained earlier in this chapter, using a constitutional-Eurosceptic strategy, illiberal Polish actors are actually undermining the national values that they rhetorically vindicate as much as they are eroding European legal integration. In action, the Eurosceptic mobilization of constitutional law, at least in Poland, does not seem to be about siding with national constitutional law against European integration. Rather, it seems to be about undermining both national constitutional values and European legal integration at the same time. There is no trade-off, just a lose–lose scenario.

2.4. The Eurosceptic Mobilization of Constitutional Law as a Party-Political Strategy

Finally, something that is worth underlining is that the Eurosceptic use of constitutional law is, at the end of the day, a political strategy. With the use of constitutional language by Eurosceptic actors, a topic that was traditionally a matter for academic discussion and that seemed to be confined to judicial politics has mutated into an important element of party politics.[61] Actually, we can

[59] For instance, Rosalind Dixon and David Landau, *Abusive Constitutional Borrowing: Legal Globalization and the Subversion of Liberal Democracy* (Oxford University Press 2021). Julian Scholtes, *The Abuse of Constitutional Identity in the European Union* (Oxford University Press 2023).
[60] Castillo-Ortiz, 'Right-Wing Eurosceptic Parties and the Strategic Use of Law' (n 37).
[61] Castillo-Ortiz, 'Right-Wing Eurosceptic Parties and the Strategic Use of Law' (n 37).

assume that if Eurosceptic parties use constitutional law, it is likely to be because they expect that it will allow them to achieve what political parties want to achieve: to get into power and implement their political agenda.

2.4.1. Mobilizing constitutional law and its reputation

The history of contemporary constitutionalism is the history of warnings against its potential abuse. Because of its reputation and core role in the legitimation of our political systems, it seems to constantly be at risk of being instrumentalized. In his famous piece on constitutionalism published in 1962, Sartori underlined the increasing prestige of constitutional terminology and warned against its political abuse.[62] This warning seems to be particularly relevant nowadays, in the light of what Kim Lane Scheppele defines as autocratic legalism.[63] In one of her works, Scheppele says something about populists that can be aptly applied to Euroscepticism:

> Populists expose the vulnerabilities in the theories that our profession has taken for granted, and those of us who have defended the democratic integrity of liberal constitutionalism have been surprised by the way that populists have deployed theoretical arguments and high-powered technical legal tools in ways that are hard for us to counter. Populists are a challenge to the political systems in which they operate, but they are also a challenge to those of us who believe in the normative defensibility of liberal constitutionalism. Populists exploit the debates that liberal constitutionalists have with each other over normative foundations. They mirror and mimic the language of constitutional liberalism in order to undermine it in practice. We—the constitutional liberals—can't turn away because we recognize ourselves in the criticisms that the populists offer.[64]

The Eurosceptic abuse of constitutional law is, in fact, a powerful political strategy. Note that the background of most of these parties is in societies with solid pro-European preferences. By using constitutional law, Eurosceptics gain

[62] Giovanni Sartori, 'Constitutionalism: A Preliminary Discussion' (1962) 56 The American Political Science Review 853.
[63] Kim Lane Scheppele, 'Autocratic Legalism' (2018) 85 The University of Chicago Law Review 545, 547–548.
[64] Kim Lane Scheppele, 'The Opportunism of Populists and the Defense of Constitutional Liberalism' (2019) 20 German Law Journal 314, 315.

a superficial reputation and respectability for their political agendas: it is easier to run on a rhetoric of protection of the national constitution than on one of opposition to European integration.[65] The lesson to be learned is that constitutionalism has a reputational capital that attracts a variety of political actors. This includes those with little interest in liberal constitutionalism. Eurosceptic narratives about constitutional law seem to be the result of a practical realization of how this reputation of constitutionalism can be turned against European integration, even by actors with little regard for constitutionalism itself.

2.4.2. The Eurosceptic mobilization of constitutional law and the exit strategy

A final aspect of the Eurosceptic instrumentalization of constitutional law that is worth mentioning is its complex relationship with the more traditional strategy of Eurosceptics: the exit strategy. This exit strategy, which materialized in the British exit from the European Union, simply consists in a party proposing that the Member State to which it belongs should abandon the relevant regional organization, in this case the European Union.

So far, we know that the Eurosceptic mobilization of constitutional law is different from, but compatible with, the exit strategy.[66] Sometimes, the Eurosceptic use of constitutional law can be preferred to the exit strategy, and parties opt for the first and not the second. By way of hypothesis, this could be the case when a party believes that the Eurosceptic use of constitutional law can be presented to voters as a more viable approach. At the end of the day, this means that the Eurosceptics do not need to propose a damaging exit from European organizations, and they can often portray their proposals in terms of simply transforming such organizations so that they are more respectful of national constitutional law. Of course, hidden behind this rhetoric is the fact that the Eurosceptic mobilization of constitutional law targets the core principles of the process of European integration, and thus has the potential to fundamentally damage it.

However, on other occasions, the Eurosceptic mobilization of constitutional law and the exit strategy can be presented as complementary approaches by, for instance, suggesting that the party will seek an exit from the EU but, for as

[65] Castillo-Ortiz, 'Right-Wing Eurosceptic Parties and the Strategic Use of Law' (n 37).
[66] Castillo-Ortiz, 'Right-Wing Eurosceptic Parties and the Strategic Use of Law' (n 37).

Table 2.1. Exit and constitutional Eurosceptic strategies

	Exit strategy	**Eurosceptic mobilization of constitutional law**
Goal (in hard versions)	Exiting the EU/CoE	Undermining the EU/CoE
Rhetoric	Independence	Law and constitution
Character	Explicit	Implicit
Tool to implement	Usually referendum	Court action

long as this does not materialize, will enforce constitutional supremacy over EU law.

It is worth emphasizing that the Eurosceptic mobilization of constitutional law can be as 'hard' a Eurosceptic strategy as the exit approach. We already elaborated on this in Chapter 1. Recall the definition of hard Euroscepticism by Taggart and Szczerbiak[67]: hard Euroscepticism is also Euroscepticism that questions the core aspects of the project of European integration. This is what Eurosceptic counter-narratives do. In so doing, Eurosceptic parties reject the primacy of EU law or the rulings of the ECJ, but without these, European supranational institutions simply cannot exist as we know them, and the process of European integration would simply fail.

It is important to emphasize that the distinction between the exit strategy and the Eurosceptic mobilization of constitutional law is not, thus, equivalent to the distinction between hard and soft Euroscepticism. Instead, these are two hard forms of Euroscepticism, even if they are radically different. The exit strategy is, of course, hard Euroscepticism in that it seeks to withdraw the country from European organizations, but the Eurosceptic mobilization of constitutional law seeks to undermine the process of European integration from within, by opposing its core principles, and it is thus hard Euroscepticism too.

As illustrated in Table 2.1, these two forms of hard Euroscepticism differ in their goals, rhetoric, character, and tools. The exit strategy often looks 'harder' because it uses a strong rhetoric of independence and is explicit about its goals: withdrawal from European organizations, often following a referendum. The Eurosceptic mobilization of constitutional law, by contrast, uses a

[67] Paul Taggart and Aleks Szczerbiak, 'Contemporary Euroscepticism in the Party Systems of the European Union Candidate States of Central and Eastern Europe' (2004) 43 European Journal of Political Research 1, 3.

rhetoric based on constitutional theory categories, and its threat to European integration is often implicit, its Euroscepticism subtler; the preferred tool here is court action. To wrap up this section, it is worth recalling that regarding their goals, the exit strategy seeks withdrawal of a specific country from the European Union or the Council of Europe, while the Eurosceptic mobilization of constitutional law seeks to undermine these European organizations from within.

2.5. Conclusion: A True Challenge for European Integration

The Eurosceptic mobilization of constitutional law is not a milder form of Euroscepticism. It is not less dangerous than other forms, either. The fact that Eurosceptics often present it as such shows precisely one of its perils: it has great potential to attract voters by using a counter-narrative which exploits the prestige of constitutionalism for electoral gain.

These Eurosceptic constitutional counter-narratives, however, may pose a real threat to European integration. They attack the core principles around which European organizations are constructed. They target the principle of the primacy of EU law. European integration has long been seen as a form of 'integration through law.'[68] Eurosceptics seem to have become aware of this, and now they aim to turn the mechanism around: disintegrating through law is their strategy.

In attacking European integration, Eurosceptics interpret constitutional law in ways that also conflict with the values that underlie the European project. European integration is also a project that wants citizens of different countries to see themselves as European citizens, but the accounts of Eurosceptics continue to say that the national people is something exclusive. European integration aims to protect values such as democracy, the rule of law and human rights, but Eurosceptic uses of constitutional law are often aimed at shielding illiberal governments and policies from these values. Eurosceptics seek to transform the open constitutionalism of the post-WWII period into a closed phenomenon in which national constitutional institutions are weaponized against supranational ones.

[68] The expression 'integration through law' originates from a series of important volumes edited by Mauro Cappelletti, Monica Seccombe, and Joseph Weiler, *Integration Through Law: Europe and the American Federal Experience, Vol 1: Methods, Tools and Institutions* (Walter de Gruyter 1986). For a critique of the integration through law approach, see most recently Robert Schütze, '"Integration-through-Law": Grand Theory, Revisionist History' (2025) 4 European Law Open 162.

In the following chapters of this book (Chapters 4–7), we analyse in depth how the Eurosceptic mobilization of constitutional law works in four different countries: Italy, the United Kingdom, Spain, and Poland. We seek to show the functioning of the Eurosceptic constitutional strategy, explaining its fundamental theoretical and doctrinal elements. However, throughout this book, we also seek to question this Eurosceptic counter-narrative about constitutional law. This book, thus, rests on a normative premise: that open constitutionalism is a fundamental premise of post-WWII constitutionalism and should be protected and preserved, since its denial would imply a violation of the common axiological ground connecting the national and supranational constitutional levels.

3

Constitutional Law and Euroscepticism

A Comparative Analysis

3.1. Introduction

Earlier in this book, we explored the idea of the Eurosceptic mobilization of constitutional law from a theoretical perspective. In the rest of this book, we show that Eurosceptic parties not infrequently mobilize constitutional ideas, rhetoric, and institutions against European integration. This strategy is a distinct strategy, albeit an often complementary one, from that which proposes exiting from European organizations. The Eurosceptic mobilization of constitutional law often seeks to undermine European integration without necessarily abandoning its organizations, by attacking the core principles that structure the legal system of the EU or the European Convention on Human Rights.

Interestingly, we still know very little about why Eurosceptic parties choose to exploit constitutional concepts, instruments, and discourses against European integration in their election campaigns—or why they sometimes choose not to. Furthermore, traditional explanations for the Euroscepticism of political parties are not necessarily helpful for understanding this specific type of opposition to European integration. The reason is that traditional, more political forms of hard Euroscepticism (such as a proposal to leave the EU) and the Eurosceptic mobilization of constitutional law do not always overlap. Manifestos such as those of AfD (2017) or Finns (2011) in national general elections openly propose leaving the European Union but do not use a strong mobilization of constitutional law against European integration. Manifestos such as those of the British Conservative Party (2010) or the Danish People's Party (2015) strongly mobilize the law against European integration, but do not propose abandoning EU organizations. The causation of forms of Euroscepticism related to constitutional law is thus probably specific and idiosyncratic, and so far remains unexplored.

The Eurosceptic Mobilization of Constitutional Law. Pablo Castillo-Ortiz and Giuseppe Martinico, Oxford University Press. © Pablo Castillo-Ortiz and Giuseppe Martinico 2026. DOI: 10.1093/9780198959205.003.0003

This chapter fills this gap for a meaningful subsample of the universe of Eurosceptic parties: right-wing Eurosceptic parties of the EU-15 countries. It then explores how the findings of the chapter can be generalized to other contexts. The chapter thus makes a contribution to the understanding of the Eurosceptic mobilization of constitutional law from an empirical and comparative perspective that combines law and politics. To do this, the chapter focuses on the use of constitutional law against European integration in party manifestos. Using configurational research with Qualitative Comparative Analysis (QCA), the chapter shows that there are three main paths to the Eurosceptic mobilization of constitutional law by these parties. First, the path applicable to Eurosceptic parties with a high proportion of the vote in countries without a tradition of the strong form of constitutional review. Second, the path of radical right-wing populist Eurosceptic parties in countries that were strongly affected by the crisis in the Eurozone. Third, the path of radical right-wing populist parties facing right-wing Eurosceptic competition in countries without a tradition of the strong form of constitutional review.

3.2. Constitutional Law versus European Integration in Election Manifestos

This chapter focuses on the manifestos of Eurosceptic right-wing parties in the main national elections in each country of the EU-15. The choice to study only the EU-15 is justified for two main reasons. First, the usual focus of literature about the use of law against European integration has been on Central and Eastern European countries,[1] which has led to a gap in the literature for countries of the EU-15. Second, the countries of the EU-15 are the older members of the European Union and are older democracies, and thus the European dynamics of their party systems are likely to be dissimilar, in important areas, from those of countries that joined the EU in subsequent enlargements. At the comparative level, this meant that selecting only countries of the EU-15 was a more cautious design strategy. However, the chapter complements this analysis

[1] Petra Bárd and Adam Bodnar, 'The End of an Era. The Polish Constitutional Court's Judgement on the Primacy of EU Law and Its Effects on Mutual Trust' [2021] CEPS Policy Insights No 2021-15; R Daniel Kelemen and Laurent Pech, 'The Uses and Abuses of Constitutional Pluralism: Undermining the Rule of Law in the Name of Constitutional Identity in Hungary and Poland' (2019) 21 Cambridge Yearbook of European Legal Studies 59; Kim Lane Scheppele, 'The Treaties without a Guardian: The European Commission and the Rule of Law' (2023) 29 Columbia Journal of European Law 93.

with a qualitative explanation of the extent to which our findings could apply to other instances, such as left-wing Eurosceptic parties or parties in countries of the EU-27 (Section 3.6).

The object of the research in this chapter—the phenomenon that we try to explain—is the Eurosceptic mobilization of constitutional law in election manifestos. For the information about it in our cases, this chapter relies on the dataset gathered by Castillo-Ortiz in an earlier piece of research.[2] This dataset systematically covers national election manifestos, identifying instances of the Eurosceptic use of constitutional supremacy for those right-wing Eurosceptic parties that are electorally of a certain size—those that obtained at least 10 per cent of the vote in the relevant election. This is because we considered those parties to be more likely to have leverage over the political agenda, and thus they were qualitatively different from less sizeable parties. The dataset covers a period of more than a decade, from the entry into force of the Lisbon Treaty until the recent decision K3/21 of the Polish Constitutional Court. We consider this timeframe to be appropriate for two reasons. First, it covers the cases since the entry into force of the current framework of EU primary legislation—the Lisbon Treaty—until 2021, when the decision of the Polish Constitutional Court marked a qualitative milestone in the phenomena that we are exploring. Second, we believe that the period is extensive enough to cover a significant number of cases, but also that it is sufficiently homogeneous in background conditions—at least when it comes to EU law and its dynamics—to make meaningful and adequate comparisons across cases. Table 3.1 presents all the cases covered by the research. As can be seen, a total of twenty-nine manifestos were included.

As can be seen, the sample ranges from traditional conservative parties (such as the British Conservative Party in the 2010 election) to very radical parties, such as Alternative für Deutschland. In the Euroscepticism dimension, there is also an interesting variation, with the sample including both more and less openly Eurosceptic parties. It is worth noting that in some countries (Ireland, Luxembourg, and Portugal), Eurosceptic right-wing parties never crossed the threshold of 10 percent of the vote in the period covered.

Some parties were hard to classify, and thus it was difficult to decide whether or not to include them in the sample. The British Conservative Party, at least in the early part of the period, could best be defined as a (moderate) right-wing party, but its Eurosceptic position was unclear: under

[2] Pablo Castillo-Ortiz, 'Right-Wing Eurosceptic Parties and the Strategic Use of Law' (2023) 61 Journal of Common Market Studies 1125.

Table 3.1. Manifestos of European Eurosceptic parties included in the sample

COUNTRY	ELECTION 1	ELECTION 2	ELECTION 3	ELECTION 4	ELECTION 5
AUSTRIA	2013: FPO (20.5%)	2017: FPO (26%)	2019: FPO (16.2%)		
BELGIUM	2010: N-VA (17.4%)	2014: N-VA (20.26%)	2019: N-VA (16%), VB (11.95%)		
DENMARK	2011: DPP (12.3%)	2015: DPP (21.1%)	2019: -		
FINLAND	2011: Finns (19.1%)	2015: Finns (17.7%)	2019: Finns (17.48%)		
FRANCE	2012: FN (17.9%)	2017: FN (33.9%)			
GERMANY	2013: -	2017: AfD (12.6%)	2021: AfD (10.3%)		
GREECE	2012 (May): ANEL (10.6%)	2012 (Jun.): -	2015 (Jan.): -	2015 (Sep.): -	2019: -
IRELAND	2011: -	2016: -	2020: -		
ITALY	2013: -	2018: Lega (17.35%)			
LUXEMBOURG	2013: -	2018: -			
NETHERLANDS	2010: PVV (15.4%)	2012: PVV (10.1%)	2017: PVV (13.1%)	2021: PVV (10.8%)	
PORTUGAL	2011: -	2015: -	2019: -		
SPAIN	2011:-	2015: -	2016: -	2019 (Apr.): VOX (10.3%)	2019 (Nov.): VOX (15.1 %)
SWEDEN	2010: -	2014: SD (12.9%)	2018: SD (17.5%)		
UK	2010: Cons (36.1%)	2015: Cons (36.9%) UKIP (12.6%)			

Data: Castillo-Ortiz, 2023.[3] Own elaboration.

David Cameron's leadership, the official position of the party was to remain in the EU, although Cameron called the UK referendum on EU membership that led to Brexit. However, the party was included in the sample because at that time it did not belong to the family of pro-European conservative

[3] Castillo-Ortiz (n 2).

parties: the European People's Party. In Italy, the difficult case was that of the 5 Star Movement: the party was affiliated with the European Freedom and Direct Democracy group of the 8th European Parliament, but, because it was difficult to characterize it as a right-wing party, it was not covered by the sample for this chapter. Although Forza Italia has at times exhibited traits of Euroscepticism, it was not included in the sample, given its affiliation to the European People's Party (EPP) and the fact that its Eurosceptic traits were softer and occasional. Finally, in the case of Vox in Spain, the problem was related to the fact that this party ran with exactly the same manifesto in the two 2019 elections that took place in the country. These were treated as two different cases.

It is also worth mentioning that, in the case of the UK, the period covered is more limited: given that in June 2016 the country narrowly voted in favour of exiting the European Union, we only cover general elections in this country until that date.

Recall that the main phenomenon that this chapter seeks to scrutinize is the mobilization of constitutional law against European integration in the election manifestos of the parties covered by the sample. For operational purposes, in this chapter, we consider that a manifesto fits this definition to the extent that it proposes making internal law prevail over the law of the European Union—thus undermining the principle of primacy—or of the Council of Europe—that is, essentially, the European Convention on Human Rights or the case law of the European Court of Human Rights. This will be the case when this is stated explicitly and directly (such as by the Italian Lega party in 2018), but also when it is stated implicitly and indirectly (such as by the Spanish Vox party in 2019). However, note that there are of course other forms of mobilization of constitutional law against European integration, as we will show in the following four case study chapters.

In total, eight cases were deemed to be instances of the mobilization of constitutional supremacy against European integration. These are described in Table 3.2. Instances not included in Table 3.2 were not considered to be cases of the Eurosceptic mobilization of constitutional law, even if some were found to be borderline. For instance, in the 2017 election, the Austrian FPÖ pledged the 'Evaluation of the European Convention on Human Rights and, if necessary, replacement by an "Austrian Convention on Human Rights"'.[4] While this case has elements of the Eurosceptic mobilization of constitutional law, it was

[4] FPÖ, 'Österreicher verdienen fairness' (2017). Our translation.

Table 3.2. Eurosceptic mobilization of constitutional law in election manifestos

Party (country)	Election	Eurosceptic mobilization of constitutional law
Conservative Party (UK)	2010	'Unlike other European countries, the UK does not have a written constitution. We will introduce a United Kingdom Sovereignty Bill to make it clear that ultimate authority stays in this country, in our Parliament'.
ANEL (Greece)	2012 (May)	'[The ANEL party] 1. Makes non-negotiable the principles of national independence and pride, popular sovereignty, the promotion of the national interest, adherence to the Constitution and parliamentary democracy. 2. Demands the repeal of the memorandum and refuses to accept the onerous, illegal debt incurred at usurious interest rates. 3. Rejects the cession of national sovereignty and the abolition of the nation-state'. 'The memoranda are unconstitutional. Therefore invalid'.
Conservative Party (UK)	2015	'The next Conservative Government will scrap the Human Rights Act, and introduce a British Bill of Rights. This will break the formal link between British courts and the European Court of Human Rights, and make our own Supreme Court the ultimate arbiter of human rights matters in the UK'.
UKIP (UK)	2015	'We will remove ourselves from the jurisdiction of the European Court of Human Rights: the Strasbourg Court whose interpretation of the European Convention of Human Rights has been known to put the rights of criminals above those of victims. Our own Supreme Court will act as the final authority on matters of Human Rights'. 'Cuts to the police force, a plethora of insidious EU directives, poor judgements from the European Court of Justice that trample on the rights of victims: all these have eroded trust and confidence in policing and our judicial and prison systems'.
DPP (Denmark)	2015	'All essential decisions that concern the Danes must be taken in the Folketing and not by judges in the EU'.
Lega (Italy)	2018	'The jurisprudence of the Constitutional Court must prevail over that of the European Court of Justice. Ordinary judges cannot set aside laws in force on the basis of an alleged opposition to the jurisprudence of the European Court of Justice, in this case they must remit the documents to the Constitutional Court'.
Vox (Spain)	2019 (Apr.)	'To recover sovereignty in the application of rulings of our courts. Terrorists, rapists and assassins will not benefit from the protection of European organisms, as has been the case so far'.
Vox (Spain)	2019 (Nov.)	'To recover sovereignty in the application of rulings of our courts. Terrorists, rapists and assassins will not benefit from the protection of European organisms, as has been the case so far'.

Translations are ours.

not considered as a case of the presence of the outcome for two reasons. First, the pledge is phrased in a hypothetical and conditional fashion. Second, it is an ambiguous pledge which, if realized, could mean a form of 'exit' from the system of the Convention rather than a form of the mobilization of constitutional law to oppose it.

3.3. Theories and Hypotheses

This section puts forward three hypotheses to respond to the research question of this chapter. In line with best practice in configurational research, these hypotheses are configurational and are based on the ideas of necessity and sufficiency.[5] By configurational we mean that our hypotheses seek to understand how factors interact in leading to a result. By necessity and sufficiency, we refer to a certain understanding of causation: one in which factors are not just *likely to cause* a result, but rather one in which factors—actually, often combinations of factors—are *necessary* or *sufficient* to lead to a result.

Our hypotheses about sufficiency are both based on theories that link contextual country-level aspects with party-level factors. They show how contexts provide for opportunities and constraints that parties utilize in different ways depending on their characteristics.

3.3.1. Scepticism about constitutional review as a strategy for successful Eurosceptic parties

Most European countries rely on strong forms of constitutional review,[6] but not all do. According to our expectations, parties in systems without strong forms of constitutional review will exploit this form of constitutional law, especially when they become sizeable and thus less likely to propose an exit from the relevant European organizations.

[5] Carsten Q Schneider and Claudius Wagemann, 'Standards of Good Practice in Qualitative Comparative Analysis (QCA) and Fuzzy-Sets' (2010) 9 Comparative Sociology 397.

[6] Tom Ginsburg and Mila Versteeg, 'Why Do Countries Adopt Constitutional Review?' (2014) 30 The Journal of Law, Economics, and Organization 587; Alec Stone Sweet, 'Constitutional Courts and Parliamentary Democracy' (2002) 25 West European Politics 77.

Constitutional review allows judicial organs to overturn decisions made by the democratically elected political branches of government.[7] In countries with such arrangements, the idea that the Court of Justice of the EU can develop a principle such as primacy will not be at odds with the political culture of the country. Likewise, the idea that democratically legitimized political actors need to comply with decisions of the European Court of Human Rights will be relatively easy to accept. In countries without a strong tradition of constitutional review,[8] however, Eurosceptic actors might exploit this. In these countries, traditional conceptions of parliamentary sovereignty or the role of the democratically elected legislator, to whom courts should show deference, are more prevalent. These aspects of national legal culture can be exploited by right-wing Eurosceptic parties, as they try to portray themselves as defenders of traditional conceptions of national democracy vis-à-vis European legalism.

In fact, this strategy is more suitable for parties that are sizeable in electoral terms. Parties with more chance of achieving power also have more chance of implementing their policy proposals. Paradoxically, this can have a constraining effect on traditional forms of hard Euroscepticism, such as the proposal to exit European organizations. At the end of the day, it is easy for a party to propose a costly exit from the European institutions when the party's poor electoral prospects are such that the proposal will not be implemented. However, parties with a chance to actually achieve power will be reluctant to propose withdrawal from European organizations.[9]

Scepticism about constitutional review thus provides a viable, easy alternative to an exit strategy that is available to sizeable parties. Constrained—paradoxically—by their electoral success into not proposing the abandonment of supranational European organizations, these parties will turn to constitutional forms of Euroscepticism because the constitutional culture of their country facilitates that strategy.

H1: The electoral success of a Eurosceptic party combined with the lack of a tradition of constitutional review will be sufficient for the use of constitutional law against European integration in the party manifesto.

[7] Tom Ginsburg, 'The Global Spread of Constitutional Review' in Keith E. Whittington, R. Daniel Kelemen, and Gregory A. Caldeira (eds), *Oxford Handbook of Law and Politics* (Oxford University Press 2008) 81; Ginsburg and Versteeg (n 6).

[8] For an early discussion of the UK case, see Francis A Trinidade, 'Parliamentary Sovereignty and the Primacy of European Community Law' (1972) 35 Modern Law Review 375.

[9] See, for the case of Greece, Sofia Vasilopoulou, 'The Party Politics of Euroscepticism in Times of Crisis: The Case of Greece' (2018) 38 Politics 311.

3.3.2. The Euro-crisis as a constraining opportunity for populist radical Eurosceptic parties

Our second theoretical line of argumentation has to do with economic shocks as alternative pathways to the use of constitutional law against European integration.

The literature suggests that poorer countries tend to be more supportive of European integration.[10] Eurosceptic parties in wealthier countries can find it easier to convince voters that pulling out of European organizations, particularly the European Union, is viable for the country. In less wealthy countries, by contrast, Eurosceptic parties might find it more difficult to defend an exit strategy, and for that reason might resort to constitutionally framed forms of Euroscepticism. This might be aggravated by strong economic shocks. Some EU countries (notably Ireland, Italy, Spain, Greece, and Portugal) suffered in 2009 from an important debt crisis. This context favoured the emergence of important Eurosceptic counter-narratives and the emphasis on national sovereignty vis-à-vis the austerity measures promoted at the European and international levels. In the case of Greece, for instance, Vasilopoulou shows that 'the economic dimension of the multiple crises facing the European Union (EU) contributed to a Eurosceptic shift in public opinion, the electoral success of Eurosceptic parties'.[11]

Populist radical parties might be particularly keen to follow this path. Populist radical parties portray themselves as defenders of the ordinary people against a corrupt elite.[12] As explained by Kim Lane Scheppele, 'in addition to the negative case they make against constitutional liberalism, some populists have begun to develop what appears to be a sophisticated theoretical framework of their own'.[13] Populist discourses about the crisis are easy to recycle into Eurosceptic constitutional counter-narratives through which a Eurosceptic party can claim to be the defender of the national constitution against the European Union. The national constitution would, in this context, be deemed to be the embodiment of national sovereignty, and disregard of European Union law would be framed as a protection of such a sovereign constitution. In the long run, the social legacy of this Eurosceptic framework could be exploited beyond the specific period of the crisis.

[10] Tobias Theiler, 'The Origins of Euroscepticism in German-Speaking Switzerland' (2004) 43 European Journal of Political Research 635, 640.

[11] Vasilopoulou (n 9) 311.

[12] Cas Mudde, 'Three Decades of Populist Radical Right Parties in Western Europe: So What?' (2013) 52 European Journal of Political Research 1.

[13] Kim Lane Scheppele, 'The Opportunism of Populists and the Defense of Constitutional Liberalism' (2019) 20 German Law Journal 314, 315.

Economic crises might thus be a constraining opportunity for populist radical right-wing Eurosceptics. The economic shock makes exit from European organizations a less—economically viable strategy, but might create the opportunity for a populist Eurosceptic mobilization of law. Therefore:

H2: The radical right populist character of Eurosceptic parties combined with the presence of the Euro-crisis in the country will be sufficient for the use of constitutional law against European integration in the party manifesto.

3.3.3. Party competition

Additionally, party competition can foster policy radicalism as a consequence of the particular election that is taking place. When there is more than one right-wing Eurosceptic party on the electoral menu, such parties will compete with one another by making more radical proposals, bidding for the sympathies of radical voters.[14] The proposal of the mobilization of constitutional law against European integration is no exception to this. *Sensu contrario*, there is unlikely to be a lack of radical Eurosceptic proposals in a scenario of strong party competition. Therefore:

H3: The absence of viable Eurosceptic competitors is a necessary condition for the absence of the use of constitutional law against European integration in the party manifesto.

3.4. Design and Methods

This research uses QCA to answer the research question of the chapter: what explains the adoption in election manifestos of strategies of the mobilization of constitutional law for Eurosceptic purposes? QCA is an approach and a method for empirical inquiry based on set theory and Boolean algebra. This method seeks to understand logically necessary and sufficient conditions for the occurrence of an outcome.[15]

[14] See, on the UK case, Tim Bale, 'Policy, Office, Votes—and Integrity. The British Conservative Party, Brexit, and Immigration' (2022) 48 Journal of Ethnic and Migration Studies 482.

[15] Dirk Berg-Schlosser, Gisèle De Meur, Benoît Rihoux, and Charles C Ragin, 'Qualitative Comparative Analysis (QCA) as an Approach' in Benoît Rihoux and Charles Ragin (eds), *Configurational Comparative Methods* (Sage 2009) 10.

QCA was selected for a number of reasons as the method for this research. First, it is particularly efficient when dealing with medium-N objects of study, when the number of cases is limited but the number of 'variables' is sizeable.[16] Second, QCA is very good at uncovering the interaction between explanatory conditions in the occurrence of an outcome. Third, QCA is very well balanced when it comes to the dilemma between complexity and parsimony, and is able 'to allow systematic cross-case comparisons, while at the same time giving justice to within-case complexity'.[17]

Table 3.3. Conditions, sources, and measures

Condition	Explanation	Source	Measure
Outcome	Eurosceptic use of constitutional law in manifesto	(Castillo-Ortiz, 2023)[18]	1: Eurosceptic use of constitutional law 0: No Eurosceptic use of constitutional law
Vote20	Share of vote obtained in the relevant election	Parlgov database	1: 20 per cent of the vote or above 0: less than 20 per cent of the vote
Ccourt	The country has a strong form of constitutional review	(Castillo-Ortiz, 2020)[19]	1: Constitutional review 0: No constitutional review
PRR	Populist radical right party	(Taggart and Pirro, 2021)[20]	1: Populist radical right party 0: All others
Partycompet	Existence of at least one other right-wing Eurosceptic party in the sample for that election	Parlgov database	1: At least one other right-wing Eurosceptic party in the sample for that election 0: No other right-wing Eurosceptic party in the sample for that election
Crisis	Gravely affected by Euro-crisis	Own research	1: Gravely affected (Italy, Spain, Greece, Ireland, Portugal) 0: All others

[16] Berg-Schlosser, De Meur, Rihoux, and Ragin (n 15) 5.

[17] Benoît Rihoux and Charles C Ragin (eds), *Configurational Comparative Methods. Qualitative Comparative Analysis (QCA) and Related Techniques* (Sage 2009) xviii.

[18] Castillo-Ortiz (n 2).

[19] Pablo Castillo-Ortiz, 'Constitutional Review in the Member States of the EU-28: A Political Analysis of Institutional Choices' (2020) 47 Journal of Law and Society 87.

[20] Paul Taggart and Andrea LP Pirro, 'European Populism before the Pandemic: Ideology, Euroscepticism, Electoral Performance, and Government Participation of 63 Parties in 30 Countries' (2021) 51 Italian Political Science Review/Rivista Italiana di Scienza Politica 281.

Table 3.3 presents the explanatory conditions and the outcome used in this chapter, and the operationalization of these. As can be seen, in this chapter, we are using the crisp set version of QCA (csQCA), in which the conditions are dichotomous (that is to say, phenomena analysed are considered to be either present or absent in each case).[21] This is for two reasons. First, the majority of our explanatory conditions and the outcome are dichotomous in nature, or are apt for dichotomization. Second, csQCA is particularly neat, straightforward, and easy to understand when it comes to illustrating membership of cases in specific sets and configurations of conditions.

QCA allows different uses of counterfactuals: configurations of conditions that are logically possible even if they did not occur empirically.[22] In this chapter, we use the intermediate solution, in which counterfactuals are used only if there are theoretical or empirical reasons to believe that they would contribute to the outcome. This type of solution is usually preferred in QCA. As explained by Schneider and Wagemann,[23] this allows for solutions that are more parsimonious than those that do not use any counterfactuals, without relying on difficult counterfactuals that contradict theoretical expectations or common sense.

Finally, a few definitions and clarifications are due at this point in order for readers to understand the analyses of this chapter. In the notation used in this chapter, the name of a condition indicates its presence, and the name of a condition preceded by the symbol '~' indicates its absence. The symbol '*' involves conjunction, meaning that the conditions appear together and interact to produce a solution (typically, they lead jointly to the outcome in an analysis of sufficiency). Additionally, 'coverage' refers to the proportion of cases with the outcome of interest that is explained by a solution, and consistency refers to the proportion of cases explained by a solution that have the outcome of interest.[24]

For replication and transparency purposes, the data matrix on which the analyses are based is presented in Table 3.7 at the end of this chapter.

[21] See Carsten Q Schneider and Claudius Wagemann, *Set-Theoretic Methods for the Social Sciences. A Guide to Qualitative Comparative Analysis* (Cambridge University Press 2013) 24.

[22] See Benoît Rihoux and Gisèle De Meur, 'Crisp-Set Qualitative Comparative Analysis (csQCA)' in Benoît Rihoux and Charles Ragin (eds), *Configurational Comparative Methods* (Sage 2009) 59.

[23] Schneider and Wagemann (n 21) 175.

[24] For more explanation of the method, see Charles Ragin, *The Comparative Method. Moving Beyond Qualitative and Quantitative Strategies* (University of California Press 1987); Rihoux and Ragin (n 17); Schneider and Wagemann (n 21).

3.5. Analysis

3.5.1. Analysis of necessary conditions

Table 3.4 presents the analysis of the necessary conditions for the presence and absence of the outcome. This analysis of the necessary conditions displays the extent to which a certain condition is necessary for the outcome to occur (i.e., whenever the outcome occurs, the condition also occurs, even if the condition can occur without the outcome taking place). The standard for deeming that a condition is necessary for an outcome is a consistency of at least 0.9,[25] and the conditions meeting this threshold are indicated in Table 3.4 in bold.

The analysis of necessary conditions shows that no condition meets the 0.9 consistency threshold for the presence of the outcome. That means that no condition can be considered necessary to the occurrence of the Eurosceptic mobilization of constitutional law in the manifestos. However, for the absence of the outcome, two conditions do. First, the absence of Eurosceptic party competition is a necessary condition for the lack of utilization of constitutional law against European integration, thus backing hypothesis 3. Second, this is also the case for countries that were not strongly affected by the Euro crisis.

Table 3.4. Analysis of necessary conditions

	Presence of Eurosceptic use of constitutional law		**Absence of Eurosceptic use of constitutional law**	
	Consistency	**Coverage**	**Consistency**	**Coverage**
Ccourt	0.38	0.21	0.53	0.79
~Ccourt	0.63	0.33	0.48	0.67
PRR	0.75	0.25	0.86	0.75
~PRR	0.25	0.40	0.14	0.6
Partycompet	0.25	0.5	0.1	0.5
~Partycompet	0.75	0.24	**0.9**	**0.76**
Crisis	0.5	1	0	0
~Crisis	0.5	0.16	**1**	**0.84**
Vote20	0.37	0.43	0.2	0.57
~Vote20	0.63	0.23	0.81	0.77

Condition labels are explained in Table 3.3.

[25] Schneider and Wagemann (n 21) 143.

3.5.2. Analysis of sufficient conditions for the presence of the outcome

In QCA, the analysis of sufficient conditions shows which combinations of factors are sufficient—but not necessary—to lead to the outcome under study—the Eurosceptic mobilization of constitutional law. The analysis of sufficient conditions for the presence of the outcome shows three paths to the utilization of constitutional law against European integration in election manifestos.

The first path covers the British Conservative Party in 2010 and 2015, and the Danish People's Party in 2015. This path consists of the interaction of two elements: the absence of a strong form of constitutional review and being a party with a high proportion of the vote. The relevance of the first of these conditions is underlined by the party manifestos themselves, which often refer to the sovereignty or the legitimacy of their national parliaments: in countries based on political constitutionalism (like the UK) or that have a weaker form of legal constitutionalism (Denmark), the idea of the primacy of EU law over the national democratic institutions can easily be exploited at the rhetorical or practical level. For instance, as we have already noted, the British Conservatives stated in their 2010 manifesto that 'Unlike other European countries, the UK does not have a written constitution. We will introduce a United Kingdom Sovereignty Bill to make it clear that ultimate authority stays in this country, in our Parliament'.[26] The Danish People's Party also claimed in its 2015 manifesto that decisions affecting the Danish people should be taken by the Danish parliament, and not by the EU judges.[27]

Table 3.5. Analysis of sufficient conditions for the presence of the outcome

Path	Raw coverage	Unique coverage	Consistency	Cases
~Ccourt*Vote20	0.375	0.375	1	Cons10, ***Cons15***, DPP15
Crisis*PRR	0.5	0.5	1	ANEL12m, Lega18, ***Vox19a, Vox19n***
~Ccourt*Partycompet*PRR	0.125	0.135	1	***UKIP15***
Solution coverage: 1 Solution consistency: 1				

Simplifying assumptions: all conditions contribute to the outcome when present, except for 'Ccourt' which contributes when absent. In bold and italics: manifestos that also proposed exiting (or an exit referendum) from European organizations. Condition labels are explained in Table 3.3.

[26] Conservative Party, 'Invitation to join the Government of Britain' (2010) 114.
[27] Dansk Folkeparti, 'Tryghed og tillid' (2015).

This condition, however, interacts in this path with the fact that these were parties with relatively high percentages of the vote (above 20 per cent). The large voting share of these parties meant that there was a real possibility that their proposals could be implemented. For this reason, in these cases, a constitutional-Eurosceptic strategy could be less risky: it allows for strong criticism and an undermining of European integration without taking the risk of proposing an overt exit from the European institutions. The case of the Conservative party in 2015 partially challenges this explanation, as in this manifesto, the Conservative party included an in/out referendum on EU membership: 'after the election, we will negotiate a new settlement for Britain in Europe, and then ask the British people whether they want to stay in the EU on this reformed basis or leave. David Cameron has committed that he will only lead a government that offers an in–out referendum. We will hold that in–out referendum before the end of 2017 and respect the outcome'.[28] However, it is worth recalling that, although the party included the referendum proposal and although this proposal ended with the British exit from the EU, the position of David Cameron as leader of the Conservative Party was, at the time, in favour of continued membership in the organization. This path backs research hypothesis 1.

The second path covers radical right populist parties in countries strongly affected by the European sovereign debt crisis (Italy, Greece, and Spain). The parties covered are Ανεξάρτητοι Έλληνες, Independent Greeks—National Patriotic Alliance (ANEL) (in the May 2012 Greek election), the Italian Lega (2018), and Vox (in the two elections in Spain in 2019). For these parties, the Euro-crisis certainly seems to have played an important role in the development of their Eurosceptic stances. The manifesto analysed for ANEL was written in a context in which Greece was already deeply affected by the crisis. Only a couple of years later, in January 2015, the party formed a coalition with the left-wing party Syriza which had a strong anti-austerity component. The case of the Italian Lega is also interesting: in 2018, this party not only took a strong legal-Eurosceptic stance but also put forward strong criticisms against the Euro currency, which it considered 'the main cause of our economic decline, a currency managed at their need by Germany and multinational [companies] and contrary to the needs of Italy and small companies'.[29] The connection between the Euro-crisis and Vox is slightly less clear, as the party

[28] Conservative Party, 'Strong Leadership, Clear Economic Plan as a Vehicle for a Brighter, More Secure Future' (2015) 72.

[29] Lega, 'Salvini Premier. La rivoluzione del bounsenso' (2018) 9. Our translation.

does not mention the crisis in its manifesto, but Spain was one of the countries most affected by the sovereign debt crisis.[30] The radical-right populist character of these parties might have led them to respond to the crises in these countries using radical proposals, consisting of legal forms of Euroscepticism. This path provides evidence to back research hypothesis 2.

The third path covers one unique case: United Kingdom Independence Party (UKIP) in 2015. As we explained above, in this election UKIP used harsh rhetoric against the judicial aspects of European integration, referring not only to the EU but also to the European Court of Human Rights: 'We will remove ourselves from the jurisdiction of the European Court of Human Rights: the Strasbourg Court whose interpretation of the European Convention of Human Rights has been known to put the rights of criminals above those of victims. Our own Supreme Court will act as the final authority on matters of Human Rights. We will also repeal Labour's Human Rights legislation. It has given European judges far too much power over British law making and law enforcement and prevented us deporting terrorists and career criminals and from implementing whole-life sentences'.[31] This path points to the populist radical right nature of the party, combined with the absence of a tradition of constitutional review in the country and with the existence of party competition (the Conservative Party in this election ran, as stated above, with a proposal for an in–out referendum on EU membership in its manifesto).

3.5.3. Analysis of sufficient conditions for the absence of the outcome

The model for the absence of the outcome (Table 3.6) tells us which combinations of conditions are sufficient for the outcome under study not to occur. The analysis presents perfect coverage and consistency (meaning respectively that all the cases of interest are explained by the solution and that the solution covers only cases of interest) and is also comprised of three paths.

The first path combines the lack of party competition, a limited impact of the Euro-crisis in the country, and the absence of a large share of votes. This is a generally radicalizing path, so in principle, the absence of the Eurosceptic mobilization of constitutional law seems paradoxical. However, this is not the

[30] See, on this, José Real-Dato and Aleksandra Sojka, 'The Rise of (Faulty) Euroscepticism? The Impact of a Decade of Crises in Spain' [2024] 29 South European Society and Politics 457.

[31] UKIP, 'UKIP manifesto 2015' (2015) 53.

Table 3.6. Analysis of sufficient conditions for the absence of the outcome

Path	Raw coverage	Unique coverage	Consistency	Cases
~Partycompet*~Crisis*~Vote20	0.61	0.48	1	***AfD17***, AfD21, ***DPP11***, ***FN12***, FPO19, ***Finns11***, Finns15, Finns19, NVA10, ***PVV10***, ***PVV12***, ***PVV17***, ***PVV21***, ***SD14***, ***SD18***
Ccourt*~Crisis*~Vote20	0.33	0.1	1	***AfD17***, AfD21, ***FN12***, FPO19, NVA10, NVA19, VB19
Ccourt*~Partycompet*~Crisis	0.43	0.19	1	FPO17, ***RN17***, ***AfD17***, AfD21, ***FN12***, FPO13, FPO19, NVA10, NVA14
Solution coverage: 1 Solution consistency: 1				

Simplifying assumptions: all conditions contribute to the outcome when absent, except for 'Ccourt' which contributes when present. In bold and italics: manifestos that also proposed exiting (or an exit referendum) from European organizations. Condition labels are explained in Table 3.3.

case. Note that many of the manifestos covered by this path do include strong forms of Euroscepticism: while they might not mobilize constitutional law against European integration, they often propose a political exit from integration organizations. This is the case for nearly 67 percent of the manifestos covered by this first path. Some of the manifestos are quite explicit in this regard. For instance, the German party AfD in 2017 states that: 'Should we not succeed with our ideas of a fundamental reform within the present framework of the European Union, we shall seek Germany's exit, or a democratic dissolution of the EU, followed by the founding of a new European economic union'.[32] The Swedish Democrats, in the 2018 election, state that the party 'protects democratic self-determination and therefore wants Sweden to leave the EU in favour of intergovernmental European cooperation'.[33] Some other parties are rather more ambiguous. For instance, the French National Front states in its 2012

[32] AfD, 'Manifesto for Germany (English Version)' (2017) 15.

[33] Sverigedemokraterna, 'Valplattform Sverigedemokraternas valplattform 2018' (2018) 16. Our translation.

manifesto that: 'In the context of Article 50 of the Treaty of the EU, a renegotiation of the treaties will be initiated with the aim of breaking up with the failure of dogmatic European construction'.[34] The reference here to article 50 might be interpreted as an implicit threat of a potential French exit from the EU.

This might be pointing at something interesting: the path does not tell us about more moderate parties that avoid turning constitutional law against European integration. Instead, the path suggests that these are often parties that take a different radical Eurosceptic approach by suggesting the abandoning of European organizations. The conditions in the path seem in line with this interpretation: the absence of the Euro-crisis and a small share of votes are not moderating factors. By contrast, small Eurosceptic parties in wealthier countries might have more incentives to take the exit approach. Additionally, a lack of competition with other Eurosceptic parties might decrease the incentive to follow a constitutional-Eurosceptic strategy, even if not to moderate exit proposals. Because these parties are not competing for Eurosceptic voters, they may not need to increase the offer by adding Eurosceptic proposals using constitutional law. Instead, they might just want to stick to the standard, traditional hard-Eurosceptic approach: the pledge to leave the European organizations. Finally, it is worth mentioning that almost all the manifestos in this path that do not propose an exit from the European organizations (except Finns in the 2015 and 2019 elections) are over-determined: that is to say, they can also be explained by other paths.

The second path has a lower explanatory power. It only covers 33 per cent of the cases, and in fact the majority of those cases are over-determined and can be explained by either the first path (oriented towards a radical exit strategy) or the third (moderating) path. Only two cases can be explained exclusively by this path: Nieuw-Vlaamse Alliantie—New Flemish Alliance (NVA) in 2019 and Vlaams Belang—Flemish Interest (VB) in 2019. The path consists of a combination of radicalizing factors (small share of votes, no Euro-crisis) with the presence of a constitutional court in the country, which should disincentivize the use of constitutional law against European integration. With this background, it could be expected that these parties would turn to exit strategies rather than to constitutional-Eurosceptic ones. While the latter part of this statement is correct, the former is not. Neither exit nor constitutional strategies are present for these two cases, which are both instances of Flemish nationalist parties in the same Belgian election of 2019.

[34] FN, 'Mon Project Pour La France et Les Français' (2012) 15. Our translation.

Finally, the third path consists of parties in countries that were not hit by the Euro-crisis and that have some form of constitutional review, and in which there was no Eurosceptic competition. All of these factors are expected to lead to the absence of Eurosceptic constitutional strategies, and so this path can be seen as an ideal combination to avoid using constitutional law against European integration, *regardless* of the use of an exit strategy. In this regard, the third path stands in contrast with the first path, which was composed of factors that seemed to incentivize an exit strategy as opposed to a constitutional one.

3.6. Eurosceptic Mobilization of Constitutional Law Beyond the Right-wing Eurosceptic Parties of the EU-15

The analyses carried out in this chapter have shed light on the reasons why parties opt for Eurosceptic constitutional strategies or opt to avoid them. In carrying it out, we used a subsample of cases: sizeable right-wing Eurosceptic parties in general elections in countries of the EU-15. The findings of this chapter refer to the subsample of cases in the period of study. Because QCA is based on modest generalization,[35] researchers should be cautious in seeking to automatically apply the findings of this chapter to other contexts. This is not to say that the findings may not be helpful in understanding other cases. In fact, they might contain some information that is very valuable for other parties and elections in Europe, but when applying the information provided by this chapter to other cases, one needs to take into account that contextual changes might affect cases in ways that are unforeseen here.

We can illustrate how this idea of modest generalization works using some examples. For instance, we have reason to think that the findings of our research may be helpful in explaining the Eurosceptic positions of some left-wing parties, in addition to those of right-wing ones. During the Euro-crisis in Spain, the radical left party Izquierda Unida mobilized constitutional law against European integration. The party denounced what it described as a 'de-constituent process' and argued that 'national sovereignty has moved away from national constitutions and towards institutions such as the European Commission, the European Central Bank and the International Monetary Fund—the Troika'.[36] The party also pledged to 'reject the mercantile principles of community law and the doctrine of the Court of Justice of the EU consisting

[35] Berg-Schlosser, De Meur, Rihoux, and Ragin (n 15) 11–12.

[36] Izquierda Unida, 'Programa para las elecciones europeas 2014' (2014) 22. Our translation.

in the application of the "principle of country of origin".[37] The context was very similar to the one described in the second path of Table 3.5: a radical party with populist undertones in a country severely hit by the Euro-crisis, Spain. However, this was a left-wing party, and the statements described were from a European Parliament election (2014) manifesto. While more research would be necessary to understand this case, we know at the very least that it is compatible with one of the paths found for right-wing parties in the QCA analysis of sufficiency.

A counterexample, however, is shown by the Polish Party Law and Justice (PiS): the findings of this chapter do not seem to be entirely able to explain its Eurosceptic mobilization of constitutional law. This party is similar to those in the sample in this chapter, but it is from a country that joined the EU at a later stage. The PiS carried out an extensive mobilization of constitutional law against the European Union in several national election manifestos. In 2011, it pledged to change the Polish Constitution to define its superiority over EU law.[38] In 2015, the party mentioned the *Kompetenz-Kompetenz* principle to argue that competence remains with the nation state.[39] In the 2019 election, the mobilization of constitutional law was more implicit than explicit, but the party again seemed to hold a Eurosceptic view of constitutional law when referring to the Constitution being the higher law in Poland, and when claiming that the European institutions should respect national constitutions.[40]

The analysis of sufficient conditions does not seem able to explain the position of PiS in these three elections. This is a party in a country that was not deeply affected by the crisis of the Eurozone and that has opted for a form of constitutionalism based on the existence of an entrenched constitution with a Constitutional Court. Thus, the analysis in Table 3.5 would not suffice to explain these instances of the Eurosceptic mobilization of constitutional law, and it is likely that a different theoretical approach would be necessary for this.

The recommendation to take a modest approach to generalization in QCA is thus illustrated by the Polish (PiS) and Spanish (Izquierda Unida) cases: although the findings of the research should not be automatically extrapolated to other contexts, they might provide insights that are helpful in understanding cases beyond the sample when those cases are sufficiently similar, as seems to

[37] Izquierda Unida (n 37) 43. Our translation.
[38] PiS, 'PiS, 'Nowoczesna Solidarna Bezpieczna Polka' (2011).
[39] PiS, 'Zdrowie Praca Rodzina' (2014).
[40] PiS, 'Polski Model Państwa Dobrobytu' (2019); Castillo-Ortiz (n 2).

be the case with Izquierda Unida. Nevertheless, the ability of the findings to shed light on those other cases should be tested in a case-by-case manner.

3.7. Conclusion

Our research had as its starting point an important factual observation: there are instances of the Eurosceptic mobilization of constitutional law in several European countries. This chapter has shown that certain combinations of factors can explain this.

In the sample covered by this chapter, only the UK Conservative Party had a position of sufficient power that would have allowed it to implement its ideas for the Eurosceptic use of constitutional law. While this question has been obscured by the fact that the UK has now left the EU, the debate is continuing in the UK but now with a focus on the European Convention on Human Rights.[41]

Other instances, however, show the implications of implementing this strategy more clearly. In Hungary and Poland, governments opting for Eurosceptic approaches to constitutional law coupled this with an illiberal takeover of the constitutional courts.[42] This allowed them to start implementing their anti-EU approach to constitutional law. In Hungary, as explained by Kim Lane Scheppele, 'The captured Hungarian Constitutional Court now routinely challenges the primacy of EU law and applies EU law in ways that raise questions about the consistent application of Union law across the Member States. For example, the Constitutional Court ruled in 2016 that it alone will be the guardian of Hungarian "constitutional identity" which, in its view, gives it the power to pick and choose which elements of EU law Hungarian courts will follow'.[43] The author also explains that 'the Hungarian government has not made secret its disdain for the primacy of EU law when it might provide a basis for challenging the concentration of power in the hands of the prime minister or when it challenges his culture war appeals'.[44]

[41] See Richard Ekins, *Protecting the Constitution* (Policy Exchange 2019); Philip Sales and Richard Ekins, 'Rights-Consistent Interpretation and the Human Rights Act 1998' (2011) 127 Law Quarterly Review 217.

[42] Laurent Pech and Kim Lane Scheppele, 'Illiberalism within: Rule of Law Backsliding in the EU' (2017) 19 Cambridge Yearbook of European Legal Studies 3; Bojan Bugarič and Tom Ginsburg, 'The Assault on Postcommunist Courts' (2016) 27 The Journal of Democracy 69.

[43] Scheppele (n 1) 117.

[44] Scheppele (n 1) 167.

Explaining the reasons behind the Eurosceptic use of constitutional law is thus not only important for the future of European integration. It might often matter for constitutional law itself. Using QCA as a methodological approach, this chapter has shed some light on this important question. We can at least identify some main ideas.

Table 3.7. Data matrix

Case	Outcome	Vote	Ccourt	PRR	partycompet	Crisis	vote20
Cons10	1	36.1	0	0	0	0	1
Cons15	1	36.9	0	0	1	0	1
FPO17	0	26	1	1	0	0	1
RN17	0	33.9	1	1	0	0	1
ANEL12m	1	10.6	0	1	0	1	0
AfD17	0	12.6	1	1	0	0	0
AfD21	0	10.3	1	1	0	0	0
DPP11	0	12.3	0	1	0	0	0
DPP15	1	21.1	0	1	0	0	1
FN12	0	17.9	1	1	0	0	0
FPO13	0	20.5	1	1	0	0	1
FPO19	0	16.2	1	1	0	0	0
Finns11	0	19.1	0	1	0	0	0
Finns15	0	17.7	0	1	0	0	0
Finns19	0	17.48	0	1	0	0	0
Lega18	1	17.35	1	1	0	1	0
NVA10	0	17.4	1	0	0	0	0
NVA14	0	20.26	1	0	0	0	1
NVA19	0	16	1	0	1	0	0
PVV10	0	15.4	0	1	0	0	0
PVV12	0	10.1	0	1	0	0	0
PVV17	0	13.1	0	1	0	0	0
PVV21	0	10.8	0	1	0	0	0
SD14	0	12.9	0	1	0	0	0
SD18	0	17.5	0	1	0	0	0
UKIP15	1	12.6	0	1	1	0	0
VB19	0	11.95	1	1	1	0	0
Vox19a	1	10.3	1	1	0	1	0
Vox19n	1	15.1	1	1	0	1	0

First, the Eurosceptic use of constitutional law and its use of exit strategies do not always coincide, and to explain them, we seem to need different causal theories.[45]

Second, the explanations as to why parties opt for using—or not using—Eurosceptic constitutional strategies are not mono-causal: very often they occur in the combinations of different circumstances that take place at different levels.

Finally, different causal paths can explain these choices in different cases, and in this chapter, we have identified some of these paths. On occasions, a situation like an economic crisis might prove both enabling and constraining for radical populist parties. This is because, in that context, such parties will need to avoid exit strategies, but the very context will create incentives for the Eurosceptic use of constitutional law. Likewise, successful Eurosceptic parties in countries without a tradition of strong constitutional review might find the Eurosceptic use of constitutional law very useful. Thus, certain contexts which combine party-level and country-level factors seem ideal for the use of constitutional law against European integration.

[45] For more detail, see Castillo-Ortiz (n 2).

4
The UK
Constitutional Law and Euroscepticism in the Country of Brexit*

4.1. Introduction

The UK, despite its recent exit from the European Union, is a fundamental laboratory for techniques in judicial Euroscepticism,[1] and for this reason, we have decided to consider it as the first of our case studies. Obviously, the UK is characterized by an evolutionary constitution[2] that is only partially codified and is inspired by the premises of political constitutionalism.[3] Constitutionalism in most European countries is synonymous with a written, codified constitution that is enforced by some sort of constitutional court. The United Kingdom is, in this landscape, a relative oddity. As Stone Sweet put it:

> After a polite nod to Westminster, parliamentary sovereignty can be pronounced dead. It was killed off during the second half of the twentieth century in successive waves of constitution-making that followed a world war, the overthrow of military dictatorship in Southern Europe, and the collapse of Communist regimes in Central and Eastern Europe. All European constitutions written after World War II establish enforceable, substantive constraints on government, including constraints on legislative and executive authority, in the form of human rights, the scope and content of which go far beyond the American Bill of Rights. With very few exceptions, all such constitutions provide for 'constitutional review' by a 'constitutional court'.[4]

* Unless otherwise indicated, all the election manifestos of the political parties discussed in this chapter are available at the following link <https://manifestoproject.wzb.eu/>.

[1] Gavin Drewry, 'The Jurisprudence of British Euroscepticism: A Strange Banquet of Fish and Vegetables' (2007) 3 Utrecht Law Review 101.

[2] John A Griffith, 'The Political Constitution' (1979) 42 Modern Law Review 1.

[3] Richard Bellamy, *Political Constitutionalism* (Cambridge University Press 2009).

[4] Alec Stone Sweet, 'Why Europe Rejected American Judicial Review: And Why It May Not Matter' (2003) 101 Michigan Law Review 2744, 2745.

The Eurosceptic Mobilization of Constitutional Law. Pablo Castillo-Ortiz and Giuseppe Martinico, Oxford University Press. © Pablo Castillo-Ortiz and Giuseppe Martinico 2026. DOI: 10.1093/9780198959205.003.0004

As suggested by Stone Sweet, Westminster is an exception to the general rule of legal constitutionalism. The country's system is still anchored in the sovereignty of Parliament, even if the understanding of this concept is, as we will see, rather disputed.[5]

For an analysis of the Eurosceptic mobilization of constitutional law, this has implications. On the one hand, the lessons learnt from the UK case are probably relatively idiosyncratic, making generalizations largely difficult. It will often be the case that the arguments for, the reasons behind, and the results of constitutional counter-narratives in the UK can only be of indirect help in understanding other countries. On the other hand, however, there are some reasons why this sui generis character of UK constitutionalism will be particularly interesting. Because it is very peculiar, UK constitutionalism will be helpful for understanding scenarios and testing conjectures that cannot be tested in other countries. The Eurosceptic mobilization of constitutional law in the UK is indeed likely to be different from that taking place in countries with strong forms of judicial review of legislation, like Italy or Germany. In the UK, there is no constitutional court whose case law can be mobilized against European integration. However, the peculiar form of British constitutionalism is amenable to nationalist mobilization by those who reject the power of the European courts.[6]

The second specificity of the UK case is Brexit. The UK joined the European Communities in 1973 and left the European Union in 2020. The UK became the first Member State to leave the organization, an event that shaped public opinion across the continent.[7] This fact, again, renders the UK a different case and complicates generalizations to other jurisdictions, but, again, allows us at the same time to understand the Eurosceptic mobilization of constitutional law in a different light, and thus is of particular analytical significance. For instance, the extent to which the exit strategy pursued by British Eurosceptics is compatible with anti-EU constitutional counter-narratives is a fascinating object of study in a country whose European trajectory is unique. In fact, as

[5] Sionaidh Douglas-Scott, *Brexit, Union and Disunion: The Evolution of British Constitutional Unsettlement* (Cambridge University Press 2023); Oliver Garner, 'The Brexit Sovereignty Problem' (17 April 2024) Review of Democracy <https://revdem.ceu.edu/2024/04/17/the-brexit-sovereignty-problem/>

[6] Pablo Castillo-Ortiz, 'The Imperfect Legitimacy of Judicial Umpires in European Multilevel Democracies' (2024) 44 Legal Studies 242.

[7] Catherine E De Vries, 'Benchmarking Brexit: How the British Decision to Leave Shapes EU Public Opinion' (2017) 55 Journal of Common Market Studies 38. See also Sarah Wheaton, Dionisios Sturis, and Anne McElvoy, 'A Divorce and a Birthday: Five Years of Brexit, 10 Years of *POLITICO*' (*POLITICO*, 17 April 2024) <https://www.politico.eu/newsletter/eu-confidential/a-divorce-and-a-birthday-five-years-of-brexit-10-years-of-politico/>.

this chapter shows, the Eurosceptic mobilization of constitutional law is a phenomenon that has been present in both pre- and post-Brexit UK. It has targeted not just the EU and its legal system, but also the European Convention on Human Rights (ECHR),[8] and it has not only been present in parties like United Kingdom Independence Party (UKIP) and Reform UK, but it has also played a protagonist role in a mainstream party like the Conservative Party.

This chapter is structured as follows. After this introduction, we explain the constitutional framework governing the connection between the UK and the European legal systems during British membership of the Union. We then explore how British constitutional ideas and institutions have been mobilized by UK Eurosceptic parties, and shed light on Eurosceptic approaches to the British Constitution in legal academia. The penultimate section outlines the rationale for an open, pro-European British constitutionalism, and the final section concludes.

4.2. UK Constitutional Law and European Integration

Before Brexit, the application of EU law in the United Kingdom gravitated around two main, connected, legal authorities. There was, on the one hand, the European Communities Act 1972 (ECA 1972) and its amendments. On the other hand, there was prolix case law on the matter, with the decision of the House of Lords in *R v Secretary of State for Transport, ex p Factortame Ltd* (*Factortame No.2*) at its core but reaching well beyond this decision. These legal authorities can be seen from the perspective of the relationship between the primacy of EU law and parliamentary sovereignty. A significant 'picture' of the impact of EU law on the UK legal order is found in the famous *Thoburn* judgment, where Laws LJ attempted to combine the need to guarantee the primacy of EU law with the idea that the sovereignty of the UK Parliament was untouchable.[9]

The ECA 1972 was a UK Act of Parliament making legal provision for the accession of the UK to the European Communities, as well as incorporating

[8] Conor Casey, 'The Sir Gerald Fitzmaurice Option: A Classical Natural Law Method for Interpreting the European Convention on Human Rights' (1 November 2024) <https://papers.ssrn.com/sol3/papers.cfm?abstract_id=5123963>.

[9] Thoburn v Sunderland City Council [2002] 1 CMLR 50. On this issue, see Henry WR Wade, 'Sovereignty and the European Communities' (1972) 88 Law Quarterly Review 1; Francis Trindade, 'Parliamentary Sovereignty and the Primacy of European Community Law' (1972) 35 Modern Law Review 375; John DB Mitchell, 'What Happened to the Constitution on 1st January 1973?' (1980) 11 Cambrian Law Review 6; See also Mark Elliott, 'Parliamentary Sovereignty and the New Constitutional Order: Legislative Freedom, Political Reality and Convention' (2002) 22 Legal Studies 340.

the law of the European Communities into the UK legal system. The ECA 1972, which was amended over the course of the years in response to changes to the European Union legal system, was repealed by the European Union (Withdrawal) Act 2018.

The ECA 1972 included provisions conferring legal effect on existing and future Community law, and provided (in s 2(4)) that 'any enactment passed or to be passed, other than one contained in this Part of the Act, shall be construed and have effect subject to the foregoing provisions of this section'. In addition, the ECA 1972 guaranteed that the UK courts would pay full respect to the jurisdiction of the European Court of Justice.[10] The ECA 1972 was seen at the time as a fundamental milestone in the evolution of the British political and constitutional system, with the potential to transform parliamentary procedures and the balance of powers in the UK.[11] The echoes of these debates still resonated in the UK at the time of the remain or leave referendum, and even following the British exit from the European Union.

The ECA 1972 underwent an important amendment in 2011, when the new European Union Act 2011 (EUA 2011) received royal assent. This Act presented two important innovations, represented by section 18, devoted to the so-called 'sovereignty' clause, and by the instrument of 'referendum locks' introduced in sections 2, 3, and 6.[12]

The aim of the sovereignty clause was to restate the powers of the sovereign Parliament over the application of EU law in the UK. However, as Gordon pointed out, 'the final text of the provision enacted in the EUA [2011] is no "sovereignty" clause at all; instead, section 18 simply confirms the narrower point that the status of EU law within the UK is ultimately dependant on its continuing statutory basis. In other words, section 18 maintains that EU law is effective and supreme over other domestic norms because an Act of Parliament, the European Communities Act 1972, makes it so'.[13]

As for the second main innovation, the aim was to introduce a 'referendum lock' on any further transfers of power from the UK to the European Union.

[10] Josef Drexl, 'Was Sir Francis Drake a Dutchman—British Supremacy of Parliament after Factortame' (1993) 41 American Journal of Comparative Law 551, 555.

[11] Geoffrey Howe, 'The European Communities Act 1972' (1973) 49 International Affairs 1; see also Henry WR Wade, 'Sovereignty: Revolution or Evolution?' (1996) 112 Law Quarterly Review 568.

[12] On this Act, see Paul Craig, 'The European Union Act 2011: Locks, Limits and Legality' (2011) 48 Common Market Law Review 1915.

[13] Michael Gordon, 'The European Union Act 2011' (*UK Constitutional Law Association*, 12 January 2012) <https://ukconstitutionallaw.org/2012/01/12/mike-gordon-the-european-union-act-2011/>. The original wording was: 'Status of EU law dependent on continuing statutory basis. It is only by virtue of an Act of Parliament that directly applicable or directly effective EU law (that is, the rights, powers, liabilities, obligations, restrictions, remedies and procedures referred to in section 2(1) of the European Communities Act 1972) falls to be recognised and available in law in the United Kingdom'.

Basically, as Gordon wrote, the Act provided that 'certain decisions can only be lawfully authorised by an Act of Parliament which makes the subsequent effectiveness of the decision contingent on whether it has been approved by a majority of the electorate voting in a referendum. The range of situations in which the EUA requires a referendum to be held to authorise action to be taken in relation to the EU is remarkably broad'.[14]

Regarding the case law, there have been some important judgments (coming from both ECJ and UK judges) that could be relevant to our topic. Focusing our attention on the most recent years, we can recall the strong impact of judgments like those in the cases of *KB*,[15] *Richards*,[16] and *P v S*,[17] under the pressure of which important reforms were made and which raised debates. Subsequently, the UK was involved in at least three famous cases (*Singh*,[18] *Zhu, and Chen*,[19] and *Akrich*[20]) concerning the right to family reunion and citizenship.

Schematically, we can distinguish different approaches to the (judicial) relationship between the internal and the European legal order. In the early years of Community membership, British judges tried to restrict the application of Community law to the uttermost limit by avoiding having to deal with 'legal positions' (*Rechtsstellung*) acknowledged by Community law provisions. If there was a legal conflict, the judge was bound to interpret national law in conformity with Community law; where this was not possible, the proposed solution was the application of the chronological criterion, according to which *lex posterior derogat priori*. According to this approach, the ECA 1972 was conceived as an ordinary statute which could not limit parliamentary sovereignty.[21] The hidden premise of this argument is the pure vision of the prevalence of the Westminster Parliament's undiminished sovereignty: looking at the dicta in the *Felixstowe Dock*[22] case, for example, we can see the reasoning

[14] Gordon, 'The European Union Act 2011' (n 13).

[15] ECJ, Case C-117/01 *KB v National Health Service Pensions Agency and Secretary of State for Health* ECLI:EU:C:2004:7.

[16] ECJ, Case C-423/04 *Sarah Margaret Richards v Secretary of State for Work and Pensions* ECLI:EU:C:2006:256.

[17] ECJ, Case C-13/94 *P v S and Cornwall County Council* ECLI:EU:C:1996:170.

[18] ECJ, Case C-370/90 *The Queen v Immigration Appeal Tribunal and Surinder Singh, ex parte Secretary of State for the Home Department* ECLI:EU:C:1992:296.

[19] ECJ, Case C-200/02 *Kunqian Catherine Zhu and Man Lavette Chen v Secretary of State for the Home Department* ECLI:EU:C:2004:639.

[20] ECJ, Case C-109/01 *Secretary of State for the Home Department v Hacene Akrich* ECLI:EU:C:2003:491.

[21] *Felixstowe Dock and Railway Company v British Transport Docks Board* [1976] 2 CMLR 655.

[22] Felixstowe Dock and Railway Company [1976] (n 21).

that 'if there were to be any conflict between UK law and Community law then it would have to be the latter which would fall'.[23]

The classic ('pure') concept of sovereignty adopted here was linked back to a certain interpretation of Dicey's works[24] and implied the impossibility that the successors of any particular parliament should be bound by its decisions; in other words: 'There is one, and only one, limit to Parliament's legal power: it cannot detract from its own continuing sovereignty'.[25]

This conception was gradually overcome due to the growing body of ECJ case law and the recognition that the ECA 1972 had been adopted when the structural principles of Community law (direct effect and primacy) were already well established.[26] In those years, Lord Denning described the Treaty 'like an incoming tide. It flows into the estuaries and up the rivers. It cannot be held back. Parliament has decreed that the Treaty is henceforward to be part of our law (. . .). The governing provision is section 2(1) of the European Communities Act 1972 (. . .). The statute is expressed in forthright terms which are absolute and all-embracing'.[27]

To understand this approach to the relationship between the UK and the EU legal systems, it is crucial to clarify the importance of the *Factortame II* decision of the House of Lords. We will not spend much ink discussing the context and facts of the Factortame saga here, as these have been well documented elsewhere,[28] but the aspects of the decision that concern the relationship between UK and EU law are worth analysing in more detail. In what is the most relevant part of the decision for the purposes of this book, Lord Bridge held that:

> Under the terms of the Act of 1972 it has always been clear that it was the duty of a United Kingdom court when delivering final judgment, to override any rule of national law found to be in conflict with any directly enforceable rule of Community law. Similarly, when decisions of the European Court of Justice have exposed areas of United Kingdom statute law which failed to

[23] Paul Craig, 'Report on the United Kingdom: Constitutional Doctrine within the United Kingdom: The Impact of the EC' in Anne M Slaughter, Alec Stone Sweet, and Joseph HH Weiler (eds), *The European Court and National Courts: Doctrine and Jurisprudence* (Hart Publishing 1998) 195–224, 198.

[24] Albert V Dicey, *An Introduction to the Study of the Law of the Constitution* (Macmillan 1959) 10.

[25] Craig, 'Report on the United Kingdom' (n 23) 197.

[26] *Aero Zipp Fasteners Ltd v YKK Fasteners (UK) Ltd* (1973) CMLR 819, 820.

[27] *Bulmer Ltd v Bollinger SA* [1974] 2 All ER 1226.

[28] Inter alia, Claire Francis, 'Factortame Ltd. v. Secretary of State for Transport' (1990) 84 American Journal of International Law 269; Paul Craig, 'Sovereignty of the United Kingdom Parliament after *Factortame*' (1991) 11 Yearbook of European Law 221; Drexl (n 10).

> implement Council directives, Parliament has always loyally accepted the obligation to make appropriate and prompt amendments. Thus there is nothing in any way novel in according supremacy to rules of Community law in those areas to which they apply and to insist that, in the protection of rights under Community law, national courts must not be inhibited by rules of national law from granting interim relief in appropriate cases.[29]

Paul Craig gave an enlightening reading of the decision when he argued that:

> Lord Bridge is speaking in broad terms about the relationship between EEC law and United Kingdom law. His dictum represents a general statement concerning the priority of EEC law over national law in the event of a clash between the two. The foundation for this reasoning is essentially contractarian: the United Kingdom knew when they joined the EEC that priority should be accorded to EEC law, and they must be taken to have contracted on those terms. If, therefore, 'blame' was to be cast for a loss of sovereignty then this should be laid at the feet of Parliament and not the courts.[30]

As with the implications of the ECA 1972, the *Factortame II* decision is still controversial in legal academia. For authors like Barber, the understandings of parliamentary sovereignty that existed before 1991 were abandoned with the decision.[31] Other authors, like Drexl, argued at the time that: 'Parliamentary sovereignty, in a modern understanding, is not necessarily an argument against European integration but a useful tool for a more active European policy to be pursued by the United Kingdom',[32] and that 'supremacy of Parliament, in a modern understanding, is designed to guarantee the continuing application of the democratic principle. It does not prevent the application of Community law in the United Kingdom, but argues for enlarged legislative powers for the European Parliament'.[33]

Looking further at the impact of *Factortame II*, it is possible to argue that the notion of sovereignty brought forward in cases like *Thoburn*[34] or *McWhirter*[35]

[29] R v Secretary of State for Transport, ex p Factortame Ltd (No 2) [1991] 1 AC 603, 658 (HL).
[30] Craig, 'Sovereignty of the United Kingdom Parliament after *Factortame*' (n 28) 249.
[31] Nicholas W Barber, 'The Afterlife of Parliamentary Sovereignty' (2011) 9 International Journal of Constitutional Law 144.
[32] Drexl (n 10) 562.
[33] Drexl (n 10) 571.
[34] *Thoburn v Sunderland City Council* [2002] 1 CMLR 50.
[35] *McWhirter v Secretary of State for Foreign Affairs* [2003] EWCA civ 384. On these two cases, see Andrea Biondi, 'Principio di supremazia e "Costituzione" inglese. I due casi "Martiri del sistema metrico" e "McWhirter and Gouriet"' (2006) <https://www.forumcostituzionale.it/wordpress/wp-content/uploads/pre_2006/101.pdf>.

introduced a new phase in the constitutional debate in the UK. In Thoburn, Laws LJ recognized the existence of a constitutional group of statutes and acts, which included the Magna Carta, the Bill of Rights 1689, the Acts of Union 1707, the Reform Acts, the Human Rights Act 1998, the Scotland Act 1998, the Government of Wales Act 1998, and the European Communities Act 1972. These all fell within the category of 'constitutional' statutes. Subsequent cases such as *HS2* seemed to confirm the existence of a hierarchy within constitutional legislation, in which EU law could take precedence.[36]

Looking at the judges' reasoning in *Thoburn*, it is possible to appreciate a further effort to reconcile the primacy of EU law with parliamentary sovereignty. According to this judgment, in fact, the primacy of EU law was based on Parliament's self-limitation; in other words, the legal basis of the UK's relationship with the EU rested on national provisions, not on EU law:

> There is nothing in the [European Communities Act] which allows the Court of Justice, or any other institutions of the EU, to touch or qualify the conditions of Parliament's legislative supremacy in the United Kingdom. Not because the legislature chose not to allow it; because by our law it could not allow it.[37]

Had EU law contravened a fundamental principle of the UK's unwritten constitution, the former would not have taken precedence over the latter. This idea of the existence of some counter-limits to EU law (that is, those national fundamental principles which national courts have raised—like impenetrable barriers—against the penetration of EU law) was again brought forward in *McWhirter*,[38] where the Court of Appeal conceived the possibility of denying the primacy of EU law whenever it challenged the constitutional principles of the British legal order.

In any case, according to other scholars,[39] one should not overestimate the importance of *Thoburn*, since the statements of Laws LJ were not confirmed by the House of Lords or the UK Supreme Court. From this, one could infer that *Factortame* still remains the reference judgment in the UK context.

[36] *R (HS2 Action Alliance Ltd) v Secretary of State for Transport* [2014] UKSC 3.

[37] Thoburn v Sunderland City Council [2002] EWHC 195 (Admin), [2003] QB 151, [59].

[38] *McWhirter* (n 35). On this point, see Biondi (n 35).

[39] 'However, it must be noted that Laws' statement in *Thoburn* came in the Court of Appeal and has not been approved by the House of Lords. As such, the more deferential approach in *Factortame* remains the binding precedent in the UK', Cian Murphy, 'Report on the UK and Ireland' in Giuseppe Martinico and Oreste Pollicino (eds), *The National Judicial Treatment of the ECHR and EU Laws: A Comparative Constitutional Perspective* (Europa Law Publishing 2010) 479–498, 486–487.

Euroscepticism has characterized the third phase of the legal relations between the UK and the EU. Brexit was, of course, the landmark event for these purposes. In legal terms, Brexit was implemented through a number of Acts of Parliament, including the European Union (Withdrawal) Act 2018 and the European Union (Withdrawal Agreement) Act 2020, as well as being channelled through EU law provisions such as art 50 TEU. However, before Brexit, an important element—one that we will also find in the Polish case—was the famous Polish and UK 'opt out'[40] (although it does not represent an 'opt out' properly speaking[41]): a protocol to the Lisbon Treaty, aimed at limiting the justiciability of some provisions of the Charter. Later on, the 'incoming tide' described by Lord Denning reached its high-water mark during the period of maximum friction: the withdrawal from the European Union. The Miller I saga serves as a definitive confirmation of this shift.[42]

On those occasions, both the High Court of England and Wales and the UK Supreme Court denied the government the ability to exercise the power of notification to the European Council of the intention to leave the Union under article 50 TEU without parliamentary involvement, through the approval of a statute. The non-revocability of the notification was one of the fundamental pillars of the judges' reasoning and served as an external—referring to a non-national norm—premise of that judgment. However, article 50 TEU offered margins for either option, as scholars had already pointed out:

> The point is arguable either way. It could be argued that since a notification to withdraw is subject to a Member State's constitutional requirements, the

[40] In order to escape the risk of being subject to such provisions, the UK and Poland insisted on signing a specific Protocol (no 30) stating in article 1 that: '1. The Charter does not extend the ability of the Court of Justice of the European Union, or any court or tribunal of Poland or of the United Kingdom, to find that the laws, regulations or administrative provisions, practices or action of Poland or of the United Kingdom are inconsistent with the fundamental rights, freedoms and principles that it reaffirms.

2. In particular, and for the avoidance of doubt, nothing in Title IV of the Charter creates justiciable rights applicable to Poland or the United Kingdom except in so far as Poland or the United Kingdom has provided for such rights in its national law.'

Art 2 of the Protocol: 'To the extent that a provision of the Charter refers to national laws and practices, it shall only apply to Poland or the United Kingdom to the extent that the rights or principles that it contains are recognised in the law or practices of Poland or of the United Kingdom'.

See, on this, the comprehensive work of Oliver Garner, *Constitutional Disintegration and Disruption: Withdrawal and Opt-outs from the European Union* (Oxford University Press 2025) 79–138.

[41] ECJ, Case C-411/10 *NS & Others v SSHD* and Case C-493/10 *M.E. and Others v Refugee Applications Commissioner, Minister for Justice, Equality and Law Reform* ECLI:EU:C:2011:865, paras 116–20; House of Lords EU Select Committee, 'The Treaty of Lisbon: An Impact Assessment', 13 March 2008 <https://publications.parliament.uk/pa/ld200708/ldselect/ldeucom/62/62.pdf>.

[42] *R (Miller) v Secretary of State for Exiting the European Union* [2016] EWHC 2768; *R (Miller) v Secretary of State for Exiting the European Union* [2017] UKSC 55. Patrick Birkinshaw, 'Brexit's Challenge to the UK's Unwritten Constitution' (2020) 26 European Public Law 29.

> Treaty therefore leaves to each Member State the possibility of rescinding that notification in accordance with those requirements. On the other hand, it could also be argued that Article 50 only provides for two possibilities to delay the withdrawal of a Member State from the EU once notification has been given (an extension of the time limit, or a different date in the withdrawal agreement). There's no suggestion that this is a non-exhaustive list. Therefore, the notification of withdrawal can't be rescinded.[43]

Over the years, UK membership of the Union has created complex rules in the etymological sense of the term[44]: a set of norms that are the result of a tangled knot between domestic law and European law. This made the reference to the law of the EU Treaties inevitable for the correct reading of the question posed to the British courts in the *Miller I* saga. The wording of article 50 TEU, moreover, refers to domestic law when it reads that 'Any Member State may decide to withdraw from the Union in accordance with its own constitutional requirements'. This confirms the legal interweaving created by the European integration process. However, precisely because of the impact that the question of revocability of the notification had on the margin of manoeuvre of the UK Parliament, commentators stressed the excessive brusqueness of some of the relevant passages in the *Miller I* judgment. They also criticized the choice not to consult with the Court of Justice in accordance with the preliminary reference mechanism governed by article 267 TFEU.[45]

After Brexit, interestingly, the relationship between EU law and UK law has continued. Retained legislation (REUL), a type of domestic law created by the

[43] Steve Peers, 'Article 50 TEU: The Uses and Abuses of the Process of Withdrawing from the EU' (*EU Law Analysis*, 8 December 2014) <http://eulawanalysis.blogspot.com/2014/12/article-50-teu-uses-and-abuses-of.html>. See also Jake Rylatt, 'The Irrevocability of an Article 50 Notification: Lex Specialis and the Irrelevance of the Purported Customary Right to Unilaterally Revoke' (*UK Constitutional Law*, 27 July 2016) <https://ukconstitutionallaw.org/2016/07/27/jake-rylatt-the-irrevocability-of-an-article-50-notification-lex-specialis-and-the-irrelevance-of-the-purported-customary-right-to-unilaterally-revoke/>; Charles Streeten, 'Putting the Toothpaste Back in the Tube: Can an Article 50 Notification Be Revoked?' (*UK Constitutional Law*, 13 July 2016) <https://ukconstitutionallaw.org/2016/07/13/charles-streeten-putting-the-toothpaste-back-in-the-tube-can-an-article-50-notification-be-revoked/>; Oliver Garner, 'Can the United Kingdom Unilaterally Revoke its Article 50 Notification to Withdraw from the EU? Wightman v Secretary of State for DexEU [2018] CSIH 62' (*European Law Blog*, 24 September 2018) <https://www.europeanlawblog.eu/pub/can-the-united-kingdom-unilaterally-revoke-its-article-50-notification-to-withdraw-from-the-eu-wightman-v-secretary-of-state-for-dexeu-2018-csih-62/release/1>

[44] Giuseppe Martinico, *The Tangled Complexity of the EU Constitutional Process: The Frustrating Knot of Europe* (Routledge 2023).

[45] Peers, 'Article 50 TEU' (n 42). See also, on this, Oliver Garner, 'Referring Brexit to the Court of Justice of the European Union: Why Revoking an Article 50 Notice Should be Left to the United Kingdom' (*European Law Blog*, 14 November 2016) <https://www.europeanlawblog.eu/pub/referring-brexit-to-the-court-of-justice-of-the-european-union-why-revoking-an-article-50-notice-should-be-left-to-the-united-kingdom/release/1>.

EU (Withdrawal) Act 2018, came into effect after the UK's post-Brexit transition period, which ended on 31 December 2020. Its primary aim was to ensure legal continuity and certainty.

On 29 June 2023, the Retained EU Law (Revocation and Reform) Bill 2023 received Royal Assent and became the Retained EU Law (Revocation and Reform) Act 2023 (REUL Act 2023). Under the REUL Act 2023, any REUL not revoked by the end of 2023 became 'assimilated law'. Unlike REUL, assimilated law is not interpreted according to EU principles, which were removed from domestic law by the REUL Act 2023, effective from 1 January 2024. The new UK government has partially slowed down this process, delaying the implementation of some key provisions of the REUL Act 2023. Returning to the set of rights introduced into the British legal system by EU law, the retained legislation passed by the UK Parliament confirms that, from a technical point of view, the constitutional scenario differs from the pre-accession status quo.

On the one hand, post-Brexit controversies about the transformations of parliamentary sovereignty continued, as evidenced by the reactions to the *Allister* case.[46] On the other hand, the power granted to national judges in light of the Simmenthal doctrine points to a fundamental shift.[47]

According to Bogdanor, the *Simmenthal* doctrine transformed the political constitution into something different.[48] Indeed, in his view, the European Union (Withdrawal) Act 2018 sought 'to do something quite unprecedented in the constitutional history of the modern world by withdrawing Britain from a protected constitution into an unprotected one'.[49] This also explains why, soon after Brexit and in response to the litigation brought against the prorogation, the populist government of Boris Johnson targeted the judiciary, and the UK Supreme Court in particular. EU integration, moreover, has created ties that bind even after the exit, and all the added value, in terms of the protection of fundamental rights, created by years of European integration, has been converted into domestic law. This confirms, again, that the 'incoming tide' has changed the geology of the British legal system. Another confirmation can be seen in the persisting role of the Court of Justice, according to the text of the Withdrawal Agreement, which maintained its jurisdiction during and even

[46] Liam Edwards, '*Allister and Others v Secretary of State for Northern Ireland*: A Summary of the "NI Protocol" Case' (10 May 2023) <https://www.diritticomparati.it/allister-and-others-v-secretary-of-state-for-northern-ireland-a-summary-of-the-ni-protocol-case/>.

[47] ECJ, Case-106/77 *Amministrazione delle Finanze dello Stato v Simmenthal SpA* ECLI:EU:C:1978:49.

[48] Vernon Bogdanor, *Beyond Brexit: Towards a British Constitution* (IB Tauris 2019).

[49] Vernon Bogdanor, 'Brexit and Our Unprotected Constitution' (*The Constitution Society*, 2018) <https://consoc.org.uk/wp-content/uploads/2018/02/Brexit-and-our-unprotected-constitution-web.pdf>.

beyond the transition period. Apart from the ECJ's jurisdiction over cases or proceedings pending at the end of the transition period or events occurring before that date, the ECJ also has some jurisdiction over entirely new cases arising after that date. In this sense, as Peers clarified, there are four different categories of 'continued jurisdiction',[50] each of which relates to specific provisions of the Withdrawal Agreement. They have to do with citizens' rights,[51] financial settlement,[52] the Protocol on Ireland and Northern Ireland, and the Protocol on Cypriot bases.

The question of the reception of the law of the ECHR in the UK deserves one final, specific, mention. The question is important because, in the UK, the ECHR and its court have been—and continue to be—a preferred target for attack by Eurosceptic actors. In the UK, it is the Human Rights Act 1998 (HRA 1998) that selectively incorporates, in a very specific way, the ECHR into the British legal system. Ewing explains that:

> [T]he Human Rights Act 1998 does not incorporate ECHR into domestic law in the way that the European Communities Act 1972 incorporates the EC Treaty. Rather what it does is to give effect to certain provisions of the Convention and some of its protocols by providing that these so-called 'Convention rights' are to have a defined status in English law. There is no question of the Convention rights in themselves 'becoming part of our substantive domestic law': rather, certain defined provisions of the Convention enjoy a defined legal status.[53]

Importantly, the HRA 1998 mandates British courts to interpret legislation in a way that is compatible with the ECHR and, if that is not possible, empowers them to issue a 'declaration of incompatibility' (see sections 3, 4, and 10). Because of this, some authors have described the HRA 1998 as an 'unprecedented transfer of political power from the executive and legislature to the judiciary, and a fundamental re-structuring of our "political constitution"'.[54] But it must be noted, nonetheless, that the declaration of incompatibility does

[50] Steve Peers, 'The End—or a New Beginning? The EU/UK Withdrawal Agreement' (2020) 39 Yearbook of European Law 122–198.
[51] Art 158 of the Withdrawal Agreement.
[52] Art 160 of the Withdrawal Agreement.
[53] Keith D Ewing, 'The Human Rights Act and Parliamentary Democracy' (1999) 62 The Modern Law Review 79, 84.
[54] Ewing (n 53) 79.

not imply the invalidation of the legislation at stake, thus ultimately respecting the principle of parliamentary sovereignty.[55]

As we show later in this chapter, controversy around the HRA 1998 persists in the UK. At the parliamentary level, the latest episode of this was the proposed Bill of Rights Bill introduced to the House of Commons in 2022. The Bill of Rights Bill sought to replace the HRA 1998, but by 2023, it was confirmed that the government would not pursue the passing of this bill. This episode, however, cannot be understood without a clear explanation of the Eurosceptic mobilization of constitutional law against the ECHR in the UK, as we will see later.

4.3. Eurosceptic Mobilization of Constitutional Law in UK Parties

This section is structured around the analysis of the election manifestos of UKIP and the Conservative Party, but also those of parties that can be seen as successors to UKIP, such as Reform UK and the Brexit Party.[56] The period covered is from 2004 (the time of the failed Constitutional Treaty) to 2024.

In addition to right-wing Euroscepticism, there has been a tradition of Euroscepticism on the left in the UK. At the time of accession and the 1975 referendum, the main political resistance to European integration came from the Labour Party, some of whose members feared not only pro-business policies but also a loss of sovereignty.[57] Furthermore, the ambiguous position at the time of the Brexit referendum of Jeremy Corbyn—the leader of the Labour Party in that period—as well as of 'Corbynism' is worth noting.[58]

Despite this, we believe that our focus on right-wing British Euroscepticism in this section is appropriate. These parties have been selected because they were protagonists in the Eurosceptic camp in the UK during the period

[55] For a critical reflection on the distinction between weak and strong forms of constitutional review, see Aileen Kavanagh, 'What's So Weak about "Weak-Form Review"? The Case of the UK Human Rights Act 1998' (2015) 13 International Journal of Constitutional Law 1008.

[56] See, on this, Karine Tournier-Sol, 'From UKIP to the Brexit Party: The Politicization of European Integration and Disruptive Impact on National and European Arenas' (2021) 29 Journal of Contemporary European Studies 380.

[57] Ben Wellings, 'Losing the Peace: Euroscepticism and the Foundations of Contemporary English Nationalism' (2010) 16 Nations and Nationalism 488, 492.

[58] Matt Bolton and Frederick Harry Pitts, 'Corbynism and Blue Labour: Post-Liberalism and National Populism in the British Labour Party' (2020) 15 British Politics 88; Jonathan Tonge, Stuart Wilks-Heeg, and Louise Thompson, 'Conclusion: The BBC and the Election: Boris, Brexit and Corbyn' (2020) 73 Parliamentary Affairs 288.

covered. Also, in their manifestos and speeches, we were able to observe open, explicit Eurosceptic counter-narratives and arguments.

Indeed, for many years, Eurosceptic politics was dominated in the UK by UKIP, led by Nigel Farage. UKIP was created in 1993 with a distinctive emphasis on Euroscepticism,[59] which the party combined with populism.[60] Research shows that UKIP often framed UK membership of the EU as a form of oppression or invasion.[61] The analysis of this party's manifestos will thus be particularly enlightening when it comes to understanding Eurosceptic constitutional counter-narratives in the UK.

In the period covered by this research, the Conservative Party was, however, the other main pillar of Eurosceptic politics in the UK. When the Conservative Prime Minister David Cameron called for a referendum on British membership of the EU, his declared intention was to secure the vote to remain and to settle the issue for at least some time. But, as Gifford puts it, Cameron's leadership of the Conservative Party always exhibited important traits of reluctancy in relation to the status quo of European integration:

> The dominant perspective within Cameron's revitalised Conservative Party continues to be that UK/EU relations are largely a zero-sum game in which UK power has been progressively eroded. It is fair to argue that at the core of this is a traditional Conservative attachment to parliamentary sovereignty as the essence of UK state authority. Nevertheless, to shore up this political principle they have increasingly appealed to the British people against the European Union. As Cameron has made clear in his attack on Brown's 'grand top-down schemes' to revive a sense of national identity: 'it is not standing up for Britishness when you undermine our Houses of Parliament by passing more and more power to Brussels without giving people the referendum you promised'.[62]

[59] Philip Lynch, Richard Whitaker, and Gemma Loomes, 'The UK Independence Party: Understanding a Niche Party's Strategy, Candidates and Supporters' (2012) 65 Parliamentary Affairs 733; Philip Lynch and Richard Whitaker, 'Rivalry on the Right: The Conservatives, the UK Independence Party (UKIP) and the EU Issue' (2013) 8 British Politics 285; Catherine MacMillan, 'Reversing the Myth? Dystopian Narratives of the EU in UKIP and Front National Discourse' (2018) 26 Journal of Contemporary European Studies 117.

[60] Tim Bale, 'Who Leads and Who Follows? The Symbiotic Relationship between UKIP and the Conservatives—and Populism and Euroscepticism' (2018) 38 Politics 263.

[61] Andrew S Ross and Aditi Bhatia, '"Ruled Britannia": Metaphorical Construction of the EU as Enemy in UKIP Campaign Posters' (2021) 26 The International Journal of Press/Politics 188.

[62] Chris Gifford, 'The UK and the European Union: Dimensions of Sovereignty and the Problem of Eurosceptic Britishness' (2010) 63 Parliamentary Affairs 321, 333.

Furthermore, after the Brexit vote, the Conservative Party took an increasingly Eurosceptic stance, which culminated during the leadership of Boris Johnson, who, unlike David Cameron, had campaigned in favour of leaving the European Union.

For the purposes of this book, what is most interesting about the British case is the way in which the Eurosceptic mobilization of constitutional law was intertwined with the exit strategy. These two strategies are conceptually different, but they appear together and are complementary in the British case. For example, in many instances, constitutional arguments were presented by Eurosceptics as part of the rationale behind their preference to leave the European Union.

The British case presents another very interesting trait: the way in which Eurosceptic parties also target the ECHR and the Strasbourg court, and the intensity with which they do so, which are not paralleled, at least in any of the other case studies. In this section, we will start with an analysis of attacks against the EU, and then we will turn to the criticisms of the ECHR.

4.3.1. Undermining our democracy? The European Union as a threat to the British Constitution

Our analysis of the Eurosceptic mobilization of constitutional law against the EU in the UK reveals one important preliminary point: this Eurosceptic mobilization is not new, and has been part of political debates in the UK for a long time, although it coexisted with calls for a complete exit from the EU.[63] In fact, the alleged antagonism between UK constitutional law and European integration seems to have been present in British political debates since the accession of the country to the European Communities. According to Gifford:

> In the case of Europe, some of the fiercest objections to UK entry into the Common Market came from those who regarded it as an attack on the British principle of parliamentary sovereignty. It enabled politicians on the right and the left, most notably Enoch Powell and Tony Benn, to find common ground and argue against membership in the 1975 referendum.[64]

[63] See on the latter, for instance, UKIP, 'We want our country back' (2005).
[64] Gifford (n 62) 324–325.

In recent years, the strategic mobilization of constitutional law against European integration was not limited to the more radical UKIP but also extended to the Conservative Party. Throughout the years, these two parties sought to mobilize constitutional ideas and concepts against the EU, with some core themes being particularly frequent.

Amongst these, the first is the rejection of the idea of the European Union as a constitutional project, which was particularly prevalent in the first decade of the century, coinciding with the attempt to ratify the Treaty Establishing a Constitution for Europe. For instance, in their manifesto for the 2004 European election, the Conservatives devoted significant attention to this matter, as the party positioned itself against this Treaty: 'The proposed new European Constitution would compound these problems: it would undermine individual Member States' ability to determine their own policies (. . .). Countries have constitutions: nation states make treaties with one another'.[65] The rejection of the idea of a European Constitution continued over the years, and in its 2009 European Parliament (EP) election manifesto, the Conservatives and Unionists still emphasized their rejection of an EU Constitution, as they saw the Lisbon Treaty as 'its near identical successor',[66] an idea that was also voiced by UKIP in its 2010 general election manifesto.[67]

Secondly, there is a theme around the EU legal system being antagonistic to the national legal system, which can be found repeatedly in the party manifestos. In 2010, for the general election, UKIP argued that 'today, a large majority of our national law is imposed by Brussels (for example, 72% of business regulation). All told, there are more than 120,000 EU directives and regulations in force in the UK. In addition, European Court of Justice verdicts, the EU Arrest Warrant, Europol and the EU's body of law, Corpus Juris, all act to undermine our legal and constitutional system'.[68] In that election, the Conservative Party was also very assertive in opposing British constitutionalism to European integration: 'Unlike other European countries, the UK does not have a written constitution. We will introduce a United Kingdom Sovereignty Bill to make it clear that ultimate authority stays in this country, in our Parliament'.[69] Along the same lines, UKIP's 2015 general election manifesto argued that EU primacy had involved an erosion of the voting capacity of the UK in international bodies such as those of the UN,[70] and after the Brexit

[65] Conservative Party, 'Putting Britain First' (2004) 1.
[66] Conservative and Unionist Party, 'Vote for Change' (2009) 3.
[67] UKIP, 'Empowering the people' (2010) 2.
[68] UKIP, 'Empowering the people' (n 67) 2.
[69] Conservative Party, 'Invitation to join the government of Britain' (2010) 114.
[70] UKIP, 'Believe in Britain' (2015) 63.

vote, in 2017, UKIP asserted that 'Parliament must resume its supremacy of law-making without restriction' as one of the 'tests' to be sure that 'the British people have got the deal they voted for'.[71] Also in 2017, in the general election, the Conservative manifesto under Theresa May still referred to the idea of British law and to the rejection of the Court of Justice of the EU: 'We will enact a Great Repeal Bill. Our laws will be made in London, Edinburgh, Cardiff and Belfast, and interpreted by judges across the United Kingdom, not in Luxembourg'.[72] This Great Repeal Bill would become, in its parliamentary form, the European Union (Withdrawal) Act 2018. In 2019, under Boris Johnson, the manifesto pledged that 'once we get Brexit done, Britain will take back control of its laws. As we end the supremacy of European law, we will be free to craft legislation and regulations that maintain high standards but which work best for the UK'.[73] After Brexit, the message was repeated, although this time it was framed as an achievement of the previous government: 'Thanks to Brexit, we have taken back control of our laws and freed British businesses from unnecessary burdens. We legislated to remove the principle of EU law supremacy and have undertaken a root-and-branch review of the more than 6,000 laws we had inherited from the EU'.[74]

Thirdly, there is the important question of referendums, which predates the debate on the leave/remain vote and has historically been intertwined with constitutional considerations. In the 2004 European election manifesto, the Conservatives not only considered it to be imperative that the Constitutional Treaty would be subject to a referendum, but also that 'referendums on future significant constitutional Treaty changes should be compulsory in Britain'.[75] The pledge to submit the European Constitution to a referendum and to campaign for a 'no' vote was repeated in the 2005 general election manifesto.[76] In the 2009 European elections, the party pledged to call a referendum on the Lisbon Treaty,[77] as well as on any further transfer of powers to the EU.[78] The Conservatives repeated the pledge to submit to a referendum any 'further extension of the EU's power over the UK' in its 2010 general election manifesto, under the heading 'Restore democratic control': 'We will amend the 1972 European Communities Act so that any proposed future Treaty that transferred

71 UKIP, 'Britain together' (2017) 7.
72 Conservative Party, 'Forward, together' (2017) 37.
73 Conservative Party, 'Get Brexit done, unleash Britain's potential' (2019) 48.
74 Conservative and Unionist Party, 'Clear plan, bold action, secure future' (2024) 11.
75 Conservative Party, 'Putting Britain first' (n 65) 7.
76 Conservative Party, 'It is time for action' (2005) 31.
77 Conservative and Unionist Party, 'Vote for change' (n 66) 3.
78 Conservative and Unionist Party, 'Vote for change' (n 66) 20.

areas of power, or competences, would be subject to a referendum—a "referendum lock"'.[79] As we explained earlier in this chapter, the 'referendum lock' became part of the European Union Act 2011, showing how sometimes these pledges become realities.

Finally, there is the antagonism towards the European courts. As we have already pointed out, the Court of Justice of the EU has received its share of attack in the British debate. In the 2004 European election manifesto, the Conservatives considered that a new 'threat from the EU Constitution' stemmed from the role of this institution: 'The Charter of Fundamental Rights will mean that European judges in Luxembourg will impose rules to restrict business freedom.'[80] In 2017 UKIP criticized Theresa May's government for 'capitulating on key issues such as (. . .) freeing the UK from the jurisdiction of European courts.'[81] In 2019, in the general election manifesto, the Conservative Party argued that 'Boris Johnson's new deal takes the whole country out of the EU as one United Kingdom. It takes us out of the customs union, allowing us to set our own tariffs and do our own trade deals. It allows us to pass our own laws and ensures that it is our courts that enforce them (. . .). There will be no political alignment with the EU. We will keep the UK out of the single market, out of any form of customs union, and end the role of the European Court of Justice.'[82] Sometimes, attacks against the Court of Justice are framed from a law and order perspective, as in the case of UKIP's 2015 general election manifesto, which included a statement from the MEP Diane James: 'Cuts to the police force, a plethora of insidious EU directives, poor judgements from the European Court of Justice that trample on the rights of victims: all these have eroded trust and confidence in policing and our judicial and prison systems. Our internal national security has never felt so undermined.'[83]

This analysis reveals that the British political debate on the EU—at least when it comes to electoral campaigning—has featured an intensive use of constitutional ideas, concepts, and considerations. Not only UKIP but also the Conservative Party have resorted to core elements of Eurosceptic constitutional counter-narratives, from the rejection of the primacy of EU law to criticisms of the Court of Justice and even the rejection of the idea of European constitutionalism *tout court*. This is, in fact, no different from Eurosceptic counter-narratives in other European countries. However, unlike in other

[79] Conservative Party, 'Invitation to join the government of Britain' (n 69) 113.
[80] Conservative Party, 'Putting Britain first' (n 65) 9.
[81] UKIP, 'Britain together' (n 71) 6.
[82] Conservative Party, 'Get Brexit done, unleash Britain's potential' (n 73) 5.
[83] UKIP, 'Believe in Britain' (n 70) 52.

countries, the British debate is marked by the special nature of the UK constitution. References are made to the sovereignty of the UK Parliament, and the opposition to the primacy of EU law on these grounds is, as expected, frequent. The specific nature of the UK constitution then allows European integration to be contraposed not just to the UK constitution but to basic notions of democracy. Because in the UK the democratically elected parliament is sovereign, the subtext in the Eurosceptic counter-narratives points to European integration undermining not just national constitutional law but also core aspects of the way in which democracy is articulated in the UK.

4.3.2. The last word on human rights: The European Court of Human Rights and the controversy around the HRA 1998

In this book, our primary focus is on EU law, which is considered sui generis due to its structural principles of primacy and direct effect. However, as anticipated in Chapter 1, this chapter devotes particular attention to the debate on Euroscepticism directed at the European Convention on Human Rights (ECHR). This is because the UK's debate on the ECHR draws heavily on many of the arguments and techniques originally developed in relation to EU law. In other words, the legal Euroscepticism examined in this book persists in the British context in forms that, while different, are nonetheless comparable—and it continues to fuel a debate that, as yet, has no equivalent in other European countries. Indeed, as is widely known, the targets of Eurosceptic criticisms in the UK have been not just the EU, but also the ECHR. These criticisms again have to be seen in the context of what Jay refers to as a distinctly British 'rights culture, based on principles such as parliamentary sovereignty and so-called common sense values'.[84] For Cowell, criticism of the ECHR in the UK is based on the notion of 'British exceptionalism', which he defines as 'the belief that the UK's domestic constitutional institutions are unique and superior to the European Convention on Human Rights, in part because of their historical provenance and longevity'.[85]

[84] Zoë Jay, 'Keeping Rights at Home: British Conceptions of Rights and Compliance with the European Court of Human Rights' (2017) 19 The British Journal of Politics and International Relations 842, 842.

[85] Frederick Cowell, 'Understanding the Causes and Consequences of British Exceptionalism towards the European Court of Human Rights' (2019) 23 The International Journal of Human Rights 1183, 1183.

Interestingly enough, in our analysis, we have been able to identify political criticism of this human rights instrument dating back decades. In its 2005 general election manifesto, UKIP included a statement whose echoes can still be heard in contemporary British political debates: 'UKIP will repeal the 1999 [sic] Human Rights Act, preferring to rely on British custom, our common law and the principles of the European Convention of Human Rights which are based on individual freedom rather than state control. Outside the EU, we shall also avoid our freedoms being overtaken by the EU's Charter of Fundamental Rights and its misguided notions of fairness'.[86]

The rejection of the ECHR is repeated over time in other manifestos and on other occasions, although the concrete phrasing changes. For instance, during the 2010 election campaign, UKIP pledged to 'Repeal the 1998 Human Rights Act and withdraw from the European Convention on Human Rights and Fundamental Freedoms. In future the British courts will not be allowed to appeal to any international treaty or convention that overrides or sets aside the provisions of any statue [sic] passed by the UK Parliament'.[87] In the 2015 general election manifesto, the argument was reframed again: 'We will remove ourselves from the jurisdiction of the European Court of Human Rights: the Strasbourg Court whose interpretation of the European Convention of Human Rights has been known to put the rights of criminals above those of victims. Our own Supreme Court will act as the final authority on matters of Human Rights. We will also repeal Labour's Human Rights legislation. It has given European judges far too much power over British law making and law enforcement and prevented us deporting terrorists and career criminals and from implementing whole-life sentences.'[88]

An interesting strategy in this regard is UKIP's attempt to intertwine criticisms of the EU and of the European Court of Human Rights (ECtHR). In the 2014 European Parliament election, the party argued that: 'The European Court of Human Rights—which the Lisbon Treaty forces all EU member states to sign up to—still wants to give prisoners the vote. It also prevents convicted terrorists from being deported. UKIP will leave the EU and the jurisdiction of the European Court of Human Rights. Parliament should decide fairer human rights laws.'[89] Likewise, in its 2015 manifesto for the general election, UKIP argued that 'British justice is still the best in the world, but is being corrupted by the EU. Unelected bureaucrats in Brussels and judges in Strasbourg

[86] UKIP, 'We want our country back' (n 63) 15.
[87] UKIP, 'Empowering the people' (n 67) 6.
[88] UKIP, 'Believe in Britain' (n 70) 53.
[89] UKIP, 'Create an earthquake' (2014) 7.

and Luxembourg, can ignore British fears about crime. It is time to bring our British legal system back under British control.'[90]

UKIP was historically not alone in its distrust of the ECtHR. The 2010 general election manifesto of the Conservative Party included a pledge to 'replace the Human Rights Act with a UK Bill of Rights'.[91] In the 2014 European Parliament election, the party, under David Cameron, not only pledged an in/out referendum on EU membership but also targeted the ECtHR. One of the key changes they pledged to fight for is the following: 'Our police forces and justice systems able to protect British citizens, unencumbered by unnecessary interference from European institutions, including the European Court of Human Rights.'[92] In that manifesto, the party also insisted on the matter by pledging to 'undertake radical reform of human rights laws and publish a detailed plan for reform that a Conservative government would implement immediately: we will scrap Labour's Human Rights Act, curtail the role of the European Court of Human Rights in the UK and make certain that the UK's Supreme Court is in Britain and not in Strasbourg'.[93]

The same combination of membership referendum regarding the EU and questioning the HRA 1998 could be found in the Conservatives' 2015 general election manifesto, which is particularly prolix on the latter matter. First, by committing to 'scrap the Human Rights Act, and introduce a British Bill of Rights. This will break the formal link between British courts and the European Court of Human Rights, and make our own Supreme Court the ultimate arbiter of human rights matters in the UK.'[94] And then, again, by promising to scrap the HRA 1998 in the following terms:

> We will scrap Labour's Human Rights Act and introduce a British Bill of Rights which will restore common sense to the application of human rights in the UK. The Bill will remain faithful to the basic principles of human rights, which we signed up to in the original European Convention on Human Rights. It will protect basic rights, like the right to a fair trial, and the right to life, which are an essential part of a modern democratic society. But it will reverse the mission creep that has meant human rights law being used for more and more purposes, and often with little regard for the rights of wider

[90] UKIP, 'Believe in Britain' (n 70) 55.

[91] Conservative Party, 'Invitation to join the government of Britain' (n 69) 79.

[92] Conservative Party, 'A stronger economy at home, renewed respect abroad, real change in Europe' (2014) 7.

[93] Conservative Party, (n 92) 16.

[94] Conservative Party, 'Strong leadership, a clear economic plan, a brighter, more secure future' (2015) 60.

> society. Among other things the Bill will stop terrorists and other serious foreign criminals who pose a threat to our society from using spurious human rights arguments to prevent deportation.[95]

In fact, the Conservative Party won the 2015 general election and formed a government. However, as Amos put it in 2017, after that election victory 'almost immediately, the new government pledged that within 100 days it would "scrap" the HRA and replace it with a British Bill of Rights that would alter the relationship between the UK and the ECtHR. This plan was soon dropped, and, more than two years later, still nothing has happened, although it has been confirmed that it is not a part of present plans for the UK to withdraw from the ECHR.'[96]

Interestingly, the Brexit vote did not seem to reverse the trend of increasing distrust of the ECtHR by these parties, and, instead, the opposite was true. In 2017, the Conservative general election manifesto had argued that: 'We will not bring the European Union's Charter of Fundamental Rights into UK law. We will not repeal or replace the Human Rights Act while the process of Brexit is underway but we will consider our human rights legal framework when the process of leaving the EU concludes. We will remain signatories to the European Convention on Human Rights for the duration of the next parliament.'[97] As explained earlier, in 2022 a Bill of Rights Bill was introduced to the House of Commons by the Conservative government, but it was never passed. In 2024, with Brexit implemented, the party pledged that 'we will run a relentless, continual process of permanently removing illegal migrants to Rwanda with a regular rhythm of flights every month, starting this July, until the boats are stopped. If we are forced to choose between our security and the jurisdiction of a foreign court, including the ECtHR, we will always choose our security.'[98] The framing of the ECtHR as a 'foreign court' is particularly noteworthy, and its nationalist undertones are particularly clear.

As we write these lines, the British debate about the ECHR is far from settled. In fact, it seems to be one important issue of political polarization in the country which overlaps with the left–right cleavage: the current Labour government has declared that it has no intention of reconsidering the terms of the UK's membership of the Council of Europe, whilst the Conservative Party and

[95] Conservative Party, (n 94) 73.
[96] Merris Amos, 'The Value of the European Court of Human Rights to the United Kingdom' (2017) 28 European Journal of International Law 763, 764–765.
[97] Conservative Party, 'Forward, together' (n 72) 37.
[98] Conservative and Unionist Party, 'Clear plan, bold action, secure future' (n 74) 36.

Reform UK, in particular, have more critical positions and, in the case of the latter, there is a clear proposal to leave the ECHR.[99]

4.4. Eurosceptic Constitutional Counter-Narratives in UK Academia

The Eurosceptic mobilization of constitutional ideas in the UK is, however, not a monopoly of political actors. Academics and think tank members in the country have also resorted to constitutional law–related arguments to justify their opposition to the EU and to the ECHR.

The most interesting aspect of justifications of Brexit based on the British Constitution is that in these arguments there is a convergence of the two most important Eurosceptic strategies: the exit approach and the mobilization of constitutional law against European integration. Scholars—particularly law scholars—positioning themselves against UK membership of the EU frequently did so with one argument: that EU law was in tension with the main features of the British political constitution, particularly the principle of parliamentary sovereignty. This is not to say that these types of arguments are particularly relevant in explaining the Brexit vote, but constitutional law-based justifications of Brexit existed nonetheless, and they seemed to strongly mirror many of the political statements analysed earlier in this chapter.

It is also worth noting that the Brexit referendum did not end the academic debate on the relationship between UK and EU law. Rather, it seems to have animated it. The work of John Finnis illustrates this.[100] For reasons of space, however, we will focus here on some of the literature that tackles the core of the relationship between UK constitutional law and EU law. A good example of this is the work of Richard Ekins. In an academic article about the topic, illustratively entitled 'Restoring Parliamentary Democracy', Ekins argues that: 'The U.K. joined the EEC in accordance with this constitutional order, but membership was always difficult to square with the principles of parliamentary democracy and the difficulty increased over time. The decision to leave the E.U. is a choice to disengage from the European legal order and thus to restore self-government.'[101] Elsewhere, the author has argued in the same line that:

[99] Reform UK, 'Our contract with you' (2024).

[100] John Finnis, 'Brexit and the Balance of Our Constitution', *Judicial Power Project*, 2 December 2016, <https://judicialpowerproject.org.uk/wp-content/uploads/2016/12/Finnis-2016-Brexit-and-the-Balance-of-Our-Constitution2.pdf>.

[101] Richard Ekins, 'Restoring Parliamentary Democracy' (2018) 39 Cardozo Law Review 997, 1017.

> The U.K.'s membership in the EU did not change the fundamentals of the U.K. constitution. However, membership was hard to square with the constitution's animating logic and spirit (. . .). As a matter of domestic law, Parliament remained free to legislate, but in practice this freedom was heavily curtailed, with EU Treaties forming, in effect, a supra-national constitution, making provision for judicial review of domestic law. Predictably, European integration compounded political alienation and encouraged political opposition within the U.K. and European law more generally.[102]

Note how those arguments resonate with Eurosceptic counter-narratives about the tension between the UK constitution and European Union law. Some of the main themes of these counter-narratives are also present in these works: the idea of EU law constraining parliamentary sovereignty, the critique of EU-level constitutionalism, and the incidental distrust of the role of the courts in the EU legal system.

Together with constitutional law-based defences of Brexit, we can find, in the intellectual debate in the UK, constitutional law-related criticisms of the ECHR and the HRA 1998. One argument in this regard has been that the case law of the ECtHR has made the Convention system unrecognizable vis-à-vis the intent of its drafters and ratifiers.[103] However, the main point of ECHR sceptics has again been the opposition between the law of the Convention and the role of Parliament in British constitutionalism, as 'the strictures of the Act, and the related reception of ECtHR jurisprudence, pose a (rising) challenge to the integrity of parliamentary self-government'.[104] This is coupled with the idea that British democracy would actually benefit from questioning the UK's approach to the ECHR:

> Concerns about rule by a foreign court are not novel or marginal as Lord Hoffmann's public contributions on point confirm. We would add that concerns about rule by any court are well-established and well made. The UK was a just, decent democracy before the ECHR existed and before the HRA was enacted. Like Australia and New Zealand, to mention two other close

[102] Richard Ekins, 'The Constitutional Dynamics of Brexit' (2022) 12 Notre Dame Journal of International & Comparative Law 46, 47–48.

[103] Conor Casey and Yuan Yi Zhu, *Revisiting the British Origins of the European Convention on Human Rights* (Policy Exchange 2025) <https://policyexchange.org.uk/publication/revisiting-the-british-origins-of-the-european-convention-on-human-rights/>.

[104] Richard Ekins and Graham Gee, 'How Not to Dismiss Human Rights Law Reform' (*Policy Exchange, Judicial Power Project*, 11 May 2016) <https://judicialpowerproject.org.uk/richard-ekins-and-graham-gee-how-not-to-dismiss-human-rights-law-reform/>.

> comparators, the UK is fully capable of governing itself well, of protecting human rights and the common good, without subjecting itself to rule by an international court.[105]

Of course, there are simultaneous criticisms of the EU and the ECHR system in UK academic debate:

> The U.K. is a signatory to the European Convention on Human Rights (ECHR), and the Human Rights Act 1998 gives it some domestic force, but U.K. courts very clearly have no authority to invalidate an Act of Parliament. For some lawyers and judges, this is an embarrassment and a problem. Much influenced by (some) continental European and North American approaches to constitutionalism, they reason that a good constitution would impose legal limits on Parliament and that the people are less a source of authority or legitimacy than a standing danger to minority rights and constitutional (limited) government. The appeal of EU membership, on this view, is that it squares a circle, subjecting both the Parliament and the government of the U.K. to hard-edged (if nonetheless often vague) legal limits, removing in practice the capacity of the people by way of their representatives to freely to legislate.[106]

It is worth noting that these positions have gone beyond mere academic and think tank publications.[107] Good examples are submissions and written evidence to the UK Parliament by academics who oppose the HRA 1998. Ekins and Gee, for instance, argued in their 2018 submission that 'in our view, the HRA should never have been enacted—it threatened to compromise the rule of law, to politicise the courts, and to distort democratic deliberation, and each of these threats has been realised'.[108] Their recommendation in this piece of written evidence was:

> It would be reasonable for Parliament to repeal the HRA (. . .). Our point is that constitutional principle confirms that repealing the HRA would help

[105] Ekins and Gee (n 104).

[106] Ekins, 'The Constitutional Dynamics of Brexit' (n 102) 49.

[107] For instance, see John Finnis, 'Terminating Treaty-Based UK Rights' (*UK Constitutional Law*, 26 October 2016) <https://ukconstitutionallaw.org/2016/10/26/john-finnis-terminating-treaty-based-uk-rights/>, which was influential in shaping the UK government's legal argument in *R (Miller) v Secretary of State for Exiting the European Union (No 1)* [2017] UKSC 5.

[108] Richard Ekins and Graham Gee, 'Written Evidence from Policy Exchange's Judicial Power Project (HRA0033)' UK Parliament, Joint Committee on Human Rights, Twenty Years of the Human Rights Act Inquiry para 2 <https://data.parliament.uk/writtenevidence/committeeevidence.svc/evidencedocument/human-rights-committee/20-years-of-the-human-rights-act/written/90593.html>.

> restore the balance of the constitution, even if Parliament would need to take care to avoid courts recreating the substance of the HRA by way of novel common law rights. Repealing the HRA would not end the UK's subjection to the ECtHR of course but it would end the direct incorporation of problematic Strasbourg case law and strengthen the UK's capacity to defy that lawless court.
>
> In the alternative, Parliament should amend the HRA. It would be reasonable for Parliament to restore the original design of the Act and to end the ten-year experiment, which is gathering pace, in going beyond Strasbourg. It would be reasonable also, if rather more likely to encourage friction with the ECtHR, for Parliament to require our courts in applying the HRA to confine themselves to interpretations of convention rights that are consistent with the text of the ECHR and the intentions of the signatory states . . . [109]

The works above illustrate how academics have played an important role in the creation and dissemination of constitutional law-related Eurosceptic ideas in the UK. The parallel between political and academic arguments is noteworthy in this regard, and they have in common the central role of a specific understanding of parliamentary sovereignty. In this understanding, there would be, at the very least, a tension between this principle and European law, exemplified by the role of the courts. This perspective on the UK constitution is, however, not the only possible one, as we show in the next section.

4.5. The Eurosceptic Mobilization of Constitutional Law in the UK: A Critique

We have seen how Eurosceptic political actors tried to portray the relationship between UK constitutionalism and European integration as antagonistic. As said, the central concept for understanding this Eurosceptic mobilization of constitutional law in the UK is that of parliamentary sovereignty. Gordon, however, has sharply criticized the use of this concept in Eurosceptic counternarratives in the UK during the Brexit referendum:

> That there exists broad consensus that the UK conception of parliamentary sovereignty had been reconciled successfully with the core precepts of EU membership (and in particular, the domestic supremacy which must be

[109] Ekins and Gee (n 108) paragraphs 26–27.

> afforded to EU law) did not seem to be significant during the course of the referendum campaign. Instead, the notion of sovereignty employed to justify Brexit was more emotive and less precise, leaving it open to debate exactly what those citizens who were persuaded by such arguments were voting to restore.[110]

Indeed, the view of the UK constitution presented by Eurosceptics is not the only possible one. One alternative reading was offered by Paul Craig as early as 1991, when he argued that:

> The 'classical' writers on the constitution, such as Blackstone and Dicey, discussed sovereignty as part of a more general vision of the constitutional ordering within the State (. . .). It is manifestly clear that the conditions for the Blackstonian balanced constitution, and the Diceyan self-correcting constitution, are no longer prevalent today. At least, however, both writers recognized that the concept of sovereignty must be analysed as part of this broader constitutional map. They both recognized that there had to be some normative justification for the degree of power accorded to Parliament (. . .) [W]e may well find that, for example, the modern embodiment of a balanced constitutional order is one which does not afford unlimited power to Parliament. We may well discover that a system of government which is both balanced and normatively justifiable is one in which there are rights-based limits on the power of Parliament, which are to be policed by our courts (. . .). Once the methodology of the classical writers is made apparent, it becomes evident that any justification for Parliamentary omnipotence must be based on arguments of principle. It may also be the case that once matters are perceived in this way there is no longer any such principled justification for legally unconstrained Parliamentary power in the modern day. Rather, that we are led to the conclusion that some species of rights-based constraints must feature in any convincing principled picture of twentieth century government.[111]

Craig's proposal, as we interpret it, had important implications. He proposed that a core aspect of British constitutionalism such as the sovereignty of Parliament must be read in context and in relation to the normative

[110] Michael Gordon, 'Brexit: A Challenge for the UK Constitution, of the UK Constitution?' (2016) 12 European Constitutional Law Review 409, 441.

[111] Craig, 'Sovereignty of the United Kingdom Parliament after *Factortame*' (n 28) 253–255.

justification of constitutionalism. Because of changes to that context, new constraints on the sovereignty of Parliament might now be justified.

Craig's proposal might be interpreted by some as an attempt to introduce legal elements into the British political constitution. Of course, those with more orthodox approaches to the political character of the British Constitution will distrust this idea, but their stances will need to confront, in turn, a paradox inherent to their arguments.

According to the more Eurosceptic line of argument, the sovereignty of Parliament would be incompatible with the preeminent application of supranational, judicialized legal norms. Furthermore, the British Parliament could not bind itself *ad futurum* to EU law because this would violate a core aspect of the British Constitution. We believe that Craig's reading can counter this position well, by showing how a certain degree of constraint on Parliament is still compatible with the telos of the work of classical British constitutional thinkers, but let us assume, for the sake of argument, that Eurosceptics have a point, and that the current British Constitution cannot and should not be compatible with supranational integration.

In other European countries in which an incompatibility has been found between EU law and the national constitution, the latter has been amended, and thus the conflict has been resolved.[112] One wonders why that could not be the case in the UK too. In principle, furthermore, the British Constitution is easily amendable: that is, precisely, one of the features of the British form of constitutionalism.

Those who mobilize the British Constitution against European integration thus have the burden of normatively justifying why the flexible British Constitution which they claim to defend is so rigid when it comes to European integration. Implicit in their argument seems to be the assumption that there is, after all, a sort of unamendable part of the British Constitution that is, precisely, the part that forces British constitutionalism to be closed to European integration, at least in its current form. We believe that Gordon advances a similar argument when he warns against 'ossifying' some principles of the UK constitution:

> The UK constitution has changed, is still changing, and this is in no small part a direct result of membership of the EU. It is a matter for debate how

[112] See, inter alia, Mattias Wendel, 'Lisbon before the Courts: Comparative Perspectives' (2011) 7 European Constitutional Law Review 96; Pablo Castillo-Ortiz, *EU Treaties and the Judicial Politics of National Courts. A Law and Politics Approach* (Routledge 2017).

> far the political constitutionalist paradigm still accurately represents the modern position in the UK. We must also be careful not to present a vision of the UK constitution which ossifies certain principles, arrangements or philosophies. Nevertheless, in my view, the political constitutionalist paradigm does still have clear salience in the UK context—both descriptively and normatively—despite the changes which have occurred. Indeed, that this constitution is continually open to reformation is (at least ostensibly) one of its defining characteristics, and the extent of change in recent history can be understood as a vindication of the continuing force of the idea of a political constitution.[113]

In any case, let us again accept this Eurosceptic point for the sake of argument. Even if we accept the alleged inherent closedness of the British Constitution to European integration in its current form, things remain difficult for Eurosceptics in the UK. In countries based on legal constitutionalism, unconstitutional constitutional amendments are usually declared to be so, if this happens at all, by a constitutional court or like body.[114] However, in the UK, precisely from a Diceyan orthodox approach, the ultimate say on constitutional matters would lie with the sovereign Parliament: exactly the institution that originally passed the 1972 European Communities Act, or the HRA 1998.[115]

This closes the circle of argument at the constitutional level. British Eurosceptics want to enforce parliamentary sovereignty against the will of Parliament. They claim to defend the British political constitution but then they imply an eternity clause to close it to European integration. At the political level, this reading renders the British Constitution closed to EU law, and thus a constraint on the capacity of British politics to enter into deep forms of cooperation with the UK's neighbours.

With regard to the ECHR and the HRA, things are probably less complicated. As explained earlier, the HRA does not give British courts the power to strike down legislation on the grounds of incompatibility with Convention rights, but simply allows them to declare this incompatibility. Parliament

[113] Gordon, 'Brexit: A Challenge for the UK Constitution' (n 110) 437.

[114] Yaniv Roznai, 'Unconstitutional Constitutional Amendments—The Migration and Success of a Constitutional Idea' (2013) 61 The American Journal of Comparative Law 657; Yaniv Roznai, *Unconstitutional Constitutional Amendments: The Limits of Amendment Powers* (Oxford University Press 2019).

[115] However, there is a debate as to whether, ultimately, the common law may impose constraints upon parliamentary sovereignty, particularly in cases of serious violations of fundamental rights. This was discussed as obiter dicta in *R (Jackson) v Attorney General* [2005] UKHL 56.

continues to have the last word. However, debates in the UK about the HRA 1998 have gone beyond the relationship between judiciary and parliamentary sovereignty, and sometimes have pointed towards executive empowerment, for instance, with the proposal to limit the power of the courts to declare secondary legislation to be incompatible with Convention rights, as opposed to quashing it. The response by Tyrrell and Young in their written evidence to the UK Parliament is enlightening on this point:

> We do not agree that courts should be limited to making declarations of incompatibility in respect of secondary legislation that cannot be read compatibly with Convention rights. The proposal risks removing an important check on executive power, is likely to dilute the protection of rights, and may create inconsistencies which are difficult to justify (. . .). The proposed change also risks upsetting the balance of powers between the institutions of state by removing an important check on executive power. If Parliament delegates to the executive the authority to make legislation, it is an uncontroversial role of the courts to supervise the exercise of that delegated authority and to be able to constrain the executive to their proper jurisdiction where they purport to exceed it. Judicial supervision is especially important where there is limited opportunity for legislative scrutiny.[116]

4.6. Conclusion

UK politics has historically displayed an extensive use of constitutional ideas as part of Eurosceptic arguments.

The specificities of the British Constitution have been skilfully mobilized in this regard. The UK system does not rely on a constitutional court whose case law can be instrumentalized by Eurosceptics, but this has not been an obstacle for actors wishing to use constitutional law as part of their rhetoric and strategy. On the contrary, UK-based Eurosceptic actors have created a discourse around parliamentary sovereignty that mobilizes the special nature of British constitutionalism against European law. In this discourse, the power of European courts, the attempts to create a more perfect European constitutionalism, or the primacy of EU law would be a threat to the British constitutional

[116] Helene Tyrrell and Alison Young, 'Written Evidence from Dr Hélène Tyrrell and Professor Alison Young (HRR0001)' (2022) UK Parliament, Joint Committee on Human Rights, Human Rights Act Reform Inquiry, paras 34–36 <https://committees.parliament.uk/writtenevidence/106528/pdf/>.

arrangements. A case in point is some criticisms of the ECHR by Conservative politicians, which often rely on elements of the British constitutional tradition:

> When Conservative Party politicians first proposed repealing the HRA, and replacing it with a British Bill of Rights they often focused on the seeming lack of democratic accountability. For example David Cameron in 2010, when he was the leader of the opposition, argued that he wanted new legislation to ensure that 'laws can no longer be decided by unaccountable judges' whilst lauding the tradition of parliamentary supremacy. When arguing that Britain should withdraw from the ECHR Theresa May, the then home secretary, claimed the ECtHR was able to 'bind the hands of Parliament'. This goes beyond simply arguing that judges have no democratic mandate but is rooted in the British tradition that Parliament protects rights and liberties.[117]

The evidence gathered in this chapter shows the adaptability of Eurosceptic constitutional counter-narratives, which are able to take root in countries based on either legal or political constitutionalism. These counter-narratives often rely on similar points on sovereignty, democracy, and nation-level constitutionalism—which are presented as being under threat from European integration. Context-specific circumstances are, however, vividly present in these counter-narratives, which are constructed around—not against, nor despite—national constitutional idiosyncrasies.

According to McHarg, Brexit opened a crisis of constitutional implications.[118] However, in the case of the UK, Eurosceptic constitutional counter-narratives did not disappear with the exit from the EU, despite the problems they created for the British Constitution.[119] These counter-narratives continue to exist and now target the ECHR. Europe continues to be a point of contention in the country. In this scenario, from a normative perspective, this shows the need to build a strong case for an open, viable, pro-European UK constitutionalism, one in which British constitutional democracy is not just reconciled with European law but is reinforced by it.

[117] Cowell (n 85) 1188.
[118] Aileen McHarg, 'Navigating without Maps: Constitutional Silence and the Management of the Brexit Crisis' (2018) 16 International Journal of Constitutional Law 952.
[119] See also Alison Young, *Unchecked Power?* (Bristol University Press 2024).

5

Italy

Constitutional Law, Euroscepticism, and Sovereignism*

5.1. Introduction

In 2024, some Lega (League) MPs presented a constitutional bill aimed at questioning the primacy of EU law over national law.[1] This is nothing new: in the previous legislature, Fratelli d'Italia (Brothers of Italy, FdI)—which had remained in opposition during the Draghi government—proposed a similar constitutional amendment.[2] The most recent constitutional bill was an initiative taken in response to the decision of a court in Catania that had disapplied[3] the so-called 'Safe Countries' decree on the grounds of conflict with EU law,[4] triggering criticism from government forces. The purpose of the Safe Countries decree was to facilitate the identification of applicants for international protection from countries considered to be safe, thus reducing the time taken to process asylum applications. From the outset, this decree was seen as being at odds

* Unless otherwise indicated, all the election manifestos of the political parties discussed in this chapter are available at the following link <https://manifestoproject.wzb.eu/>.

[1] Bill n 1917, 13 June 2024, 'Elenco delle proposte emendative (262) in I Commissione in sede referente pubblicate nel Bollettino delle Giunte e Commissioni del 05/11/2024 (n. 396) riferite al C. 1917, in ordine di pubblicazione' <https://documenti.camera.it/apps/emendamenti/getProposteEmendativeSeduta.aspx?contenitorePortante=leg.19.eme.ac.1917&tipoSeduta=1&sedeEsame=referente&urnTestoRiferimento=urn:leg:19:1917:null:null:com:01:referente&dataSeduta=20241105&tipoListaEmendamenti=1>. In particular, see amendments 7.02 and 7.03, published on 5 November 2024. 'At every stage and in every type of judicial proceeding, at every level and in every instance, the Constitution shall not constitute, in any of its provisions, a source subordinate to the Treaties and other acts of the European Union' (/7.02). 'After Article 7, add the following: Art. 7-bis. 1. To Constitutional Law No. 87 of 11 March 1953, after Article 23, add the following: "Art. 23-bis. 1. If, in the course of a judgment, the judicial authority finds a conflict between a provision of law or an act having the force of law and a directly applicable European provision, it shall raise the question of constitutionality"' (7.03).

[2] Bill n 291, 23 March 2018 <https://documenti.camera.it/leg18/pdl/pdf/leg.18.pdl.camera.291.18PDL0003090.pdf>.

[3] Tribunale di Catania, Section immigration, sentenza of 4 November 2024 <https://www.sistemapenale.it/pdf_contenuti/1730797521_tribcatania-3112024-non-convalida-trattenimento-disapplica-dl-23102024-ok-ok.pdf>.

[4] Decree-Law No. 158 of 23 October 2024 <https://www.gazzettaufficiale.it/eli/id/2024/10/23/24G00177/sg>.

The Eurosceptic Mobilization of Constitutional Law. Pablo Castillo-Ortiz and Giuseppe Martinico, Oxford University Press. © Pablo Castillo-Ortiz and Giuseppe Martinico 2026. DOI: 10.1093/9780198959205.003.0005

with EU law, in particular Directive 2013/32/EU[5] on common procedures for granting and withdrawing international protection status. We will return to the contents of the amendment tabled by the League later in the chapter, but this is an example that says a lot about the current approach to EU law of the political majority in power.

We have selected Italy as a case study for this book because it is a founding Member State, and, in particular, because it is currently governed by a coalition with important Eurosceptic components. This allows us to understand the evolution of the Eurosceptic uses of constitutional law, from opposition to government.

One of the main characteristics of the current phase of Italian Euroscepticism is that it is widespread even in the intellectual debate. Many of the arguments used by Italian Eurosceptic movements with reference to domestic law have in fact been developed by this intelligentsia. This explains the existence of a large section in this chapter devoted to the arguments of those authors who describe themselves as sovereignists.

Italy has long been regarded as a staunchly pro-European nation.[6] However, since the Eurozone crisis if not before, the dynamics of its political landscape have shifted.[7] On the left, there has been intense criticism of the measures implemented to address the economic crisis, often accompanied by pointed critiques of European supranational institutions. More recently, the Italian political spectrum has witnessed the rise of far-right actors who openly and assertively espouse Eurosceptic views.

[5] Directive 2013/32/EU of the European Parliament and of the Council of 26 June 2013 on common procedures for granting and withdrawing international protection. The interpretation of Directive 2013/32 is at the heart of Case C-758/24, *Alace*, ECLI:EU:C:2025:591. The judgment established that Member States may designate a country as a 'safe country of origin', but national courts can review this designation. Notably, the ruling was criticized by the Meloni government, both through a post on X (formerly Twitter) by President Giorgia Meloni <https://x.com/GiorgiaMeloni/status/1951220267356688659>, and via an official statement published on the website of the Italian Presidency of the Council of Ministers <https://www.governo.it/it/articolo/decisione-della-corte-di-giustizia-ue-merito-ai-paesi-sicuri-la-nota-di-palazzo-chigi/29389>.

[6] 'If at the beginning of the 1950s there was deep polarisation on the question of the integration of Western European democracies—one reflecting the broader polarisation of the Italian party system—by the early 1990s the situation was instead one of convergence, with all parties (excluding the irrelevant extremes) sharing not only broad support for the integration process, but also specific support for its trajectory represented by the EU', Nicolò Conti, Francesco Marangoni, and Luca Verzichelli, 'Euroscepticism in Italy from the Onset of the Crisis: Tired of Europe?' (2020) 25 South European Society and Politics 1, 2.

[7] On this shift, see Christophe Roux and Luca Verzichelli, 'Italy: Still a Pro-European, but not a Fully Europeanised Elite?' (2010) 15 South European Society and Politics 11; Nicolò Conti, 'The Italian Political Elites and Europe: Big Move, Small Change?' (2017) 38 International Political Science Review/Revue internationale de science politique 534; Manuela Caiani and Nicolò Conti, 'In the Name of the People: The Euroscepticism of the Italian Radical Right' (2014) 15 Perspectives on European Politics and Society 83.

Political scientists[8] have argued that Italy used to be characterized by general support for the EU process, and this too can be explained in different ways. In the case of the extreme right, this was also due to the fact that the European Communities (ECs) were seen as an opportunity to emancipate the country from US and Soviet influence.[9] This has also been the subject of some recent contributions by Lorimer, in which the author, taking her cue from the French and Italian cases, argued that the EU process functioned 'as a powerful ideological resource for far-right parties looking for legitimation because it allowed them to refashion their political message in a more acceptable form, while maintaining the allegiance of their core voters and supporters'.[10] It is probable, however, that all the Italian political forces also tried to see different things in the ECs because of the uncertainty of the political potential of a process that presented itself, first and foremost, as a strategy of economic cooperation. This obviously also applied to the extreme right and the Movimento Sociale Italiano (Italian Social Movement),[11] the Italian post-fascist force from which the Fratelli d'Italia party[12] would later be born. The position of the extreme left, particularly the Partito Comunista Italiano (PCI), has greatly changed over the years. Initially, the prevailing position was one of opposition to the creation of the ECs, seen as a possible alternative to the Soviet bloc and, especially, as an extension of the North Atlantic alliance. The economic matrix of the European integration process was then seen as another factor for criticism by the PCI, which saw this as a process inspired only by capitalist logic. The PCI's position changed in the 1960s, particularly with the first evident cracks in the relationship with the Soviet Union, and, in particular, after the Soviet repression of demonstrators in Budapest in 1956 and then in Prague in 1968. Later, in the 1980s, the PCI would participate in the elections for the European Parliament (EP) and, under Berlinguer's leadership, would develop a form of Europeanism (seen as different from 'internationalism'[13]) that, although sui generis, would

[8] Conti, Marangoni, and Verzichelli (n 6).

[9] Gregorio Sorgonà, 'The Italian Right-Wing and the European Integration Process: The Case of the Italian Social Movement' (2022) 27 Journal of Modern Italian Studies 383.

[10] Marta Lorimer, *Europe as Ideological Resource European Integration and Far Right Legitimation in France and Italy* (Oxford University Press 2024) 2.

[11] For a recent overview of the Movimento Sociale Italiano, see Marco Tarchi and Antonio Carioti, *Le tre età della fiamma* (Solferino 2024).

[12] For a recent analysis in English, see Davide Vampa, *Brothers of Italy. A New Populist Wave in an Unstable Party System* (Springer 2023).

[13] Antonio Varsori, *La Cenerentola d'Europa? L'Italia e l'integrazione europea dal 1947 ad oggi* (Rubbettino 2010) 313; Marco Di Maggio, 'Internazionalismo, socialismo ed europeismo nel Pci di Berlinguer' (2016) 18 Dimensioni e problemi della ricerca storica 55. Internationalism here refers to the need for loyal alignment with the global communist movement and the Soviet Union.

lay the foundations for a supportive approach to EU dynamics.[14] To refer to this new approach, historians use the concept of 'Eurocommunism', by which they mean a reinterpretation of communism that aimed to reconcile the values of Marxism with the principles of liberal democracy, marking a significant departure from Soviet orthodoxy.[15]

Two examples may be cited as evidence of the country's Europhile orientation. First of all, the only EU-related referendum held in Italy took place in 1989, and it was consultative in nature. It asked whether Italian voters supported the transformation of the ECs into a European Union equipped with a government accountable to the EP, and an EP empowered to draft a constitution for Europe. The outcome was overwhelmingly positive, with 88.03 per cent voting in favour and only 11.97 per cent against.[16]

Generally speaking, the first cracks in this general Europhile approach appeared as reactions to the Maastricht Treaty[17] and, more recently, to the principles that guided the EU in managing the financial crisis of 2010, with the notorious season of austerity that caused so much criticism of the Union.[18] When the Maastricht Treaty was ratified, and despite broad cross-party

[14] Calogero Laneri, 'Il Pci di Enrico Berlinguer e le elezioni europee attraverso la lettura della stampa comunista (1979–1984)' (2017) 32 Diacronie [Online] 1.

[15] Santiago Carrillo, *Eurocomunismo y estado* (Editorial Critica 1977). On the notion of Eurocommunism, see also Donald Sassoon, 'Eurocommunism, the Labour Party and the EEC' (1979) 50(1) The Political Quarterly 86.

[16] Nevertheless, the referendum was intended to have symbolic value rather than legal effect, which was also because, under the Italian legal system, referendums are permitted only to abrogate parliamentary laws (as per article 75 of the Constitution) or to confirm a constitutional law revising the Constitution (as per article 138). In this respect, a specific constitutional law (Law No 2 of 3 April 1989) was adopted to allow for such a 'consultative referendum' on the future of the European Union.

[17] 'Finally, at the extremes of the political spectrum, euroscepticism became a solid feature after 1994, although it was mainly verbal rather than policyseeking (. . .). On the one side, the PRC (Partito della Rifondazione Comunista—Refounded Communist Party, a rather small party that played a relevant role in coalition formation, supporting the Italian government in 1996 and 2006) voted against the Maastricht treaty and the launch of the Monetary Union. The party represented the EU as an instrument of Americanisation and as an international technocratic power (often associated with IMF and WTO). The communists mainly focused on the negative outcomes of the integration process, particularly in terms of the domestic impact of the EU, considered to be responsible for the diminishing quality of life of the lower classes and of the most disadvantaged social groups. On the other side of the spectrum, the main radical right-wing party, Lega, which at the time was also a regionalist party, strongly criticised the results achieved by the EU, whose institutions they accused of replacing the nation-state with a new "super-state" that prevents local identities and powers from developing and becoming more independent. Overall, Lega expressed a pessimistic evaluation of the impact of the EU on the main party goal of the time—the self-determination of the northern regions of Italy—as well as on its targeted social groups, such as farmers, milk producers, and small firms', Conti, Marangoni, and Verzichelli (n 6) 4. See also: Eleonora Poli and Mark Valentiner, 'From Albertini to Anti-Europeanism: Shades of Euroscepticism in Italy' (2014) 54 L'Europe en Formation Revue d'études sur la construction européenne et le fédéralisme 66, 67.

[18] This can be traced back to a broader trend: Andrea LP Pirro and Stijn van Kessel, 'United in Opposition? The Populist Radical Right's EU-pessimism in Times of Crisis' (2017) 4 Journal of European Integration 405.

agreement, an interesting debate emerged regarding the need for a constitutional amendment to account for the new powers transferred to the EU, even if the possibility of a constitutional amendment was ultimately ruled out.[19]

The second example is the fact that, on European issues—including parliamentary votes on laws authorizing the ratification of European Treaties—there is a long-standing tradition of broad political support. This applies even to international treaties indirectly linked to European integration, such as the highly contested Fiscal Compact.[20]

Indeed, as Conti, Marangoni, and Verzichelli pointed out, the European elections of 2014 represented a fundamental turning point:

> One year after its first electoral success, on the occasion of the European elections, M5S campaigned against the euro and in support of a referendum on Italy's exit from the eurozone, the rejection of the major EU financial constraints like the Fiscal Compact, and in favour of creating a Euro-Mediterranean community alternative to the EU community. On the same occasion, other opposition and radical right parties (Lega, FdI) also aligned themselves with the M5S on many European issues. Forza Italia, although cooperating with the national government and not having the profile of a challenger party, represented the EU as an enemy (more vehemently than ever in the past), with a campaign that made use of such slogans as 'less Europe in Italy' and of stories of an EU conspiracy against Italian interests (at a moment of widespread public concern about the economic situation of the country consequent to the effects of the financial crisis).[21]

Building on these considerations, in this chapter, we will first remind readers of the relevant constitutional framework employed to justify the structural principles of EU law (mainly, primacy and direct effect) in the Italian system. Second, we shall focus on some Eurosceptic movements, paying particular attention to the most recent developments, but without neglecting the historical dimension to stress both the continuity and the discontinuity in their evolution. Subsequently, we shall concentrate on Euroscepticism in the academic and intellectual discourse, which is particularly relevant in the Italian case.

[19] On this debate, see Sergio Bartole, *Interpretazioni e trasformazioni della Costituzione repubblicana* (Il Mulino 2004) 307.

[20] Leonardo Pierdominici, *Constitutional Change through Euro Crisis Law: Italy* (2014) European University Institute <https://eurocrisislaw.eui.eu/wp-content/uploads/sites/55/2019/05/Italy.pdf>, 24, 27, and 49.

[21] Conti, Marangoni, and Verzichelli (n 6) 4.

The chapter concludes with a response to Eurosceptic constitutional counter-narratives in Italy.

5.2. Italian Constitutional Law and European Integration

After the Court of Justice's (ECJ) landmark judgments in *Van Gend en Loos*[22] and *Costa*,[23] the reception at the national level of the doctrines of direct effect and primacy became an obvious theme of scholarly debate. Scholars and authors[24] from different backgrounds were involved in this discussion: this was the case, in particular, for international law scholars, including those who had specialized in the field of EC law since the 1980s, constitutional law scholars, and practitioners and officials of the EC institutions at work on the European integration process. The result was a wide and rich debate, animated by different legal sensitivities and accompanying the evolution of the Constitutional Court's case law.[25]

The diversity of views was clear from the early case law[26] of the Constitutional Court. As is well known, after some initial reluctance the Constitutional Court found, in article 11 of the Italian Constitution, the legal grounds for recognizing the direct effect and primacy of EC law,[27] as article 11 provides that Italy agrees, on conditions of equality with other states, to the limitations of sovereignty that may be necessary to a world order ensuring peace and justice among nations.[28]

The full acceptance of primacy, however, did not occur immediately, but was the result of a long process. One reason for this was the absence of an

[22] ECJ, Case 26/62, *NV Algemene Transport- en Expeditie Onderneming Van Gend en Loos v Netherlands Inland Revenue Administration* ECLI:EU:C:1963:1.

[23] ECJ, Case 6/64 *Flaminio Costa v E.N.E.L.* ECLI:EU:C:1964:66.

[24] On the changing arguments used by scholars to explain the structural principles of EU law, see Giulio Itzcovich, *Teorie e ideologie del diritto comunitario* (Giappichelli 2006).

[25] A clear and concise account of this debate is provided by Giandonato Caggiano, 'La dottrina italiana nella fase costituente dell'ordinamento giuridico comunitario' (2013) 8 Studi sull'integrazione europea 441.

[26] For instance, Corte costituzionale, sentenza 14/1964 < www.cortecostituzionale.it>.

[27] In case n 14/1964 the Italian Constitutional Court interpreted the relationship between national and Community acts in the light of the chronological criterion lex posterior derogat priori (since the enabling domestic act ratifying the Treaties was an ordinary legislative act); later on, in case n 183/1973, the Italian Constitutional Court changed its position and claimed that the constitutional basis of Community law primacy can be found in article 11 of the Italian Constitution.

[28] The full text of article 11 of the Italian Constitution reads: 'Italy rejects war as an instrument of aggression against the freedom of other peoples and as a means for the settlement of international disputes. Italy agrees, on conditions of equality with other States, to the limitations of sovereignty that may be necessary to a world order ensuring peace and justice among the Nations. Italy promotes and encourages international organisations furthering such ends'.

explicit European clause in the Italian Constitution. In the Italian Constituent Assembly, the constituent body operating from 1946 to 1948 and tasked with writing a constitution for the new Italian Republic, there was a brief exchange between Emilio Lussu and Aldo Moro on the possibility of codifying an explicit reference to a possible (future) European organization, as we will see when we return to this point later.

This situation, which was quite similar to that in other EC/EU Member States, changed in 2001 when an explicit reference to EU obligations was introduced in the new text of article 117 of the Constitution. Article 117 of the Italian Constitution now reads as follows: 'Legislative powers shall be vested in the State and the Regions in compliance with the Constitution and with the constraints deriving from EU legislation and international obligations'. Another feature of the Italian Constitutional Court's approach to EU law is the counter-limits doctrine, devised by the Corte costituzionale in the *Frontini* judgment of 1973[29] (or even earlier, see decision 98/1965[30]) soon after the well-known judgment of the ECJ in *Internationale Handelsgesellschaft*. In this judgment, the European Court of Justice pointed out the primacy of Community law over national law including national constitutional norms.[31] As the formula suggests, counter-limits are those supreme principles that represent the untouchable core of the Italian constitutional order; they cannot be set aside in the process of European legal integration. From *Frontini* onwards, the Italian Constitutional Court has theoretically provided itself with the possibility of declaring Italian law authorizing the ratification of European Treaties unconstitutional because of the violation of one of the counter-limits (which are not a priori identified by the Constitutional Court, by the way).

In this respect, the Italian position—along with the German one[32]—is relevant for a complete understanding of the reasons behind the national judicial 'resistance' of those years. The constitutional courts have claimed that they are maintaining their role as the guardians of the national constitutional identity without exceptions. From their perspective, the constitutional courts have sought to mitigate the original approach taken by the Court of Justice in its

[29] Corte costituzionale, sentenza 183/73 *Frontini* [1974] 2 CMLR 372, but see also case 170/84, the so-called *Granital* judgment: Corte costituzionale, sentenza 180/1974 *Granital* [1984] CMLR 756. For more on this, see Marta Cartabia, *Principi inviolabili e integrazione europea* (Giuffrè 1995).

[30] Corte costituzionale, sentenza 98/1965 <https://www.cortecostituzionale.it/default.do>.

[31] 'Therefore the validity of a Community measure or its effect within a member State cannot be affected by allegations that it runs counter to either fundamental rights as formulated by the constitution of that State or the principles of its constitutional structure', ECJ Case 11/70 *Internationale Handelsgesellschaft mbH v Einfuhr- und Vorratsstelle für Getreide und Futtermittel* ECLI:EU:C:1970:114, para 3.

[32] BVerfGE 37, 271 ff, in <https://www.bundesverfassungsgericht.de/EN/Home/home_node.html>.

interpretation of the relationship between legal systems. They have raised ultimate barriers against the penetration of EU law in the definition of the fundamental principles of the legal orders of which they are the guardians.

The consequence of a possible declaration of invalidity could have been Italy's withdrawal from the EU, but we should take into account that there was no provision comparable to Article 50 TEU at the time. According to Cartabia,[33] the counter-limits test was originally conceived as a way to exert an exceptional control in respect of the conditions for the constitutionality of the Italian accession to the ECs.

Later on, with decision 232/1989 (the so-called '*Fragd* judgment'),[34] the nature of the counter-limits doctrine changed; it was transformed from an exceptional control into a 'simple' control of the compatibility of EU law with the Constitution that does not question Italy's membership in the EU.

Because of the 'transformation' of this doctrine, the counter-limits have worked as a limitation to European primacy. According to the same scholarship, starting with the *Fragd* judgment, the Italian Constitutional Court implicitly admitted that a possible conflict with the Italian Constitution would not cause the invalidity of the national law of execution of the Rome Treaty but merely the non-applicability of the EC rule.[35]

The above-mentioned 2001 constitutional reform included an explicit reference to EU law in article 117. Soon after the reform, the interpretation of this provision created a division among scholars. According to some, article 117, paragraph 1, simply codifies the pre-existing situation, granting a sort of a posteriori assent to the European primacy[36] developed by the ECJ and accepted across the ECs. Other scholars, on the other hand, emphasized the importance of the constitutional status given to European primacy and asserted that article 117 paved the way for the acceptance of the Italian monist thesis.[37]

Another manifestation of the progressive (but still partial) convergence between the ECJ and the Italian Constitutional Court is seen in the developments in the field of the preliminary ruling mechanism. On 15 April 2008, for

[33] Cartabia (n 29) 110.

[34] Corte costituzionale, sentenza 232/1989 <www.cortecostituzionale.it>. In English: *Fragd* [1990] 27 CMLR 93.

[35] See Marta Cartabia and Joseph HH Weiler, *L'Italia in Europa* (Bologna 2000) 171–172.

[36] Cesare Pinelli, 'I limiti generali alla potestà legislativa statale e regionale e i rapporti con l'ordinamento comunitario' (2001) 125 Foro italiano 194.

[37] Francesco Paterniti, 'La riforma dell'art. 117, 1° co. della Costituzione e le nuove prospettive dei rapporti tra ordinamento giuridico nazionale e Unione Europea' (2004) 49 Giurisprudenza costituzionale 2101; Alessandro Pajno, 'Il rispetto dei vincoli derivanti dall'ordinamento comunitario come limite alla potestà legislativa nel nuovo Titolo V della Costituzione' (2003) 23 Le Istituzioni del federalismo 814.

the first time in its history, the Italian Court agreed to refer a preliminary question to the ECJ.[38]

This convergence has also produced important cases of judicial dialogue in recent years, but it has not eliminated the occasional tensions. In this sense, the growing importance of the EU Charter of Fundamental Rights has generated interpretative conflicts and has renewed the constitutional conflicts between the primacy of EU law and constitutional supremacy. An example of these tensions can be found in the well-known *Taricco* saga,[39] a series of cases revolving around the enforcement of EU law against financial fraud, specifically involving VAT (value added tax), and the implications for domestic legal principles, particularly Italy's constitutional prohibition on retroactive criminal penalties. This saga, according to many Italian constitutional law scholars, represented a turning point in the relationship between the courts.[40] In 2019, the Italian Constitutional Court also recognized the constitutional nature of the Charter of Fundamental Rights, holding that it was 'endowed with particular characteristics due to the typically constitutional stamp of its contents'. Indeed, 'the principles and rights laid out in the Charter largely intersect with the principles and rights guaranteed by the Italian Constitution (and by other Member States' constitutions)'.[41]

[38] Corte costituzionale, ordinanza n 103/2008 <https://www.cortecostituzionale.it/default.do>.

[39] ECJ C-105/14 *Ivo Taricco* et al. ECLI:EU:C:2015:555; Corte costituzionale, ordinanza 24/2017; ECJ, C-42/17 *M.A.S., M.B.* ECLI:EU:C:2017:936; Corte costituzionale, sentenza 115/2018.

[40] Massimo Luciani, 'Il brusco risveglio. I controlimiti e la fine mancata della storia costituzionale' (2016) 6 *Rivista AIC* 1. See the contributions included in Alessandro Bernardi and Cristiano Cupelli (eds), *Il caso Taricco e il dialogo tra le corti. L'ordinanza 24/2017 della Corte costituzionale* (Jovene 2017). For further information on the evolving relationship between the Italian Constitutional Court and the Court of Justice, see Vittoria Barsotti, Paolo G Carozza, Marta Cartabia, and Andrea Simoncini, *Italian Constitutional Justice in Global Context* (Oxford University Press 2016) 205; Roberto Mastroianni, 'La Corte costituzionale si rivolge alla Corte di giustizia in tema di "controlimiti" costituzionali: è un vero dialogo?' (2017) 14 *Federalismi.it. Rivista di diritto pubblico italiano, comparato, europeo* 1; Giacomo Di Federico, *L'identità nazionale degli stati membri nel diritto dell'Unione europea. Natura e portata dell'art. 4, par. 2, TUE* (Editoriale Scientifica 2017); Daniele Gallo, 'Challenging EU Constitutional Law: The Italian Constitutional Court's New Stance on Direct Effect and the Preliminary Reference Procedure' (2019) 25 European Law Journal 434.

[41] Corte costituzionale, sentenza 269/2017 <https://www.cortecostituzionale.it/default.do>. This decision created many anxieties that were then partly assuaged by subsequent case law. The Constitutional Court argued that: '[T]he emergence of the guarantees found in the EUCFR and those provided by the Italian Constitution can generate competing legal remedies. In light of this, for cases of "double prejudice" [doppia pregiudizialità]—i.e. disputes that may give rise to questions of constitutionality and, simultaneously, questions of compliance with Union law—the ECJ has, in turn, affirmed that Union law "does not preclude" the overriding character of the constitutional determination that falls under the competence of the national constitutional courts, provided that the ordinary judges are free to submit to the ECJ "any question that it considers necessary, at whatever stage of the proceedings it considers appropriate, even at the end of an interlocutory procedure for the review of constitutionality;" and "to adopt any measure necessary to ensure the provisional judicial protection of the rights conferred under the European Union's legal order;" to disapply, at the conclusion of the interim judgment of constitutionality, the national legislative provision at issue which has survived constitutional scrutiny, whenever, on other grounds, they consider it to conflict with Union law'. In spite of these tensions,

5.3. Patterns of Eurosceptic Mobilization of Constitutional Law by the Italian Parties

5.3.1. Italian politics, hard Euroscepticism and the exit strategy

In Italy at present, examples of hard Euroscepticism[42] focused on the exit strategy are of marginal importance, but it should not be forgotten that in the past even parties with great relevance, such as Lega, MoVimento Cinque Stelle (M5S, 'Five Star Movement'), and Fratelli d'Italia, took hard Eurosceptic positions, even if they have now softened them (especially in the case of Fratelli d'Italia).

Today, the exit option is supported by No Europa per l'Italia—ItalExit con Paragone ('No Europe for Italy—ItalExit with Paragone'),[43] a party created by Gianluigi Paragone, a journalist and former member of the Five Star Movement. This party is modelled on Farage's Brexit Party and has no members in the Italian parliament because of its poor performance in the 2022 elections. In 2022, the party changed its name to Per l'Italia con Paragone ('For Italy with Paragone'), maintaining its Eurosceptic (and anti-NATO) and sovereignist position. Other political forces that present themselves as characterized by hard Euroscepticism are certainly Forza Nuova ('New Force', FN) and CasaPound ('House of [Ezra] Pound', CP),[44] two neo-fascist parties. In

cooperation has not been absent. In 2024, the Italian Constitutional Court seemed to abandon a subversive reading of the obiter dictum included in decision 269/2017, renouncing 'the antithesis or an order of priority between these instruments', Corte costituzionale, sentenza 181/2024 <https://www.cortecostituzionale.it/default.do>. See also Corte costituzionale, sentenze 1/2025, 7/2025, 21/2025, 24/2025 <https://www.cortecostituzionale.it/default.do>.

[42] Paul Taggart and Aleks Szczerbiak, 'Theorising Party-Based Euroscepticism: Problems of Definition, Measurement and Causality' (2023) SEI Working Paper No 69 <https://aei.pitt.edu/6562/>.

[43] See the official website <https://italexitperlitalia.it/>.

[44] 'The name CasaPound had a great symbolic meaning, with a clear reference to the American poet and modernist Ezra Pound, who wrote extensively during the war against housing rent as usury, as well as anti-Semitism. Pound was the incarnation of the ideal fascist revolution, meaning by that the struggle against plutocracy. The symbol of the party is a stylized turtle, embodying the right to housing. The turtle carries its own home and is among the animals that live longest. But this symbol also refers to the Roman formation called Testudo, the army of Rome that, in the words of cpi, showed the greatness and force of the Empire, which emerged "from a vertical order and from a hierarchical principle." Contextually, the octagonal shape is reminiscent of the historical monument Castel del Monte, built by the "last Cesare" in Italy, the emperor Federico II. The arrow is the same we find in other far-right movements' flags in Europe, such as that of The Nordic Resistance Movement (nrm) in Scandinavia (. . .). The Forza Nuova party (FN) was founded in September 1997, two years after Fiuggi, and was meant to be a new reference point for both the youth fringes of the Italian radical right and conservative right-wing traditionalists; a party for parliamentary deputies, autonomous groups and skinheads', Elisabetta Cassina Wolff, 'CasaPound Italia: "Back to Believing. The Struggle Continues"'(2019) 8 Fascism 61, 61 and 82.

particular, the leader of CasaPound stated that: 'We are not running to change the EU from within (. . .) because it is impossible, but to sink it because it is now a prison. There is no alternative to collecting signatures at the moment, considering that Salvini and M5S have abandoned their battles against the euro and the EU and Meloni has even made Fitto's conservatives join her party. *CasaPound* will be the only party on the ballot that will clearly tell the Italians that the only solution is Exit'.[45] These declarations are confirmed by a reading of CasaPound's manifesto.[46] Roberto Fiore, the leader of Forza Nuova, justified his anti-EU position as follows: 'There are two Europes. One in Strasbourg—bureaucratic, anti-Christian, led by lobbyists. The other represents the Christian world. The only group of people with a Roman concept of peace and relations between people, where there is no domination and slavery'.[47] This opposition between two Europes is also an element of the rhetoric of sovereignism, as we will see in the next section.

Also present on the radical left are forces that are relevant from our point of view, such as Democrazia Sovrana e Popolare ('Sovereign and Popular Democracy', DSP), the movement coordinated by Marco Rizzo, a central figure in Italian sovereignism, as we shall see. This tiny political force takes up some of the points of anti-Europeanism developed by the PCI in the 1950s, emphasizing the capitalist and neo-liberal character of the process of supranational integration and combining these anti-NATO (and even pro-Putin) elements with a pacifist rhetoric that has led to criticism of the EU sanctions against Russia and the decision to fund the Ukrainian resistance. This element is also partly present in the Five Star Movement.[48]

These arguments are combined with the sovereignist element that characterizes the rhetoric of the left-wing sovereignist politician Marco Rizzo. Marco Rizzo's position on the EU has always been critical, but over the years, it has acquired a more radical tone. In past years, Rizzo maintained a Eurosceptic outlook while recognizing some useful aspects of European cooperation. However, recently, as leader of Democrazia Sovrana e Popolare, he has taken an even harder line: he openly supports Italy's exit from the EU and NATO,

[45] Alberto Ferrarese, 'Casapound alle europee senza programma per uscire dall'Ue' (16 May 2019) <https://www.policymakermag.it/fact-checking/casapound-europee-senza-programma-uscire-ue/>. Our translation.

[46] For instance, it is available on their website: <https://www.casapounditalia.org/il-programma/>. See also the 2018 general election manifesto: CasaPound, 'Elezioni CAMERA E SENATO 2018 Programma politico CasaPound Italia' (2018) <https://dait.interno.gov.it/documenti/trasparenza/politiche2018/Doc/6/6_Prog_Elettorale.pdf>.

[47] See the official website of Forza Nuova <https://www.forzanuova1997.it/>. Our translation.

[48] Amy Kazmin, 'Five Star Party Splits as Ukraine War Shakes Italian Politics' *Financial Times* (22 June 2022) <https://www.ft.com/content/f34eba5a-9ca8-4ca5-bc50-21fcca81068b>.

stating that these institutions limit Italian sovereignty and are now serving US policies, especially in the military and geopolitical sphere.

Rizzo believes that Europe is too involved in US-led geopolitical issues, such as the war in Ukraine, and that this has significant economic costs and risks for Italy. In his view, the EU has damaged the continent's economy and peace, and he therefore proposes that Italy detaches itself to create a future in which Italy and Europe focus more on their sovereignty and geopolitical neutrality. In 2019, Marco Rizzo said: 'We are the only force truly against the EU, the euro and NATO'.[49] Although these parties often have no representation in Parliament, they should not be underestimated, as they contribute to shaping a political language that frequently draws on references (often dubious and questionable ones) to constitutional law, and they often end up conditioning the positions of more influential parties.

5.3.2. Euroscepticism through constitutional law arguments in Italy

In addition to these parties focused on exit strategies, the Italian electoral landscape presents many other forces that are certainly sceptical but are not calling for Italy's withdrawal from the EU.

For the purpose of this section, we shall look at three political forces: Lega, Fratelli d'Italia, and MoVimento Cinque Stelle. In so doing, we shall analyse their manifestos to emphasize both the continuities and the discontinuities in their evolution. The period covered starts in the aftermath of the rejection of the Constitutional Treaty, although we must note that two of these parties (MoVimento Cinque Stelle and Fratelli) were actually only created later, in the early 2010s, and that most instances of the use of these constitutional strategies date from precisely that decade.

All these three parties are referred to by the PopuList[50] as populist movements. Two of them (Fratelli d'Italia and Lega) are right wing, while today—despite its origins—the 5 Star Movement has, under Giuseppe Conte's leadership, partly changed its approach by transforming itself into a more

[49] Il Redazione Politica, 'La sfida del comunista Rizzo: "Brexit anche in Italia, ma prima torniamo al socialismo"' *Corriere della Serra* (19 April 2019) <https://www.corriere.it/politica/19_aprile_19/sfida-comunista-rizzo-brexit-anche-italia-ma-prima-torniamo-socialismo-4e2b7faa-627d-11e9-a7fc-361228882fb7.shtml>.

[50] The PopuList, 'Country Report on Italy' <https://popu-list.org/wp-content/uploads/2023/09/Italy.pdf>. On the nexus between populism and Euroscepticism in Italy, see Selcen Öner, 'Growing Fusion of Populism and Euroscepticism in Italy: A Comparative Analysis of the League and The Five Star Movement' (2020) 24 Tripodos 13.

traditional party that can now be considered a left-wing force. Lega and MoVimento Cinque Stelle have defined themselves as populist movements, and they formed part of the same government coalition in 2018, before splitting. Fratelli d'Italia is a far-right party that still has some post-fascist elements in its extreme wings.[51] The mobilization of the idea of constitutional supremacy over EU law is present in many of the manifestos analysed and is sometimes coupled with interpretations that run counter to constitutional case law.

The League is a chameleon-like political force that has changed its nature multiple times and, in the past, has occasionally taken a positive view of the process of European integration, as when, for example, it considered the EU to be a means of overcoming the Italian central state, which it perceived as inefficient or oppressive.[52] However, it can now clearly be considered to be a Eurosceptic party. For instance, it is interesting to note that the 2018 general election manifesto of Lega[53] denied the conclusion—despite consistent case law of the Italian Constitutional Court on this point—that article 11 of the Italian Constitution can be used, from a constitutional point of view, to justify the limitations of sovereignty arising from the EU.[54] Instead, the party argued in its manifesto that:

> [O]ur Constitution clearly defines in its Fundamental Principles (art. 11) that Italy can renounce spaces of sovereignty in favor of international organizations whose objective is the achievement of peace and justice among nations. The EU is not among these organizations. For this reason, also the German Federal Constitutional Court, which also has a Constitution that places limits on the transfer of sovereignty, clarified that any European law or treaty that is in conflict with the Constitution must be rejected.[55]

The 2018 manifesto of Lega is very prolix on this question and continues by stating that:

[51] Think of the controversy caused by the Fan Page investigation: 'Gioventù Meloniana: inchiesta su giovani di FdI' 2024 <https://www.fanpage.it/backstair/story/gioventu-meloniana-inchiesta-su-giovani-di-fdi/>; Giulia Merlo, 'I giovani fascisti spaccano Fratelli d'Italia: il clan Meloni sotto accusa' 28 June 2024 <https://www.editorialedomani.it/politica/italia/giovani-fascisti-fratelli-italia-partito-diviso-meloni-mudy34p0>.

[52] On the history and origins of Lega, see Ilvo Diamanti, *Il male del Nord: Lega, localismo, secessione* (Donzelli 1996).

[53] Lega, 'Salvini Premier. La rivoluzione del buonsenso' (2018) 9.

[54] Lega, 'Salvini Premier' (n 53).

[55] Lega, 'Salvini Premier' (n 53). Our translation.

> The European Court of Justice claims to have the final say in all matters to which the EU's jurisdiction extends, that is now practically on everything. This leads to even the Constitutional Court being subordinated to the caselaw of a European court that is not only unrepresentative, but also completely irresponsible. The Court of Justice claims to be the direct reference for all Italian judges, being able to order disapplication of Italian laws when deemed to conflict with European norms and principles (. . .). The text of article 117 paragraph 1 of the Constitution as amended in 2001 must therefore be clarified in the sense that the last word on the laws voted by the Parliament still belongs to the Constitutional Court (. . .). In short the jurisprudence of the Court of Justice must stop before the jurisprudence of the Constitutional Court.[56]

Lega was not the only party, in that election, to question the primacy of the EU legal system. In its manifesto for the 2018 general election,[57] Fratelli d'Italia called for the renunciation of austerity policies and excessive regulations that hinder development, and a revision of the EU Treaties (in an unspecified way). Under the motto 'More politics, less bureaucracy in Europe', it also advocated a reduction in the surplus of Italy's annual payments to the EU budget and, above all, the prevalence of the Italian Constitution over EU law.

One year later, Fratelli repeated their willingness to 'restate the supremacy of the Italian Constitution and legal system over European rules', in the first point of their manifesto for the 2019 EP election.[58] Interestingly, Fratelli d'Italia's manifesto for the 2022 general election seemed to mitigate some aspects of its Euroscepticism, referring to 'full adherence to the European integration process, with the prospect of a more political and less bureaucratic Union'.[59]

Finally, it is worth noting that direct appeals to the undermining of the principle of primacy on the grounds of constitutional supremacy are often coupled with more indirect criticisms of the EU's legal system through attacks on the EU courts. A good example of this is Lega's 2014 EP election manifesto, in which the party targets the Court of Justice of the EU because 'with its caselaw [it] is progressively cancelling entire parts of national law'.[60] Rhetorical

[56] Lega, 'Salvini Premier' (n 53) 31. Our translation.

[57] Fratelli d'Italia, 'Un programma per l'Italia' (2018) <https://dait.interno.gov.it/documenti/trasparenza/politiche2018/Doc/97/97_Prog_Elettorale.pdf>.

[58] Fratelli d'Italia, 'Programma Elezioni Europee' (2019), 1. Our translation.

[59] Fratelli d'Italia, 'Per L'Italia. Accordo quadro di programma per un Governo di centrodestra' (2022) 2 <https://dait.interno.gov.it/documenti/trasparenza/POLITICHE_20220925/Documenti/68/(68_progr_2_)-programma.pdf>. Our translation.

[60] Lega, 'Elezioni Europee 25 maggio 2014. Programma elettorale' (2014), 3. Our translation.

attacks against the EU and its principles are sometimes operationalized into attempts to reform the Italian Constitution along Eurosceptic lines. In 2017, Fratelli d'Italia's La Russa, who is currently President of the Senate, proposed, as first signatory, a constitutional bill to reform articles 11 and 117 of the Italian Constitution.[61] In the words of La Russa: 'This proposed constitutional law, which provides for the reformulation of Articles 11 and 117, paragraph 1, of the Constitution, intends, in essence, to revive the original content of the Charter, as established by the Founding Fathers'. La Russa himself presented this initiative as a 'virtuous return to the past, which we could also call a "return to the future"'.[62] This bill aimed to amend article 117, paragraph 1, of the Constitution by removing the reference to the limits deriving from international and EU obligations for state and regional laws.

In 2018, a similar constitutional bill was presented by Giorgia Meloni.[63] These constitutional bills aimed to set down in black and white that the Italian Constitution prevailed over EU Treaties and secondary legislation,[64] thus in part revisiting the case law of the Italian Constitutional Court, which, as we have seen, hinges on counter-limits, understood as supreme principles of the Constitution that cannot be renounced. For the Italian Constitutional Court, in other words, EU law, unlike other international treaties such as the ECHR (which is instead required to comply with the entire Constitution), must necessarily respect only the supreme principles of the Constitution.[65]

These proposed amendments, furthermore, did not seem to be improvised, but were part of the fundamental demands of the parties as expressed in their manifestos. In fact, in their 2018 election manifesto, Fratelli had, as the second point in their list of fifteen priorities, the creation of a 'supremacy clause in the Constitution to block agreements and directives that are damaging Italy like the Bolkestein Directive and the Dublin Regulation'.[66] Likewise, as explained above, Lega pledged in that same year to reform the text of article 117

[61] Bill n 4387 'Proposta di Legge costituzionale Modifiche agli articoli 11 e 117 della Costituzione, concernenti l'introduzione del principio di sovranità rispetto all'ordinamento dell'Unione europea' (23 March 2017) <https://documenti.camera.it/apps/CommonServices/getDocumento.ashx?sezione=documenti&tipoDoc=lavori_testo_pdl_html&codice=17PDL0050990&idLegislatura=17>.

[62] Bill n 4387 (n 61). Our translation.

[63] Bill n 291 (n 2).

[64] By stating that: 'The norms of the Treaties and other acts of the European Union are applicable on an equal footing and only insofar as they are compatible with the principles of sovereignty, democracy and subsidiarity and with the other principles of the Italian Constitution' Bill n 4387 (n 61). Our translation.

[65] Corte costituzionale, sentenze 348/2007 and 349/2007 <https://www.cortecostituzionale.it/>.

[66] Fratelli d'Italia, 'Un programma per l'Italia' (2018) (n 57) 2. Our translation.

paragraph 1 of the Constitution, as amended in 2001, to 'clarify' that 'the last word on the laws voted by the Parliament still belongs to the Constitutional Court'.[67]

More recently, as we saw at the outset of this chapter, initiatives such as these have been put forward by the League. Think of the amendment tabled to the constitutional bill concerning the introduction of a paragraph to the current version of article 11 of the Constitution, according to which 'at all stages and types of judgement, of whatever order and degree, the Constitution shall not constitute, in all its provisions, a source subordinate to the treaties and other acts of the EU'.[68] The Five Star Movement now seems to have significantly changed its position on Europe, leaving behind, at least formally, its anti-euro position. From the manifesto presented in April 2014, one cannot but notice the proposal for a euro exit referendum, something that would be very difficult to carry out under article 75 of the Italian Constitution, which prohibits a referendum like this in the words: 'No referendum may be held on a law regulating taxes, the budget, amnesty or pardon, or a law ratifying an international treaty'.[69]

In 2015, MoVimento Cinque Stelle proposed and collected signatures for a referendum on the euro,[70] an idea that was also relaunched in 2017.[71]

In 2018, the party argued that 'in our current system, it has been possible to gradually transfer sovereignty to European institutions without citizens being asked for their opinion! From now on, we want any changes to the Treaties governing Italy's participation in the European Union to be put to a mandatory

[67] Lega, 'Salvini Premier' (n 53) 31. Our translation.

[68] Bill n 1917 (n 1). Our translation.

[69] Article 75 of the Italian Constitution. 'Building its EP electoral campaign around several anti-EU arguments, the Five Star Movement used populist rhetoric to leverage on widespread social discontent with the Fiscal Compact and the euro, gathering support from electorates' conviction of the desperate necessity to change the model of the EU27. For instance, the party defined Europe as an expensive, large and inefficient bureaucratic organization that does not represent its people. The party's European agenda consisted of seven points that included a referendum on the euro and an immediate abolishment of the Fiscal Compact, which were both held responsible for the downfall of the Italian economy. According to the Five Star Movement, a coalition of Mediterranean economies would turn out to be an alternative to the German dictat, that rather favoured the necessities of Northern countries', Poli and Valentiner (n 17) 72.

[70] Paolo Martone, 'Il M5S deposita le firme per il referendum sull'euro' *La Stampa* (8 June 2015) <https://www.lastampa.it/politica/2015/06/08/news/il-m5s-deposita-le-firme-per-il-referendum-sull-euro-1.35249781/>.

[71] Domenico Giovinazzo, 'Il Movimento 5 Stelle rilancia il referendum sull'euro, ma non darà indicazioni di voto' *EU News* (23 March 2017) <https://www.eunews.it/2017/03/23/il-movimento-5-stelle-rilancia-il-referendum-sulleuro-ma-non-dara-indicazioni-di-voto/>; 'Europa ed Euro, come è cambiata in 5 anni la linea M5S' *Il Sole 24 Ore* (3 September 2019) <https://www.ilsole24ore.com/art/europa-ed-euro-come-e-cambiata-linea-pentastellata-cinque-anni-ACogTmh>.

referendum before ratification. Only in this way will the Italian people be able to have a say in European policymaking'.[72]

A final point which allows us to connect with the intellectual Eurosceptic debates in Italy is the emphasis on sovereignty as conceived in antagonistic terms vis-à-vis European integration, often with legal implications. This can often be found in the manifestos of this period, especially in the case of Lega.

In its 2014 EP election manifesto, Lega argued that 'sovereignty is being replaced by a governance of universal powers: on the one hand the secular branch, the new *Sacro Romano Impero* with its site in Brussels; on the other hand the new papacy, the European Court of Human Rights, with its site in Strasbourg'.[73] The manifesto also argued that 'It is not for the European Court of Justice to define the constitutional identities of each Member State, lest their sovereignty become purely formal'.[74]

In its manifesto for the 2018 general election, Lega called for a return to the pre-Maastricht Treaty EU, that is, a return to the EU seen as 'a form of free and peaceful cooperation between states of a purely economic nature; a profound correction of the functioning of the internal market is indispensable, aimed at: eradicating the phenomena of dumping within the Union; abolishing rules that are alien to the different legal traditions of the Member States'.[75]

The 2024 Lega manifesto for the EP election highlighted a number of key issues in line with its Eurosceptic and sovereignist vision.[76] It can be noted that, in spite of the rhetoric used in the past (Salvini was a spokesman for Ital-exit demands[77]), the League did not call for an exit from the European Union in its 2024 manifesto. Instead, the 2024 manifesto promoted a strengthening of the sovereignty of the Member States, in opposition to what Lega saw as excessive interference by EU institutions. The manifesto more generally reflected Lega's political line as an alternative to pro-European parties, seeking to build a 'Europe of nations' based on intergovernmental cooperation and a downsizing of central powers in Brussels.

[72] MoVimento 5 Stelle, 'Programma affari costituzionali' (2018), 5. Our translation.

[73] Lega, 'Elezioni Europee 25 maggio 2014. Programma elettorale' (n 60) 4. Our translation.

[74] Lega, 'Elezioni Europee 25 maggio 2014. Programma elettorale' (n 60) 6. Our translation.

[75] Lega, 'Salvini Premier' (n 53). Our translation.

[76] Lega, 'Più Italia, Meno Europa' (2024). The manifesto can be found here <https://cdn.pagellapolitica.it/wp-content/uploads/2024/05/programma-lega-europee.pdf>.

[77] Lara Rastellino, 'Salvini pronto alla spallata contro l'Europa dopo l'ennesimo rifiuto: 7 giorni per 'salvare' l'Ue. E invoca l'Italexit' *Secolo d'Italia* (30 March 2020) <https://www.secoloditalia.it/2020/03/salvini-pronto-alla-spallata-contro-leuropa-dopo-lennesimo-rifiuto-7-giorni-per-salvare-lue-e-invoca-litalexit/>.

5.4. The Importance of the Intellectual Factor: Italian Sovereignism

Many of the manifesto and policy proposals presented above were not born in a vacuum. Eurosceptic parties have developed arguments that started elsewhere, and academic and intellectual factors may have played an important role in this laboratory. This idea is partly confirmed by the importance for Italian Euroscepticism (and sovereignism) today of realities such as *Asimmetrie* ('Asymmetries'), a think tank supported by, among others, Lega Senator Alberto Bagnai, who is also professor of economic policy at the Gabriele d'Annunzio University. Over the years, Asimmetrie has organized an extensive series of conferences and cultural activities to bring together some of the most important Eurosceptic academic voices,[78] and represents a sovereignist hub in Italy.[79] Sovereignism refers to a current of thought that developed in Russia[80] and spread to Eastern Europe before reaching the rest of the European continent. It has been defined as the claim of national sovereignty against the dependence of domestic politics (and law) on international constraints.[81] Between Euroscepticism and sovereignism, there is a partial overlap, in the sense that sovereignists tend to be structurally Eurosceptic (while the reverse is not necessarily true), contesting the alleged limitation of sovereignty caused by the constraints of the integration process. Sovereignists do not necessarily support radical Euroscepticism, as we saw when commenting on the recent evolution of Lega, Fratelli d'Italia, and MoVimento Cinque Stelle. A Eurosceptic may also not necessarily be a sovereignist, as his or her attitude to the EU may depend on reasons other than the impact on national sovereignty.

Sovereignism and populism are, in theory, autonomous phenomena, but they also have a contingent overlap.[82] This combination of populism and sovereignism has been labelled 'PopSovism' by some political scientists, in which the 'sovereignist component advocates a return to an international order in which the nation-state, guided by the self-identified interests of the native

[78] Many of these events can be watched on the YouTube channel of Asimmetrie <https://www.youtube.com/user/asimmetrie>. This is obviously not the only case.

[79] Although smaller in numbers, we also point out—on the left wing—the Centro Studi sulla Costituzione e sulla Prima Repubblica (Centre for the Study of the Constitution and the First Republic), whose website can be found here: <https://www.youtube.com/@CentroStudiCPR/videos>.

[80] Vladislav I Surkov, 'Nationalization of the Future: Paragraphs pro Sovereign Democracy' (2009) 47 Russian Studies in Philosophy 8.

[81] Luigi Ferrajoli, 'L'alleanza perversa fra sovranismi e liberismo' (2019) 2 costituzionalismo.it 1.

[82] Linda Basile and Oscar Mazzoleni, 'Introduction: Sovereignist Wine in Populist Bottles?' in Linda Basile and Oscar Mazzoleni (eds), *Sovereignism and Populism: Citizens, Voters and Parties in Western European Democracies* (Routledge 2022) 1, 2.

ethno-cultural population, maintains or re-asserts sovereign control over its laws, institutions, and the terms of its international interactions.'[83]

However, it is difficult to suggest precise genealogies, given the patchwork of ideologies behind the shared use of the concept of sovereignism, and this 'syncretism' also explains the terminological and conceptual inconsistencies that characterize these approaches.

Scholars have identified two main versions of sovereignism in Europe: 'identitarian sovereignism' and 'democratic sovereignism'.[84] For an identitarian sovereignist, the European Union would be a threat to traditional and historical values, while for a self-proclaimed democratic sovereignist, it would be a danger to the social justice which is one of the achievements of post-World War II (WWII) constitutionalism. Sovereignism can be explained as part of a general tendency to rediscover sovereignty and to interpret it, as we shall see, in a closed way.

For the purposes of this chapter, we shall look at the arguments developed by some intellectual figures who have played the role of champions of sovereignism, such as Paolo Becchi and Giuseppe Valditara; the latter is currently Minister of Education and Merit in the Meloni government.

The first author to be mentioned is Paolo Becchi, professor of legal philosophy at the University of Genova. Becchi has authored different works devoted to sovereignism[85] and was initially very close to MoVimento Cinque Stelle and, more recently, to Lega.[86] Becchi wrote, among other things, a volume entitled *Manifesto Sovranista* ('Sovereignist Manifesto'),[87] in which one can find all the recurring elements of Italian sovereignism, including its evident anti-EU flavour. The EU is portrayed as a part of a homogenizing globalization. It is often defined as an expression of a 'global elite' against the peoples.[88] As such, the EU has enslaved the European peoples. His sovereignism, he claims, is different from the old sovereignism because it is not nationalist.[89] Indeed, his sovereignism is described as pro-European, but it stands for a

[83] Stephan De Spiegeleire, Clarissa Skinner, and Tim Sweijs, 'The Rise of Populist Sovereignism: What It Is, Where It Comes from and What It Means for International Security and Defense' (The Hague Centre for Strategic Studies 2017) ii.

[84] Alessandro Somma, 'Un sovranismo democratico per un nuovo europeismo' (2018) MicroMega <https://www.micromega.net/>.

[85] Paolo Becchi, *Italia sovrana* (Sperling & Kupfer 2018).

[86] Matteo Salvini himself authored the preface to a volume that Becchi wrote with Giuseppe Palma: Paolo Becchi and Giuseppe Palma, *Dalla Seconda alla Terza Repubblica. Come nasce il governo Lega-M5S* (Paesi edizioni 2018).

[87] Paolo Becchi, *Manifesto sovranista: per la liberazione dei popoli europei* (Giubilei Regnani 2019).

[88] Becchi, *Manifesto sovranista* (n 87) 9 and 19.

[89] Becchi, *Manifesto sovranista* (n 87) 8–9.

Europe which should be understood as different from the European Union.[90] The subtitle of his book is 'For the Liberation of the European Peoples', and he drafts a charter of the rights of the European peoples[91] in one of the chapters.

According to Becchi, the euro was the product of a coup d'état; Becchi himself wrote a book entitled *Colpo di Stato permanente* ('permanent coup d'état'[92]) and argues that Italian membership of the EU was based on a manipulation of article 11 of the Italian Constitution. Becchi entitles the last part of the *Manifesto Sovranista* 'The European Union and Italy: The legal reconstruction of an enslavement',[93] and in this he denounces the alleged misinterpretation of article 11 of the Italian Constitution. In his view, compared to the mechanisms envisaged by countries such as Germany, Italy had one main issue, which was the absence of an explicit clause devoted to its relationship with the EU.[94]

For Becchi, it is possible to argue, from the preparatory works of the Constituent Assembly, that the founding fathers explicitly wanted to exclude membership of the European integration project from the scope of article 11.[95] He derives this interpretation from the previously mentioned exchange between two members of the Constituent Assembly, Emilio Lussu and Aldo Moro.[96] This reading of the Italian Constitution is also questionable in the light of what we said earlier. As a matter of fact, when the European Coal and Steel Community (ECSC) was set up, there were no explicit provisions devoted to it in the constitutions of its founding Member States. As in Italy, the German Constitutional Court admitted direct effect and primacy on the basis of constitutional provisions generally devoted to the international community. In this sense, the main difference between Italy and Germany was that Germany was faster to amend its Basic Law to include an explicit reference to the ECs (now article 23 of the German Basic Law), since it did so in 1992, while Italy made the amendment in 2001. However, in both countries, the national constitutional courts accepted the structural principles of Community law much earlier, by giving a broad reading to their constitutional clauses devoted to the international community (in Germany article 24, and in Italy article 11). This happened simply because the entry into force of the European Treaties occurred later than the entry into force of these two national constitutions. The same thing happened in the other Member States. The second erroneous point

[90] Becchi, *Manifesto sovranista* (n 87) 21.
[91] Becchi, *Manifesto sovranista* (n 87) 31–39.
[92] Paolo Becchi, *Colpo di Stato permanente: Cronache degli ultimi tre anni* (Marsilio 2014).
[93] Becchi, *Manifesto sovranista* (n 87) 101.
[94] Becchi, *Manifesto sovranista* (n 87) 111.
[95] Becchi, *Manifesto sovranista* (n 87) 126.
[96] Becchi, *Manifesto sovranista* (n 87) 126.

in Becchi's reconstruction regards the exchange between Lussu and Moro; Moro clarified that there was no need to include Europe in the wording of article 11 because it was too early to constitutionalize a reference to a possible European federation or confederation and because the wording of article 11 was already broad enough to cover any such arrangement.[97] Here, one can find the cherry-picking approach that characterizes the strategy employed by Eurosceptic authors when presenting such a constitutional counter-narrative.

The point that membership of the Eurozone can be seen as a possible coup d'état deserves further discussion, since it is shared by Barra Caracciolo,[98] a member of the Italian State Council—the supreme administrative law court in Italy—and a former under-secretary (*sottosegretario*) for European affairs. In his books, Barra Caracciolo has openly challenged the principle of the primacy of EU law. He also runs a blog, called *orizzonte48*, where he frequently publishes very harsh posts against the EU.[99]

In his works, Becchi recalls an old academic article written by an eminent public law scholar and former Minister for Finance, Giuseppe Guarino, whose position cannot be described as sovereignist.[100] In his article, Guarino argued that the entry into force of the euro was based on an invalid Regulation, namely Regulation 1466/1997, because this was in conflict with the European Treaties, namely with article 104C of the TEU. This Regulation governed the strengthening of the surveillance of budgetary positions and the surveillance and coordination of economic policies. The argument is very technical, but it can be summed up as follows: Regulation 1466/1997 is a legal source that cannot breach the EU Treaties, which represent 'the basic constitutional charter'[101] of the EU. For Guarino, 'the rules laid down in the Regulation are different from, indeed opposed to, those of the Treaty',[102] because 'the Treaty sets an objective for growth in accordance with Article 2, whose attainment is entrusted to the economic policies of the individual member states, each of which was to take account of the concrete, specific conditions of its own economy'.[103] According to Guarino, 'the regulation abolishes all this. The Member State's

[97] The mini-report of the relevant working session of the Constituent Assembly held on 24 January 1947 can be found here: <https://www.nascitacostituzione.it/01principi/011/index.htm?art011-003.htm&2>.

[98] As we have seen, this is an idea that is present even in the thinking of left-wing sovereignists; see, for instance, Marco Rizzo, *Il golpe europeo. I comunisti contro l'Unione* (Baldini Castoldi Dalai 2012).

[99] <http://orizzonte48.blogspot.com/>.

[100] Becchi, *Manifesto sovranista* (n 87) 132.

[101] ECJ, Case 294/83 *Parti écologiste 'Les Verts' v European Parliament* ECLI:EU:C:1986:166, para 23.

[102] Giuseppe Guarino, 'The "Truth" about Europe and the euro. A Second Essay' (2014) 26 Nomos. Le attualità del diritto, 25, 32.

[103] Guarino (n 102) 33.

economic policies are cancelled. As a consequence, every possible contribution by Member States is cancelled'.[104] On this basis, Guarino concluded that this Regulation suppressed democracy by producing a 'coup d'état'.[105]

This debate has not resonated significantly beyond Italy[106] and, notwithstanding this theory, Regulation 1466/1997 has never been declared invalid, despite EU law providing remedies to challenge it.

This thesis has been retrieved to attack the so-called 'Fiscal Compact', formally the Treaty on Stability, Coordination and Governance in the Economic and Monetary Union (TSCG).

The argument made by Professor Guarino was also brought to the attention of the EP and the Commission by Claudio Morganti (Lega Nord at that time), who was then a member of the EP, and recalled the essays by Guarino in two written questions[107] presented in the EP. On 6 February 2013, the President of the Commission officially responded by saying:

> The main contention of the essay quoted by the Honorable Member is that the preventive part of the SGP [Stability and Growth Pact] and the Fiscal Compact, by introducing the obligation for MS to attain and maintain a medium-term budgetary objective (MTO), in principle more demanding than the deficit reference value of 3%, exceed what could be legally required. The Commission does not share this assessment. The balanced budget rule provides for a balanced medium term budgetary objective to guarantee the 3% limit *ex ante*. The first aim of the MTO is thus precisely that of providing an adequate safety margin against the breaching of the deficit reference value. In other words, and consistent with the wording of the Treaty, the deficit reference value should not be intended as an objective but a limit that should not be trespassed under normal cyclical fluctuations. This demands that MS pursue an objective that, taking into account normal cyclical fluctuations, should be more demanding than the reference value. Otherwise, at least in

104 Guarino (n 102) 33.

105 'Technically speaking, the suppression of democracy can be termed "the de facto installation of a new regime," which is an even graver violation than what we call a "coup d'état". To deprive a complex community of its democratic regime is a hazardous, perilous operation. Regulation 1466 managed the trick in a simple if unforeseeable manner'. Guarino (n 102) 33, 37.

106 For a synthesis of this debate, see Marco Baldassarri, 'The Resilient Governance of the EU: Towards a Post-democratic Society' in Marco Baldassarri, Emanuele Castelli, Matteo Truffeli, and Giovanni Vezzani (eds), *Anti-Europeanism: Critical Perspectives Towards the European Union* (Springer 2020) 77.

107 See the written questions presented by Hon. Member Claudio Morganti available at the following links: <https://www.europarl.europa.eu/sides/getDoc.do?pubRef=-//EP//TEXT+WQ+E-2012-010892+0+DOC+XML+V0//EN>. and <https://www.europarl.europa.eu/sides/getDoc.do?pubRef=-//EP//TEXT+OQ+O-2013-000075+0+DOC+XML+V0//EN>.

the negative phase of the cycle, it could be expected that MS would breach the reference value, which is clearly in contradiction with the Treaty.[108]

As argued earlier, the financial crisis and the response of the EU (by means of both EU law measures and international treaties signed by some of its Member States) appear to have facilitated, among other things, the emergence of sovereignism.

This idea of 'stolen democracy' has become very influential because of this group of authors. A similar conclusion[109] can be found in a work by Giuseppe Valditara,[110] currently a minister in the Meloni government and professor of Roman Law at the University of Turin. For him, sovereignism is a reaction to progressivism, and his book *Sovranismo*[111] also has a preface written by Thomas Williams, the Breitbart Rome Bureau Chief.

Germany has been the other recurrent protagonist in the sovereignist plot, at least until 2021. On this basis, the only way for the Italian people to be emancipated is to leave the European Union, but in Italy, a referendum such as the one that was held in the UK is not possible. According to this approach, there is an 'impossible coexistence' between the EU Treaties and the Italian Constitution.[112]

It is interesting to note that there have also been attempts to present a left-wing version of sovereignism. An example is the so-called 'democratic sovereignism'[113] presented by Alessandro Somma, professor of comparative law at La Sapienza University, Rome. According to him, we need a new type of Europe, which must depart from the neo-liberal orthodoxy that characterizes the EU, since a 'United Europe does not promote peace and justice, nor does it respect equality between States'.[114] For him, the EU does not respect social rights and solidarity and has been secured by the principle of the primacy of EU law, which does not have 'a constitutional basis'.[115] However, arguments like these have at least two flaws. First of all, the Italian Constitutional Court

[108] 'Answer given by Mr Barroso on behalf of the Commission' 6 February 2013, Official Journal of the European Union <https://eur-lex.europa.eu/legal-content/IT/TXT/HTML/?uri=OJ:C:2013:339E:FULL&from=MT>.

[109] For an overview, see Francesco Giubilei, 'Oggi tutti parlano di "sovranismo" ma (quasi) nessuno spiega che cosa sia' *Il Giornale* (11 December 2018) <http://www.ilgiornale.it/news/spettacoli/oggi-tutti-parlano-sovranismo-quasi-nessuno-spiega-che-cosa-1614631.html>.

[110] Giuseppe Valditara, *Sovranismo. Una speranza per la democrazia* (Book Time 2017).

[111] Valditara (n 110).

[112] Luciano Barra Caracciolo, *Euro e (o?) democrazia costituzionale. La convivenza impossibile tra costituzione e trattati europei* (Dike Giuridica Editrice 2013).

[113] Somma, 'Un sovranismo democratico' (n 84).

[114] Somma, 'Un sovranismo democratico' (n 84). Our translation.

[115] Somma, 'Un sovranismo democratico' (n 84). Our translation.

itself has accepted the principle of the primacy of EU law, making it conditional upon respect for the supreme principles called counter-limits,[116] as we saw earlier. Second, the argument could be replicated for all the other Member States that did not have a constitutional basis when the Court of Justice delivered its judgment in the *Costa/Enel* case.[117]

Additionally, certain aspects of the principle of primacy are recognized by article 117 of the Italian Constitution after the 2001 constitutional reform. The solution, according to Somma, consists in the re-nationalization (defined as 'inevitable'[118]) of economic policies, understood as an 'essential prerequisite for reactivating popular sovereignty and social conflict as the foundations of economic democracy'.[119] In his view, if this does not happen and if what he calls 'ideological Europeanism' does not cease, identitarian sovereignism (as opposed to what Somma calls 'democratic sovereignism') will prevail. For Somma, the 'EU has developed as an institution devoted to depoliticising markets through a neoliberal federalist approach, thus becoming an institution which has denied the reasons for its own existence'.[120]

5.5. Responding to Eurosceptic Constitutional Counter-Narratives

In our view, the supporters of legal sovereignism have created false dichotomies, one of which is the (alleged) dichotomy between the European Treaties and the Constitution, as reconstructed by authors such as Barra Caracciolo, for example.[121]

The supporters of this dichotomy conceive sovereignty as a closed and holistic entity and, based on this assumption, understand it only as a claim, a unilaterally activated shield to protect the national interest. However, as post-totalitarian comparative law shows, sovereignty is not only a *shield* but also, and above all, a *key* to participating in multilateral international organizations. If this is true, there is then no conflict between the Treaties and the

[116] *Frontini* (n 29). However, Somma defines this doctrine and the counter-limits as 'opiates' capable of reassuring legal practitioners of the existence of an emergency brake. The same definition can be found in Andrea Guazzarotti, 'Sovranità e integrazione europea' (2017) 7 Rivista AIC 1.

[117] *Costa* (n 23).

[118] Somma, 'Un sovranismo democratico' (n 84). Our translation.

[119] Somma, 'Un sovranismo democratico' (n 84). Our translation.

[120] Alessandro Somma, 'Europa, sovranità e ordine economico nel prisma delle teorie federaliste' (2020) 10 DPCE online 427, 427.

[121] Barra Caracciolo (n 112).

Constitution, but mutual enrichment, especially with reference to the Treaties that protect *constitutional goods* such as fundamental rights.

One only has to look at the language of post-WWII constitutions to appreciate their characteristic openness,[122] as we saw in the Preface to this book. Indeed, it is necessary to remember how the Italian Constitution understands the role of the Italian Republic in the international and European arenas, stressing the difficulties encountered by the Italian Constitutional Court in putting into practice the difficult balance struck by the Constituent Assembly,[123] where sovereignty (not sovereignism) should be read in the light of the new constitutional values stemming from post-WWII constitutionalism.[124] Moreover, contrary to sovereignist claims, the Italian Constitutional Court has not relinquished sovereignty, constitutional identity, or national democracy, as if it were an accomplice to an alleged European or global coup d'état.

Indeed, the Italian Constitutional Court has frequently threatened to use the counter-limits doctrine, not only against the Court of Justice of the EU but also against the International Court of Justice,[125] and there have been similar dynamics with regard to the case law of the Strasbourg Court.[126] These periodic disagreements show that the Italian Constitutional Court is acquainted with the possibility of limits to constitutional openness when it considers that fundamental principles are at stake. Similar approaches can be found elsewhere and show that post-WWII constitutionalism has tried to favour international openness[127] without renouncing the ability to have the last word when it comes to the relationship between national and supranational law.[128] This has nothing to do with the nostalgic sovereignism that characterizes the majority

[122] Paolo Carrozza, 'Constitutionalism's Post-Modern Opening' in Martin Loughlin and Neil Walker (eds), *The Paradox of Constitutionalism: Constituent Power and Constitutional Form* (Oxford University Press 2008) 169.

[123] Antonio Cassese, 'Politica estera e relazioni internazionali nel disegno emerso alla Assemblea Costituente' in Ugo de Siervo (ed), *Scelte della Costituente e cultura giuridica. I: Costituzione italiana e modelli stranieri* (Il Mulino 1980) 505, 519.

[124] See Antonio Cassese, 'Modern Constitutions and International Law' (1985) 122 Collected Courses of the Hague Academy of International Law 331.

[125] Corte costituzionale, sentenza 238/2014 <www.cortecostituzionale.it>.

[126] For instance Corte costituzionale, sentenza 49/2015 <www.cortecostituzionale.it>.

[127] Alejandro Saiz Arnaiz, *La apertura constitucional al derecho internacional y europeo de los derechos humanos. El artículo 10.2 de la Constitución Española* (Centro de Estudios Políticos y Constitucionales 1999); Eric Stein, 'International Law in Internal Law: Toward Internationalization of Central-Eastern European Constitutions?' (1994) 88 American Journal of International Law 427, 429; Carrozza (n 122).

[128] Giuseppe Martinico, 'National Courts and Judicial Disobedience to the ECHR. A Comparative Overview' in Oddný Mjöll Arnardóttir and Antoine Buyse (eds), *Shifting Centres of Gravity in Human Rights Protection: Rethinking Relations between the ECHR, EU, and National Legal Orders* (Routledge 2016) 59.

of Eurosceptic forces in Italy,[129] which conceive the Italian legal system as self-referential and disconnected from the international community and its international obligations.

Sovereignists tend to invoke a playbook in which Italy is the constant victim of an international conspiracy guided by a global elite, with the EU being a manifestation of this conspiracy. In this scenario, the euro and EU membership are based on a coup d'état that was accepted by a supranational and national elite without the possibility of the national constitutional identity being preserved,[130] through a Europeanization that undermines the basis of national democracy. In the light of this, they frequently argue that no coexistence between the EU Treaties and the Italian Constitution is possible.[131]

We, however, reject this reading. Certainly, sovereignty is a part of what, in the first chapters of this book, we have called the constitutional counter-narrative of Italian Eurosceptic movements, that is, the strategic and selective instrumentalizing of categories of constitutional theory and law. Here we return to a point mentioned at the outset: the overlap between populism and sovereignism in the context of Italian Euroscepticism. We saw this when we analysed some of the arguments used by the political parties in manifestos and speeches by the champions of sovereignism. The concept of sovereignty is also cited in the reading of the EU, portrayed as a threat to Italian sovereignty and an obstacle to true democracy. This image explains the frequent reference made to article 1 of the Italian Constitution, which is selectively and arbitrarily referred to by the populist component present in the League and the Five Star Movement and, to some extent, in the nativism of Fratelli d'Italia. Suffice it to compare here the speech given by the then Italian Prime Minister Giuseppe Conte at the United Nations in 2018 (when he was leading the coalition government with the League) to the call for popular sovereignty made by Meloni and Salvini. In these interpretations, only one part of article 1 is mentioned:

> When some accuse us of souverainism or populism, I always enjoy pointing out that Article 1 of the Italian Constitution cites sovereignty and the people, and it is precisely through that provision that I interpret the concept of sovereignty and the exercise of sovereignty by the people.[132]

[129] Daniele Amoroso, 'Italy' in Fulvio Palombino (ed), *Duelling for Supremacy: International Law vs. National Fundamental Principles* (Cambridge University Press 2019) 184.
[130] Becchi, *Manifesto sovranista* (n 87) 8–9.
[131] Barra Caracciolo (n 112).
[132] Giuseppe Conte, 'Remarks by Giuseppe Conte to the 73rd Session of the United Nations General Assembly' 26 September 2018 <http://www.voltairenet.org/article203153.html>.

Here, one can see the attempt to find a reading consistent with the text of the Italian Constitution by stretching, at the same time, some of its key concepts and—most importantly—exercising a sort of cherry-picking approach to the Constitution.[133] Indeed, when referring to article 1 of the Italian Constitution, populists tend to mention only a part of the relevant provision (the part recognizing the principle of 'popular sovereignty') in order to find confirmation of their approach to the fundamental charter, and to reinforce the false dichotomy between themselves (the people voted in by the people) and the 'others'. In so doing, they tactically omit the fact that the same article 1 of the Italian Constitution subsequently clarifies that popular sovereignty should be understood as being limited by the Constitution itself, as the provision reads: 'Sovereignty belongs to the people and is exercised by the people in the forms and within the limits of the Constitution'.[134] This approach is very telling of the way in which populists try to legitimize themselves as political forces consistent with the Constitution; at the same time, when looking for a literal link with the text of the Constitution, they advance an alternative reading of two of the constitutional concepts mentioned in that provision, 'people' and 'popular sovereignty', by relying on the constitutive ambiguity of these concepts.[135]

In this interpretation, these forces advance a reading of the Constitution that ends up being allergic to the very idea of limits to power. If we apply this majoritarian approach to the constitutional provisions on participation in the international community, the rejection of a limit inevitably leads to the contestation of international and supranational constraints, which are portrayed as factors altering democratic balances. As we tried to explain at the beginning of this volume, this way of reducing the European integration process to a series of constraints ends up (strategically) omitting the added value that EU law actually provides to national democracies. A similar radical majoritarian reading of the principle of popular sovereignty was put forward by Giorgia Meloni and Fratelli d'Italia.[136]

We have analysed the sovereignist discourse to capture the origin of many of the legal arguments used by the relevant Italian Eurosceptic movements. These

[133] This approach is not completely new in Italy. See also the examples given by Marco Revelli, *Populismo 2.0* (Einaudi 2017).

[134] Article 1 of the Italian Constitution.

[135] On 'popular indeterminacy' and populism, see Paulina Ochoa Espejo, 'Populism and the Idea of The People' in Cristóbal Rovira Kaltwasser, Paul A. Taggart, Paulina Ochoa Espejo, and Pierre Ostiguy (eds), *The Oxford Handbook of Populism* (Oxford University Press 2017) 607, 610.

[136] Governo Italiano, Presidenza del Consiglio dei Ministri, 'Presidente Meloni. Intervista del Presidente Meloni con Maurizio Belpietro a "Il giorno de La verità"' 4 May 2024 <https://www.governo.it/it/articolo/intervista-del-presidente-meloni-con-maurizio-belpietro-il-giorno-de-la-verit/25783>.

are mainly arguments that come from identitarian sovereignism and conceive the EU as a threat to traditional values. Moreover, as argued elsewhere, the illiberal component that characterizes identitarian sovereignism ends up instrumentalizing the conservative argument of tradition, and manipulating the religious, historical, and moral arguments.[137]

Finally, it is worth underlining the marginal role played by the concept of 'motherland' (*patria*) in Italian Eurosceptic discourse. A partial exception is represented by the reference to article 52 of the Constitution[138] by Salvini and Meloni with regard to the burning issue of migration.[139] The argument here is that sovereignists have a duty to protect their homeland and identity against the alleged threats posed by immigrants. Of course, this kind of approach completely neglects the duties that the Italian Republic has under international law.[140] It must be said that anti-migrant positions have also been expressed by left-wing sovereignists. This is the case with Sergio Rizzo, the post-communist leader of Democrazia Sovrana e Popolare. Rizzo defines himself as a 'right-wing communist' and has declared that he is against the battles for civil rights (especially the rights of LGBTIQ+ couples), which he defines as a 'mass distraction'.[141] On other occasions, he has declared himself to be against immigration and in favour of a naval blockade.[142] Confirmation of this convergence between right-wing and left-wing sovereignism is also evident in the fact that, in the past, Rizzo joined forces with Gianni Alemanno,[143] the former Mayor of

[137] Giuseppe Martinico, 'Populists in Power and Constitutional Counternarratives' (2024) 45 Cardozo Law Review 1527.

[138] Article 52 of the Italian Constitution: 'Defence of the motherland is a sacred duty for every citizen. Military service is obligatory within the limits and in the manner set by law. Its fulfilment shall not prejudice a citizen's job, nor the exercise of their political rights. The organisation of the armed forces shall be based on the democratic spirit of the Republic'.

[139] 'Salvini per difendersi cita a sproposito la Costituzione: "La difesa della Patria è sacro dovere di ogni cittadino"' *Globalist* (4 February 2020) <https://www.globalist.it/politics/2020/02/04/salvini-per-difendersi-cita-a-sproposito-la-costituzione-la-difesa-della-patria-e-sacro-dovere-di-ogni-cittadino-2052524.html>).

[140] Anja Palm and Luca Barana, 'Italy's Migration Policy: A Self-Defeating Approach Spells Marginalisation in Europe' (Istituto Affari Internazionali 2019) <https://www.iai.it/en/pubblicazioni/italys-migration-policy-self-defeating-approach-spells-marginalisation-europe>; Simone Penasa, 'The Italian Way to Migration: Was It "True" Populism? Populist Policies as Constitutional Antigens' in Giacomo Delledonne, Giuseppe Martinico, Matteo Monti, and Fabio Pacini (eds), *Italian Populism and Constitutional Law. Strategies, Conflicts and Dilemmas* (Palgrave 2020) 255.

[141] 'Marco Rizzo, comunista di destra. Come smonta la linea Pd su migranti e diritti' *Il Tempo* (15 August 2023) <https://www.iltempo.it/personaggi/2023/08/15/news/marco-rizzo-comunista-di-destra-linea-pd-su-migranti-diritti-guerra-trump-36638148/>.

[142] Francesco Barana, 'Rizzo, il compagno Kojak in corsa per la Provincia: "Io comunista di destra. I diritti civili? Distrazione di massa"' *Il T Quotidiano* (24 August 2023) <https://www.iltquotidiano.it/articoli/rizzo-il-compagno-kojak-in-corsa-per-la-provincia-io-comunista-di-destra-i-diritti-civili-distrazione-di-massa/>.

[143] 'Gianni Alemanno e Marco Rizzo, insieme per "costruire il cambiamento"' *OglioPoNews* (14 November 2023) <https://www.oglioponews.it/2023/11/14/gianni-alemanno-e-marco-rizzo-insieme-per-costruire-il-cambiamento/>.

Rome, former minister of the Italian Republic, and, above all, former secretary of the National Movement for Sovereignty, a right-wing political force.

Article 52 codifies some of the essential duties linked to the concept of solidarity. In the design of the Italian Constitution, the concept of solidarity has to do with the language of duties, starting with those of contributing, through taxes,[144] to community services and ending with those related to health, which, according to article 32 of the Constitution, is not only a right of the individual but also a 'collective interest'.[145]

Solidarity does not seem to belong to the rhetoric of these Eurosceptic forces: the Meloni government on the one hand indirectly attacked the Italian income revenue authority, comparing taxes to 'state protection money',[146] and, on the other hand, flirted with and benefited from the votes of those in the anti-vax movements. In particular, Fratelli d'Italia has taken the lead in setting up a parliamentary inquiry committee into the management of the health emergency caused by the epidemic spread of the SARS-CoV-2 virus and the measures taken to prevent and tackle it.[147]

5.6. Conclusion

In this chapter, after reminding readers of the constitutional framework and the relevant case law of the Italian Constitutional Court on the relationship between EU law and domestic law, we analysed the landscape of Euroscepticism in the Italian political system. In doing so, we first analysed the hard forms of exit-based Euroscepticism that are supported in Italy by marginal political forces that are often unrepresented in Parliament. We then focused on certain political forces that are characterized today by forms of Euroscepticism that give a prominent role to constitutional counter-narratives: Lega, MoVimento Cinque Stelle, and Fratelli d'Italia. For each of these political forces, we tried to highlight the shift from strong forms of Euroscepticism to less radical positions, as the case of MoVimento Cinque Stelle, in particular, shows. As we saw, Lega and MoVimento Cinque Stelle are certainly definable as populist, given that both Salvini and Conte have described themselves as such. Fratelli

[144] See Article 53 of the Italian Constitution.

[145] See Article 32 of the Italian Constitution.

[146] 'Meloni: Lotta all'evasione non sia pizzo di Stato contro i piccoli commercianti' (27 May 2023) <https://www.youtube.com/watch?v=qwy7r7i6elo>.

[147] Established by Law No. 22 of 5 March 2024, <https://www.gazzettaufficiale.it/eli/id/2024/03/13/24G00038/SG>.

d'Italia, on the other hand, is an extreme right-wing party that has tried to present itself (especially in foreign policy) as slightly more moderate, particularly since leading the coalition government with Lega and Forza Italia. As we have tried to highlight, a central aspect of the Italian case is the combination of sovereignist and Eurosceptic arguments, present in both left- and right-wing political forces. As noted, in fact, by political scientists, radical left parties and radical right parties:

> [H]ave both cued voters on economic sovereignism, blaming the international/supranational institutions for the worsening conditions of citizens (. . .). In doing so, these parties have pledged to regain the nation-state control of budgetary, fiscal and monetary policies. These sovereignist appeals have been complemented by the opposition to EU integration, with Euroscepticism being more likely to be found on the 'extremes' of the political poles.[148]

Since the Meloni government began, initiatives such as these that frontally attack the primacy of EU law seem to have been advanced by the League, which often acts as a destabilizing factor for the centre-right coalition, as the tensions during the European election campaign have shown.[149] After all, these are two allied political forces, but they belong to two different parliamentary groups at the European level. While Lega (together with Fidesz and Rassemblement national) is part of the Patriots for Europe group, Fratelli d'Italia is part of the European Conservatives and Reformists (ECR) group. This analysis seems to suggest that, at the time this chapter is being written, the de facto most Eurosceptic political force in the governing coalition is the League. However, as we have seen, today even the League does not go as far as to advocate Italy's exit from the EU.[150]

More in general, confirmation of the Eurosceptic nature of Meloni's government also comes from its refusal, for the time being, to ratify the reform of

[148] Luca Carrieri and Davide Vittori, 'Defying Europe? The Euroscepticism of Radical Right and Radical Left Voters in Western Europe' (2021) 43 Journal of European Integration 955, 956.

[149] Giulia Merlo, 'I quattro fronti che dividono Lega e Fratelli d'Italia' *La Stampa* (15 February 2024) <https://www.lastampa.it/politica/2024/02/15/news/lega_fdi_quattro_fronti-14072781/>.

[150] Although it does not, however, renounce more openly radical positions, as evidenced, for example, by the candidature of former General Vannacci, known for his xenophobic and anti-gay views, who was elected as a member of the European Parliament in 2024 on the ticket of Lega, which he later left. Giorgio Ghiglione, 'How an Obscure General Became the Star of Italy's Far Right' Foreign Policy (10 May 2024) <https://foreignpolicy.com/2024/05/10/italy-roberto-vannacci-far-right-meloni-eu-election/>.

the European Stability Mechanism (ESM).[151] This reform has long been opposed, particularly by the Five Star Movement and the League. The ESM is regarded as the quintessence of European conditionality and is often invoked by sovereigntists as a symbol of the EU's role in reducing national democracy to a set of external constraints aimed at depoliticizing domestic political processes.[152]

[151] Stefano Feltri, 'Why Is the ESM so Controversial (Only) in Italy? A Conversation with Klaus Regling' (Bocconi Institute for European Policymaking, 15 January 2024) <https://iep.unibocconi.eu/publications/why-esm-so-controversial-only-italy-conversation-klaus-regling-0>.

[152] Leonardo Pierdominici, 'Teoria e ideologia del vincolo esterno: è predicabile un suo significato costituzionale?' in Giuseppe Martinico and Leonardo Pierdominici (eds), *Miserie del sovranismo giuridico. Il valore aggiunto del costituzionalismo europeo* (Castelvecchi 2023) 109.

6
Spain
Constitutionalism and Euroscepticism in a Traditionally Europhile Country

6.1. Introduction

Spain was traditionally regarded as a Europhile country.[1] However, since the Eurozone crisis, if not before, things have changed in the Spanish political landscape. On the one hand, on the left there was ferocious criticism of the measures to deal with that economic crisis, which included attacks on European supranational organs. On the other hand, more recently, there has been the emergence in Spain of political actors on the radical right, whose Eurosceptic stances are bold and clear.

With this background, this chapter offers an in-depth analysis of the Eurosceptic mobilization of constitutional law arguments in Spain. The country was selected as a case study for two reasons. First, it provides an interesting example not only of right-wing Euroscepticism but also of the use by left-wing parties of counter-narratives with Eurosceptic undertones. Second, such left-wing parties—including Podemos—were in power in the country as part of coalition agreements with the socialist party PSOE.

In Spain, the party traditionally on the left of the pro-European socialist party PSOE was Izquierda Unida, a coalition of left-wing parties structured around the leadership of the Spanish Communist Party (PCE, Partido Comunista de España). However, during the mid-2010s, new parties emerged in the Spanish political system. One of them, Podemos, featured a populist left-wing platform and soon became an important protagonist in the politics of the country. Different combinations of coalitions integrating Izquierda Unida, Podemos, and other smaller left-wing parties subsequently formed occasional alliances, such as Unidad Popular or Sumar. In most instances, these parties

[1] Rafael Vázquez García, Santiago Delgado Fernández, and Miguel Jerez Mir, 'Spanish Political Parties and the European Union: Analysis of Euromanifestos (1987–2004)' (2010) 11 Perspectives on European Politics and Society 201.

The Eurosceptic Mobilization of Constitutional Law. Pablo Castillo-Ortiz and Giuseppe Martinico, Oxford University Press. © Pablo Castillo-Ortiz and Giuseppe Martinico 2026. DOI: 10.1093/9780198959205.003.0006

very significantly mobilized constitutional law in support of Euroscepticism. Furthermore, these parties emphasized their criticisms of the management of the Euro-crisis in Spain and the related reform of the Spanish Constitution.[2] They often saw this episode as a form of the hollowing out of sovereignty from the Spanish Constitution.

On the far right of the Spanish political party system, we find Vox. This party gained representatives in the Spanish Congreso de los Diputados for the first time in 2019. In that year, general elections took place in April, and because the Spanish Parliament was unable to appoint a president of the government, new elections were held in November. In these two elections, Vox obtained first 24 seats and then 52 seats in the lower chamber of the parliament, the Congreso de los Diputados, which has 350 members. In both of these two elections, Vox ran with the same manifesto: a '100 proposals' document with a range of pledges, many of which were manifestly contrary to the Spanish Constitution.[3] This 2019 election manifesto was brief and ambiguous when it came to the party's European policy, although discourses by its leaders were more assertive. The manifesto included little more than unspecific pledges to abandon 'supranational organisms if they are contrary to the interests of Spain',[4] without even mentioning the EU at this point. The party, however, elaborated on its European policy in subsequent elections. In the case of Vox, the Eurosceptic mobilization of constitutional law concepts seems to be one more instance of the use by this party of constitutional law as part of their political rhetoric.[5] Furthermore, by the 2024 European Parliament (EP) election, the party had an extreme-right competitor, Se Acabó la Fiesta, a hard Eurosceptic party which gained three MEPs at this election despite running without a manifesto document.

The findings of this chapter confirm many of the intuitions regarding the Eurosceptic mobilization of constitutional law arguments that we put forward in Chapter 2. The constitutional counter-narrative of these parties emphasizes their view that the process of European integration is a risk for national constitutional law. However, left-wing and right-wing Eurosceptics show great differences when it comes to the specific ways in which these counter-narratives are constructed. The right-wing Eurosceptic party Vox included in its manifestos

[2] See, on this, José Real-Dato and Aleksandra Sojka, 'The Rise of (Faulty) Euroscepticism? The Impact of a Decade of Crises in Spain' [2024] 29 South European Society and Politics 457.

[3] Pablo Castillo-Ortiz, 'Constitutionalism and the Radical-Right: The Case of the Spanish Party Vox' (2023) 2 International Journal of Constitutional Law 733.

[4] Vox, '100 medidas para la España viva' (2018). Our translation.

[5] Castillo-Ortiz (n 3).

a greater element of judicial conflict and a far less constructive approach to the process of European integration. The left-wing parties, on the other hand, seemed to put more emphasis on their dissatisfaction with the management of the Euro-crisis in the country and had a somewhat more constructive approach to the process of European integration: they often discussed the idea of a constituent process for Europe.

The remainder of this chapter is structured as follows. After this brief introduction, we summarize the legal technicalities of the relationship between Spanish and EU law. Next, we present our analysis of party manifestos,[6] showing the frequent articulation of constitutional counter-narratives targeting the process of European integration. We then discuss Eurosceptic constitutional counter-narratives in Spain at the level of civil society, beyond party manifestos. In the following section, we discuss these constitutional counter-narratives in the light of our doctrinal understanding of the Spanish constitutional system. The last section concludes.

6.2. Spanish Constitutional Law and European Integration

Spain joined the European Communities in January 1986. At that time, the new Spanish democratic Constitution was relatively young, dating back to just 1978. Before that, the country had suffered a four-decade-long dictatorship, and one of the many effects of this was the relative isolation of the country from its Western European democratic neighbours.

The Spanish Constitution of 1978 lacks an explicit and comprehensive European clause.[7] In fact, the European Union was not mentioned in the Constitution until 2011, when article 135 was amended to include, inter alia, the principle of budget stability and a limit to the structural deficit.[8] As we show below, this reform was highly controversial and became part of constitutionally related criticisms of the EU.

The absence of an explicit European clause in the Spanish Constitution was not, however, an obstacle to membership of Spain in the European project: the

[6] Unless otherwise indicated, all the election manifestos of the political parties discussed in this chapter are available at the following link <https://manifestoproject.wzb.eu/>.

[7] See, on this matter, Miguel Herrero de Miñón, 'Constitución Española y Unión Europea: Comentarios al Artículo 93 de La Constitución Española' (1992) 26 Revista de las Cortes Generales 7; Miguel Herrero y Rodríguez de Miñón, José María Jover Gómez-Ferrer, Áurea Roldán Martín, and José Amérigo Alonso, 'La Respuesta Constitucional a la Integración Europea' (2005) 25 Revista Española de Derecho Constitucional 239.

[8] See, for an analysis, Violeta Ruiz Almendral, 'Estabilidad Presupuestaria y Reforma Constitucional' (2012) 41 Revista Española de Derecho Europeo 33.

Spanish Constitution has several provisions that open it up to supranational integration and to international law more generally. The most important of these is probably article 93, which states:

> By means of an organic law, authorisation may be granted for concluding treaties by which powers derived from the Constitution shall be vested in an international organisation or institution. It is incumbent on the *Cortes Generales* or the Government, as the case may be, to guarantee compliance with these treaties and with the resolutions emanating from the international and supranational organisations in which the powers have been vested.

Indeed, the constitutional issues surrounding EU accession have been addressed on the basis of the original text of the 1978 Constitution, defined at first as a procedural precept and, only later, re-evaluated as a substantive norm,[9] lacking explicit provisions on European primacy. Another relevant provision is article 96(1), according to which 'validly concluded international treaties, once officially published in Spain, shall form part of the internal legal order. Their provisions may only be repealed, amended or suspended in the manner provided in the treaties themselves or in accordance with the general rules of international law'.

The Constitutional Court[10] conceived of article 93 of the Spanish Constitution as a basis for the primacy of Community law without giving the Community law a constitutional status in the legal sources system. One of the fathers of the Spanish Constitution, Miguel Herrero de Miñón, saw the provision in article 93 as opening up the Spanish constitutional system to international law generally and to supranational law specifically, albeit while safeguarding

[9] See judgement 28/1991 of the Spanish Constitutional Court, BOE n 64, 15 March 1991. On art 93 of the Spanish Constitution, see Antonio López Castillo, 'La Unión Europea «en constitución» y la Constitución estatal en (espera de) reformas. A propósito de la DTC 1/2004 de 13 diciembre' in Antonio López Castillo, Alejandro Saiz Arnaiz, and Víctor Ferreres Comella (eds), *Constitución española y constitución europea* (Centro de Estudios Políticos y Constitucionales 2005) 13, 22; see also Alejandro Saiz Arnaiz, 'De primacía, supremacía y derechos fundamentales en la Europa integrada: la Declaración del Tribunal Constitucional de 13 diciembre de 2004 y el Tratado por el que establece una Constitución para Europa' in Antonio López Castillo, Alejandro Saiz Arnaiz, and Víctor Ferreres Comella (eds), *Constitución española y constitución europea* (Centro de Estudios Políticos y Constitucionales 2005) 51.

[10] For a useful overview of Spanish case law, see 'Prontuario de jurisprudencia del Tribunal Constitucional sobre el Derecho de la Unión Europea' (2020) <https://www.tribunalconstitucional.es/es/jurisprudencia/InformacionRelevante/Prontuario%20jurisprudencia%20constitucional%20sobre%20Derecho%20de%20la%20UE.pdf>; Pablo Pérez Tremps *Constitución Española y Comunidad Europea* (Civitas 1993); Antonio López Castillo, *Constitución e integración. El fundamento constitucional de la integración supranacional europea en España y en la RFA* (Centro de Estudios Políticos y Constitucionales 1996); Luis María Díez-Picazo, 'El Derecho comunitario en la jurisprudencia constitucional española' (1998) 18 Revista española de derecho constitucional 2552; Ricardo Alonso García, *El juez español como juez comunitario* (Tirant lo Blanch 2003).

Spanish sovereignty.[11] Manuel Aragón, a former judge of the Constitutional Court, considered that while article 93 cannot be used to amend the Spanish Constitution, it allows alterations of the competences of the public authorities to accommodate European integration, as these alterations are foreseen by the Constitution itself.[12] The Spanish Constitutional Court has confirmed the idea that these provisions operate to form the basis of the openness of Spanish constitutional law towards supranational and international law. Regarding article 93, the Court very graphically established that 'metaphorically, it could be said that Art. 93 CE operates as a "hinge" ['*bisagra*' in Spanish] through which the Constitution itself allows the entry of other legislations into our constitutional system through the transfer of the exercise of competences'.[13]

In addition to this, article 10(2) of the Spanish Constitution provides that 'the principles relating to the fundamental rights and liberties recognised by the Constitution shall be interpreted in conformity with the Universal Declaration of Human Rights and the international treaties and agreements thereon ratified by Spain'. This provision, opening up Spanish law to supranational and international human rights instruments, plays a major role when it comes to European human rights law. Given the economic matrix of EU law, article 10(2) has not been called into question for supranational treaties. However, the nature of EU law changed with Lisbon, given the binding nature of the Charter of Fundamental Rights, and today it is difficult to deny that 'in reality, in the area of fundamental rights, it is evident that the decision of the Court of Justice is constitutionally relevant to the purposes of Art.10.2'[14] of the Spanish Constitution.

The seeds of this change can be found in the Court's *Declaración* 1/2004 on the Constitutional Treaty. On that occasion, the majority of the judges of the Spanish Constitutional Court stressed the valuable ability of that provision to open up the Spanish system of fundamental rights to supranational and international human rights law:

> It is the reiterated doctrine of this Court that the international treaties and agreements referred to by Art 10.2 of the Constitution 'constitute valuable

[11] Herrero de Miñón (n 7).

[12] Manuel Aragón Reyes, 'La Constitucion Española Y El Tratado De La Union Europea: La Reforma De La Constitucion' (1994) 42 Revista Española de Derecho Constitucional 9.

[13] Declaración 1/2004 of the Spanish Constitutional Court, 13 December 2004, part II.2. Our translation.

[14] Pedro Cruz Villalón and Juan Luis Requejo Pagés, 'La relación entre la cuestión prejudicial y la cuestión de inconstitucionalidad' (2015) 50 Revista de Derecho Comunitario Europeo 173, 191. Our translation.

> interpretative criteria for the meaning and scope of the rights and freedoms recognised by the Constitution', in such a way that they must be considered 'in order to corroborate the meaning and scope of the specific fundamental right which (. . .) has been recognised by our Constitution (. . .).' [STC 292/2000, of 30 November, FJ 8, precisely with reference to the Charter of Nice; also STC 53/2002, of 27 February, FJ 3 b)]'.[15]

Declaración 1/2004 of the Spanish Constitutional Court on the Constitutional Treaty also clarified an important point regarding the relationship between Spanish and European Union law: the question of primacy. The Spanish Constitution declares its own supremacy in its article 9. In the Declaración, the majority of the Constitutional Court declared that there was compatibility between constitutional supremacy and the primacy of EU Law. Even if the argument is quite long, it is worth reproducing some excerpts from this Declaración on this point:

> Supremacy and primacy are categories which are developed in differentiated orders. The former, in that of the application of valid regulations; the latter, in that of regulatory procedures. Supremacy is sustained in the higher hierarchical character of a regulation and, therefore, is a source of validity of the lower regulations, leading to the consequent invalidity of the latter if they contravene the provisions set forth imperatively in the former. Primacy, however, is not necessarily sustained on hierarchy, but rather on the distinction between the scopes of application of different regulations, principally valid, of which, however, one or more of them have the capacity for displacing others by virtue of their preferential or prevalent application due to various reasons. In principle, all supremacy implies primacy (which leads to its occasional equivalence, as in our DTC 1/1992, FJ 1), unless the same supreme regulation has set forth, in some scope, its own displacement or non-application. The supremacy of the Constitution is therefore compatible with application systems which award applicative preference to regulations of another legislation other than the national legislation as long as the Constitution itself has set forth said provision, which is what happens exactly with the provision set forth in Art. 93, which enables the transfer of competences resulting from the Constitution in favour of an international institution thus enabled constitutionally for the regulatory provision of matters until then reserved

[15] Declaración 1/2004 of the Spanish Constitutional Court, 13 December 2004, part II.6. Our translation.

> for constituted internal powers and the application thereto. In short, the Constitution has accepted, by virtue of Art. 93, the primacy of the Union legislation in the scope inherent to said Law, as now recognised expressly in Art. I-6 of the Treaty.[16]

The Constitutional Court, however, added an interesting caveat:

> In the unlikely case where, in the ulterior dynamics of the legislation of the European Union, said law is considered irreconcilable with the Spanish Constitution, without the hypothetical excesses of the European legislation with regard to the European Constitution itself being remedied by the ordinary channels set forth therein, in a final instance, the conservation of the sovereignty of the Spanish people and the given supremacy of the Constitution could lead this Court to approach the problems which, in such a case, would arise. Under current circumstances, said problems are considered inexistent through the corresponding constitutional procedures . . .[17]

This caveat has been underlined and discussed by Spanish constitutional scholars. At the time, Rodríguez Iglesias argued, in line with the Declaración, that it would not be reasonable to expect a constitutional court to renounce the possibility of addressing such hypothetical problems, and that, unlike other European counterparts, the Spanish Constitutional Court had phrased its decision in a way that excluded any risk to legal certainty with regards to the primacy principle.[18] Another relevant issue concerns the scope of article 93 of the Spanish Constitution or, in other words, the (implicit) material limits to European integration: state sovereignty, basic constitutional structures, and constitutional values and principles. This is a new development that was not found in previous Spanish constitutional case law and is discussed in *Fundamento Jurídico* (Legal Basis) 2 *in fine*. These material limits are not expressly stated in the constitutional provision but are implicitly derived from the Constitution and the essential meaning of the provision itself.

[16] Declaración 1/2004 of the Spanish Constitutional Court, 13 December 2004, part II.4. Our translation.

[17] Declaración 1/2004 of the Spanish Constitutional Court, 13 December 2004, part II.4. Our translation.

[18] Gil Carlos Rodríguez Iglesias, 'No Existe Contradicción Entre La Constitución Española y La Constitución Europea: La Declaración Del Tribunal Constitucional' (2005) 9 Revista de Derecho Comunitario Europeo 5, 12.

Martín y Pérez de Nanclares took a more critical approach to the caveat to primacy in this part of the decision.[19] In addition to criticizing its odd wording, which indeed is rather muddled in Spanish, the author sees this passage as a Spanish version of *Solange II*, and suggests that on this point the Constitutional Court could have emphasized loyal cooperation and solidarity with the Court of Justice as opposed to conflict and confrontation.[20]

It is possible to note a strong evolution in the case law of the Constitutional Court from the judgment 28/1991[21] and Declaración 1/1992[22] up to Declaración 1/2004. In this case, the Constitutional Court adopted a more substantive reading of article 93 of the Constitution, no longer conceiving of it only as a procedural clause.

The position of EU law in the domestic ranking is, however, ambiguous. Since constitutional courts have renounced a (pure) dualistic strategy—according to which EU laws would be sources external to their domestic legal order—they have often accepted the erosion of the boundary between legal orders by 'devising' a new step in the hierarchy of legal sources. This new step is 'super-legislative' but also 'sub-constitutional'. In this way, courts guarantee the prevalence of EU law over domestic law without infringing constitutional supremacy. The Spanish Constitutional Court represents no exception to this trend. This attempt has, however, created confusion in the case law of the constitutional courts themselves, as demonstrated by the contradictions found in decisions of the Spanish Constitutional Court. In case 28/1991, in fact, the Constitutional Court used two formulae to define the legal strength of EU law—'non-constitutional law' and 'infra-constitutional law'—while in other cases it has used the formula 'constitutionally relevant [law]'.[23] Consequently, according to the Constitutional Court, the contrast between EU law and national law cannot be seen as a manifestation of the lack of constitutionality of the national rule: it is a legality issue which has to be resolved by ordinary judges.

[19] José Martín y Pérez de Nanclares, 'Hacia Una Nueva Concepcion Del Articulo 93 de La Constitucion: Comentario a La Declaracion 1/2004 Del Tribunal Constitucional' (2005) 57 Revista Española de Derecho Internacional 799.

[20] Martín y Pérez de Nanclares (n 19) 812.

[21] Tribunal Constitucional, sentencia 28/1991 <https://www.tribunalconstitucional.es/es/Paginas/default.aspx>.

[22] Tribunal Constitucional, declaración 1/1992 <https://www.tribunalconstitucional.es/es/Paginas/default.aspx>. On this, see Pérez Tremps (n 10).

[23] See Tribunal Constitucional, sentencia 28/1991 <https://www.tribunalconstitucional.es/es/Paginas/default.aspx>. Concerning the terminology used by the Constitutional Court, see Carlos Vidal Prado, *El impacto del nuevo derecho europeo en los Tribunales Constitucionales* (Editorial Colex 2004).

> However, the aforementioned link does not mean that, for the sake of Article 93, the rules of European Community Law have been given constitutional status and force, nor does it in any way mean that the possible infringement of those rules by a Spanish provision necessarily entails at the same time a violation of the aforementioned Article 93 EC.[24]

As a consequence, EU law does not imperil the supremacy of the national Constitution, which, according to the perspective of the Constitutional Court, remains the highest law. In summary, the Spanish Constitution is generally acknowledged to be open to supranational integration. The question concerns the extent of this openness and how this openness can be connected with the idea of constitutional supremacy and national sovereignty. As we will see, Eurosceptic discourses in Spain take their own approach to this connection, and sometimes seek to use it to undermine the process of European integration, to question EU institutions, or to attack specific policies. Although the Spanish Constitutional Court has shown itself to be relatively open on the fundamental issues of European integration, starting with the recognition of primacy, it has nevertheless traditionally been reluctant to accept direct dialogue with the Court of Justice under article 267 TFEU. In fact, it has raised the EU law preliminary question only once, in the famous *Melloni* case.[25] This preliminary question had drawn attention from scholars for at least two reasons: first of all, it was raised by the Spanish Constitutional Court, which for the first time had decided to use Article 267 TFEU (and in this sense it represented a link in a longer chain of preliminary questions raised by national constitutional courts); the second reason was that the ECJ was expected to say something important about article 53 of the Charter of Fundamental Rights of the EU, concerning the burning issue of the relationship between the standard of protection given to the same right at different levels.

In the *Melloni* case, the ECJ refused a minimalist interpretation of article 53, saying that the 'Charter would undermine the principle of the primacy of EU law inasmuch as it would allow a Member State to disapply EU legal rules which are fully in compliance with the Charter where they infringe the fundamental rights guaranteed by that State's constitution' (para 58). The ECJ then added at para 60:

[24] Tribunal Constitucional, sentencia 28/1991 <https://www.tribunalconstitucional.es/es/Paginas/default.aspx>. Our translation.

[25] Case C-399/11 *Stefano Melloni v Ministerio Fiscal* EU:C:2013:107.

> It is true that Article 53 of the Charter confirms that, where an EU legal act calls for national implementing measures, national authorities and courts remain free to apply national standards of protection of fundamental rights, provided that the level of protection provided for by the Charter, as interpreted by the Court, and the primacy, unity and effectiveness of EU law are not thereby compromised.

This was seen as a return to an absolute conception of primacy,[26] and in general sounded very tough. On 13 February 2014, in its follow-up to the *Melloni* decision of the Luxembourg Court, the Spanish Constitutional Court reversed its case law and abided by the indications of the ECJ.[27] The Spanish follow-up to the *Melloni* case was a little ambiguous because 'while the outcome does fulfil the mandates of EU law, the reasoning proves quite unsettling'.[28] At the same time, although it does not regularly use the preliminary ruling procedure under article 267 TFEU, the Spanish Constitutional Court has sought to ensure that ordinary courts comply with that procedure. For example, the Constitutional Court acknowledged[29] the exhaustibility of the *recurso de amparo* (a remedy for the protection of constitutional rights) when an ordinary judge refuses to refer a preliminary question to the ECJ pursuant to article 234 ECT (267 TFEU). If this refusal implies the violation of a fundamental right guaranteed by the *recurso de amparo*, it is possible to proceed before the Constitutional Court for a violation of article 24 of the Spanish Constitution.[30] With this decision, the Constitutional Court has balanced its initial refusal to accept the mechanism of preliminary rulings by ensuring the loyalty of its national judges. The Constitutional Court specified that a refusal to refer a preliminary question to the ECJ is relevant for the admission of the *recurso de amparo* whenever the domestic judge is obliged to refer to the ECJ according to article 267 TFEU and when there is no precedent ruling by the ECJ on an analogous or identical case. A mere refusal to refer a preliminary question does

[26] To quote the words used, also recently, by some scholars: Stephan W Schill and Armin von Bogdandy, 'Overcoming Absolute Primacy: Respect for National Identity under the Lisbon Treaty' (2011) 48(5) Common Market Law Review 1417.

[27] Tribunal Constitucional, sentencia 26/2014 <https://www.tribunalconstitucional.es/es/Paginas/default.aspx>.

[28] Aida Torres Pérez, 'Melloni in Three Acts: From Dialogue to Monologue' (2014) 10(2) European Constitutional Law Review 308.

[29] Tribunal Constitucional, sentencia 58/2004 <https://www.tribunalconstitucional.es/es/Paginas/default.aspx>.

[30] Tribunal Constitucional, sentencia 58/2004 <https://www.tribunalconstitucional.es/es/Paginas/default.aspx>.

not, on its own, give rise to the possibility of using the *recurso de amparo*; in this sense, EU law continues not to have constitutional status.

6.3. Patterns of the Eurosceptic Mobilization of Constitutional Law Arguments by Spanish Parties

As explained earlier, Spain is an interesting case study because of the coexistence of left-wing and right-wing Eurosceptic discourses in a country traditionally perceived as Europhile. The two forms of Euroscepticism have displayed both areas of overlap and significant differences. On the one hand, both have resorted to the mobilization of constitutional law against European integration. On the other hand, however, right-wing actors have been more assertive in their general Euroscepticism, while the left-wing parties have usually taken a more constructive and integrationist approach when it comes to imagining what European constitutionalism could look like. In this section, we group together, by themes, the main elements of all these forms of Eurosceptic constitutional counter-narrative.

6.3.1. European integration as a threat to the Spanish Constitution: Counter-narratives from left and right

A very distinctive form of the Eurosceptic counter-narrative in Spain is the claim that the process of European integration hollows out or threatens the Spanish Constitution.

The left-wing approach to this claim emphasized the management of the Euro-crisis in Spain and its effects on the country's constitutional system. For instance, the Izquierda Unida coalition authored a very comprehensive critique in its 2014 European election manifesto, and repeated it in its 2019 EP election manifesto.[31] In the part of the manifesto devoted to 'the directive role of the troika: ECB, IMF and European Commission', the coalition argued that:

> This crisis is the result of the process of regional integration defended by the European majority parties. A neoliberal project that since Maastricht and until the Budgetary Stability Treaty, concretised a coup d'état (. . .) These structural reforms have a double area of acting; in the economic space, in

[31] Izquierda Unida, 'Tu izquierda. Programa para las elecciones al Parlamento Europeo' (2019) 4.

> which they seek to impact the job market and public services, and on the other hand, in the political space, in which they proceed to a de-constituent process that consecrates the anti-democratic character and facilitates economic reforms (. . .). National sovereignty is displaced from national constitutions to institutions like the European Commission, European Central Bank and the International Monetary Fund—the Troika (. . .). In 2011, the constitutional amendment of Article 135, agreed by PP and PSOE (. . .) was the political expression of PSOE and PP to make the European project gravitate around this neoliberal dogma.[32]

Criticisms of the management of the Euro-crisis are, however, not the only criticisms put forward by these parties when it comes to their view of the national Constitution in the context of European integration. More generally, these parties seem to be suspicious of the democratic credentials of the constitutional changes related to European Union politics. There are a number of examples of this. In the 2014 EP election, the Podemos party had an approach to the articulation between EU law and national constitutional law that can be considered as populist, and was in line with the trajectory of that party, especially in that period. Podemos focused generally on the impact of EU law on Member States' constitutions, with relatively vague phrasing but a very specific proposal consisting of the introduction of 'democratic ratification':

> [T]he inclusion in the normative framework in force of a need for democratic ratification with effective popular participation of changes that affect the constitutions of Member States. To guarantee that any decision taken by European institutions that is of great relevance for citizens must be ratified compulsorily by the latter.[33]

The party also argued that:

> The new legal system must include binding referendums and people's legislative initiatives as a key aspect of democratic participation (. . .) The Spanish Constitution to be reformed to guarantee the holding of referendums in such cases and the withdrawal of measures that have been approved without democratic popular participation.[34]

[32] Izquierda Unida, 'Programa para las elecciones europeas 2014' (2014) 6–7. Our translation.
[33] Podemos, 'Podemos. Documento final del programa colaborativo' (2014) 29. Our translation.
[34] Podemos (n 33) 29–30. Our translation.

In fact, a similar proposal already existed in the 2011 general election manifesto of Izquierda Unida, which demanded 'the introduction in the Constitution of a number of areas that require a mandatory popular consultation, such as integration into supranational organizations'.[35] A similar pledge might be found in the 2015 general election manifesto of Unidad Popular, which pledged that 'the passing and modification of primary treaties of the European Constitution or of any rule of European constitutional reach must be subject to referendum of all Member States'.[36] This party also called for a constituent process after criticizing the push to 'institutionalize the reforms and cutbacks in rights and freedoms carried out since 2010, in the framework of austerity policies mandated by the Troika for the so-called Europe of the Euro'.[37] Left-wing parties in Spain do not, however, have a monopoly on the idea that European integration might threaten the national Constitution. Among the most prominent proposals in the 2023 Vox manifesto is the articulation of a clear strategy of Euroscepticism through law. The party pledged to defend 'the primacy of the Constitution over European law and, in general, of national law in issues that affect the common good of Spain and the general interests of the State'.[38] Of course, the party did not define what it meant by the common good or the general interests of the state, but this makes this pledge particularly concerning. At the end of the day, vagueness gives elasticity to content, so that it can be manipulated and construed to cover the widest variety of situations.

For the 2024 EP election, Vox repeated some of the themes and pledges that it had put forward in the previous election, often with identical phrasing. We can again find the pledge to 'defend the primacy of the Spanish Constitution over European law'.[39] Curiously enough, in this election, the left-wing party Sumar also touched upon this issue, albeit with a softer rhetoric: 'it is necessary to underline the incompatibility of many European rules, especially those promoting austerity, with the constitutional texts of the Member States'.[40]

Overall, both radical left-wing and radical right-wing Eurosceptic parties in Spain seem to distrust the way in which the process of European integration has affected the Spanish Constitution. Criticisms of the management of the Euro-crisis, proposals for referendums, and the assertion of constitutional supremacy are three very different expressions of this distrust, but they seem to

35 Izquierda Unida, 'Propuestas electorales Izquierda Unida elecciones 2011' (2011) 23.
36 Unidad Popular, 'Por un nuevo país' (2015) 13. Our translation.
37 Unidad Popular (n 36) 22. Our translation.
38 Vox, 'Un programa para lo que importa' (2023) 134. Our translation.
39 Vox, 'Nos van a oir' (2024) 6. Our translation.
40 Sumar, 'Un programa que marca el rumbo en Europa' (2024) 45. Our translation.

have something in common: the idea that the Spanish Constitution is not safe in the status quo but is under threat from EU institutions.

6.3.2. European courts and national courts

The question of the relationship between national and supranational courts is linked to the above discussion. It seems logical for parties that distrust the impact of EU institutions on the national constitution to distrust the impact of European courts on the national court system as well.

Parties on the left had less critical stances on the European courts. However, these parties still devoted some proposals to the ECJ in their manifestos. In the 2009 EP Election, the manifesto of Izquierda Unida argued, with somewhat odd wording, that 'the rules present in the European Higher Court of Justice constitute a frontal attack to collective bargaining and labour regulations'[41] and claimed to 'reject the subordination of social components and trade unions to the standards of the market as held by the European Higher Court of Justice'.[42] This was a criticism of the ECJ from a left-wing perspective, which however did not target the court from a constitutional law angle. The manifesto of Izquierda Unida for the 2014 EP election also included other criticisms of the EU judicial institutions. First, the party pledged 'rejection of mercantilist principles of Community law and the doctrine of the European Court of Justice consisting in the application of the "country of origin" principle'.[43] Second, the party proposed the 'control and election of the members of the Court of Justice by the European Parliament'.[44] These two points were repeated in the party's 2019 manifesto.[45]

The radical right-wing party Vox did, however, attack the European judicial institutions using constitutional counter-narratives. The 2019 election manifesto of Vox pledged to recover 'national sovereignty in the application of rulings of our courts'.[46] This proposal, albeit vague, seemed to be targeted at European supranational courts in general and aimed to question compliance with their decisions. Additionally, in the 2024 EP Vox election manifesto, there is a long paragraph devoted to courts in which the party pledges to:

[41] Izquierda Unida, 'Tu voz en Europa' (2009) 12. Our translation.
[42] Izquierda Unida (n 41) 43. Our translation.
[43] Izquierda Unida (n 32) 43. Our translation.
[44] Izquierda Unida (n 43). Our translation.
[45] Izquierda Unida, 'Programa para las elecciones al Parlamento Europe' (2019) 56.
[46] Vox, '100 medidas para la España viva' (n 4). Our translation.

> Boost the recovery of national sovereignty in the application of rulings of our courts. To ensure respect to decisions of Spanish judges, pushing for a reform of the European Arrest Warrant to eliminate the possibility that individuals with pending criminal cases can benefit from the protection of European organisms, as has happened until now.[47]

The party thus chose to frame the question of the relationship between national and supranational judicial institutions in terms of sovereignty that had to be 'recovered' when it comes to Spanish courts. On this point, the question of courts thus overlaps with the counter-narrative on sovereignty, which featured strongly for some of these parties and which we develop in more detail just below.

6.3.3. European integration as a threat to sovereignty

We explained earlier that Izquierda Unida considered the process of European integration to be a threat to national sovereignty.[48] The 2019 EP election manifesto of this party is a very good example of this stance, combining three criticisms of the European Union: the ideas of a de-constituent process, an attack on national sovereignty, and a process of de-democratization. These three elements are combined in the following manner:

> In the political arena, they proceed to a de-constituent process that consecrates the anti-democratic character and facilitates the implementation of economic reforms (. . .). This de-constituent process has its roots in the very process of construction of the EU. For decades they have been delegating the effective capacity to take decisions (. . .) to supranational institutions. This process has gone together with the internal dismantling of democratic structures that form the backbone of the States (. . .). This way, national sovereignty is effectively displaced from the national constitution to institutional forms of new roles such as the European Commission, the European Central Bank and the International Monetary Fund—the Troika.[49]

47 Vox, 'Nos van a oir' (2024) 6. Our translation.
48 Izquierda Unida, 'Programa para las elecciones europeas 2014' (2014) 6–7.
49 Izquierda Unida, 'Tu izquierda' (2019) 25. Our translation.

Interestingly enough, on the opposite side of the political spectrum, the radical right-wing party Vox also had strong criticism of the way in which the EU institutions allegedly undermined Spanish sovereignty. In its 2024 EP election manifesto, the party accused the EU of renouncing the principle of subsidiarity and of attacking 'the sovereignty of Nations'.[50] In this regard, it pledged that:

> The European Union will stop behaving as a political commissary that attacks the legitimate freedom and autonomy of national democracies, and instead will be at the service of Member States respecting the principle of subsidiarity and their sovereignty.[51]

Sovereignty and subsidiarity were thus two core concepts in Vox's constitutional counter-narrative during the 2024 election. Regarding the first, the party also argued that 'despite the pretences of bureaucrats in Brussels, the European Union is not a sovereign State. Sovereignty resides in the different Nations that are part of the European Union'.[52] Regarding sovereignty, the party argued that:

> All directives approved in Brussels are then applied in national legislation. Therefore, it is necessary to reformulate, reinforce and give efficacy to the mechanisms available to community institutions to ensure respect for the principles of subsidiarity and proportionality, and especially to improve the procedures for Member States to oppose in a well-founded way the decisions and legislative acts of the Union that attack their interests and those of their nationals.[53]

These discussions by Vox about sovereignty and subsidiarity seemed to culminate in an accusation against what the party considered the expansive powers of the EU, and in particular against 'the disproportionate and contrary to the treaties growth of competences of community institutions, the growing and complex community normative framework'.[54] The discussions also converged in a proposal that the EU 'respect national sovereignty of their Member States singularised in their Parliaments. [Vox will] push for a new European treaty returning to Member States the protagonist role against the bureaucracy of an unelected European Commission'.[55] Finally, this rhetoric also

[50] Vox, 'Nos van a oir' (2024) 26.
[51] Vox (n 39) 28. Our translation.
[52] Vox (n 39) 31.
[53] Vox (n 39) 30–31.Our translation.
[54] Vox (n 39) 31. Our translation.
[55] Vox (n 39) 32. Our translation.

materialized in a pledge to 'abrogate or reform Art. 7 of the Lisbon Treaty so as to prevent the meddling of Brussels in the political Constitution and the democratic decisions of the Member States'.[56]

The manifesto also criticized the sanctions on Hungary 'for protecting underage people from the indoctrination of gender lobbies'.[57] The manifesto included more general criticisms of the European Court of Human Rights, saying that it had 'on occasions been at the service of the enemies of Spain'.[58] Interestingly enough, another Spanish party, Izquierda Unida, which had also included Eurosceptic proposals in its manifestos, had a different take on the Hungarian case. In their 2014 EP election manifesto, the party asked for 'sanctions on countries that pass discriminatory legislation against LGBTI people, such as the Hungarian Constitution passed in 2012'.[59]

Criticisms of the impact of EU institutions on national sovereignty thus featured from both the radical left and the radical right in Spain. However, left-wing criticisms in this regard seemed to be more linked to the specific way in which the Euro-crisis had been managed, while Vox's position seemed to be more radically at odds with the current construction of the European Union.

6.3.4. The reform of article 135 of the Spanish Constitution

As we have repeatedly argued in this chapter, an important aspect of Eurosceptic constitutional counter-narratives in Spain had to do with the management of the Euro-crisis. As a result of this management, the Spanish Constitution was reformed in 2011 to include, in article 135, the principles of, inter alia, budget stability and a limit to the structural deficit. Solanes and Torres explain the context for this amendment:

> The constitutional amendment was prompted by the so-called Euro-Plus-Pact, a package of measures adopted by the European Council in March 2011 to respond to the crisis and preserve financial stability, and, more particularly, by the French–German summit held on 16 August 2011. Several months after the constitutional amendment, the Treaty on Stability, Coordination and Governance in the Economic and Monetary Union (TSCG), signed on 2 March 2012, incorporated the so-called 'golden rule', i.e., the requirement

[56] Vox (n 39) 32.
[57] Vox (n 39) 26. Our translation.
[58] Vox (n 39) 5. Our translation.
[59] Izquierda Unida (n 32) 67. Our translation.

> that 'the budget position of the general government must be balanced or in surplus' (Art. 3(1)(a)). Moreover, according to Art. 3(2), there is an obligation to give effect to the financial provisions of Art. 3(1) in national law 'through provisions of binding force and permanent character, preferably constitutional, or otherwise guaranteed to be fully respected and adhered to throughout the national budgetary processes'.[60]

The reform was controversial at the academic and political levels. In legal academia, some colleagues questioned whether it would be acceptable that 'the interests of the markets' resulted in the undermining of the 'constitutional consensus' in Spain.[61] Politically, some parties, especially on the radical left, were very critical of this reform. A good example is Unidad Popular, which argued in its 2015 general election manifesto that 'the crisis has been used as an excuse to empty the constitutional legal systems of EU countries and an example is the imposition that implies the reform of Art. 135.2 of the Spanish Constitution, with which PP and PSOE prioritize the payment of debt before social needs'.[62] Izquierda Unida—which was part of the Unidad Popular coalition—presented its own manifesto for this election too, and it pledged to derogate the reform of article 135.[63]

Similarly, Podemos included the reform of article 135 of the Spanish Constitution in its 2016 general election manifesto.[64] It also included, in its manifesto for the April 2019 general election, 'the derogation of the rules that institutionalised austerity and the lost decade of Spain (Art. 135 Spanish Constitution and the Law on Budgetary Stability)'.[65] The party thus proposed the 'derogation of article 135 bis of the Spanish Constitution and the Law on Budgetary Stability'.[66]

In the 2019 EP election, Izquierda Unida argued that 'in 2011, the constitutional amendment of Art. 135, agreed by PP and PSOE and which established the concept of "budgetary stability" and the priority in the payment of debt and its interests was the political expression of the consensus amongst PSOE and

[60] Joan Solanes Mullor and Aida Torres Pérez, 'The Constitution of Spain: The Challenges for the Constitutional Order under European and Global Governance' in Anneli Albi and Samo Bardutzky (eds), *National Constitutions in European and Global Governance: Democracy, Rights, the Rule of Law: National Reports* (TMC Asser Press 2019) 547.

[61] Maria Josefa Ridaura Martinez, 'La Reforma Del Articulo 135 de La Constitución Española: ¿Pueden Los Mercados Quebrar El Consenso Constitucional?' (2012) 29 Teoría y Realidad Constitucional 237, 259.

[62] Unidad Popular, 'Por un nuevo país' (2015) 22. Our translation.

[63] Izquierda Unida, 'Por un nuevo país' (2015) 95.

[64] Podemos, 'Cambiar España. 50 pasos para gobernar juntos' (2016) 3.

[65] Podemos, 'Las razones siguen intactas' (2019) 94. Our translation.

[66] Izquierda Unida (n 31) 9. Our translation.

PP to make the European project turn towards this neoliberal dogma which asphyxiates and cuts down the social model'.[67]

Criticisms of the reform of article 135 of the Constitution can still be found in the most recent manifestos of the left-wing parties in Spain. In the 2024 EP election, the left-wing Sumar party argued that the EU institutions themselves and the Member States 'fail to comply with the Treaties (. . .). The forced reform of Art. 135 of our Constitution, executed nocturnally and with treachery whilst Germany used diverse forms of financial engineering that have now been declared unconstitutional, is a good example of that'.[68]

6.3.5. Eurosceptics and Eurocritics: Proposals for a different Europe

So far, we have focused on the Eurosceptic criticisms and constitutional counter-narratives of the radical left- and right-wing parties in Spain. The parties of both the radical left and the radical right show important quantities of distrust in the process of European integration, even if they are often focused on different aspects or structure their counter-narratives around different key ideas.

One important difference, however, is that the left-wing parties seem to have a more constructive attitude, one in which they put forward proposals for the future of European integration. Many of these proposals are embedded in political stances where constitutionalism plays an important role.

A good example can be found by looking at the 2008 general election in Spain and the 2009 EP election, which took place only a few years after the failed ratification of the European Constitutional Treaty. In that general election, Izquierda Unida called for a 'true European constituent process located in the European Parliament'.[69] In their 2009 EP election manifesto, they called for a 'true constituent process (. . .) emanating from a constituent assembly elected by direct universal suffrage of all citizens of the European Union (. . .)'.[70]

This sort of stance continued over time in subsequent elections. In their 2011 general election manifesto, Izquierda Unida called for a 'unitary European response (. . .) that allows us to move towards a new European constituent process to build a social Europe of rights and not a Europe at the service of markets'.[71] In their 2014 EP election manifesto, Izquierda Unida claimed that:

[67] Izquierda Unida (n 31) 5.
[68] Sumar (n 40) 45. Our translation.
[69] Izquierda Unida, 'Más izquierda' (2008) 152. Our translation.
[70] Izquierda Unida, 'Tu voz en Europa' (2009) 45. Our translation.
[71] Izquierda Unida, (n 35) 82. Our translation.

> [A] European democracy is not possible in the frame of the current treaties (. . .). An alternative project won't be possible unless a true constituent process is started, a refoundation of the EU and the institutions of the Spanish political system (. . .). This constituent process would involve at the very least the calling of a European Constituent Assembly elected by universal suffrage to determine a true democratic architecture of European institutions. The goal to build a social and environmentally sustainable Europe that the current Stability Treaty brings to an end, the principle of de-regulation of the market, the single currency without a European Public Treasury, the European Central Bank as an entity not controlled democratically.[72]

Other parties on the left shared this tone and this sort of proposal. In the 2014 EP election, Podemos, which was at the time a new party in Spain, had a similar pledge in its manifesto. It first briefly mentioned a 'European constituent process'[73] and then went on to request:

> Derogation from the Lisbon Treaty to ensure that public services are not subject to the principle of competition, nor can they be commodified in the same manner as those underpinning the neoliberal and antidemocratic Europe; the initiation of a process leading to a refoundation of EU institutions through a constituent assembly.[74]

The idea of a European constituent process appears again in the 2019 manifesto of Izquierda Unida, which states that the goal is 'to build a social and environmentally sustainable Europe that brings an end to the Stability Treaty'.[75]

The radical left-wing parties in Spain thus combined Eurosceptic criticisms of the EU institutions and strong constitutional counter-narratives with some proposals for a constitutional future of Europe. Whether they are realistic or not, the fact is that these proposals were not matched by the radical right-wing party Vox, which remained much more sceptical on this point too and stuck to the idea of a Europe of sovereign nations that can be found in the most radical discourses of Eurosceptic parties around the continent.

72 Izquierda Unida, 'Programa para las elecciones europeas 2014' (2014) 22. Our translation.
73 Podemos, 'Documento final del programa colaborativo' (2014) 23.
74 Podemos, 'Documento final del programa colaborativo' (2014) 28. Our translation.
75 Izquierda Unida, 'Tu izquierda' (2019) 26. Our translation.

6.4. Civil Society and the Mobilization of Constitutional Law Arguments Against the Primacy of EU Law in Spain

Spanish civil society does not present anti-European mobilization phenomena comparable to the Polish case, nor does its intelligentsia make arguments for the constitutional counter-narrative as in the Italian case. In the Spanish case, however, there is an interesting contrast in the utilization of constitutional counter-narratives between Spanish nationalist parties like Vox and nationalist actors in some Autonomous Communities like Catalonia. The former mobilize constitutional supremacy against EU law. The latter, by contrast, mobilize EU law against the Spanish Constitution. These two phenomena may appear to be opposed to each other, but they are not; in fact, they are, in a way, united by a common approach to legal systems—one that portrays different legal systems as closed and in opposition to one another, rather than open and interconnected.

6.4.1. The Catalan independence movement and the mobilization of EU law against the Spanish Constitution

We will start with the use of EU law against Spanish constitutional law in the case of Catalan secessionism. A good example is the use made, in the secessionist approach, of provisions such as article 4(2) TEU.[76] Moreover, the case law of the Court of Justice has been referred to by the supporters of secession to justify the so-called 'internal enlargement thesis',[77] as noted by Ignacio Molina:

[76] For instance, Bossacoma referred to this provision to emphasize that EU law does not oppose secession: 'Neither primary nor secondary EU law contains specific rules that regulate or limit the right of internal secession of sub-state territories. Thus, to clarify the issue we will have to resort, among other arguments, to the legal principles of the Union and, subsidiarily, to international law. There is a notable tension, particularly if the secession is unilateral, between the principles and values of freedom—in a collective sense—and of democracy (art. 2 TEU), the protection of minorities and respect for pluralism (arts. 2 and 3.3 TEU) and European citizenship (arts. 3.2 and 9 TEU) versus those of the rule of law (art. 2 TEU), institutional autonomy, respect for territorial integrity and respect for the national and constitutional identity of the Member States (art. 4.2 TEU)', Pau Bossacoma Busquets, 'Secesión e integración en la Unión Europea Cataluña ¿nuevo Estado de la Unión?' (2017) <http://www.gencat.cat/governacio/pub/sum/iea/ieaR_01_esp.pdf>.

[77] On this thesis, see also: Araceli A Mangas Martín, 'La secesión de territorios en un Estado miembro: efectos en el Derecho de la Unión Europea' (2013) 25 Revista de Derecho de la Unión Europea 47; Phoebus Athanassiou and Stéphanie Laulhé Shaelou, 'EU Accession from within? An Introduction' (2014) 33 Yearbook of European Law 335; Paula García Andrade, 'La ciudadanía europea y la sucesión de Estados: a vueltas con las implicaciones de una separación territorial en el seno de la UE' (2014) 49 Revista de Derecho Comunitario Europeo 997.

> Internal enlargement accepts the logical premise that, after secession, the parent state continues to exist and remains an EU member. However, it adds that the newly independent state wishing to join the EU could benefit from automatic accession, not so much through a formal succession under international law, but rather based on four EU law principles: (a) the Treaties do not regulate this scenario, so under a vague general principle of law, what is not prohibited is possible; (b) a seceded territory would, by definition, already comply with the acquis communautaire; (c) its citizens would have acquired rights from years of EU membership; and (d) the EU only foresees voluntary exit, not expulsion.[78]

These arguments vary in complexity. The first relies on the idea that 'what is not explicitly prohibited is permitted', while the fourth suggests that denying automatic enlargement to an independent Catalonia would contradict the prohibition on expulsion, since the EU Treaties only provide for voluntary withdrawal (article 50 TEU). However, this reasoning assumes as a premise (Catalonia's automatic accession) what should be proved, as the ban on expulsion only applies to existing EU Member States. According to this argument, 'the loss of EU citizenship due to the separation of part of a member state's territory would make the automatic exit of the secessionist region from the EU impossible'.[79]

This explains the Generalitat de Catalunya's references to supranational case law in official reports and academic publications at the time of the secessionist attempt,[80] and the emphasis on the progressive emancipation of EU citizenship from national citizenship. Notably, references to article 11(2) of the Spanish Constitution—which states that 'no Spaniard by origin may be deprived of their nationality'—are much rarer. This may be a strategic choice, positioning EU law as the primary source of an alternative legal framework.

[78] Ignacio Molina, 'Independentismo e integración europea (I): la imposible adhesión automática a la UE de un territorio secesionado' (2012) <https://www.files.ethz.ch/isn/155537/ARI80-Molina_UE_Escocia_Catalunya.pdf>. Our translation.

[79] García Andrade (n 77) 999. Our translation.

[80] Consell Assessor per a la Transició Nacional, *Les vies d'integració de Catalunya a la Unió Europea* (2014) <https://www.municipisindependencia.cat/wp-content/uploads/2014/04/140414-les-vies-integracio-de-catalunya-a-la-unio-europea.pdf>.

6.4.2. Vox's Spanish nationalists and the mobilization of the Spanish Constitution against EU law

Vox represents the reverse twin of the rhetoric of the Catalan nationalists, as this party seeks to mobilize the Spanish Constitution against European integration. However, in addition to Euroscepticism—reflected in Vox's current membership of the Patriots for Europe group—the party and its networks emphasize the defence of *Hispanidad*, now rebranded as the 'Iberosphere'. This concept extends beyond Spanish nationalism to frame a broader cultural and political identity encompassing Spanish-speaking nations, reinforcing Vox's vision of Spain as the leader of a civilization.

Since we have already covered, in detail, the constitutional counter-narrative of this party, in this section, we only give a summary description of the sovereignist intellectual sphere associated with Vox in Spain, and we briefly sketch the mobilization of constitutional law arguments by Vox's networks.

The book *Soberanía* by Jorge Buxadé[81] gives an interesting account of the ideas that populate Vox's ideational space. Jorge Buxadé is a Spanish lawyer and right-wing politician who was elected to the European Parliament in 2019; since February 2020, he has served as the spokesperson for the right-wing Vox party. The book describes itself as an analysis and defence of Spanish national sovereignty in the face of internal and external threats. It focuses on Spain as a sovereign nation and analyses various internal issues such as autonomous communities, the party system, and separatism. The second part of the book addresses broader issues such as the 'false progressive consensus', 'Agenda 2030', 'false elites', and globalism. Finally, the work touches on specific topics such as immigration and Europe and proposes an 'alternative'. This vaguely defined alternative includes strategies and concrete first steps to be taken at the European level and in Spanish economic policy.

Disenso[82] is Vox's official foundation and serves as a vehicle for ideological dissemination. Its activities are closely aligned with Vox's broader agenda, focusing on national sovereignty, cultural conservatism, and Eurocritical counter-narratives. In some of its publications, we find, for instance, criticism of what they consider to be the EU's 'financial blackmail of Poland' in relation to the rule of law backsliding in that country,[83] as well as attacks on the EU and the Court of Justice for allegedly 'twisting' the basis of EU competences.[84]

[81] Jorge Buxadé, *Soberanía: Por qué la Nación es valiosa y merece la pena defenderla* (Homo Legens 2021).

[82] Its official website can be found at the following link: <https://fundaciondisenso.org/>.

[83] <https://fundaciondisenso.org/el-chantaje-financiero-de-la-union-europea-a-polonia/>.

[84] <https://fundaciondisenso.org/ue-cesion-o-confiscacion-de-soberania/>.

On the periphery of Vox, but still within its ideological orbit, is ISSEP (Instituto de Ciencias Sociales, Económicas y Políticas), the Madrid branch of the *Institut des Sciences Sociales, Économiques et Politiques* founded by Marion Maréchal. ISSEP plays a key role in training political cadres for Vox, offering courses aimed at shaping future party leaders and intellectuals.

Finally, in academia, there remains a persistent Schmittian influence,[85] which is part of a long-standing intellectual tradition in Spain that draws on the work of Carl Schmitt to critique liberal democracy, advocate for strong state authority, and challenge the European integration project. These works resonate with Vox's emphasis on national sovereignty and executive power, placing them within the broader ideological constellation of Spanish right-wing thought.[86]

6.5. Eurosceptic Mobilization of Constitutional Law in Spain: A Critique

Spanish Eurosceptic parties have articulated diverse counter-narratives to mobilize the Spanish Constitution against European integration. Although each party, and possibly each manifesto, is different in the way they do this, there are some overlaps: certain arguments cut across parties, elections, and sometimes even ideologies, and these constitute the core elements of the Eurosceptic counter-narratives that we have scrutinized in this chapter.

In this section, we would like to present our take on what we consider to be the two most important elements of those Eurosceptic counter-narratives: the ideas of European integration as a threat to the Spanish Constitution and as a threat to national sovereignty.

On the one hand, the idea that European integration is a threat to the Spanish Constitution is present, particularly, at the doctrinal level. This tells us something about how the Eurosceptic parties interpret the text of the Spanish Constitution. Of course, the manifestos of the parties are not (always) as precise as to mention specific constitutional provisions when they attack EU institutions, but ideas such as the mobilization of constitutional supremacy against EU law can clearly be linked to a certain understanding of article 9 of the

[85] José Díaz and Jerónimo Molina, *Los enemigos de España son mis enemigos. Bibliografía panhispánica de Carl Schmitt (1926–2022)* (Editorial Comares 2022).

[86] On the Spanish right, see Pau Hernández Delgado, 'La nueva derecha española. Una experiencia intelectual entre el tardofranquismo y la globalización' (2024) 9 Tiempo devorado: revista de historia actual 4.

Spanish Constitution. Likewise, proposals such as the use of referendums to decide on important issues pertaining to European integration can be linked to article 93 of the Constitution as well as the different constitutional provisions that regulate the use of referendums in Spain.

The clearest instance of an opposition between constitutional supremacy and the primacy of EU law is given by Vox, especially in its 2024 EP election manifesto.[87] This opposition, however, is generally at odds with the view of the majority of the judges of the Spanish Constitutional Court in its Declaración 1/2004, as we explained earlier in this chapter. The only caveat to this in the reasoning of the majority of the judges of the Constitutional Court has to do with the potential that a piece of EU legislation is 'irreconcilable with the Spanish Constitution', which could lead the Constitutional Court to address the problem to guarantee 'the conservation of the sovereignty of the Spanish People', even if the Court warned that it considered this situation unlikely.[88] This nuance in the reasoning of the Constitutional Court is somewhat odd, as it seems to run contrary to the rest of the ruling. However, it is worth noting that even this caveat is not enough to justify Vox's assertive tone when it seeks to undermine the primacy of EU law on the grounds of constitutional supremacy. Vox's interpretation of article 9 of the Spanish Constitution is not the same as the reading provided by the Spanish Constitutional Court, whose aim seems to be to reconcile, to the extent possible, the constitutional and European legal systems. The Spanish Constitution depicted by the Spanish Constitutional Court in Declaración 1/2004 is open to integration, with just a minor—yet significant—caveat.[89] The understanding of the Spanish Constitution mobilized by Vox is closed to supranational integration and is set against the European legal system.

On the other hand, there are attacks on European integration because of its alleged threat to national sovereignty. To a certain extent, these criticisms seem to be based on a very specific understanding of sovereignty: one in which the demos or the nation is unconstrained, so that any constraints on the sovereign people are illegitimate and undemocratic. On the left, this criticism addressed the management of the Euro-crisis in the country, which allegedly undermined the sovereignty of the Spanish people. The understanding of sovereignty here

[87] Vox, 'Nos van a oir' (2024) 6.

[88] Declaración 1/2004 of the Spanish Constitutional Court, 13 December 2004, part II.4 <https://www.tribunalconstitucional.es/es/Paginas/default.aspx>.

[89] See, on this, Ricardo Alonso García, 'The Spanish Constitution and the European Constitution: The Script for a Virtual Collision and Other Observations on the Principle of Primacy' (2005) 6 German Law Journal 1001; Camilo B Schutte, 'Spain Tribunal Constitucional on the European Constitution. Declaration of 13 December 2004' (2005) 1 European Constitutional Law Review 281, 289.

reflects a strong parallel to a certain understanding of a twin concept, that of constituent power. As Verdugo explains, the classical approach to this idea holds that the constituent power resides in the people and is understood as original, unlimited by legal constraints, and sovereign in nature.[90] This depiction, however, fails to understand the reality of constitutionalism: 'The suggestion that constituent power is unconstrained is dubious in many, if not most, cases (. . .). Constraints always exist since constitutions are not created in a vacuum, they require a regulated procedure including electoral rules, and there are institutions, factions, officers, and sectors of the society trying to influence the process'.[91] Something similar occurs with sovereignty: the idea of an unconstrained sovereign is at odds with the reality of empirical politics, in which the people's sovereignty is exercised in complex contexts. The Euro-crisis was an example of this. Debtor countries were sovereign in the sense that they could accept bail-outs in exchange for conditions imposed by the creditors, or they could reject those conditions and then lose the bail-outs, but they were not sovereign in the sense that they could decide to take the credit and simultaneously to reject the conditions attached to it. There can be a debate on whether the conditions attached to the bail-outs were fair or unfair, sensible or not, but the episode showed that sovereignty is not unconstrained in the real world. Approaching the issue from the perspective of a people whose sovereignty is undermined implies that the criticism is based on an unrealistic understanding of this concept.

On the right, the attacks by Vox focused on what, in their view, were the expansive powers of the EU, which would again undermine Spanish sovereignty. Implicit in these criticisms, however, seems to be the idea that supranational integration is at odds with national sovereignty, which cannot be pooled with the sovereignty of other demoi. Again, there is a strong parallel here with some criticisms of the traditional understanding of unconstrained constituent power, which can lead to 'an undemocratic notion of the people as an organ, which is necessarily a non-inclusive notion (. . .). Who belongs in the people? The Catholics? The nationals? The poor? The majority?'.[92] This criticism can be redirected to the Eurosceptic understanding that EU institutions undermine national sovereignty. This is because European integration can also be understood as a way in which to exercise sovereignty in common with other peoples. This understanding, however, is not possible if one takes

[90] Sergio Verdugo, 'Is It Time to Abandon the Theory of Constituent Power?' (2023) 21 International Journal of Constitutional Law 14, 23.
[91] Verdugo (n 90) 34.
[92] Verdugo (n 90) 38.

an exclusionary view of the demos according to which cooperation is an illegitimate constraint on national sovereignty.

6.6. Conclusion

This chapter has analysed the Eurosceptic mobilization of constitutional law in Spain. The focus on this country allowed us to carry out interesting research on the nuanced differences and the surprising similarities between left-wing and right-wing Eurosceptic constitutional counter-narratives. Spain has traditionally been seen to be a strongly Europhile country, despite the existence of some Eurocritical parties like Izquierda Unida. However, in the transformation of the Spanish political landscape in recent years, parties such as Podemos (on the radical left) and Vox (on the radical right) have emerged, questioning—and at times attacking—the status quo of the European integration process. To do this, all these parties resort to different forms of constitutional counter-narratives. This is consistent with findings in the political science literature:

> [R]ejection of the EU by the extreme parties is due to different causes. Podemos argues that the integration of Spain into the European Union accelerated the penetration of neoliberalism. In turn, Vox opposes membership because European integration would boost the transfer of competences to a supranational tier of governance and undermine Spanish national sovereignty. (. . .) it seems that Podemos is more Eurocritic than Eurosceptic; its rejection of the EU has more to do with the current management of the EU than with its nature. It is worth noting that Vox maintains a very ambiguous position on the EU.[93]

These ideas have been directly translated into counter-narratives integrating and mobilizing constitutional concepts. For parties on the left, the Euro-crisis seemed to be an important catalyst in the construction of their most recent constitutional counter-narratives. For these parties, the reform of article 135 of the Spanish Constitution was an attack on Spanish constitutional sovereignty. Interestingly, on the right, Vox also considered that Spanish sovereignty and the Spanish Constitution were undermined by the process of European

[93] Beatriz Carrasco, Elena González, and Jean-Baptiste Harguindéguy, 'Euroscepticism in Spain: A Phenomenon of Extremes?' in Xavier Coller and Leonardo Sánchez-Ferrer (eds), *Politicians in Hard Times: Spanish and South European MPs Facing Citizens after the Great Recession* (Springer International Publishing 2021) 264.

integration. This party, however, did not focus on the Euro-crisis. Instead, it made a general criticism of what it considered to be an expansive approach to its powers by the EU.

Thus, the same core concepts—constitutionalism, sovereignty, and even democracy—are present in the Eurosceptic counter-narratives of parties on the left and the right, but they are articulated in different ways and take place in the context of divergent discourses about the relationship between Spain and the process of European integration. Perhaps the most significant difference has to do with the proposals and the visions of these parties for the future of Europe. While parties like Izquierda Unida and Podemos have advocated for alternative forms of the constitutionalization of Europe, Vox appears to reject this idea altogether. Instead, it has adopted an assertive, nationalist approach to the Spanish Constitution—going so far as to assert the absolute and unconditional supremacy of the national Constitution over EU law and to challenge the authority of the ECJ.

7

Continuity and Discontinuity in Polish Euroscepticism

Before, During, and After the Government of Illiberal Populists*

7.1. Governing the Transition: Why Polish Euroscepticism (Still) Matters

Poland is a fascinating mix of Euroscepticism, illiberalism,[1] and populism, as well as a system undergoing a delicate political transition. Nawrocki's election as president before the summer of 2025 reflects the complexity of the political context. Indeed, the new government—headed by Donald Tusk—faces significant challenges, having inherited a system deeply affected by the illiberal policies of the Prawo i Sprawiedliwość ('Law and Justice', PiS) government.[2] The Polish case, then, is a context characterized by a government that is not Eurosceptic but yet exhibits some friction with the European Union due to the pockets of resistance still present in the judiciary after the court-packing[3] carried out during Mateusz Morawiecki's government(s).

In this respect, the new government is facing a real dilemma concerning making the Polish judiciary less illiberal without violating the ideal of the rule of law. This is a real conundrum that is the focus of attention of numerous

* Unless otherwise indicated, all the election manifestos of the political parties discussed in this chapter are available at the following link <https://manifestoproject.wzb.eu./>.

[1] Illiberalism is a much-used word in the literature, but for the purposes of this book, this concept refers to a gradual moving away from the protection of liberal values. In other words, it can be used to describe a phase of transition, a detachment or a partial divergence from liberal values. This is why we also accept the distinction made by authors such as Walker between anti-liberalism and illiberalism. According to this distinction, 'illiberalism views the purpose and priorities of government by other standards, according to which liberal values are treated as secondary and at least in some measure dispensable', Neil Walker, 'Illiberalism and National Sovereignty' in András Sajó, Renata Uitz, and Stephen Holmes (eds), *The Routledge Handbook of Illiberalism* (Routledge 2022) 250, 250.

[2] Among others, see Wojciech Sadurski, *Poland's Constitutional Breakdown* (Oxford University Press 2023).

[3] On court-packing in a comparative perspective, see David Kosař and Katarína Šipulová, 'Comparative Court-packing' (2023) 21 International Journal of Constitutional Law 80, 85–86.

The Eurosceptic Mobilization of Constitutional Law. Pablo Castillo-Ortiz and Giuseppe Martinico, Oxford University Press. © Pablo Castillo-Ortiz and Giuseppe Martinico 2026. DOI: 10.1093/9780198959205.003.0007

scholars[4]—and of the Venice Commission of course[5]—and makes the Polish case a unique one for those interested in how to repair a system affected by the damage of illiberal reforms.[6]

As we have seen in previous chapters, we regard populism and Euroscepticism as two abstractly distinguishable phenomena, but we also think that in practice there can often be overlaps. Indeed, Kopecký and Mudde,[7] who wrote a fundamental piece on Euroscepticism several years ago, treated the Polish case as emblematic, describing PiS as an 'authoritarian and populist platform'.[8]

Scholars have pointed out that the Polish context is a laboratory of great interest for the study of populism, as populism has been seen as a distinctive trait of all the mainstream parties in Poland.[9] In this sense, it has been said that the characteristics of populism in Central and Eastern European countries are different from those in Western European countries. In fact, in the case of the Eastern European countries, the particular features of local populism are also partly related to the transformation of the political systems that took place in the post-communist phase.[10] In this respect, it has been argued that, unlike the populist wave in Western Europe, the driving forces in Poland were less the

[4] Gábor Halmai, 'Can the Rule of Law Be Restored by Violating Its Principles? The Current Polish Debate' 3 January 2025 <https://verfassungsblog.de/can-the-rule-of-law-be-restored-by-violating-its-principles/>; see also Kim Lane Scheppele, 'Blinded by Legality' (23 December 2024) <https://verfassungsblog.de/blinded-by-legality/>.

[5] European Commission for Democracy through Law, 'CDL-AD(2024)029-e Poland—Joint Opinion of the Venice Commission and the Directorate General Human Rights and Rule of Law on European standards regulating the status of judges, adopted by the Venice Commission at its 140th Plenary Session' (Venice, 11–12 October 2024) <https://www.venice.coe.int/webforms/documents/?pdf=CDL-AD(2024)029-e>; European Commission for Democracy through Law, 'CDL-AD(2024)035-e Poland – Opinion on the draft constitutional amendments concerning the Constitutional Tribunal and two draft laws on the Constitutional Tribunal, adopted by the Venice Commission at its 141st Plenary Session' (Venice, 6–7 December 2024) <https://www.venice.coe.int/webforms/documents/?pdf=CDL-AD(2024)035-e>.

[6] Tom Gerald Daly, 'Constitutional Repair: A Comparative Theory' DEM-DEC Constitutional Repair Working Paper No 2-2023 <https://static1.squarespace.com/static/5abb53e6372b9691939ac577/t/6579c25840e061704144ad1a/1702478428708/DEM-DEC+WP_2-2023_Daly.pdf>. See also Tom Gerald Daly, '"Good" Court-Packing? The Paradoxes of Constitutional Repair in Contexts of Democratic Decay' DEM-DEC Constitutional Repair Working Paper No 1-2022 <https://static1.squarespace.com/static/5abb53e6372b9691939ac577/t/62319932d81fcf4a32a9e2e0/1647417654829/DEM-DEC+WP_2022-1_Daly_v2.pdf>.

[7] Petr Kopecký and Cas Mudde, 'The Two Sides of Euroscepticism: Party Positions on European Integration in East Central Europe' (2002) 3 European Union Politics 297, 310–313.

[8] Kopecký and Mudde (n 7) 312.

[9] Natasza Styczyńska, 'Contesting European Union from the "Heart of Europe": A Peculiar Case of Polish Populist Euroscepticism after 2015' (2023) 0 Political Studies Review 1, 3.

[10] 'While in Western Europe populism emerged on the fringes of the political spectrum and is often stimulated by disappointment with democracy, the case of CEE is different. In the post-communist CEE region, populism developed during the post-communist transformation period together with the construction of democratic institutions and currently occupies the mainstream of politics', Styczyńska (n 9) 2–3.

result of economic factors—such as the effects of austerity policies—and more the result of values and identity issues. As we shall see, these issues were also central to the mobilization led by the Eurosceptic movements.

This populist substratum in the rhetoric of many Polish parties has, to some extent, fostered the explosion of the recent Eurosceptic wave. The beginnings of this wave can be traced back to the post-enlargement past, starting with the coalition between PiS and the League of Polish Families and Self-Defence of the Republic of Poland in 2005–2007[11] and going through to 2015 and the outbreak of the refugee crisis.

This combination of populism and Euroscepticism has led to a particular understanding of the well-known dichotomous approach that is characteristic of populisms:

> Since 2015 the populist and anti-elitist narrative moved to the mainstream of the political and public discourse pointing out the dichotomy between 'pure people' and the 'corrupted elite'. According to the parties in power, the latter one is located either on the international level (EU institutions) or is organised around the opposition parties who are still informally influencing Polish politics through the so-called post-communist 'clique' (. . .). The populist worldview of the ruling PiS-led coalition is applied to the EU level where the elite is located in Brussels or large member states (e.g. Germany), while pure people are understood as Poles (nation) rather than the 'European people'. EU institutions, especially the European Commission, are criticised for not being democratic enough as are not directly elected. Moreover, they are accused of imposing a certain way of life and attempting to undermine traditional values, national identity and the role of religion.[12]

Another important element, which we also find in the Italian case, is that the Euroscepticism of the old governing majority, particularly PiS, does not present itself as radically anti-European. Here, in fact, we again find the distinction already encountered elsewhere between Europe and the European Union, the latter seen as dominated by Western values imbued by liberalism, the protection of minority rights, secularism, and multiculturalism. Another element common to the Italian and Polish cases is the anti-German rhetoric

[11] Aleksandra Moroska-Bonkiewicz, 'Political Responses to the Extreme Right in Poland. Motivations and Constraints for Collaboration in the Executive Arena' (2019) 47 Studia Polityczne 65.
[12] Styczyńska (n 9) 4.

that characterizes the Eurosceptic approach in these two countries.[13] In this rhetoric,

> Poland is portrayed as the 'heart of Europe', but also the last frontier consequently making Eastern Europe a bulwark of Christianity and true European values (...). Both the PiS-led coalition and nationalistic Konfederacja claim that Western Europe lost their moral compass, and nowadays we are facing a struggle between the Christian-rooted values of Europe and the 'decadent influence of the West'.[14]

This identitarian component and the polemic about the idea of the EU as a threat to Christian values can be found in the Hungarian case, together with a certain amount of nativism, at least with reference to the refugee issue (with the partial exception of refugees from the Ukrainian context). Poland is also presented as the 'heart of Europe', positioned as the catalyst for a radical change in the EU. This idea can be compared with what was written about Italian identitarian sovereignism. It led PiS to instrumentalize the argument of tradition[15] and religion, with an indirect impact on the case law of the Polish Constitutional Court once it had been captured by the then Eurosceptic and populist majority. Indeed, during its years in government, PiS developed conservative policies, including, for example, a series of policies aimed at banning abortion and developing anti-LGBTIQ+ rhetoric.[16] From this perspective, too, Poland is a laboratory.

Against this background, the Polish case is comparable to the Hungarian one, as there are many similarities with regard to the handling of power by the Hungarian government and by the former Polish one. At the same time, we will in this chapter highlight some crucial differences, one of them being, of course, the parliamentary numbers, which prevented the previous majority from making the same use of constitutional amendments as was done in Hungary. This is certainly an important difference, but, as we have tried

[13] Commons Library Research Briefing, 13 February 2024 <https://researchbriefings.files.parliament.uk/documents/CBP-9868/CBP-9868.pdf>.

[14] Styczyńska (n 9) 5.

[15] 'When studying contemporary CEE, neo-traditionalist political narratives are often placed in the context of the post-communist transformation and closer integration with Western Europe', Natasza Styczyńska and Jan Meijer, 'Populist Euroscepticism in Poland: Towards a Framework for Analysis' in Haris Dajč and Natasza Styczyńska (eds), *Faces of Populism in Central and South-Eastern Europe* (Jagiellonian University Press 2023) 177, 183.

[16] Stefano Fella, 'Poland: The Law and Justice Government and Relations with the EU, 2015–2023' Commons Library Research Briefing (13 February 2024) <https://researchbriefings.files.parliament.uk/documents/CBP-9868/CBP-9868.pdf>.

to emphasize elsewhere,[17] the impact of populisms on constitutional democracies is not limited to the (albeit very important) issues of unconstitutional constitutional amendments[18] or the abuse of emergency powers,[19] but is much more subtle. Populisms tend to erode the structures of constitutional democracy by following other strategies, for instance through the creation of constitutional counter-narratives. Indeed, populists do not always succeed in amending the constitution, and such an amendment is not the only strategy followed by populists to attack the constitution:

> Populists in power usually stay away from constitutional amendment and tend to prefer constitutional replacement, or unilateral major constitutional changes, as in the cases of Venezuela, Ecuador and Turkey (. . .). Constitutional replacement may be preceded by specific amendments, removing any possible constitutional hurdles to the populist project of constitutional replacement. This was the case in Hungary. However, constitutional amendment is not always available as a constitutional tool (in the sense used by Blokker's "instrumentalism";[. . .]) serving populists' projects of constitution-making.[20]

Poland is also an excellent case study because, unlike Spain and Italy, it is not a member of the Eurozone. This also allows us to compare the Polish case with the British case described in Chapter 4.

Poland still uses its national currency, the Polish *złoty*.[21] Moreover, there is another factor of (potential) asymmetry that applies to both the Polish and the UK cases, Poland and the UK having negotiated the adoption of a specific Protocol (No 30) aimed at limiting the justiciability of certain provisions of the Charter of Fundamental Rights of the EU.[22]

[17] Giuseppe Martinico, *Filtering Populist Claims to Fight Populism: The Italian Case in a Comparative Perspective* (Cambridge University Press 2021).

[18] Using a concept described by Yaniv Roznai, *Unconstitutional Constitutional Amendments: The Limits of Amendment Powers* (Oxford University Press 2019).

[19] Patrick Gardiner, 'Conflating the Powers of the Commissarial and the Sovereign Dictator in Tunisia' 29 November 2022 <https://verfassungsblog.de/conflating-the-powers-of-the-commissarial-and-the-sovereign-dictator-in-tunisia/>.

[20] Pietro Faraguna, 'Populism and Constitutional Amendment' in Giacomo Delledonne, Giuseppe Martinico, Matteo Monti, and Fabio Pacini (eds), *Italian Populism and Constitutional Law. Strategies, Conflicts and Dilemmas* (Palgrave 2020) 97, 105.

[21] 'Prime Minister Morawiecki warned against Polish membership of the euro in a news conference in January 2023. He also referred to the recent adoption of the euro in Croatia and said this had caused "chaos" and a cost-of-living spike with prices increasing to "exorbitant" levels. He said this should serve as a warning to Poland, and that Polish adoption of the euro would similarly increase inflation, which at that point was above 17% in Poland' Fella (n 16) 15.

[22] Protocol (No 30) reads: '1. The charter does not extend the ability of the Court of Justice of the European Union, or any court or tribunal of Poland or of the United Kingdom, to find that the laws,

This Protocol has sometimes been portrayed as an opt-out, but such a characterization would not be accurate.[23] However, the ECJ clarified its view on this Protocol in the *NS* judgment, by confirming that Protocol No 30 'does not call into question the applicability of the Charter in the United Kingdom or in Poland'.[24]

In this chapter, we first try to reconstruct the constitutional frame[25] of reference and then examine the arguments used by Eurosceptic forces in constructing their constitutional counter-narratives. We will also discuss these Eurosceptic arguments in connection with illiberalism and civil society actors, as well as their practical implementation. We then present a critique of these arguments before concluding the chapter.

7.2. Polish Constitutional Law and European Integration in a Comparative Perspective

The Polish Constitution is part of a constitutional wave with cross-country commonalities. Albi, commenting on the text of Eastern European constitutions, describes them as being characterized by a great emphasis on the protection of sovereignty.[26] In other words, although these constitutions recognize

regulations or administrative provisions, practices or action of Poland or of the United Kingdom are inconsistent with the fundamental rights, freedoms and principles that it reaffirms. 2. In particular, and for the avoidance of doubt, nothing in Title IV of the charter creates justiciable rights applicable to Poland or the United Kingdom except in so far as Poland or the United Kingdom has provided for such rights in its national law'.

[23] 'The opt-out is not an opt-out at all', Catherine Barnard, 'The "Opt-out" for the UK and Poland from the Charter of Fundamental Rights: Triumph of Rhetoric over Reality?' (The Lisbon Treaty and the Future of European Constitutionalism conference, 11–12 April 2008, EUI, Fiesole), on file with author. Confirmation of this hypothesis can be found in the words of the House of Lords EU Select Committee: 'The Protocol is not an opt-out from the Charter. The Charter will apply in the UK, even if its interpretation may be affected by the terms of the Protocol. The Preamble itself of the document does not use the qualification in terms of opt-out, its goal consists of the clarification of certain aspects of the application of the Charter', House of Lords EU Select Committee, 'The Treaty of Lisbon: An Impact Assessment' 13 March 2008 <https://publications.parliament.uk/pa/ld200708/ldselect/ldeucom/62/62.pdf>.

[24] ECJ, Case C-411/10 *NS & Others v SSHD* and Case C-493/10 *M.E. and Others v Refugee Applications Commissioner, Minister for Justice, Equality and Law Reform* ECLI:EU:C:2011:865: 'In those circumstances, Article 1(1) of Protocol (N. 30) explains Article 51 of the Charter with regard to the scope thereof and does not intend to exempt the Republic of Poland or the United Kingdom from the obligation to comply with the provisions of the Charter or to prevent a court of one of those Member States from ensuring compliance with those provisions' (paras 116–120).

[25] On the Polish constitutional system, see Miroslaw Granat and Katarzyna Granat, *The Constitution of Poland. A Contextual Analysis* (Hart Publishing 2019).

[26] Anneli Albi, '"Europe" Articles in the Constitutions of Central and Eastern European Countries' (2005) 42 Common Market Law Review 399; Anneli Albi, 'Bringing Parliaments into the Equation of "Co-operative Constitutionalism"' (2007) 3 European Constitutional Law Review 25.

the authority of EU law—either by devoting specific clauses to it or by absorbing the reference into norms relating to international law—they almost always add a caveat. This openness to external law, they specify, cannot affect constitutional supremacy or national sovereignty (normally distinguished from the concept of independence).[27] This is not just a rhetorical point; as we shall see, this element also has an important substantive component. Another relevant factor is the mindset of jurists in these countries: as Rodin and Kühn[28] have observed, a jurist in these countries follows an approach of textual positivism, which clashes with the heavy use of teleological interpretation in the case law of the ECJ.[29]

Concerning the constitutional framework in Poland, article 8 of the Constitution provides that '1. The Constitution shall be the supreme law of the Republic of Poland. 2. The provisions of the Constitution shall apply directly, unless the Constitution provides otherwise'. Another relevant provision is article 9, which states that 'The Republic of Poland shall respect international law binding upon it'.[30] Also noteworthy is article 90, which concerns the possibility of delegating 'to an international organization or international institution the competence of organs of State authority in relation to certain matters'.[31] International agreements are listed in article 87[32] as being among the binding legal sources, and a ratified international agreement shall be 'applied directly, unless its application depends on the enactment of a statute' (article 91(1)).

[27] 'The former implies internal sovereignty, referring to the State's power competences, and the latter denotes external sovereignty—connoting an independent statehood in the international arena', Albi, '"Europe" Articles' (n 26) 403.

[28] Zdeněk Kühn, 'The Application of European Law in the New Member States: Several (Early) Predictions' (2005) 6 German Law Journal 563; Siniša Rodin, 'Discourse and Authority in European and Post-Communist Legal Culture' (2008) 1 Croatian Yearbook of European Law and Policy 1.

[29] Albi, 'Bringing Parliaments into the Equation' (n 26) 33.

[30] Article 9 of the Polish Constitution.

[31] Article 90 of the Polish Constitution:

> The Republic of Poland may, by virtue of international agreements, delegate to an international organization or international institution the competence of organs of State authority in relation to certain matters.
>
> A statute, granting consent for ratification of an international agreement referred to in para 1, shall be passed by the Sejm by a two-thirds majority vote in the presence of at least half of the statutory number of Deputies, and by the Senate by a two-thirds majority vote in the presence of at least half of the statutory number of Senators.
>
> Granting of consent for ratification of such agreement may also be passed by a nationwide referendum in accordance with the provisions of Article 125.
>
> Any resolution in respect of the choice of procedure for granting consent to ratification shall be taken by the Sejm by an absolute majority vote taken in the presence of at least half of the statutory number of Deputies.

[32] Article 87 of the Polish Constitution: 'The sources of universally binding law of the Republic of Poland shall be: the Constitution, statutes, ratified international agreements, and regulations. Enactments of local law issued by the operation of organs shall be a source of universally binding law of the Republic of Poland in the territory of the organ issuing such enactments'.

According to article 91(2): 'An international agreement ratified upon prior consent granted by statute shall have precedence over statutes if such an agreement cannot be reconciled with the provisions of such statutes'.[33]

Article 188 of the Constitution empowers the Polish Constitutional Court to adjudicate on the conformity of national laws with ratified international agreements and, at the same time, to check the conformity of international agreements with the Constitution, seen as the supreme law of the land.[34] Finally, article 193 of the Constitution empowers national courts to raise *incidenter* questions to the Constitutional Court in the case of conflict with a ratified international agreement or statute, 'if the answer to such a question is decisive for the determination of an issue pending before such court'.[35]

EU law has had a significant impact on the Polish system. The first important decisions in which the Polish Constitutional Court dealt with the issue of the primacy of EU law were the Accession Treaty case[36] and the European Arrest Warrant case.[37] In the first of these, the Constitutional Court verified the constitutionality of the Accession Treaty on the basis of article 188 of the Constitution, rejecting all the grounds raised by the applicants. However, as Kowalik-Bańczyk stressed:

> [T]he sole fact of accepting the competence to control legality of [the] Accession Treaty might be seen as problematic: it implicitly indicates that the Constitutional Tribunal considers that the national Constitution can be a basis for this type of control. However, it is mainly the reasoning of the Constitutional Tribunal that seems quite particular and raises the serious question of acceptance (or rather lack of acceptance) of supremacy of European law over Constitution in Poland.[38]

[33] Krystyna Kowalik-Bańczyk, 'Report on Poland' in Giuseppe Martinico and Oreste Pollicino (eds), *The National Judicial Treatment of the ECHR and EU Laws* (Europa Law Publishing 2010) 327, 330.

[34] Article 188 of the Polish Constitution: 'The Constitutional Tribunal shall adjudicate regarding the following matters:

> the conformity of statutes and international agreements to the Constitution;
> the conformity of a statute to ratified international agreements whose ratification required prior consent granted by statute;
> the conformity of legal provisions issued by central State organs to the Constitution, ratified international agreements and statutes;
> the conformity to the Constitution of the purposes or activities of political parties;
> complaints concerning constitutional infringements, as specified in Article 79, para. 1'.

[35] Article 193 of the Polish Constitution: 'Any court may refer a question of law to the Constitutional Tribunal as to the conformity of a normative act to the Constitution, ratified international agreements or statute, if the answer to such question of law will determine an issue currently before such court'.

[36] Polish Constitutional Court, decision K 18/04, 11 May 2005 <https://trybunal.gov.pl/>.

[37] Polish Constitutional Court, decision P 1/05, 27 April 2005 <https://trybunal.gov.pl/>.

[38] Krystyna Kowalik-Bańczyk, 'Should We Polish It Up? The Polish Constitutional Tribunal and the Idea of Supremacy of EU Law' (2005) 6 German Law Journal 1355, 1363–1364.

In the second case, the Constitutional Court exerted pressure on the Polish Parliament to induce a constitutional amendment,[39] while nonetheless maintaining that 'the Constitution remains the most important source of law, superior over international instruments (including EU law)'.[40] This decision is paradoxical, as the Constitutional Court appeared highly deferential towards the EU legal order, even though it ultimately declared a national provision enacted to implement the Framework Decision on the European Arrest Warrant to be invalid.[41]

Indeed, although in this judgment the Polish Constitutional Court declared the national law to be unconstitutional, some authors have argued that the decision is significantly more Europeanist than the ruling concerning the Accession Treaty, because of the remarkable effort made by the Court to find a possible conforming interpretation—for example, by attempting to distinguish between extradition and surrender.[42] What happened was that the wording of article 55 of the Constitution—prohibiting the extradition of Polish citizens—left the Court with no room for manoeuvre: the literal text of the Polish Constitution was simply too clear to allow the national provisions to be upheld.

In this respect, the decision on the Accession Treaty[43] was less pro-European. On that occasion, the Constitutional Court declared the Treaty to be consistent with the Constitution, but at the same time sent a strong message to the ECJ, emphasizing the existence of a hard constitutional nucleus that could not be affected by European integration, and drawing a distinction between constitutional sovereignty and the primacy of EU law.

However, the Polish Constitutional Court appeared to accept the primacy of EU law over national legislation (the relationship with the Constitution is, as noted, more complex), as well as the disapplication of national law in cases

[39] As Kowalik-Bańczyk has written: 'The Tribunal therefore used all the means available to it to milder its judgment and allow Poland continue fulfilling its EU obligations. Taking into account those arguments, it seemed that in this judgment the Tribunal went further than the existing practice—it implicitly accepted the supremacy of EU law over constitutional norms. It however denied that supremacy only two weeks later in the judgment on Accession Treaty', Kowalik-Bańczyk, 'Should We Polish It Up?' (n 38) 1361.

[40] Kowalik-Bańczyk, 'Should We Polish It Up?' (n 38) 1356; Kowalik-Bańczyk, 'Report on Poland' (n 33) 334. Polish Constitutional Court, decision K 18/04, 11 May 2005 <https://trybunal.gov.pl/>.

[41] 'Paradoxically, the first one—invalidating a provision of Polish Criminal Procedure Code—might be seen as a sign of respect for Polish international obligations stemming from the EU law. The second, confirming the validity of Accession Treaty of 2003, is a clear refusal of supremacy of this Treaty over national Constitution', Kowalik-Bańczyk, 'Should We Polish It Up?' (n 38) 1358.

[42] Kowalik-Bańczyk, 'Should We Polish It Up?' (n 38).

[43] Polish Constitutional Court, decision K 18/04, 11 May 2005 <https://trybunal.gov.pl/>.

of conflict with EU provisions.[44] Nevertheless, the primacy of EU law was regarded as the result of a self-limitation by the state.[45]

The Polish courts, after some initial tensions, accepted the *Simmenthal* doctrine[46] and same applies (in spite of the recent developments that we will come to later) to the traditional case law of the Polish Constitutional Court.[47]

The Constitutional Court has referred a preliminary question to the ECJ.[48] As mentioned above, article 193 of the Constitution permits judges to raise *incidenter* questions to the Constitutional Court in case of a conflict with a ratified international agreement or statute, 'if the answer to such a question is decisive for the determination of an issue pending before such court'. The duty of the judges in these cases has been interpreted in different ways by the Supreme and the Constitutional Courts.[49] In its case law, the Constitutional Court has argued that it 'does not require the national courts to raise the *incidenter* question where the conflict between the EU and Polish provisions appears. The courts are expected to either independently disapply the conflicting Polish provision or to ask the preliminary question to the ECJ'.[50]

The Polish Constitutional Court also joined the club of constitutional courts that have decided on the compatibility of the Lisbon Treaty and the Constitution. By engaging in extended reflections on sovereignty and comparative constitutional doctrine, the Polish Court endorsed the possibility of ultra vires control over EU acts, implicitly signalling to the Court of Justice its intention to defend the core principles of the Polish Constitution.[51]

Among the most significant rulings of the Polish Constitutional Court, which has been captured by political power, are three decisions that have also been the subject of studies commissioned by the European Parliament's Committee on Legal Affairs.[52]

[44] Polish Constitutional Court, order P 37/05 (19 December 2006) <https://trybunal.gov.pl/>.

[45] Polish Constitutional Court, decision P 1/05 (27 April 2005) <https://trybunal.gov.pl/>.

[46] Warsaw Administrative Court, judgments of 12 October 2005, III SA/Wa 2219/05, of 4 August 2006, III SA/Wa 1381/06 of 21 June 2006, III SA/Wa 656/6, of 5 April 2007, III SA/Wa 223/07 of 14 June 2006, III SA/Wa 1101/06; Lublin Administrative Court, judgment of 25 May 2005, I SA/Lu 77/; Białystok Administrative Court, judgment of 6 February 2007, I SA/Bk 406/06. All reported in Kowalik-Bańczyk, 'Report on Poland' (n 33).

[47] Polish Constitutional Court, order P 37/05 (19 December 2006) <https://trybunal.gov.pl/>.

[48] ECJ, Case C-390/15 *Rzecznik Praw Obywatelskich (RPO)* ECLI:EU:C:2017:174.

[49] Kowalik-Bańczyk, 'Report on Poland' (n 33).

[50] Kowalik-Bańczyk (n 33) 339.

[51] Polish Constitutional Court, decision K 32/09 <http://www.trybunal.gov.pl>.

[52] Fryderyk Zoll, Katarzyna Południak-Gierz, and Wojciech Bańczyk, 'Primacy of EU Law and Jurisprudence of Polish Constitutional Tribunal' Policy Department for Citizens' Rights and Constitutional Affairs Directorate-General for Internal Policies PE 732.475, 2022 <https://www.europarl.europa.eu/RegData/etudes/STUD/2022/732475/IPOL_STU(2022)732475_EN.pdf>.

The first significant ruling is U 2/20,[53] in which Polish constitutional judges declared a decision of the Supreme Court—issued in accordance with three rulings from the Court of Justice[54]—to be incompatible with the Constitution. This ruling constituted an indirect attack on the principle of primacy, which was justified by the Constitutional Court on the grounds that the Supreme Court had not adequately implemented the Court of Justice's decision. However, this justification was merely a superficial argument that, in reality, served to undermine the proper implementation of supranational case law and was in fact pronounced at the request of the prime minister.[55]

The second judgment was P 7/20,[56] and was given in response to interim measures ordered by the Court of Justice, consisting in the suspension of provisions relating to the powers of the Disciplinary Chamber of the Supreme Court 'to rule, both at first instance and on appeal, in disciplinary cases concerning judges'.[57] On that occasion, the Court of Justice had spoken of 'a panel that does not meet the requirements of independence defined, inter alia, in the judgment of 19 November 2019, A. K. and Others'.[58]

The Court of Justice would later return to the issue in Case C-791/19,[59] condemning Poland for, among other things, failing to guarantee the independence and impartiality of the Disciplinary Chamber. The interim measures requested by the Court of Justice triggered the reaction of the Polish Constitutional Court. For the Constitutional Court, the provisional measures requested by the Court of Justice amounted to ultra vires obligations—that is, they exceeded the competences of the EU—because they affected the organization of the Polish judiciary, a matter reserved to the national legislator. As these obligations went beyond the scope of supranational competences, the decision of the Polish Constitutional Court was presented as being in line with the principle of the primacy of EU law, which applies only when EU acts touch on competences reserved to itself. Furthermore, the Court argued that, in this case, there had been a violation of constitutional supremacy. In any event, it stressed the need for a strict interpretation of the transfers of sovereignty permitted by

[53] Polish Constitutional Court, decision U 2/20 <http://www.trybunal.gov.pl>.
[54] ECJ, Joined Cases C-585/18, C-624/18, and C-625/18 *A.K. and Others v Sąd Najwyższy* ECLI:EU:C:2019:982.
[55] Zoll, Południak-Gierz, and Bańczyk (n 52) 20.
[56] Polish Constitutional Court, decision P 7/20 <http://www.trybunal.gov.pl>.
[57] ECJ, Case C-791/19 R, Order of the Court (Grand Chamber) *European Commission v Republic of Poland* ECLI:EU:C:2020:277.
[58] ECJ, Case C-791/19 R, Order of the Court (Grand Chamber) *European Commission v Republic of Poland* ECLI:EU:C:2020:277.
[59] ECJ, Case C-791/19 *European Commission v Republic of Poland* ECLI:EU:C:2021:596.

the Polish Constitution. For this reason, it concluded that the decision did not amount to a challenge to the primacy of EU law as such.

Finally, the most radical judgment, which we will analyse later, was judgment K 3/21[60] in which the Polish Constitutional Court ruled that certain provisions of the TEU conflict with the Polish Constitution. It argued that interpreting EU law in a way that compels Polish courts to issue rulings disregarding the Polish Constitution or applying unconstitutional laws violates several constitutional provisions.[61] Moreover, it ruled that article 19(1) TEU, when read with article 4(3) TEU, unlawfully allows Polish courts to apply laws that have previously been declared unconstitutional.[62] Lastly, the Court declared that article 19(1) TEU, when interpreted in conjunction with article 2 TEU to mean that courts are empowered to review judicial appointments made by the President or the National Council of the Judiciary, contradicts certain provisions of the Polish Constitution.[63]

7.3. Patterns of Eurosceptic Mobilization of Constitutional Law Arguments in Poland

The Eurosceptic mobilization of constitutional law has been common in Poland too, and here Eurosceptic actors have actually challenged the EU legal system in practice. In this chapter, we focus on the PiS party, as it has led some Polish governments that were characterized not only by strong Eurosceptic rhetoric but also by actual confrontation with the EU.

[60] Polish Constitutional Court, decision K 3/21 <http://www.trybunal.gov.pl>. This ruling has also led to proceedings brought by the European Commission against the Republic of Poland, which have now been decided by the Court of Justice, holding that Poland has failed to fulfil its obligations under EU law: ECJ, C-448/23 *European Commission v Republic of Poland* ECLI:EU:C:2025:975. On this, see Giacomo Di Federico, 'In the Name of Primacy. Opinion C-448/23 and the EU's Existential Principle of Primacy' (22 April 2025) <https://verfassungsblog.de/polishing-broken-tribunal/>.

[61] Namely articles 2 ('The Republic of Poland shall be a democratic state ruled by law and implementing the principles of social justice'), 7 ('The organs of public authority shall function on the basis of, and within the limits of, the law'), and 8(1), read together with articles 8(2), 90(1), 91(2), and 178(1) ('Judges, within the exercise of their office, shall be independent and subject only to the Constitution and statutes') of the Polish Constitution.

[62] Namely articles 2, 7, and 8(1), read together with articles 8(2), 91(2), 90(1), and 178(1), as well as article 190(1), of the Polish Constitution.

[63] Namely article 8(1), read together with articles 8(2), 90(1), 91(2), 144(3) (about presidential official acts needing the countersignature of the Prime Minister, with exceptions), 17 ('by means of a statute, self-governments may be created within a profession in which the public repose confidence, and such self-governments shall concern themselves with the proper practice of such professions in accordance with, and for the purpose of protecting, the public interest. Other forms of self-government shall also be created by means of statute. Such self-governments shall not infringe the freedom to practice a profession nor limit the freedom to undertake economic activity') and 186(1) ('the National Council of the Judiciary shall safeguard the independence of courts and judges').

PiS is a far-right party that was created by the Kaczyński twins in 2001; initially, it had a conservative approach, and it has gradually become more radical over the years. One of its founders, Lech Kaczyński, was President of Poland from 2005 to 2010, until he died in a plane crash. PiS presents itself as a conservative, anti-immigration, Eurosceptic, and anti-Russian political force, the latter feature being decisive on the issue of aid to Ukraine after Russian aggression. The party was first in government with Samoobrona Rzeczpospolitej Polskiej ('Self-Defence of the Republic of Poland') and the Liga Polskich Rodzin ('League of Polish Families') after the 2005 elections. Samoobrona Rzeczpospolitej Polskiej and the Liga Polskich Rodzin[64] have de facto disappeared from the Polish party landscape, but PiS, in contrast, returned to power from 2015 to 2023. During the last PiS-led government, the coalition was formally known as Zjednoczona Prawica ('United Right'). The other members of this coalition were Solidarna Polska ('United Poland', SP), led by Zbigniew Ziobro and perhaps an even more radical force than PiS on issues of national sovereignty and criticism of the European Union, and Porozumienie ('Agreement'), founded by Jarosław Gowin. Porozumienie left the coalition in 2021, causing the coalition to weaken. PiS is characterized by a nationalist and conservative vision of Poland and emphasizes the importance of traditional values, Catholicism, and national sovereignty. The party opposes what it sees as foreign influence, particularly from the European Union and liberal Western elites.

Scholars[65] have analysed the identity and evolution of PiS, starting with its Political Manifesto of June 2001. It is interesting to examine the evolving nature of PiS over time, particularly its transformation in relation to the Christian component of its conservatism:

> In its founding manifesto of 2001, the party did not openly avow any political or historical tradition, bar anti-communism. Yet it positively noted the periods and actions described as 'heroic'. These were, specifically, the interwar Second Polish Republic (1918–1939), the struggle against German and Soviet oppression, and the activities of Solidarity. In foreign policy, the party endorsed a pro-Western orientation (. . .). What is surprising from

[64] The former leader of the League of Polish Families, Roman Giertych, has become a strong critic of PiS and aligned himself with opposition groups during the PiS government.

[65] Adam Folvarčný and Lubomír Kopeček, 'Which Conservatism? The Identity of the Polish Law and Justice Party' (2020) 16 Politics in Central Europe 159; Klaudia Cymer, 'The Rise of Euroscepticism on the Political Scene in Poland—The Case of the Party Law and Justice' (2022) 10 European Studies Quarterly 89, 93; Melissa Stolfi, 'The "Revival" of PiS: The Transformation of Campaign Strategies from the Kaczyński Twins to Andrzej Duda' (2024) 10 Journal of Liberty and International Affairs 14.

> today's perspective is that there was originally no strong identification of the party with the Catholic Church, although the manifesto did, of course, mention Christianity. This started to change around 2005.[66]

The 2001 manifesto touched upon the question of possible (at that time) EU membership, and devoted one section, entitled 'Our Place in Europe', to it. In that passage, EU membership was seen as the fruit of a well-considered choice that should not, however, in any way undermine the country's national identity.[67]

This form of Euroscepticism did not seem to disappear, and indeed went on to feature in the political practice of the party, albeit that PiS used constitutional law arguments to do so. A good example is the 2011 election manifesto, in which the party pledged to amend the Constitution to define its superiority with regard to EU law, both primary and secondary.[68]

Another good example is the 2015 election manifesto, in which there was a section devoted to 'Poland in Europe and the World', which stated that the European Union should be transformed 'as a tool for the realisation of Polish national interests and not as an end in itself and the end of Polish subjectivity'.[69] That manifesto also mentioned the need for an 'Act on the Exercise of State Sovereignty' to prevent the EU from becoming a federal state and to codify the supremacy of the Polish Constitution over EU law, even citing the Accession Treaty and Lisbon Treaty decisions of the Polish Constitutional Court.[70]

There were also passages that radically challenged the strategies undertaken by the EU to address the economic crisis. More broadly, the phenomenon of competence creep attributed to EU law was criticized, and the EU bureaucracy—perceived as an emanation of supranational technocracy—was strongly attacked. The European Union was portrayed as both unsustainable and problematic. Once again, we find an intimation of the so-called 'Eurorealistic'[71] approach, which mirrors the strategy observed in the Italian case: a narrative setting the EU as a bureaucratic machine against the idea of a 'real' Europe.

[66] Folvarčný and Kopeček (n 65) 169.
[67] Cymer (n 65) 93.
[68] PiS, 'Nowoczesna Solidarna Bezpieczna Polska' (2011) 219.
[69] PiS, 'Program Prawa i Sprawiedliwości 2014. Zdrowie, Praca, Rodzina' (2014) 149–150, as cited and translated into English by Cymer (n 65) 93.
[70] PiS, 'Zdrowie, Praca, Rodzina' (2014) 151.
[71] Cymer (n 65) 94.

'Eurorealism' is also a key word in the 2019 election programme, which called for the EU to respect national sovereignty and subsidiarity[72] and to build a 'Europe of the homeland'. The manifesto for that election is slightly more subtle, however, in its mobilization of constitutional law arguments against European integration, or at least is less explicit. In that manifesto, however, the party continued to insist that the highest law in Poland is the Constitution, linking this claim to the idea that EU law is only valid in its 'literal form'.[73] This approach is particularly revealing in highlighting the overlap between illiberalism and Euroscepticism in the case of PiS. The underlying message is that, in seeking to address the erosion of the rule of law in Poland, the EU is undermining the Polish Constitution and acting beyond its competences. The 2023 manifesto of the party continued to target EU institutions. On that occasion, it was the Court of Justice that was criticized for promoting a 'competence creep' and allegedly making decisions without a proper legal basis.[74] Interestingly, the manifesto mentioned the possibility of creating a special chamber within the ECJ tasked with assessing the competences of EU institutions—an idea that somewhat resembles the proposal floated by the so-called 'Group of Twelve' in 2023.[75] However, in the version put forward by PiS, there would be a presumption in favour of Member State competence, with what appears to be a high threshold for national judges to rebut that presumption.[76]

Also, in the same electoral programme, PiS insisted on the need to adopt 'appropriate steps taken to protect Polish values primarily' and 'consistently counteract solutions that are unfavourable to Poland and Poles, including in migration, agricultural, energy, raw materials and social policies'.[77]

We will return to the defence of Polish values when discussing civil society and think tanks such as Ordo Iuris.

While in Italy the Eurosceptic political forces have introduced to the debate some of the arguments used by voices from the cultural and academic world, here we do not have anything really comparable. Although there has been no shortage of academics who have offered arguments to the illiberal majority, in

[72] PiS, 'Program Prawa i Sprawiedliwości 2019. Polski model państwa dobrobytu' (2019) 20, as quoted and translated into English by Cymer (n 65) 94.

[73] PiS, 'Polski model państwa dobrobytu' (2019) 52. Our translation.

[74] PiS, 'Bezpieczna Przyszłość Polaków' (2023) 165.

[75] Group of Twelve, 'Sailing on High Seas: Reforming and Enlarging the EU for the 21st Century' (2023) <https://www.diplomatie.gouv.fr/IMG/pdf/20230919_group_of_twelve_report_updated14.12.2023_cle88fb88.pdf>.

[76] PiS, 'Bezpieczna Przyszłość Polaków' (2023) 166.

[77] PiS, 'Program Prawa i Sprawiedliwości 2019. Polski model państwa dobrobytu' (2019) 20, as quoted and translated into English by Cymer (n 65) 94. Other sources analysed by scholars to study PiS's disguised Euroscepticism are interviews with key political figures; for instance, see Cymer (n 65) 94.

general academia has been subject to significant constraints that have limited its pluralism.[78] Some names from the academic world have played a role in the illiberal shift in Poland; for instance, there is Przemysław Czarnek, known for his anti-LGBTIQ+ and anti-migrant views and for his public statements against women's rights and in favour of corporal punishment in children's education.[79] Another academic with a similar profile, who has also played various political roles, is Ryszard Legutko, a PiS member and philosopher. His background aligns more with that of a politician than of an academic intellectual. He has written extensively against liberalism[80] and in his works 'liberalism is denounced as displaying suspicion towards collective societal institutions, such as the family, while human rights are frequently understood as arbitrary claims of specific political groups raised against the common good'.[81]

7.4. The Seeds of Polish Euroscepticism and the Transition to Illiberalism in Poland

Kopecký and Mudde argued that 'Poland, the largest of the four prospective EU members from East Central Europe (ECE), has had the strongest elite consensus on EU membership in the ECE context, combined with the most critical (though not necessarily outright negative) and worried electorate'.[82]

These lines reveal much about the continuity and discontinuity in the relationship between Poland and the European Union, and they allow us to trace the roots of what occurred under the previous government's majority. As we said at the beginning of this chapter, Poland does not belong to the Eurozone. Indeed, when it joined the EU in 2004, Poland, like all new Member States,

[78] 'Syllabi are controlled, and video surveillance systems are being installed in classrooms. An interesting example of an adaptation strategy can be observed among gender studies scholars who are now continuing their same research under the umbrella of "family studies" instead of gender studies. Ministers of science in illiberal states are even taking the liberty of creating new disciplines like family studies, which is replacing gender studies in Hungary, or Poland's jettisoning of anthropology in favor of the study of culture and religion, thus demonstrating the impact of polypore science policy on science', Andrea Pető, 'Current Comment: The Illiberal Academic Authority. An Oxymoron?' (2021) 44 Berichte zur Wissenschaftsgeschichte 461, 467.

[79] Adam Leszczyński, 'Dowodził, że bicie dzieci jest zgodne z konstytucją. Za co poseł Czarnek został profesorem?' (11 September 2020) <https://oko.press/dowodzil-bicie-dzieci-jest-zgodne-z-konstytucja-za-co-posel-czarnek-zostal-profesorem>.

[80] Among others, Ryszard Legutko, 'What's Wrong with Liberalism?' (2008) 50 Modern Age 7; Ryszard Legutko, 'Why I Am Not a Liberal' (1 March 2020) <https://firstthings.com/why-i-am-not-a-liberal>; Ryszard Legutko, *The Demon in Democracy: Totalitarian Temptations in Free Societies* (Encounter Books 2016).

[81] Paul Blokker, 'Populist Understandings of the Law: A Conservative Backlash?' (2021) 16 PArtecipazione e COnflitto 1434, 1442.

[82] Kopecký and Mudde (n 7) 310.

pledged to adopt the euro once it met the convergence criteria set by the Maastricht Treaty. However, at the moment, it has not set a date for adopting the euro and has not yet joined the European Exchange Rate Mechanism II (ERM II), which is a preliminary step to joining the Eurozone.

There are political, economic, and social reasons, including the desire to retain control over national monetary policy, behind the reluctance to adopt the euro. This is relevant because, as in other contexts analysed in this book, the debt crises and austerity policies adopted by the European Union have certainly conditioned the emergence of Eurosceptic dynamics. However, the Polish case shows that the wave of Euroscepticism (and the populist wave) can probably only be partially explained by economic factors, but must also be read in the light of other (cultural and political) factors that we will analyse in this chapter.

Having examined the roots of Polish Euroscepticism, we can now turn to the legal arguments and strategies employed to challenge the domestic legal order and to question the primacy of EU law.

One element that characterizes the Polish case is the 'militarization' of the judiciary, which occurred through what has been called the 'hermeneutic tampering' with domestic law.[83] This is an important difference from, for example, the Italian case. This is not the place to analyse in detail the numerous reforms that were part of a broad court-packing design that has undermined the independence of the Polish judiciary[84] and that has been the subject of attention from not only the EU institutions (including the Court of Justice) but also the Venice Commission[85] and the European Court of Human Rights.[86]

The militarization of the judiciary was made possible through a series of legal measures, after the PiS government 'forced judges on to the Constitutional Court, politicized the National Judicial Council, mass-fired court presidents, compromised the judicial appointments process and installed about

[83] Jan Sawicki, 'La collisione insanabile tra diritto europeo primario e diritto costituzionale interno come prodotto della manomissione ermeneutica di quest'ultimo' (2021) 11 DPCE Online 3601.

[84] On the democratic deterioration in Poland, see Wojciech Sadurski, *Poland's Constitutional Breakdown* (n 2); Tímea Drinóczi and Agnieszka Bień-Kacała, *Illiberal Constitutionalism in Poland and Hungary. The Deterioration of Democracy, Misuse of Human Rights and Abuse of the Rule of Law* (Routledge 2022); Tomasz Tadeusz Koncewicz, 'When Legal Fundamentalism Meets Political Justice: The Case of Poland' (2022) 55 Israel Law Review 302; Tomasz Tadeusz Koncewicz, 'Unconstitutional Capture and Constitutional Recapture. Of the Rule of Law, Separation of Powers and Judicial Promises' Jean Monnet Working Paper No 3/17 <https://jeanmonnetprogram.org/paper/unconstitutional-capture-and-constitutional-recapture-of-the-rule-of-law-separation-of-powers-and-judicial-promises/>.

[85] For instance: European Commission for Democracy through Law, 'CDL-AD(2024)035-e' (n 5).

[86] ECtHR, Application no 4907/18 *Xero Flor w Polsce sp. z o.o. v Poland* <https://hudoc.echr.coe.int/eng#{%22itemid%22:[%22001-210065%22]}>.

one-quarter of the entire Polish judiciary through this politically tainted process. In addition, it created two new Supreme Court chambers to bring the rest of the judiciary under political control'.[87]

Simplifying, one can identify five major lines of reform that produced this militarization of the judiciary:

1. measures redefining the composition of the Constitutional Court;[88]
2. measures reforming the National Council of the Judiciary;[89]
3. measures affecting the composition of the Supreme Court by lowering the retirement age for former judges;[90]
4. establishment of the Disciplinary Chamber within the Supreme Court;[91] and
5. adoption of the so-called 'muzzle law'[92] prohibiting national judges from questioning the legitimacy of courts and constitutional bodies or ascertaining or assessing the legitimacy of the appointment of judges.[93]

[87] Scheppele (n 4).

[88] 'Between 2015-2023, Poland's judiciary was hijacked by a governing party with autocratic ambitions bent on the consolidation of power. The PiS government illegally forced judges onto the Constitutional Court, politicized the National Judicial Council, mass-fired court presidents, compromised the judicial appointments process and installed about one-quarter of the entire Polish judiciary through this politically tainted process. In addition, it created two new Supreme Court chambers to bring the rest of the judiciary under political control. Both the European Court of Human Rights (ECtHR) and the European Court of Justice (ECJ) determined that many of these actions were violations of EU and ECHR law. These assaults on the judiciary, almost all authorized by formal law, also violated the Polish Constitution, though after the Constitutional Tribunal was captured, there was no independent institution that could say so', Scheppele (n 4).

[89] Krajowej Radzie Sądownictwa (Law on the National Council of the Judiciary) of 12 May 2011 (Dz U No 126 of 2011, item 714), as amended by the ustawa o zmianie ustawy o Krajowej Radzie Sądownictwa oraz niektórych innych ustaw (Law amending the Law on the National Council of the Judiciary and certain other laws) of 8 December 2017 (Dz U of 2018) ('Law on the KRS').

[90] See ustawa o Sądzie Najwyższym (Law on the Supreme Court) of 8 December 2017 (Dz U of 2018) ('the New Law on the Supreme Court'), which entered into force on 3 April 2018.

[91] See ustawa o Sądzie Najwyższym (Law on the Supreme Court) of 8 December 2017 (Dz. U. of 2018) ('the New Law on the Supreme Court').

[92] 'These reforms are better known as the muzzle law because they introduced, inter alia, new disciplinary offences and sanctions for judges and rules to prevent them—with the exception of two disciplinary chambers created within the Supreme Court—from questioning the legitimacy and independence of any national court', Martina Coli, 'Don't Try to Discipline Your Judges (And Prevent Them from Applying EU Law): The Court of Justice's Judgment in Commission v. Poland (C-204/21)' *Diritti Comparati* (12 July 2023) <https://www.diritticomparati.it/dont-try-to-discipline-your-judges-and-prevent-them-from-applying-eu-law-the-court-of-justices-judgment-in-commission-v-poland-c-204-21/>.

[93] On this set of measures, see the case law of the ECJ: Joined Cases C-585/18, C-624/18 and C-625/18 *A.K. and Others v Sąd Najwyższy* ECLI:EU:C:2019:982. See also Jakub Kościerzyński (ed), *Justice under Pressure—Repressions as a Means of Attempting to Take Control Over the Judiciary and the Prosecution in Poland. Years 2015–2019* (2020) <https://ruleoflaw.pl/wp-content/uploads/2020/02/Raport_EN.pdf>.

While we will not go into detail on the first three measures, we want to stress the provisions of the so-called 'muzzle law' that directly undermined the supranational mandate of the national judges[94] and thus openly opposed the primacy of EU law.

This was one of the points made by the ECJ in its case law. The ECJ made it clear that the principle of the primacy of EU law obliges national courts to ensure the full effect of EU law in cases before them. This means that they must disapply any conflicting national rule or practice when EU law has direct effect, without awaiting legislative or constitutional action.[95] Article 47 of the Charter and the second subparagraph of article 19(1) TEU, both of which have direct effect, reinforce this obligation. Polish laws preventing courts from disapplying provisions contrary to directly effective EU law violate the principle of primacy.[96]

In particular, the Polish Constitutional Court was the subject of a 'Legislative Bombardment' and was transformed from 'an Activist Court, to a Paralysed Tribunal, to a Governmental Enabler',[97] in Sadurski's words. Indeed, the Polish Constitutional Court, which had attempted to thwart the illiberal agenda of the political majority with some of its rulings,[98] was disempowered, with the introduction of a number of exceptions to its constitutionality scrutiny[99] and other measures such as a ban on the publication of some of its rulings. This led to the loss of its role as a counter-majority actor.

At the time of writing, the Tusk government has not succeeded in adopting measures to overcome the situation produced by the previous government, partly because some of the proposed measures were seen as problematic in terms of respecting the principle of legality.[100] These difficulties make the Polish case particularly compelling for those studying political transitions.

[94] Monica Claes, *The National Courts' Mandate in the European Constitution* (Hart 2006).

[95] ECJ, Case C-106/77 *Amministrazione delle finanze dello Stato v Simmenthal* ECLI:EU:C:1978:49.

[96] ECJ, Case C-204/21 *European Commission v Republic of Poland* ECLI:EU:C:2023:442 paras 227–231.

[97] Wojciech Sadurski, 'Polish Constitutional Tribunal Under PiS: From an Activist Court, to a Paralysed Tribunal, to a Governmental Enabler' (2019) 11 Hague Journal on the Rule of Law 63, 73.

[98] For instance, Polish Constitutional Court K 47/15, judgment of 9 March 2016, by which the Constitutional Court struck down the law on the CT of 22 December 2015. This judgment is cited by Sadurski, 'Polish Constitutional Tribunal Under PiS' (n 97) 74.

[99] Article 1(10) of the statute of 22 December 2015 (found unconstitutional as a whole by the CT on 9 March 2016, K 47/15); article 38(3-6) of the statute on the CT of 22 July 2016 (found partly unconstitutional on 11 August 2016, K 39/16), as cited by Sadurski, 'Polish Constitutional Tribunal Under PiS (n 97) 72.

[100] Andrzej Schultz and Jakub Sawicki, 'Polish(ing) Broken Tribunal. The New Polish Coalition Government's Package to Restore the Constitutional Tribunal—A Wobbly Constitutional Reset?' 22 March 2024 <https://verfassungsblog.de/polishing-broken-tribunal/>.

7.5. Euroscepticism and Civil Society

The Polish case cannot be understood by limiting ourselves to the programmes and actions of the previous political majority, or to the Law and Justice party. In fact, as scholars[101] have rightly emphasized, Law and Justice succeeded in exploiting a broader conservative wave, fuelled in part by factors already present within Polish civil society and stemming from the legacy of the post-communist transition. If communism had strongly limited religious freedom in general,[102] and Catholic religious freedom in particular, the end of the regime initiated a profound transformation within the Catholic community,[103] which began to express itself in both more moderate and more conservative forms. On this basis, scholars have emphasized the importance of the religious factor[104] (and its exploitation) in the affirmation of important conservative currents that provided a favourable context for the policies of the old majority. Scholars have also described the strategies employed by genuine cultural entrepreneurs in Poland, who have 'deliberately engineered public culture',[105] initiating a process of what has been termed the 'symbolic thickening of public culture':[106]

> On the cultural side, the process involved the intensifying ideological campaign and cultural mobilization by right-wing populists of various hues, ranging from cultural clubs and youth sections of right-wing populist parties to far-right associations and football hooligan clubs. Other actors, with less explicit political agendas but with a palpable determination to redefine public culture, included several circles of conservative intellectuals, a significant

[101] Dorota Szelewa, 'Populism, Religion and Catholic Civil Society in Poland: The Case of Primary Education' (2021) 20 Social Policy and Society 310; Paul Blokker, 'Constitutional Politics and Populist Conservatism: The Contrasting Cases of Poland and Romania' (2021) 24 European Politics and Society 132.

[102] Dariusz Wadowski, 'Religion and Religiosity in Contemporary Poland' (2020) 1 Central European Journal for Contemporary Religion 35, 37.

[103] Christopher Garbowski, 'Catholicism in the New Poland: A Religion and Society in Transition' (2020) 40 Occasional Papers on Religion in Eastern Europe 35.

[104] Blokker wrote about cultural wars that had been brewing since the 1990s and then exploded after 2015; Blokker, 'Constitutional Politics and Populist Conservatism' (n 101).

[105] Marta Kotwas and Jan Kubik, 'Symbolic Thickening of Public Culture and the Rise of Right-Wing Populism in Poland' (2019) 33 East European Politics and Societies and Cultures 435, 442.

[106] 'We elucidate a specific supply-side cultural mechanism (symbolic thickening of public culture) and offer a theoretical account of how it interacts with a political mechanism of ideological thickening of populism to intensify a specific understanding of Polishness and enhance the popularity and influence of right-wing populism. In this task, we are aided by the concept of discursive opportunity structure', Kotwas and Kubik (n 105) 442–443.

> segment of the Catholic clergy, some Catholic media (Radio Maryja most prominently), and a few lay Catholic organizations.[107]

All of this makes the Polish case an example of a broader global phenomenon that scholars have termed the 'transnational culture wars',[108] in which courts—particularly top courts, such as the US Supreme Court and the European Court of Human Rights—are deliberately involved as part of strategic litigation. Obviously, there are also sections of Catholic civil society that expressed dissent with the policies of the illiberal government, and it is no coincidence that scholars have emphasized the variety within Polish Catholicism.[109] Nevertheless, PiS has promoted a vision of politics closely linked to traditional Catholic values, often in collaboration with the Polish Catholic Church. Key examples of this connection include restrictive abortion policies, as well as positions on education, and civil rights. Other examples include the vision of the family, which has influenced various official stances on gender and the LGBTIQ+ community. Similarly, Poland has been presented as the home of Catholic values that oppose the EU and globalization, which are seen as vehicles for the degeneration of traditional values. The exploitation of the Catholic Church's conservative arguments has also led to the polarization of civil society on many sensitive issues. Polish traditional values have been utilized by illiberal Polish thinkers, who present themselves as champions of Catholic values, particularly national Catholicism. This approach has found a prominent voice in the programmes of Radio Maryja, which has played an important supporting role.

The EU is a favourite target of conservative attacks by Polish Catholic and nationalist forces, as is also demonstrated by the *Catholic Poland in Christian Europe* programme, published by PiS, which states the following:

> Rejection of the invocation to God in the Constitutional Treaty is a sign of this civilizational orientation. Policy of the EU partly disregards a social order

[107] Kotwas and Kubik (n 105) 460.

[108] Christopher McCrudden, 'Transnational Culture Wars' (2015) 13 International Journal of Constitutional Law 434; Pasquale Annicchino, 'The Geopolitics of Transnational Law and Religion: Wars of Conscience and the Framing Effects of Law as a Social Institution' in Susanna Mancini and Michel Rosenfeld (eds), *The Conscience Wars: Rethinking the Balance between Religion, Identity, and Equality* (Cambridge University Press 2018) 258; Kristina Stoeckl, 'Traditional Values, Family, Homeschooling: The Role of Russia and the Russian Orthodox Church in Transnational Moral Conservative Networks and Their Efforts at Reshaping Human Rights' (2023) 21 International Journal of Constitutional Law 224.

[109] Arkadiusz Modrzejewski, 'Catholic and Nationalist Populism in the Current Poland' (2017) 10 Perspective Politice 21, 23.

> and even partly directly fights against this order. We can find here the rejection of normative character of Christian morality (...). Policy of the European Union is prejudiced to faith, national bond and family (so, to all values which reveal dignity of human nature) but in the extreme cases this policy supports degenerations, moral pathologies or even crimes treated as an expression of human freedom and signature of 'open society'.[110]

The Polish Catholic think tank Ordo Iuris also played a central role in this affair. It was founded in 2013, emerging from a conference supported by the American organization Alliance Defending Freedom (ADF). Over the years, it has become an influential, extremist lobby that pioneered a model that has been used by many mayors to declare their cities to be 'LGBTIQ+ free', and led a campaign to criminalise the voluntary termination of pregnancy in all its forms. Ordo Iuris focuses on promoting 'family and traditional values' through research, advocacy, and legal action. In conclusion, these forces of civil society have acted as an amplifier of the illiberal constitutional counter-narrative and have targeted the EU as a threat to traditional values and Polish identity. Ordo Iuris is also part of a transnational alliance of hyper-conservative think tanks, including Corvinus Collegium (MCC) and the Heritage Foundation. It is no coincidence that the EU has also been accused of favouring immigration and the arrival of refugees, seen as sources of insecurity and contamination of the national identity. In this, these conservative forces have also mobilized themselves by fuelling forms of 'moral panic',[111] portraying 'the European Union as a promoter of politics of multiculturalism as well as power of relativisation of Christian and national values'.[112]

7.6. Constitutional Counter-Narratives in Action

As in the Italian case, one can identify elements in the Polish case that contribute to a constitutional counter-narrative. Among these, the concept of

[110] Cited and translated by Modrzejewski (n 109) 29.
[111] Szelewa (n 101) 313.
[112] Modrzejewski (n 109) 29. In recent months, it has contributed to the drafting of a document entitled 'The Great Reset: Restoring Member State Sovereignty in the 21st Century' (<https://legrandcontinent.eu/fr/wp-content/uploads/sites/2/2025/03/The_Great_Reset_Restoring_Member_State_Sovereignty_0-2.pdf>). It has also advocated transforming the European Union into a 'European Community of Nations', thereby weakening its supranational and institutional components. Szabolcs Panyi, 'Renaming the EU, Dismantling the Commission: Polish, Hungarian Illiberals Seek U.S. Backing' (10 March 2025) <https://vsquare.org/heritage-foundation-mcc-ordo-iuris-russia-european-union-european-court-of-justice/>.

constitutional identity acquires considerable centrality. It is precisely the concept of national identity that has been the subject of enormous criticism in the literature and, in particular, constitutional pluralists have been accused of offering arguments to autocrats and justifying violations of the values set out in article 2 TEU:

> In EU law—as so often in life—the road to hell is paved with good intentions. The scholars who developed the theory of constitutional pluralism had the best of intentions in mind, but their creation is having destructive consequences that threaten the entire EU legal order (. . .) the theory of constitutional pluralism had inherent flaws, but it could function as a serviceable fudge so long as all the courts involved engaged in sincere cooperation, dialogue and mutual accommodation. However, with the emergence and ongoing consolidation of competitive authoritarian regimes in Hungary and Poland, the days when one could assume all national judiciaries would engage in sincere cooperation and mutual accommodation have ended and the dangers that were always inherent in the concept of constitutional pluralism and the connected concept of constitutional identity have become manifest for all to see.[113]

Not everyone agrees with this line of argument, however. Avbelj, for instance, rejected these accusations against constitutional pluralism, arguing that this criticism:

> (D)ue to its truncated, exclusively positivist understanding of constitutional pluralism, (. . .) has failed to take into account pluralism's normative core. The latter presents itself an antipode to authoritarianism, which means that autocratic regimes simply cannot credibly avail themselves of the theory of constitutional pluralism to justify their authoritarian actions.[114]

In this regard, the Polish case, and, in particular, decision K 3/21 of its Constitutional Court, is very relevant. As we know, the Court of Justice has played a crucial role in challenging the constitutional counter-narrative

[113] R Daniel Kelemen and Laurent Pech, 'Why Autocrats Love Constitutional Identity and Constitutional Pluralism. Lessons from Hungary and Poland' Reconnect Working Paper No 2 (2018) <https://reconnect-europe.eu/wp-content/uploads/2018/10/RECONNECT-WorkingPaper2-Kelemen-Pech-LP-KO.pdf>.

[114] Matej Avbelj, 'Constitutional Pluralism and Authoritarianism' (2020) 21 German Law Journal 1023, 1031.

advanced by the Polish Constitutional Court, beginning with its famous judgments concerning the Regulation on a general system of conditionality for the protection of the Union budget.[115] However, the European Parliament and the Commission have also been struggling to know what to do with Poland after the judgment of the Polish Constitutional Court in which it rejected the principle of the primacy of EU law.[116]

The previous national government and the Polish courts exploited the argument of the protection of national identity, as enshrined in article 4(2) TEU. One only has to think of a Polish government white paper on the reform of the judiciary in which the theory of constitutional pluralism was instrumentally cited. We quote the relevant passage in full:

> The legal system of the European Union is based on **constitutional pluralism** of the member states. It means that there are multiple constitutional systems—on one side there are national systems of the Member States, on another, the European framework, having its 'constitutional charter' in the Treaties: Treaty of the European Union and Treaty on the Functioning of the European Union (see: ECJ opinion No 1/91, ECR 1991/10, s. I-6102). Each country has specific constitutional solutions that are rooted in its history and legal traditions and these differences are protected by the treaty law of the European Union. Article 4 of the Treaty on European Union quoted above shows that the Union respects national identity which is inherent in the fundamental political and constitutional structures of the member states. **Constitutional identity, a core value of each national community, determines not only the most fundamental values and resulting tasks for state authorities, but also sets the limit for regulatory intervention of the European Union.**[117] (emphasis added).

The argument for the instrumentalization of the national constitutional identity is certainly a common point between Polish and Hungarian case law, but there are also important differences. With reference to the Hungarian case law that we discussed in Chapter 2, scholars have argued that the academic debate surrounding Poland's constitutional identity is still in its infancy, and this

[115] Regulation (EU, Euratom) 2020/2092 of the European Parliament and of the Council of 16 December 2020.

[116] Polish Constitutional Court, decision K 3/21 <http://www.trybunal.gov.pl>.

[117] The Chancellery of the Prime Minister, 'White Paper on the Reform of the Polish Judiciary' (7 March 2018) <https://www.statewatch.org/media/documents/news/2018/mar/pl-judiciary-reform-chanceller-white-paper-3-18.pdf>.

was explained by reference to the relative youth of Poland's Constitution and the absence of an eternity clause or unamendable provisions (a feature shared by the Hungarian Basic Law), which often serve as a foundation for articulating constitutional identity. The first explicit invocation of identity emerged in the Lisbon case,[118] but the Polish Constitutional Court did not develop it in depth. As scholars have suggested, the identity argument (unlike in Hungary) remained largely absent from the case law of the Constitutional Court between 2016 and 2019, even after its unconstitutional capture.[119]

An important change in this respect is represented by a 2021 ruling in which the Polish Constitutional Court directly challenged the primacy of EU law by declaring that articles 1(1), 2, 4(3), and 19(1) TEU are in conflict with the Constitution.[120] However, looking at the official translation of the operative part of the ruling on the website of the Polish Constitutional Court, one does not find explicit references to the concepts of 'national identity' or 'constitutional identity'.

In the Polish version of the judgment, by contrast, the word *tożsamość* (identity) is cited 58 times,[121] so it is possible to confirm that the Constitutional Court used this concept extensively. This is an oddity that, according to local

[118] See, for instance, this passage: 'In the view of the Constitutional Tribunal, the sovereignty of the Republic of Poland and its independence—construed as the separateness of Poland's statehood within its present borders, in the circumstances of the membership in the EU in accordance with the rules specified in the Constitution—mean confirmation of the primacy of the Polish Nation to determine its own fate. The normative manifestation of that principle is the Constitution, and in particular the provisions of the Preamble, Article 2, Article 4, Article 5, Article 8, Article 90, Article 104(2) and Article 126(1), in the light of which the sovereignty of the Republic of Poland is expressed in the inalienable competences of the organs of the state, constituting the constitutional identity of the state', decision K 32/09 <http://www.trybunal.gov.pl>.

[119] '[T]he academic discussion on the Polish constitutional identity has just been started. It may be understandable when we take into account the young age of our Constitution and a lack of eternity clause or unamendable constitutional provisions. They are often a natural base for reconstruction of the constitutional identity. Direct references to the identity appeared in the Lisbon case for the first time and they have never been developed by the Polish Constitutional Tribunal so far ... the constitutional identity argument had been directly used to justify the constitutional crisis in Poland only once. Unfortunately, it was not elaborated and exemplified. Contrary to the Hungarian example, even after the Constitutional Tribunal was unconstitutionally captured, it avoided using the identity argument in its 2016-2019 case-law', Michał Ziółkowski and Barbara Grabowska-Moroz, 'Enforcement of EU Values and the Tyranny of National Identity—Polish Examples and Excuses' (26 November 2019) <https://verfassungsblog.de/enforcement-of-eu-values-and-the-tyranny-of-national-identity-polish-examples-and-excuses/>.

[120] 'It is hard not to observe that constitutional identity has become a favourite argumentative tool of populist-authoritarian politicians, judges and scholars who oppose a vigorous control of national laws and practices under the norms of EU law', Aleksandra Gliszczyńska-Grabias and Wojciech Sadurski, 'Is It Polexit Yet? Comment on Case K 3/21 of 7 October 2021 by the Constitutional Tribunal of Poland' (2023) 19 European Constitutional Law Review 163, 177.

[121] I extend my gratitude to Agnieszka Bień-Kacała for her assistance in locating the Polish version of the judgment.

scholars, can be explained by the fact that the actual judgment was published more than one year after the announcement of the decision.[122]

The importance of the national (constitutional) identity argument is confirmed by the press release:[123]

> The subject matter belongs to the Polish constitutional identity, which has been pointed out by the Constitutional Tribunal a number of times before, also in its recent judgment ref. no. P 7/20 (...). The Constitutional Tribunal stressed that also Article 2 of the TEU—which contains the catalogue of values on which the Union is based—may not constitute the source of the CJEU's competences to adjudicate on the organisational structure of Polish courts. The values mentioned in Article 2 of the TEU are merely of axiological significance, and they are not legal principles. The organisational structures of the judicial systems in EU Member States do not at all fall under the common constitutional identity of the Member States, which apply different procedures for appointing judges.[124]

In these lines, one can also note the attempt to question the nature of the values in article 2 TEU, by calling them 'non-legal principles'. This is an approach refuted by the Court of Justice in its first judgments on the validity of the conditionality regulation. Scholars have presented numerous doubts concerning the justification for this decision:[125]

> The oral justification from October 2021 was mainly focused on the principle of conferral. The 'conferral argument' became supported by referencing the rule of law as a set of general and more political values which need to be developed on a national constitutional level. The second core argument of the oral justification was the need to protect the constitutional identity. The written

[122] 'It took more than a year for the Polish Constitutional Tribunal (CT) to justify in writing the judicial bomb it dropped in 2021 on the primacy of the EU law, a judicial dialogue with the Court of Justice (CJEU) and a mechanism of providing the rule of law conditions by the Member States. At the beginning of November 2022, the CT finally released the complete justification of why it considered Articles 1(1), 2, 4(3) and 19(1) TEU unconstitutional', Michał Ziółkowski, 'Heavy Clouds, No Rain. Unmasking the Polish Constitutional Tribunal Challenging the Primacy of the EU Law and the Court of Justice in case K 3/212' (2024) 16 Krytyka Prawa. Niezależne Studia nad Prawem 421, 423.

[123] Polish Constitutional Court, 'Assessment of the conformity to the Polish Constitution of selected provisions of the Treaty on European Union' <https://trybunal.gov.pl/en/news/press-releases/after-the-hearing/art/11664-ocena-zgodnosci-z-konstytucja-rp-wybranych-przepisow-traktatu-o-unii-europejskiej>.

[124] Gliszczyńska-Grabias and Sadurski (n 120). Polish Constitutional Court, decision P 7/20 <https://trybunal.gov.pl>.

[125] Ziółkowski (n 122).

> justification from November 2022 is somewhat different. The main focus was placed on the CJEU's powers, concepts and limits placed upon the method of interpreting EU law. More references to the German FCC's approach and concepts appeared. The reference to constitutional identity became almost vanished. Thus, the CT pretends to be less confrontational. It included long passages emphasising that the CJEU is essential for the EU and how valuable the judicial dialogue is.[126]

This asymmetry between the oral and the written arguments is also found in the judgment in Case K 20/20, concerning abortion.[127] It has been suggested in that case that the identity argument present in the oral justification vanished in the written justification.[128] Polish scholars have commented on how these curious changes assisted the Constitutional Court's need to align itself with the strategy employed by the (at that time) contingent majority vis-à-vis the EU Commission,[129] thus confirming the disappearance of its counter-majoritarian mission.

7.7. Countering Eurosceptic Counter-Narratives in Poland

Decision K 3/21 of the Polish Constitutional Court has, however, been much criticized by scholars from Poland and beyond for various reasons, both procedural and substantive.

For example, Jaraczewski[130] emphasized how the Court's decision aligned with the arguments of the 129-page application prepared by the Polish Prime Minister. In the application in which the arguments of national identity were used, constitutional pluralism was instrumentally invoked, and passages of foreign case law (such as rulings of the German Constitutional Court) were selectively presented.[131]

126 Ziółkowski (n 122) 428.

127 Polish Constitutional Court, decision K 20/20 <https://trybunal.gov.pl/>.

128 'At first, the judge-rapporteur suggested a constitutional identity argument in the oral justification, but then the argument disappeared in the written justification, replaced by bold statements concerning the choice of the constitution-makers. In my view, the CT had good reasons to postpone the publication of its written justification. It took time to listen and adapt its justification to the legal debate. It also supported the governmental strategy in its struggles with the Commission', Ziółkowski (n 122) 430.

129 Ziółkowski (n 122) 430.

130 Jakub Jaraczewski, 'Gazing Into the Abyss. The K 3/21 Decision of the Polish Constitutional Tribunal' (12 October 2021) <https://verfassungsblog.de/gazing-into-the-abyss/>.

131 'One important strand of the Prime Minister's argumentation were the multiple references to laws and constitutional court judgments coming from the other EU Member States, with the German FCC's 2020 PSPP judgment being most prominent', Jaraczewski (n 130). On the difference between

From a procedural point of view, scholars have pointed out that the Polish Constitutional Court agreed to carry out the review suggested by the Prime Minister's application. Indeed, the Polish Prime Minister's application in Case 3/21 challenged not the EU Treaties themselves but rather the ECJ's case law, bypassing article 188 of the Polish Constitution, which in theory only allows the Constitutional Court to review treaties, not court rulings. The Polish Constitutional Court, ignoring this limitation, engaged in 'legal acrobatics'[132] by disregarding article 9, which mandates respect for international law, and by overlooking its previous case law.[133]

Not surprisingly, this pronouncement drew an unprecedented reaction from former judges of the Constitutional Court, who responded with a letter contesting all the main points made in the K 3/21 ruling. It is worth quoting the former judges' arguments in full:

> It is not true that the judgment of the Constitutional Tribunal of 7 October 2021 was issued in order to guarantee the supremacy of the Constitution over EU law, since such a position of the Constitution has been sufficiently established in the previous case law of the Tribunal (in cases K 18/04, K 32/09, SK 45/09); It is not true that the judgment of the Constitutional Tribunal of 7 October 2021 itself falls within the competence of the Tribunal and is consistent with the Constitution; It is not true that EU law and the previous case law of the CJEU question or violate the supremacy of the Constitution in the Polish legal order; It is not true that the CJEU requires Polish courts to desist from observing and applying the Constitution as the supreme law of the Republic; It is not true that the application of EU law by Polish courts cannot be reconciled with their application of the Constitution; It is not true that the questioning by EU institutions of the breach by Polish statutes and practice of their application of the principles of independence of Polish judges, who also adjudicate in the fields covered by Union law, goes beyond the competence conferred on the European Union by Article 90(1) of the Constitution; It is not true that European Union law and the case-law of the CJEU encroach upon the regulation of the organisation of justice in Poland, since the defence of judicial independence is not part of the organisation of justice; it is not

the German and the Polish case law, see Alexander Thiele, 'Whoever Equates Karlsruhe to Warsaw is Wildly Mistaken' (10 October 2021) <https://verfassungsblog.de/whoever-equals-karlsruhe-to-warsaw-is-wildly-mistaken/>.

[132] Jaraczewski (n 130).

[133] In particular, Polish Constitutional Court, decision K 18/04 (11 May 2005) <https://trybunal.gov.pl/>.

> true that the judgment of the Constitutional Tribunal of 7 October 2021 will be able to produce legal effects other than exerting pressure on the judicial activity of Polish judges and threatening them with disciplinary proceedings; It is not true that the Constitutional Tribunal has the authority to review the constitutionality of CJEU rulings and to decide whether Poland, as a Member State, should selectively respect CJEU case law; it is not true that constitutional courts of other Member States in matters concerning relations between national law and EU law have issued judgments similar to the one issued by the Constitutional Tribunal on October 7, 2021.[134]

This text says a lot about the split between the old (pre-2018) and the new judges, which scholars interested in the law-in-context approach have recently dealt with in depth.[135] Indeed, the court-packing introduced by the old political majority has created a clear division within the Polish judiciary. If, at first, the new judges accused the old ones of being politicized and defended themselves against the same accusation by emphasizing the need to ensure the neutrality of the law,[136] more recently their strategy has changed in the face of the Tusk government's attempts at reform. After the December 2023 change in government, the new judges adopted obstructionist tactics to delay rule of law reforms. They founded Prawnicy dla Polski ('Lawyers for Poland')[137] to oppose the restoration efforts, claiming that they threatened constitutional institutions. Using alternative media, they framed the scrutiny of their status

[134] 'Statement of Retired Judges of the Polish Constitutional Tribunal' (11 October 2021) <https://verfassungsblog.de/statement-of-retired-judges-of-the-polish-constitutional-tribunal/>.

[135] Katarzyna Krzyżanowska, 'Legal Mobilisation within the Populist Supreme Court in Poland' (2024) 20 International Journal of Law in Context 324.

[136] 'One could expect that the narratives constructed by judges elected in a process influenced by PiS politicians would visibly disregard legal standards, but the opposite is true: this discourse invokes a variety of arguments that are founded on a narrowly understood rule of law associated with legalism and dogmatism. Even though these narratives are pragmatic, reactionary and self-contradictory, they still operate within a particular legalist mindset. The meta-argument, relating to legal ontology, is that law is a technical, non-political tool; is organised hierarchically; and has a limited ability to accommodate foreign sources of law (especially the judgments of the CJEU). In this positivistic vision, law is a technical tool that has the ultimate task of coordinating society; law is thus an external object that is understandable only to qualified lawyers (. . .). Thus, the new judges, accused of being political usurpers breaching juridical autonomy, defend their position by invoking the established Polish preconceptions about the law. Interestingly, there is a consensus among politicians and judges that the former should not in any way influence the outcome of the judicial process, which stresses the exceptionally autonomous position of the juridical field (. . .). In this sense, the Polish crisis of legal knowledge in the SC has not led to lawyers producing responses to problems like discretionary power or the relations between law and politics (. . .). Instead, the narratives mirror the other side's arguments but do not engage with them. It is noticeable that new judges discursively construct the opposition group—the judicial elite, the old judges—but at the same time, there is a limited sense of togetherness among the newcomers', Krzyżanowska (n 135) 331–332.

[137] Michał Stambulski, 'Schrödinger's Judges. Challenges to the Rule of Law Restoration in Poland' (19 December 2024) <https://verfassungsblog.de/schrodingers-judges/>.

as political persecution. Seeking legitimacy, they referred to the ECJ, as only recognized judges can do so, effectively delaying the verification of their position.[138] EU law, not just national constitutional law, has become part of the internal war, giving rise to forms of lawfare.

The restoration of high standards of rule of law protection will thus be intimately related to the restoration of an open, pro-European approach to constitutionalism in the country.

7.8. Conclusion

In this chapter, we analysed the Polish case. As we argued earlier, Poland represents a crucial laboratory for studying transitions following a wave of illiberal and populist governments, especially in light of the election of the nationalist Nawrocki as President of Poland before the summer of 2025.

Polish Euroscepticism has deep roots, which can be found in the first years of the country's European membership and in its constitutional specificities. For this reason, we started from the constitutional framework, placing it in the broader context of Eastern European constitutions, based on the work of Albi, among others. Our subsequent analyses, focused on PiS, were devoted to the scrutiny of the Eurosceptic mobilization of constitutional law not only in election manifestos and political rhetoric but also in action.

Our findings in the Polish case point at a strong intertwining of several concepts that are in principle different: illiberalism, populism, and Euroscepticism. While it is theoretically possible to find these three aspects separately, in the Polish case of PiS they are intimately interlinked. As we write these lines, Poland is in the process of walking back on the reforms of Law and Justice, re-consolidating its rule of law whilst at the same time becoming a reliable partner for the process of European integration. The main difficulties will thus be related to the depth of the challenges posed by the former PiS-led governments to both the rule of law and the EU.

[138] Stambulski (n 137).

8
Disintegration Through (Constitutional) Law? Final Remarks

8.1. The Path We Have Proposed to Our Readers

In the pages that follow, we pursue two aims. First, we summarize the main findings of our journey. Second, we show the added value that, in our view, this volume offers to the existing literature. These closing reflections complete our research path and clarify what we believe our work contributes to the field. Additionally, towards the end of the chapter, we offer some 'food for thought' in the form of brief reflections: once we have provided a better understanding of the phenomenon of the Eurosceptic mobilization of constitutional law, we try to shed light on the route ahead.

The book addresses a form of Euroscepticism that has not yet been thoroughly studied, despite its potentially far-reaching impact on the process of European integration: the use of constitutional law to challenge the foundations of EU law. As authors, we made it clear from the outset that this is not a self-defence manual for pro-European readers:[1] instead, this is a volume that seeks to scrutinize a complex phenomenon from a strictly academic angle. However, we do have a normative view on how best to understand national constitutional law and on why this is compatible with and open to European integration. Our central argument is that these movements exhibit a deep and instrumental interest in constitutional law. Rather than positioning themselves merely as opponents of European integration, Eurosceptic actors seek to incorporate constitutional law into their political arsenal to consolidate power and legitimize their claims.

We thus use the concept of 'mobilization' to describe the process by which constitutional law arguments are converted into political weapons deployed for strategic ends. In the title of this book, we refer to the concept of mobilization,

[1] Sergio Fabbrini, Manuale di autodifesa europeista. Come rispondere alla sfida del sovranismo (LUISS University Press 2019).

The Eurosceptic Mobilization of Constitutional Law. Pablo Castillo-Ortiz and Giuseppe Martinico, Oxford University Press. © Pablo Castillo-Ortiz and Giuseppe Martinico 2026. DOI: 10.1093/9780198959205.003.0008

drawing on the influential debate initiated by Bob's seminal 2019 book *Rights as Weapons: Instruments of Conflict, Tools of Power*.[2] Bob's book explores the complex and multifaceted nature of rights, demonstrating that they are far from being solely instruments that protect the vulnerable. Instead, rights are frequently deployed offensively, as instruments of conflict and power. Bob emphasizes that, contrary to idealistic perceptions, rights are malleable political tools employed by all sides in a conflict—including by powerful actors who may use them against weaker opponents.

The notion of mobilization is thus central to Bob's analysis of rights in political conflict. It reflects a broader understanding of rights, not as neutral guarantees but as resources strategically activated to galvanize support, unify aggrieved constituencies, and attract third-party allies. Rights discourse, in this sense, becomes a vehicle for enhancing political leverage and contesting institutional power.

Building on this conceptual framework—and following the work of Blokker[3]—we extend the analysis beyond rights to encompass other constitutional goods that form part of the broader language of liberal constitutional law. Like rights, these goods can be strategically mobilized in pursuit of political objectives. Our aim is to explore how such mobilization operates and how concepts traditionally seen as stabilizing and integrative—such as sovereignty and democracy—can also be instrumentalized in struggles for power and legitimacy.

There are two primary reasons for this mobilization. First, constitutional law arguments lend a semblance of legitimacy, reputation, and respectability to political agendas that might otherwise be perceived as radical or disruptive. Second, it is often more persuasive to present oneself as a defender of the national constitution than as a critic of European integration per se. Within this framework, the European Union is routinely portrayed as the adversary, a symbol of transnational elitism, especially by governments that combine populist rhetoric with sovereignist goals.

Chapters 3 to 7 anchor our theoretical intuitions in real-world cases. To do this, the book adopts theoretical, doctrinal, and empirical lenses. Before turning to the book's central question ('*how* do Eurosceptics mobilize constitutional law against European integration?'), we first examine *why* certain political

[2] Clifford Bob, *Rights as Weapons: Instruments of Conflict, Tools of Power* (Princeton University Press 2019).

[3] Paul Blokker, 'Using Liberal–Legal Tools for Illiberal Gains: The European Court of Human Rights and Legal Mobilisation by Conservative Right-Wing Actors' (2024) 20 International Journal of Law in Context 401.

parties opt for using this strategy while others do not. Using Qualitative Comparative Analysis (QCA), the book scrutinizes right-wing Eurosceptic parties in the EU-15 to identify three distinct routes to this form of Euroscepticism. Each route reflects a specific combination of conditions, including a party's electoral strength and competition, the state's constitutional traditions, or the domestic fallout from the Eurozone crisis. The findings underscore the fact that Eurosceptic appeals to constitutional law do not all have the same cause. They arise from intersecting factors at multiple levels.

In Chapters 4 to 7, the book then asks how Eurosceptic parties mobilize constitutional law, ideas, and institutions against European integration. It also explores the effects of this strategy, its different varieties, and the possibility of pro-European responses consistent with the tradition of *open constitutionalism*. The ways in which constitutional law is mobilized against European integration vary significantly across countries, political parties, and timeframes. In some cases, this mobilization is accompanied by explicit proposals to exit the EU; in others, these intentions remain implicit.

This mobilization frequently gives rise to constitutional counter-narratives,[4] by which we mean the cherry-picking and instrumental use of constitutional law arguments. As we show in the book, constitutional counter-narratives do not develop solely through the adoption of constitutional amendments—these are often proposed but not always approved. Government-led Euroscepticism is typically more subtle and often proceeds through alternative channels. To avoid limiting our analysis to the question of formal constitutional amendments, we have chosen to include legal systems in which this instrument has played a marginal role. This is the case of Poland, for instance, which has experienced an illiberal turn. As is well known, the PiS government lacked the parliamentary majority necessary to dismantle the rule of law through formal constitutional amendments, but this did not prevent it from significantly undermining the Polish constitutional system through other means.[5]

These counter-narratives rely on a selective and often superficial invocation of constitutional provisions and concepts—sometimes through biased selections, sometimes through merely cosmetic references—deployed strategically to advance Eurosceptic political goals. This approach is presented as distinct from, though frequently complementary to, the more familiar call for withdrawal from the EU. The objective is typically to undermine European

[4] Giuseppe Martinico, *Filtering Populist Claims to Fight Populism: The Italian Case in a Comparative Perspective* (Cambridge University Press 2021).

[5] Wojciech Sadurski, *Poland's Constitutional Breakdown* (Oxford University Press 2019).

integration from within, by attacking its foundational principles rather than by exiting its institutions outright.

This part of the book relies on an in-depth study of the United Kingdom, Italy, Spain, and Poland, countries that acceded to the EU at different stages and represent different constitutional traditions. Italy, Spain, and Poland belong to the post-WWII tradition of legal constitutionalism, characterized by openness to international law, entrenchment clauses, and robust systems of judicial review of legislation. The UK, while historically distinct, has also undergone significant constitutional developments that align it, at least in part, with the values of post-WWII constitutionalism. Each chapter examines the national constitutional framework, its relationship with European integration, and the positions and constitutional law arguments of Eurosceptic actors.

Across the various national case studies, a set of recurring themes emerges in the Eurosceptic mobilization of constitutional law. These counter-narratives consistently portray European integration as a threat to the national constitution and frame the EU as an external force undermining national sovereignty. A key strategy involves invoking 'constitutional identity' as a shield against supranational authority, and this is often accompanied by a strong representation of the allegedly conflictual relationship between the national courts and the Court of Justice of the European Union. These elements are not isolated; rather, they form part of a broader political strategy whose aim is to reshape the constitutional foundations of the European legal order from within. In general, Eurosceptic parties, regardless of their country or ideology, tend to mobilize similar concepts, among them sovereignty, identity, and democracy, in their constitutional counter-narratives. However, the specific ways in which these concepts are articulated in the counter-narratives vary significantly according to ideologies and national contexts.

In Italy, Lega has taken steps to entrench the prevalence of the Italian Constitution over EU law through proposed constitutional amendments. Significant elements of Euroscepticism are also present in Fratelli d'Italia and the Five Star Movement, as demonstrated by the debate on the reform of the European Stability Mechanism (ESM). All this is enriched by various forms of sovereignism that characterize Lega and some of the minority parties on both the right and the left. The Italian case is noteworthy for the prominent role of actors outside the political parties, with the sovereignty debate being shaped in part by academic and intellectual discourse portraying EU membership as incompatible with, or even harmful to, the national constitution.[6]

[6] Paolo Becchi, *Colpo di Stato permanente: Cronache degli ultimi tre anni* (Marsilio 2014).

The United Kingdom chapter revisits key legal and political moments in the relationship between the UK and the EU. It begins with the *Factortame II* decision, continues with the debates around Brexit and the triggering of article 50 TEU, and examines the residual jurisdiction of the ECJ even after formal withdrawal. Political actors such as UKIP and significant segments of the Conservative Party repeatedly presented the EU as a threat to British sovereignty, and sometimes proposed assertive policies to deal with this threat.[7] In the United Kingdom, too, forms of left-wing Euroscepticism emerged, most notably within the Labour Party during Jeremy Corbyn's leadership. More generally, the debate triggered by the 'Great Repeal Bill' was emblematic of a desire to reassert parliamentary supremacy and erase the principle of the primacy of EU law. At the same time, the chapter questions whether a vision of open, pro-European constitutionalism remains viable in the UK context, or whether Brexit has permanently reshaped the country's constitutional identity.

In Spain, Eurosceptic constitutional counter-narratives cut across the political spectrum. On the left, parties like Izquierda Unida and Podemos have linked their criticism of European integration to the EU's handling of the sovereign debt crisis. They have characterized the crisis management mechanisms as a 'coup d'état'[8] and have called for the repeal of the 2011 reform of article 135 of the Constitution, which allegedly prioritized debt repayment.[9] Their proposals often include the idea of launching a constituent process at the European level[10] in a search for a new democratic foundation of the Union. On the right, Vox combines nationalist rhetoric with legal strategies focused on judicial sovereignty. The party has pledged to 'recover sovereignty' in the domestic enforcement of judicial decisions[11] and defends the primacy of the Spanish Constitution in the face of what it sees as overreach by EU institutions.[12]

Poland offers perhaps the most fully developed case of constitutional resistance to the EU. It has become a laboratory for rule-of-law backsliding in which constitutional law is explicitly used to challenge European norms. During the previous government, the Law and Justice party (PiS) framed its political project in terms of a battle between a virtuous, homogeneous 'people' and a corrupt, cosmopolitan elite, often associated with Brussels. The Polish Constitutional Court has taken an active role in this rhetoric, invoking

[7] Conservative Party, 'Invitation to join the Government of Britain' (2010) 114.
[8] Izquierda Unida, 'Tu izquierda' (2019) 4.
[9] Izquierda Unida, 'Por un nuevo país' (2015) 95.
[10] Izquierda Unida, 'Más izquieda' (2008) 152.
[11] Vox, '100 medidas para la España viva' (2018) 4.
[12] Vox, 'Un programa para lo que importa' (2023).

constitutional identity to justify the rejection of EU law primacy.[13] PiS manifestos openly advocate legislation reaffirming the supremacy of the national constitution and regularly depict the EU as a bureaucratic apparatus disconnected from the values of a 'real', culturally rooted, Europe.[14]

Taken together, these cases illustrate how constitutional law—once a vehicle for deeper integration—has become a battleground for national actors seeking to reverse or halt the European project. Through legal rhetoric and institutional conflict, Eurosceptics aim not simply to exit the Union but also to transform its constitutional architecture from within.

In summary, despite their differences, these countries exhibit recurring patterns in their Eurosceptic constitutional counter-narratives, which can be analysed on three levels:

1. **Theoretical-constitutional level.** Eurosceptic forces insist on the existence of a singular national demos, whose national democratic constitution is under threat from European integration. Scholarly debates are sometimes co-opted and distorted to support this view.
2. **Judicial politics.** The ECJ is attacked and delegitimized, while national courts and political actors are called upon to oppose it.
3. **Party politics.** Constitutional rhetoric is instrumentalized in political manifestos to enhance the prestige and resonance of Eurosceptic agendas.

These three levels should not be understood as mutually exclusive, in the sense that there may be overlaps. In some systems, one level may be of greater interest than others, but in the case studies in this book, we have tried to include them all. This has led us to analyse a variety of actors, parties, and courts, but also the role of think tanks and intellectuals.

In these Eurosceptic counter-narratives, the demos is constructed in exclusionary terms, identity is framed as static and rooted in traditional national values, and sovereignty is portrayed as an absolute and unilateral claim. These framings often invoke moral, religious, and historical arguments to legitimize positions, depicting the EU as a mechanism of depoliticization that constrains democratic expression—what might be called a *dispositif* of technocratic

[13] Petra Bárd and Adam Bodnar, 'The End of an Era. The Polish Constitutional Court's Judgement on the Primacy of EU Law and Its Effects on Mutual Trust' [2021] CEPS Policy Insights No 2021-15.

[14] PiS, 'Nowoczesna Solidarna Bezpieczna Polka' (2011); PiS, 'Zdrowie Praca Rodzina' (2014); PiS, 'Polski Model Państwa Dobrobytu' (2019).

control. The EU is imagined as a vampire draining vitality from national democracies.

Such counter-narratives neglect the tangible benefits of European integration, including enhanced protection of rights, judicial remedies, regulatory capacities, and institutional checks and balances. Even the UK Supreme Court acknowledged these benefits in the *Miller* ruling. By contrast, Eurosceptic actors propagate the idea of an 'impossible coexistence' between the EU Treaties and national constitutions, championing the supremacy of the latter. From their perspective, the primacy of EU law, as established by the ECJ, is a constitutional aberration.

Should these constitutional counter-narratives be accepted as doctrinally sound deployments of constitutional discourse? We argue that they should not, for two key reasons. First, they contradict the fundamental tenets of post-WWII constitutionalism in Europe, and therefore do not stand up to scrutiny under comparative constitutional law. Post-WWII constitutions are marked by a commitment to openness, a principle that facilitates dialogue between domestic and international legal systems. This openness is deeply embedded in constitutional texts, many of which reference international human rights instruments and permit limitations on sovereignty for the sake of multilateral cooperation. This lineage can be traced back even to the interwar reflections of scholars such as Mirkine-Guetzévitch, who wrote about the 'internationalization of constitutional law'.[15]

Second, Eurosceptic counter-narratives often ignore—or explicitly deny—the content of the EU Treaties. Article 2 of the TEU articulates a set of common values that are not merely aspirational or ethical but are legally binding and shared between national and EU legal orders. These are what international lawyers might call 'multi-sourced equivalent norms',[16] by which they mean equivalent norms belonging simultaneously to different legal systems. In this sense, article 2 establishes a presumption of 'structural compatibility'[17] between national constitutions and EU law. Interpretative disagreement over these shared values is possible and, at times, productive. Indeed, constitutional

[15] Boris Mirkine-Guetzévitch, *Les nouvelles tendances du droit constitutionnel* (Giard 1936) 72.

[16] Tomer Broude and Yuval Shany (eds), *Multi-Sourced Equivalent Norms in International Law* (Hart Publishing 2011).

[17] Structural compatibility is the term used by Armin von Bogdandy, 'Founding Principles' in Armin von Bogdandy and Jürgen Bast (eds), *Principles of European Constitutional Law* (Hart Publishing 2009) 11, 22. On article 2 TEU as a clause of homogeneity at the supranational level, see Giacomo Delledonne, *L'omogeneità costituzionale negli ordinamenti composti* (Editoriale Scientifica 2017) 215. On the idea of an untouchable core in EU law, see Pablo Cruz Mantilla de los Ríos, 'European Constitutional Identity as the Unamendable Core of the EU Treaties' (2024) 20 European Constitutional Law Review 545.

conflicts can foster dialogue.[18] However, the confrontations fuelled by the abusive mobilization of constitutional law arguments are of a different nature: they are orchestrated to undermine shared commitments, hollow out the EU legal order, and betray the very constitutional texts that Eurosceptic actors purport to defend.

In sum, the Eurosceptic mobilization of constitutional law is not a neutral or benign exercise. It is a strategic, politicized, and often abusive deployment of legal language aimed at eroding both supranational and national constitutional commitments. At the normative level, we argue against such instrumentalization and defend the foundational principles of liberal constitutionalism in both its national and its European dimensions.

Of course, the Eurosceptic use of constitutional language does not always result in extreme forms of legal or political rupture. However, when Eurosceptic actors challenge the presumption of structural compatibility between national constitutional law and EU law—a presumption enshrined in article 2 TEU and affirmed through decades of integration—they reveal the abusive nature of their mobilization of domestic constitutional law arguments. This strategy not only contests the special status of EU law but also serves to legitimize broader attacks on the foundational principles of post-WWII constitutionalism, including openness, internationalism, and the rejection of authoritarian nationalism.

Conversely, when the constitutional core of post-war European legal orders is not directly contested, we may be observing a more restrained or non-abusive mobilization of national constitutional law. However, even in such cases, the practice raises significant concerns from the perspective of EU law, as it introduces legal friction, questions the primacy of EU law, and contributes to a broader atmosphere of constitutional uncertainty. At the same time, as we have argued elsewhere, constitutional conflicts are not inherently detrimental.[19] Historical examples show that they can generate productive tensions, particularly when they are used to promote dialogue between legal orders. For instance, in the 1970s, national constitutional courts challenged the absolute conception of primacy in order to safeguard fundamental rights as constitutional goods, a move that ultimately contributed to a partial convergence

[18] Giuseppe Martinico, 'The "Polemical" Spirit of European Constitutional Law: On the Importance of Conflicts in EU Law' (2015) 16 German Law Journal 1343; Ana Bobić, *The Jurisprudence of Constitutional Conflict in the European Union* (Oxford University Press 2022).

[19] Giuseppe Martinico, *Lo spirito polemico del diritto europeo: studio sulle ambizioni costituzionali dell'Unione* (Aracne 2011).

between national and supranational systems, now reflected in the language of the EU Treaties.

In contrast, in cases of abusive mobilization, Eurosceptic forces deploy constitutional law arguments not to foster such dialogue but to subvert it. Their aim is to advance a model that could be described as 'disintegration through (constitutional) law'.[20] This dynamic evokes what political theorists such as Nadia Urbinati[21] have described as the parasitic logic of populism—a strategy that co-opts the language and forms of constitutional democracy in order to erode it from within.

This book focuses on the mobilization of constitutional law by Eurosceptic forces; it is not, strictly speaking, a book about abusive mobilization per se. As we clarify in Chapter 2, we chose not to offer a general or abstract systematization of the various forms of the abuse of constitutional law categories. There are two main reasons for this decision. First, several excellent essays have already explored this subject in depth,[22] including in relation to EU law.[23] Second, as argued elsewhere,[24] it is difficult to develop a typology in the abstract without adopting a case-by-case approach.

Starting from the idea of the presumption of structural compatibility outlined in article 2 TEU, any mobilization that seeks to radically challenge the primacy of EU law is potentially abusive. This potential violation must of course be assessed for each case individually, taking into account the principles not only of primacy but also of competence and sincere cooperation.

That said, the analytical treatment in the case studies does provide numerous examples of abusive mobilization. One such example is the problematic constitutional bill promoted by most of the current Italian government—in particular Lega—which seeks to question the primacy of EU law and, through

[20] Scholars have recently made frequent reference to the idea of disintegration through law, although they have applied it to contexts that do not always coincide with those of this book. See, for example, Oliver Garner, *Constitutional Disintegration and Disruption: Withdrawal and Opt-Outs from the European Union* (Oxford University Press 2025); Vincenzo Cannizzaro, 'Disintegration through Law?' (2016) 1 European Papers 3. Obviously, the expression 'disintegration through law' deliberately plays on the title of the seminal series edited by Mauro Cappelletti, Monica Seccombe and Joseph Weiler, *Integration Through Law: Europe and the American Federal Experience, Vol 1: Methods, Tools and Institutions* (Walter de Gruyter 1986), highlighting how law can be mobilized not only to integrate but also, under certain conditions, to fragment or resist supranational authority.

[21] Nadia Urbinati, 'Democracy and Populism' (1998) 5 Constellations 110.

[22] See, for instance, Rosalind Dixon and David Landau, *Abusive Constitutional Borrowing. Legal Globalization and the Subversion of Liberal Democracy* (Oxford University Press 2021).

[23] Julian Scholtes, *The Abuse of Constitutional Identity in the European Union* (Oxford University Press 2023) 205.

[24] Giuseppe Martinico, *The Tangled Complexity of the EU Constitutional Process: The Frustrating Knot of Europe* (2nd edn, Routledge 2022) 190.

the amendments proposed in November 2024, also undermines the core of the *Simmenthal* mandate.[25]

Another example, this time involving the case law of a captured constitutional court, is the Polish judgment K 3/21,[26] which we discuss extensively in Chapter 7. In that case, the concept of constitutional identity was misused through a decontextualized reference to article 4(2) TEU, mirroring what occurred in the Hungarian case of 2016, which is illustrated in Chapter 2.

8.2. Why the Eurosceptic Mobilization of Constitutional Law Matters: On the Added Value of This Book

All of the above matter. The Eurosceptic mobilization of constitutional law is not merely a technical choice devoid of strategic and political implications. In the Polish case study chapter, we show that threats of the use of constitutional law against European integration can materialize into specific action, and in the UK case study chapter, we show that these constitutional counter-narratives are not only compatible with the exit strategy but are also often used to reinforce arguments about withdrawing from European organizations. At a time in which Eurosceptic populists are on the rise in so many European countries, these constitutional counter-narratives need to be taken seriously.[27] This is particularly true after Brexit, which has demonstrated how costly it is to leave the EU. Given the absence—for now at least—of a *domino effect* following Brexit, Eurosceptics have integrated their classic strategy.[28]

[25] Bill n 1917, 13 June 2024, 'Elenco delle proposte emendative (262) in I Commissione in sede referente pubblicate nel Bollettino delle Giunte e Commissioni del 05/11/2024 (n 396) riferite al C. 1917, in ordine di pubblicazione' <https://documenti.camera.it/apps/emendamenti/getProposteEmendativeSeduta.aspx?contenitorePortante=leg.19.eme.ac.1917&tipoSeduta=1&sedeEsame=referente&urnTestoRiferimento=urn:leg:19:1917:null:null:com:01:referente&dataSeduta=20241105&tipoListaEmendamenti=1.>. 'At every stage and in every type of judicial proceeding, at every level and in every instance, the Constitution shall not constitute, in any of its provisions, a source subordinate to the Treaties and other acts of the European Union' (Amendment 7.02). 'After Article 7, add the following: Art. 7-bis. 1. To Constitutional Law No. 87 of 11 March 1953, after Article 23, add the following: "Art. 23-bis. 1. If, in the course of a judgment, the judicial authority finds a conflict between a provision of law or an act having the force of law and a directly applicable European provision, it shall raise the question of constitutionality"' (Amendment 7.03). This is evidently in contrast with the case law of the ECJ (for instance Case C-106/77 *Amministrazione delle finanze dello Stato v Simmenthal*, ECLI:EU:C:1978:49).

[26] Polish Constitutional Court, decision K 3/21 <http://www.trybunal.gov.pl>.

[27] For a general analysis of the impact of populism on the EU and the national constitutional systems of Member States, see Alberto Nicotina, 'Measuring the Impact of Populism in the Face of EU Multi-level Governance: Politics and Constitutional Change' in Akritas Kaidatzis, Eleni Kalampakou, Ifigeneia Kamtsidou, Christos Papastylianos, and Costas Stratilatis (eds), *The People's Constitution: The Populist Transformation of Constitutional Law?* (Springer 2024) 205.

[28] On the impact of Brexit on the current state of integration, see, for example, Oliver Garner, 'Bridging Brexit and the Values Crisis: From Constitutional Resistance to Deliberation?' re:constitution

Despite this, and probably because political science is its main focus, the field of Euroscepticism studies has so far focused on political actors and political strategies.[29] Legal considerations have been less frequent in this area of study. This book seeks to remedy this, filling the gap with exhaustive evidence and analysis.

In this regard, we have insisted that, in our view, the Eurosceptic mobilization of constitutional law can be as much a form of 'hard Euroscepticism' as the exit strategy. The reason, using the classical definition of Taggart and Szczerbiak,[30] is that this strategy involves a rejection of the process of European integration as a whole through the denial of some of its basic principles. To do so, they portray national constitutional law and European law as if they were ultimately antagonists, as if they could not be open to each other. Once they have created a narrative of antagonisms in this allegedly irresolvable tension, they radically side with the national constitution and against European law. Paradoxically (or maybe not), this is often accompanied by a strong disregard for actual national constitutional law: in the Polish case, the PiS government mobilized constitutional rhetoric against European law whilst undermining national constitutional law, as evidenced by abundant literature in the field.[31] The Polish case, as we have seen, is interesting for several reasons. It confirms the damage that Euroscepticism, when combined with illiberalism, can inflict on constitutional systems and highlights the challenges of addressing such damage in the long term.[32] Moreover, it serves as a case study of a broader trend of 'transnational

Working Paper 33/2024<https://www.reconstitution.eu/fileadmin/bilder/re_constitution/33-2024_WP_reconstitution_Garner_finalDOI.pdf>.

29 See, inter alia, Paul Taggart and Aleks Szczerbiak, 'Contemporary Euroscepticism in the Party Systems of the European Union Candidate States of Central and Eastern Europe' (2004) 43 European Journal of Political Research 1; Catherine E De Vries and Erica E Edwards, 'Taking Europe to Its Extremes: Extremist Parties and Public Euroscepticism' (2009) 15 Party Politics 5; Sofia Vasilopoulou, 'Varieties of Euroscepticism: The Case of the European Extreme Right' (2009) 5 Journal of Contemporary European Research 3; Nathalie Brack and Nicholas Startin, 'Introduction: Euroscepticism, from the Margins to the Mainstream' (2015) 36 International Political Science Review 239; Paolo Marzi, 'Euroscepticism: A Meta-Analysis' (2025) 60 Acta Politica 704.

30 Taggart and Szczerbiak (n 29).

31 Tímea Drinóczi and Agnieszka Bień-Kacała, 'Illiberal Constitutionalism: The Case of Hungary and Poland' (2019) 20 German Law Journal 1140; Kriszta Kovács and Kim Lane Scheppele, 'The Fragility of an Independent Judiciary: Lessons from Hungary and Poland—and the European Union' (2018) 51 Communist and Post-Communist Studies 189.

32 Tom Gerald Daly, 'Constitutional Repair: A Comparative Theory' Democratic Repair and Renewal, Working Paper No 2-2023 <https://static1.squarespace.com/static/5abb53e6372b9691939ac577/t/6579c25840e061704144ad1a/1702478428708/DEM-DEC+WP_2-2023_Daly.pdf>. See also Tom Gerald Daly, '"Good" Court-Packing? The Paradoxes of Constitutional Repair in Contexts of Democratic Decay' Democratic Repair and Renewal, Working Paper No 1-2022 <https://static1.squarespace.com/static/5abb53e6372b9691939ac577/t/62319932d81fcf4a32a9e2e0/1647417654829/DEM-DEC+WP_2022-1_Daly_v2.pdf>.

culture wars',[33] in which the EU is portrayed as a threat to traditional values, particularly through an instrumental and hyper-conservative interpretation of the historical, moral, and religious dimensions of tradition.

Ultimately, the Eurosceptic mobilization of constitutional law can seriously harm the process of European integration. European Union law is based on the principle of primacy. Without it, the uniformity of the rules that sustain the supranational legal space would collapse. Without it, the trust amongst Member States would disappear. Without it, the binding force of the EU legal system would be fatally damaged. Member States would opt into and opt out of parts of EU law at will, thus completely undermining the law and policies of the EU. Something similar would happen with the decisions of the ECJ: by choosing when they wanted to comply with these decisions and when they did not, member countries would weaken the authority of the Luxembourg Court and question the whole edifice of European supranational integration.

The fact that constitutional law has become the preferred tool to do this is particularly striking. This is where this book displays its full added value. By analysing this phenomenon in detail, we hope to have addressed this important gap in the literature. In understanding the causes of this phenomenon, we hope to enrich public and policy debate about this topic. In shedding light on its consequences and implications, we hope to have put the focus on an important question of European law and politics that often goes unnoticed, as hard Euroscepticism is often exclusively identified with proposals to exit European organizations.

8.3. Food for Thought

In this book, we have aimed to reconstruct the way in which Eurosceptic forces mobilize constitutional law. The question of how to respond when this mobilization becomes abusive falls beyond the scope of our research. Numerous attempts in the literature address these abuses point by point.[34] Here, we limit

[33] Christopher McCrudden, 'Transnational Culture Wars' (2015) 13 International Journal of Constitutional Law 434; Pasquale Annicchino, 'The Geopolitics of Transnational Law and Religion: Wars of Conscience and the Framing Effects of Law as a Social Institution' in Susanna Mancini and Michel Rosenfeld (eds), *The Conscience Wars: Rethinking the Balance between Religion, Identity, and Equality* (Cambridge University Press 2018) 258; Kristina Stoeckl, 'Traditional Values, Family, Homeschooling: The Role of Russia and the Russian Orthodox Church in Transnational Moral Conservative Networks and Their Efforts at Reshaping Human Rights' (2023) 21 International Journal of Constitutional Law 224.

[34] Fabbrini (n 1); András Jakab and Lando Kirchmair, *Saving the European Union from Its Illiberal Member States* (Oxford University Press 2025).

ourselves to offering general observations, as citizens who are interested not so much in defending but in improving the European Union and the constitutional systems of its Member States, in the light of the aforementioned presumption of structural compatibility.

In this respect, we believe it is crucial to reclaim key concepts that certainly belong to constitutional theory, with identity and sovereignty being among the most significant of them. Too often, these foundational ideas are monopolized by Eurosceptic narratives, which is deeply unhealthy for democratic discourse and constitutional stability. If left unchallenged, this monopolization risks distorting the concepts and undermining their potential to foster inclusive and resilient political orders.

An example of this is identity. The concept of identity has always been a subject of debate, dividing the academic community: for some, it is a notion that should be abandoned,[35] while for others, it is a category that is not necessarily negative.[36] Other examples concern the rehabilitation of concepts such as sovereignty, which, as we have seen in post-WWII comparative European constitutional law, should be understood in an open sense and not only as a shield that can be unilaterally invoked to violate international obligations.

How, then, can we rehabilitate the concept of identity, for instance? Philosophers have long cautioned against reducing identity to a mere 'wall' that divides and excludes. Rather, identity should be understood as both a 'mirror' and a 'bridge'—a dynamic process that enables transformation through interaction with the other.[37] In this perspective, identity is not a fixed or rigid essence, nor is it confined to the Schmittian logic of friend versus enemy. Instead, it evolves by engaging with pluralism and difference, thereby enriching itself through dialogue and mutual recognition.

[35] Francesco Remotti, *Contro l'identità* (Laterza 1996).

[36] Francis Fukuyama, *Identity: The Demand for Dignity and the Politics of Resentment* (Deusto 2019).

[37] Furio Cerutti, 'Political Identity and Conflict: A Comparison of Definitions' in Furio Cerutti and Rodolfo Ragionieri (eds), *Identities and Conflicts* (Palgrave 2001) 9. 'Furio Cerruti has, in a text dealing with group identities and political identities, suggested two metaphorical concepts that can be used as analytical tools: the mirror-identity and the wall-identity. The mirror identity is dependent on the values, normative principles, life forms and life styles, within which a group recognises itself. This process essentially consists of the group members recognising or mirroring themselves in those values, and through this mirroring they form their image as a group "Self", as something that gives sense to their behaviour as a group. The mirror identity creates a "we" but it does not create an "other". The wall-identity, on the other hand, is more ambivalent. A wall gives support; it gives consistency to a group, preventing disintegration in times of political or social crises. A wall is also enclosing; it separates the group from other groups; it efficiently shuts out the Other. Which of the two walls will dominate or prevail depends on the wall's constitutive elements (universal integrative or self centred-exclusive) as well as on the trials (e.g. existential or political threats) to which the group is subjected', Karl G Hammarlund, 'Between the Mirror and the Wall: Boundary and Identity in Peter Weiss' Novel *Die Ästhetik des Widerstands*' in Karl G Hammarlund (ed), *Borders as Experience* (Forskning i Halmstad 2009) 117, 117.

This conceptual rehabilitation of identity finds resonance in the case law of the ECJ, particularly in its rulings on the Rule of Law Conditionality Regulation.[38] On that occasion, the ECJ confirmed the validity of the Regulation, clarified the binding legal nature of the values of article 2 of the TEU, and used the language of identity hitherto monopolized by illiberal populisms, stating that:

> In that regard, it must be borne in mind that Article 2 TEU is not merely a statement of policy guidelines or intentions, but contains values which, as noted in paragraph 127 above, are an integral part of the very identity of the European Union as a common legal order, values which are given concrete expression in principles containing legally binding obligations for the Member States.
>
> Even though, as is apparent from Article 4(2) TEU, the European Union respects the national identities of the Member States, inherent in their fundamental structures, political and constitutional, such that those States enjoy a certain degree of discretion in implementing the principles of the rule of law, it in no way follows that that obligation as to the result to be achieved may vary from one Member State to another.
>
> Whilst they have separate national identities, inherent in their fundamental structures, political and constitutional, which the European Union respects, the Member States adhere to a concept of 'the rule of law' which they share, as a value common to their own constitutional traditions, and which they have undertaken to respect at all times.[39]

This passage attracted the attention of some academics who saw this decision (also) as a response to the use of national identity by illiberal populists and their national constitutional courts.[40]

In these decisions, the ECJ emphasized that identity is not solely about demarcation or separation; it also encompasses the shared foundational values enshrined in article 2 TEU. These values unite a Union marked by cultural, linguistic, and political diversity. The Court's recognition of identity as a

[38] Regulation (EU, Euratom) 2020/2092 of the European Parliament and of the Council of 16 December 2020.

[39] ECJ, Case C-156/21 *Hungary v Parliament and Council* ECLI:EU:C:2022:97, paras 232–234.

[40] Tímea Drinóczi and Pietro Faraguna, 'The Constitutional Identity of the EU as a Counterbalance for Unconstitutional Constitutional Identities of the Member States' in Jurgen de Poorter, Gerhard van der Schyff, Maarten Stremler, Maartje De Visser, Ingrid Leijten, and Charlotte van Oirsouw (eds), *European Yearbook of Constitutional Law 2022. A Constitutional Identity for the EU?* (Springer 2023) 57.

common normative core—despite cultural differences—sends a powerful and constructive message about the nature of constitutional belonging in the EU.

In defending such concepts from Eurosceptic capture, constitutional theory can reclaim its normative vitality and contribute to a more inclusive, pluralistic understanding of political community—one that embraces difference without descending into fragmentation.

The ECJ's choice to use the language of identity in its judgment on the Conditionality Regulation (later taken up by other judgments[41]) is not entirely new. In fact, from a substantive point of view, the ECJ has attempted to reconstruct a core of indispensable elements that characterize the structure of the supranational order; it is sufficient to think of the *Kadi* saga[42] or even the infamous Opinion 2/13.[43]

Defenders of the 'no demos' thesis[44] might question this strategic choice by the Court of Justice, contesting the possibility of speaking of a common supranational identity. However, in doing so, they would end up relying on a widespread cliché in constitutional law studies, according to which there must first be a people before there can be a constitution. This reading is refuted by suggestions from comparative law.[45]

A particularly symbolic historical example is the US Federal Constitution, often described as emblematic of the popular role in constitutional genesis. As Morgan explained so well, the 'We the People' that opens the US Constitution did not crystallize an already existing people, but was the premise used for the invention of popular sovereignty.[46] It is no coincidence that, for example, the so-called 'antifederalists' opposed the formula that opens the preamble to the Federal Constitution. For them, only the peoples of the states existed, as argued by Patrick Henry[47] and, later, John Calhoun, the champion of the *Compact*

[41] ECJ, Case C-808/21 *European Commission v Czech Republic* ECLI:EU:C:2024:962, paras 160–162; ECJ, C-448/23 *European Commission v Republic of Poland* ECLI:EU:C:2025:975, paras 108, 177, 193.

[42] See, in particular, *Kadi I* in the Court of Justice (ECJ, Joined Cases C-402/05 P and C-415/05 P *Yassin Abdullah Kadi and Al Barakaat International Foundation v Council of the European Union and Commission* ECLI:EU:C:2008:461). On the *Kadi* saga, see Matej Avbelj, Filippo Fontanelli, and Giuseppe Martinico (eds), *Kadi on Trial: A Multifaceted Analysis of the Kadi Trial* (Routledge 2014).

[43] ECJ, Opinion 2/13 ECLI:EU:C:2014:2454.

[44] Dieter Grimm, 'Does Europe Need a Constitution?' (1995) 1 European Law Journal 282.

[45] Grimm addresses these legal considerations, at least in part. Dieter Grimm, *Sovereignty: The Origin and Future of a Political and Legal Concept* (Columbia University Press 2015) 55.

[46] Edmund S Morgan, *Inventing the People: The Rise of Popular Sovereignty in England and America* (W Norton & Company 1989).

[47] 'I have the highest veneration for those gentlemen; but, sir, give me leave to demand, What right had they to say, We, the people? My political curiosity, exclusive of my anxious solicitude for the public welfare, leads me to ask, Who authorized them to speak the language of, We, the people, instead of, We, the states? States are the characteristics and the soul of a confederation. If the states be not the agents of this compact, it must be one great, consolidated, national government, of the people of all the states. I have the highest respect for those gentlemen who formed the Convention, and, were some of them not

theory, among others. For these authors and politicians, the origin of the constitutional pact lay in the will of the states, as confirmed by the wording of Article VII of the U.S. Constitution, which refers to the document as a 'Constitution between the states so ratifying the same'.[48] In fact, the decision to include the phrase 'We the People' in the federal constitutional preamble was made by the Committee of Style to avoid inserting the names of the states before they ratified the Constitution.[49] Since at that time there was no federal citizenship—at least until the 14th Amendment—and since, according to the defenders of the Compact theory, only the people of the states existed, the states were considered to be the defenders of their rights (since the federal Bill of Rights was not considered to apply to the states). In some cases, the states had constitutions that were older than the Federal Constitution and, in the protection of rights in general, were considered more mature actors than the federation.

The American experience, therefore, shows us very clearly that constitutions rarely reflect the existence of a pre-existing people characterized by cultural, linguistic, and value homogeneity, as the defenders of constituent power would like.

Only a superficial reading could suggest that constitutions actually project the pre-existence of a homogeneous popular subject with a static identity. On the contrary, the study of constitutional processes shows us that constitutions contribute to the forging of the identity of the constitutional subject,[50] rather than merely reflecting a pre-existing identity. Through their processes, constitutions channel differences towards common values. According to the reasoning of the ECJ, the EU Treaties do something similar, performing a comparable performative function, and it is no coincidence that, in its case law

here, I would express some testimonial of esteem for them. America had, on a former occasion, put the utmost confidence in them—a confidence which was well placed; and I am sure, sir, I would give up any thing to them; I would cheerfully confide in them as my representatives. But, sir, on this great occasion, I would demand the cause of their conduct. Even from that illustrious man who saved us by his valor [George Washington], I would have a reason for his conduct: that liberty which he has given us by his valor, tells me to ask this reason; and sure I am, were he here, he would give us that reason. But there are other gentlemen here, who can give us this information. The people gave them no power to use their name. That they exceeded their power is perfectly clear. It is not mere curiosity that actuates me.' Patrick Henry, 'We the People? or We the States?' (1788) <https://press-pubs.uchicago.edu/founders/documents/preambles14.html>.

[48] Article VII of the US Constitution.

[49] Luigi M Bassani, 'Gli avversari della Costituzione americana: "antifederalisti" o "federalisti autentici"?' in Luigi M Bassani, *Gli Antifederalisti. I nemici della centralizzazione in America (1787–1788)* (IBL Libri 2011) 48.

[50] Michel Rosenfeld, *The Identity of the Constitutional Subject: Selfhood, Citizenship, Culture, and Community* (Routledge 1994); Gary Jeffrey Jacobsohn, *Constitutional Identity* (Harvard University Press 2010).

since the 1980s, the ECJ has defined the European Treaties as the 'fundamental constitutional charter' of the EU.[51]

It seems to us that this approach is shared by other books published in this prestigious series—for example, Julian Scholtes' *The Abuse of Constitutional Identity in the European Union*,[52] in which the author focuses on the relationship between abuse and constitutional identity. In that volume, Scholtes convincingly demonstrates that constitutional identity is not a concept to be abandoned or left in the hands of illiberal actors.[53] He offers compelling arguments for rehabilitating the concept and using it to guide actors within the European context to engage responsibly with supranational interlocutors.

Only history will tell whether or not the ECJ's strategy will succeed, but in principle, we are not inclined to condemn the Court for deciding to fight for control over the interpretation of a key concept, that of identity, which also belongs to the language of the Treaties and should therefore not be monopolized by illiberal and Eurosceptic forces.

[51] ECJ, Case 294/83 *Parti écologiste 'Les Verts' v European Parliament* CLI:EU:C:1986:166, para 23.

[52] Scholtes (n 23) 205.

[53] This does not, of course, preclude possible criticism of the Court of Justice's case law on the concept of national identity, as we have argued elsewhere: Giacomo Di Federico and Giuseppe Martinico, 'Official Languages, National Identities and the Protection of Minorities: A Complex Legal Puzzle: Court of Justice (Grand Chamber) 7 September 2022, Case C-391/20, *Boriss Cilevičs* et al., ECLI:EU:C:2022:638' (2023) 19 European Constitutional Law Review 346.

Selected Bibliography

Albi, Anneli, '"Europe" Articles in the Constitutions of Central and Eastern European Countries' (2005) 42 Common Market Law Review 399.

Albi, Anneli, 'Bringing Parliaments into the Equation of "Co-Operative Constitutionalism"' (2007) 3 European Constitutional Law Review 25.

Alexander, Larry and Schauer, Frederick, 'Defending Judicial Review' (2002) 17 Oxford Journal of Legal Studies 1.

Alonso García, Ricardo, *El juez español como juez comunitario* (Tirant lo Blanch 2003).

Alonso García, Ricardo, 'The Spanish Constitution and the European Constitution: The Script for a Virtual Collision and Other Observations on the Principle of Primacy' (2005) 6 German Law Journal 100.

Alonso, Sonia and Rovira-Kaltwasser, Cristóbal, 'Spain: No Country for the Populist Radical Right?' (2015) 20 South European Society and Politics 21.

Alter, Karen J, 'The European Court's Political Power' (1996) 19 West European Politics 458.

Alter, Karen J, Gathii, James T, and Helfer, Laurence R, 'Backlash against International Courts in West, East and Southern Africa: Causes and Consequences' (2016) 27 European Journal of International Law 293.

Alter, Karen J and Zürn, Michael, 'Theorising Backlash Politics: Conclusion to a Special Issue on Backlash Politics in Comparison' (2020) 22 The British Journal of Politics and International Relations 739.

Amos, Merris, 'The Value of the European Court of Human Rights to the United Kingdom' (2017) 28 European Journal of International Law 763.

Amoroso, Daniele, 'Italy' in Fulvio Palombino (ed), *Duelling for Supremacy: International Law vs. National Fundamental Principles* (Cambridge University Press 2019).

Annicchino, Pasquale, 'The Geopolitics of Transnational Law and Religion: Wars of Conscience and the Framing Effects of Law as a Social Institution' in Susanna Mancini and Michel Rosenfeld (eds), *The Conscience Wars: Rethinking the Balance between Religion, Identity, and Equality* (Cambridge University Press 2018) 258.

Aragón Reyes, Manuel, 'La Constitucion Española Y El Tratado De La Union Europea: La Reforma De La Constitucion' (1994) 42 Revista Española de Derecho Constitucional 9.

Arato, Andrew, *Post Sovereign Constitution Making: Learning and Legitimacy* (Oxford University Press 2016).

Arnull, Anthony, 'What Is a General Principle of EU Law?' in Stefan Vogenauer (ed), *Prohibition of Abuse of Law: A New General Principle of EU Law?* (Hart Publishing 2017) 7.

Athanassiou, Phoebus and Laulhé Shaelou, Stéphanie, 'EU Accession from within? An Introduction' (2014) 33 Yearbook of European Law 335.

Avbelj, Matej, 'Supremacy or Primacy of EU Law—(Why) Does It Matter?' (2011) 17 European Law Journal 744.

Avbelj, Matej, 'Constitutional Pluralism and Authoritarianism' (2020) 21 German Law Journal 1023.

Avbelj, Matej (ed), *The Future of EU Constitutionalism* (Hart 2023).

Avbelj, Matej, Fontanelli, Filippo, and Martinico, Giuseppe (eds), *Kadi on Trial: A Multifaceted Analysis of the Kadi Trial* (Routledge 2014).

Bale, Tim, 'Policy, Office, Votes—and Integrity. The British Conservative Party, Brexit, and Immigration' (2022) 48 Journal of Ethnic and Migration Studies 482.

Bale, Tim, 'Who Leads and Who Follows? The Symbiotic Relationship between UKIP and the Conservatives—and Populism and Euroscepticism' (2018) 38 Politics 263.

Baldassarri, Marco, 'The Resilient Governance of the EU: Towards a Post-Democratic Society' in Marco Baldassarri, Emanuele Castelli, Matteo Truffeli, and Giovanni Vezzani (eds), *Anti-Europeanism: Critical Perspectives Towards the European Union* (Springer 2020) 77.

Barber, Nicholas W, 'The Afterlife of Parliamentary Sovereignty' (2011) 9 International Journal of Constitutional Law 144.

Bárd, Petra and Bodnar, Adam, 'The End of an Era. The Polish Constitutional Court's Judgement on the Primacy of EU Law and Its Effects on Mutual Trust' CEPS Policy Insights No 2021-15.

Barnard, Catherine, 'The "Opt-Out" for the UK and Poland from the Charter of Fundamental Rights: Triumph of Rhetoric over Reality?' (The Lisbon Treaty and the Future of European Constitutionalism conference, 11–12 April 2008, EUI, Fiesole), on file with author.

Barra Caracciolo, Luciano, *Euro e (o?) democrazia costituzionale. La convivenza impossibile tra costituzione e trattati europei* (Dike Giuridica Editrice 2013).

Barsotti, Vittoria, Carozza, Paolo G, Cartabia, Marta, and Simoncini, Andrea, *Italian Constitutional Justice in Global Context* (Oxford University Press 2016).

Bartole, Sergio, *Interpretazioni e trasformazioni della Costituzione repubblicana* (Il Mulino 2004).

Basile, Linda and Mazzoleni, Oscar, 'Introduction: Sovereignist Wine in Populist Bottles?' in Linda Basile and Oscar Mazzoleni (eds), *Sovereignism and Populism: Citizens, Voters and Parties in Western European Democracies* (Routledge 2022) 1.

Bassani, Luigi M, 'Gli avversari della Costituzione americana: "antifederalisti" o "federalisti autentici"?' in Luigi M Bassani and Gli Antifederalisti, *I nemici della centralizzazione in America (1787–1788)* (IBL Libri 2011) 48.

Baquero Cruz, Julio, 'The Legacy of the Maastricht-Urteil and the Pluralist Movement' (2007) European University Institute RSCAS Working Paper 2007/13.

Becchi, Paolo, *Colpo di Stato permanente: Cronache degli ultimi tre anni* (Marsilio 2014).

Becchi, Paolo, *Italia sovrana* (Sperling & Kupfer 2018).

Becchi, Paolo, *Manifesto sovranista: per la liberazione dei popoli europei* (Giubilei Regnani 2019).

Becchi, Paolo and Palma, Giuseppe, *Dalla Seconda alla Terza Repubblica. Come nasce il governo Lega-M5S* (Paesi edizioni 2018).

Bellamy, Richard, *Political Constitutionalism* (Cambridge University Press 2009).

Berg-Schlosser, Dirk, Meur, Gisèle De, Rihoux, Benoît, and Ragin, Charles C, 'Qualitative Comparative Analysis (QCA) as an Approach' in Benoît Rihoux and Charles Ragin (eds), *Configurational Comparative Methods* (Sage 2009) 10.

Bernardi, Alessandro and Cupelli, Cristiano (eds), *Il caso Taricco e il dialogo tra le corti. L'ordinanza 24/2017 della Corte costituzionale* (Jovene 2017).

Betlem, Gerrit and Nollkaemper, André, 'Giving Effect to Public International Law and European Community Law before Domestic Courts. A Comparative Analysis of the Practice of Consistent Interpretation' (2003) 14 European Journal of International Law 569.

Betti, Emilio, *Teoria generale della interpretazione*, vol II (Giuffrè 1955).
Bickel, Alexander, *The Least Dangerous Branch* (Yale University Press 1986).
Bin, Roberto, 'L'interpretazione conforme. Due o tre cose che so di lei' (2015) 5 Rivista AIC 1.
Biondi, Andrea, 'Principio di supremazia e "Costituzione" inglese. I due casi "Martiri del sistema metrico" e "McWhirter and Gouriet"' (2006) <https://www.forumcostituzionale.it/wordpress/wp-content/uploads/pre_2006/101.pdf>.
Birkinshaw, Patrick, 'Brexit's Challenge to the UK's Unwritten Constitution' (2020) 26 European Public Law 29.
Bleckmann, Albert, 'Die Völkerrechtsfreundlichkeit der deutschen Rechtsordnung' (1979) 32 Die Öffentliche Verwaltung 309.
Blokker, Paul, 'Constitutional Politics and Populist Conservatism: The Contrasting Cases of Poland and Romania' (2021) 24 European Politics and Society 132.
Blokker, Paul, 'Populist Understandings of the Law: A Conservative Backlash?' (2021) 16 PArtecipazione e COnflitto 1434.
Blokker, Paul, 'Using Liberal–Legal Tools for Illiberal Gains: The European Court of Human Rights and Legal Mobilisation by Conservative Right-Wing Actors' (2024) 20 International Journal of Law in Context 401.
Bob, Clifford, *Rights as Weapons: Instruments of Conflict, Tools of Power* (Princeton University Press 2019).
Bobek, Michal and Kosař, David, 'Report on the Czech Republic and Slovakia' in Giuseppe Martinico and Oreste Pollicino (eds), *The National Judicial Treatment of the ECHR and EU Laws: A Comparative Constitutional Perspective* (Europa Law Publishing 2010) 133.
Bobic, Ana, *The Jurisprudence of Constitutional Conflict in the European Union* (Oxford University Press 2022).
Bobic, Ana and Dawson, Mark, 'Making Sense of the "Incomprehensible": The PSPP Judgment of the German Federal Constitutional Court' (2020) 57 Common Market Law Review 1953.
Bogdanor, Vernon, *Beyond Brexit: Towards a British Constitution* (IB Tauris 2019).
Bogdanor, Vernon, *Brexit and Our Unprotected Constitution* (2018) <https://consoc.org.uk/wp-content/uploads/2018/02/Brexit-and-our-unprotected-constitution-web.pdf>.
Bogdandy, Armin von, 'Founding Principles' in Armin von Bogdandy and Jürgen Bast (eds), *Principles of European Constitutional Law* (Hart Publishing 2009) 11.
Bolton, Matt and Pitts, Frederick Harry, 'Corbynism and Blue Labour: Post-Liberalism and National Populism in the British Labour Party' (2020) 15 British Politics 88.
Bossacoma Busquets, Pau, 'Secesión e integración en la Unión Europea Cataluña ¿nuevo Estado de la Unión?' (Think Tank 2017) <http://www.gencat.cat/governacio/pub/sum/iea/ieaR_01_esp.pdf>.
Brack, Nathalie and Startin, Nicholas, 'Introduction: Euroscepticism, From the Margins to the Mainstream' (2015) 36 International Political Science Review 239.
Broude, Tomer and Shany, Yuval (eds), *Multi-Sourced Equivalent Norms in International Law* (Hart Publishing 2011).
Bugarič, Bojan and Ginsburg, Tom, 'The Assault on Postcommunist Courts' (2016) 27 The Journal of Democracy 69.
Buxadé, Jorge, *Soberanía: Por qué la Nación es valiosa y merece la pena defenderla* (Homo Legens 2021).
Caiani, Manuela and Conti, Nicolò, 'In the Name of the People: The Euroscepticism of the Italian Radical Right' (2014) 15 Perspectives on European Politics and Society 83.
Caggiano, Giandonato, 'La dottrina italiana nella fase costituente dell'ordinamento giuridico comunitario' (2013) 8 Studi sull'integrazione europea 441.

Calamandrei, Piero, 'Cenni introduttivi sulla Costituente e i suoi lavori', in Piero Calamandrei, *Scritti e discorsi politici, vol II* (La Nuova Italia 1966) 421.

Calamandrei, Piero, 'La Costituzione e le leggi per attuarla', in Piero Calamandrei, *Opere giuridiche*, vol III (Morano 1965) 553.

Cannizzaro, Vincenzo, 'Disintegration through Law?' (2016) 1 European Papers 3.

Cappelletti, Mauro, Seccombe, Monica, and Weiler, Joseph (eds), *Integration Through Law: Europe and the American Federal Experience, Vol 1: Methods, Tools and Institutions* (Walter de Gruyter 1986).

Carrasco, Beatriz, González, Elena, and Harguindéguy, Jean-Baptiste, 'Euroscepticism in Spain: A Phenomenon of Extremes?' in Xavier Coller and Leonardo Sánchez-Ferrer (eds), *Politicians in Hard Times: Spanish and South European MPs Facing Citizens after the Great Recession* (Springer International Publishing 2021) 264.

Carrillo, Santiago, *Eurocomunismo y estado* (Editorial Critica 1977).

Carrieri, Luca and Vittori, Davide, 'Defying Europe? The Euroscepticism of Radical Right and Radical Left Voters in Western Europe' (2021) 43 Journal of European Integration 955, 956.

Carrozza, Paolo, 'Constitutionalism's Post-Modern Opening' in Martin Loughlin and Neil Walker (eds), *The Paradox of Constitutionalism: Constituent Power and Constitutional Form* (Oxford University Press 2008) 169.

Cartabia, Marta, *Principi inviolabili e integrazione europea* (Giuffrè 1995).

Cartabia, Marta and Weiler, Joseph HH, *L'Italia in Europa* (Bologna 2000).

Casey, Conor, 'The Sir Gerald Fitzmaurice Option: A Classical Natural Law Method for Interpreting the European Convention on Human Rights' (1 November 2024) <https://papers.ssrn.com/sol3/papers.cfm?abstract_id=5123963>.

Casey, Conor and Zhu, Yuan Yi, *Revisiting the British Origins of the European Convention on Human Rights* (Policy Exchange 2025) <https://policyexchange.org.uk/publication/revisiting-the-british-origins-of-the-european-convention-on-human-rights/>.

Cassese, Antonio, 'Politica estera e relazioni internazionali nel disegno emerso alla Assemblea Costituente' in Ugo de Siervo (ed), *Scelte della Costituente e cultura giuridica. I: Costituzione italiana e modelli stranieri* (Il Mulino 1980) 505.

Cassese, Antonio, 'Modern Constitutions and International Law' (1985) 122 Collected Courses of the Hague Academy of International Law 331.

Castillo-Ortiz, Pablo, 'Constitutional Review in the Member States of the EU-28: A Political Analysis of Institutional Choices' (2020) 47 Journal of Law and Society 87.

Castillo-Ortiz, Pablo, 'Constitutionalism and the Radical-Right: The Case of the Spanish Party Vox' (2023) 2 International Journal of Constitutional Law (ICON) 733.

Castillo-Ortiz, Pablo, *EU Treaties and the Judicial Politics of National Courts. A Law and Politics Approach* (Routledge 2017).

Castillo-Ortiz, Pablo, 'Right-Wing Eurosceptic Parties and the Strategic Use of Law' (2023) 61 Journal of Common Market Studies 1125.

Castillo-Ortiz, Pablo, 'The Illiberal Abuse of Constitutional Courts in Europe' (2019) 15 European Constitutional Law Review 48.

Castillo-Ortiz, Pablo, 'The Imperfect Legitimacy of Judicial Umpires in European Multilevel Democracies' (2024) 44 Legal Studies 242.

Cerutti, Furio, 'Political Identity and Conflict: A Comparison of Definitions' in Furio Cerutti and Rodolfo Ragionieri (eds), *Identities and Conflicts* (Palgrave 2001) 9.

Claes, Monica, 'The "European Clauses" in the National Constitutions: Evolution and Typology' (2005) 24(1) Yearbook of European Law 81.

Claes, Monica, *The National Courts' Mandate In The European Constitution* (Hart 2006).

Claes, Monica, 'National Identity: Trump Card or Up for Negotiation?', in Alejandro Saiz Arnaiz and Carina Alcoberro Llivina (eds), *National Constitutional Identity and European Integration* (Intersentia 2013).

Claes, Monica, *National Identity in EU Law* (Hart 2015).

Closa, Carlos, 'National Higher Courts and the Ratification of EU Treaties' (2013) 36 West European Politics 97.

Cloots, Elke, *National Identity in EU Law* (Hart 2015).

Coli, Martina, 'Don't Try to Discipline Your Judges (And Prevent Them from Applying EU Law): The Court of Justice's Judgment in Commission v. Poland (C-204/21)' (12 July 2023) <https://www.diritticomparati.it/dont-try-to-discipline-your-judges-and-prevent-them-from-applying-eu-law-the-court-of-justices-judgment-in-commission-v-poland-c-204-21/>.

Conti, Nicolò, 'The Italian Political Elites and Europe: Big Move, Small Change?' (2017) 38 International Political Science Review/Revue internationale de science politique 534.

Conti, Nicolò, Marangoni, Francesco, and Verzichelli, Luca, 'Euroscepticism in Italy from the Onset of the Crisis: Tired of Europe?' (2020) 25 South European Society and Politics 1.

Cope, Kevin L, 'The Intermestic Constitution: Lessons from the World's Newest Nation' (2013) 53 Virginia Journal of International Law 667, 670.

Cowell, Frederick, 'Understanding the Causes and Consequences of British Exceptionalism towards the European Court of Human Rights' (2019) 23 The International Journal of Human Rights 1183.

Craig, Paul, 'Sovereignty of the United Kingdom Parliament after Factortame' (1991) 11 Yearbook of European Law 221.

Craig, Paul, 'Report on the United Kingdom: Constitutional Doctrine within the United Kingdom: The Impact of the EC' in Anne M Slaughter, Alec Stone Sweet and Joseph HH Weiler (eds), *The European Court and National Courts: Doctrine and Jurisprudence* (Hart Publishing 1998) 195.

Craig, Paul, 'The European Union Act 2011: Locks, Limits and Legality' (2011) 48 Common Market Law Review 1915.

Cruz Mantilla de los Ríos, Pablo, 'European Constitutional Identity as the Unamendable Core of the EU Treaties' (2024) 20 European Constitutional Law Review 545.

Cruz Villalón, Pedro and Pagés, Requejo, and Luis, Juan, 'La relación entre la cuestión prejudicial y la cuestión de inconstitucionalidad' (2015) 50 Revista de Derecho Comunitario Europeo 173.

Cymer, Klaudia, 'The Rise of Euroscepticism on the Political Scene in Poland—The Case of the Party Law and Justice' (2022) 10 European Studies Quarterly 89.

Dajč, Haris and Styczyńska, Natasza (eds), *Faces of Populism in Central and South-Eastern Europe* (Jagiellonian University Press 2023).

Daly, Tom Gerald, 'Constitutional Repair: A Comparative Theory' DEM-DEC Constitutional Repair Working Paper No 2-2023 <https://static1.squarespace.com/static/5abb53e6372b9691939ac577/t/6579c25840e061704144ad1a/1702478428708/DEM-DEC+WP_2-2023_Daly.pdf>.

Daly, Tom Gerald, '"Good" Court-Packing? The Paradoxes of Constitutional Repair in Contexts of Democratic Decay' DEM-DEC Constitutional Repair Working Paper No 1-2022 <https://static1.squarespace.com/static/5abb53e6372b9691939ac577/t/62319932d81fcf4a32a9e2e0/1647417654829/DEM-DEC+WP_2022-1_Daly_v2.pdf>.

Dani, Marco and Menéndez, Agustín J, 'European Constitutional Imagination: A Whig Interpretation of the Process of European Integration?' (2020) iCourts Working Paper Series No 243, 42 <https://papers.ssrn.com/sol3/papers.cfm?abstract_id=3807102>.

Dann, Philipp and Engelhardt, Marie von, 'The Global Administrative Order through a German Lens: Perception and Influence of Legal Structures of Global Governance in Germany' (2011) 12 German Law Journal 1371.

De la Porte, Caroline and Jensen, Mads Dagnis, 'The Next Generation EU: An Analysis of the Dimensions of Conflict Behind the Deal' (2021) 55 Social Policy & Administration 388.

De Poorter, Jurgen, van der Schyff, Gerhard, Stremler, Maarten, De Visser, Maartje, Leijten, Ingrid and van Oirsouw, Charlotte (eds), *European Yearbook of Constitutional Law 2022. A Constitutional Identity for the EU?* (Springer 2023).

Del Vecchio, Giorgio, 'Les bases du droit comparé et les principes généraux du droit' (1960) 12 Revue internationale de droit comparé 493.

Delledonne, Giacomo, *L'omogeneità costituzionale negli ordinamenti composti* (Editoriale Scientifica 2017).

Delledonne, Giacomo, Martinico, Giuseppe, Monti, Matteo, and Pacini, Fabio (eds), *Italian Populism and Constitutional Law. Strategies, Conflicts and Dilemmas* (Palgrave 2020).

De Vries, Catherine E, 'Benchmarking Brexit: How the British Decision to Leave Shapes EU Public Opinion' (2017) 55 Journal of Common Market Studies 38.

De Vries, Catherine E, 'Public Opinion in European Union Politics' Oxford Research Encyclopedia of Politics (2020) 10 <https://oxfordre.com/politics/view/10.1093/acrefore/9780190228637.001.0001/acrefore-9780190228637-e-1049>.

De Vries, Catherine E and Edwards, Erica E, 'Taking Europe to Its Extremes: Extremist Parties and Public Euroscepticism' (2009) 15 Party Politics 5.

Diamanti, Ilvo, *Il male del Nord: Lega, localismo, secessione* (Donzelli 1996).

Díaz, José and Molina, Jerónimo, *Los enemigos de España son mis enemigos. Bibliografía panhispánica de Carl Schmitt (1926–2022)* (Editorial Comares 2022).

Dicey, Albert V, *An Introduction to the Study of the Law of the Constitution* (Macmillan 1959).

Díez-Picazo, Luis María, 'El Derecho comunitario en la jurisprudencia constitucional española' (1998) 18 Revista española de derecho constitucional 2552.

Di Federico, Giacomo, L'identità nazionale degli stati membri nel diritto dell'Unione europea. *Natura e portata dell'art. 4, par. 2, TUE* (Editoriale Scientifica 2017).

Di Federico, Giacomo, 'In the Name of Primacy. Opinion C-448/23 and the EU's Existential Principle of Primacy' (22 April 2025) <https://verfassungsblog.de/polishing-broken-tribunal/>.

Di Federico, Giacomo and Martinico, Giuseppe, 'Official Languages, National Identities and the Protection of Minorities: A Complex Legal Puzzle: Court of Justice (Grand Chamber) 7 September 2022, Case C-391/20, Boriss Cilevičs et al., ECLI:EU:C:2022:638' (2023) 19 European Constitutional Law Review 346.

Di Maggio, Marco, 'Internazionalismo, socialismo ed europeismo nel Pci di Berlinguer' (2016) 18 Dimensioni e problemi della ricerca storica 55.

Dixon, Rosalind and Landau, David, *Abusive Constitutional Borrowing. Legal Globalization and the Subversion of Liberal Democracy* (Oxford University Press 2021).

Douglas-Scott, Sionaidh, *Brexit, Union and Disunion: The Evolution of British Constitutional Unsettlement* (Cambridge University Press 2023).

Drewry, Gavin, 'The Jurisprudence of British Euroscepticism: A Strange Banquet of Fish and Vegetables' (2007) 3 Utrecht Law Review 101.

Drexl, Josef, 'Was Sir Francis Drake a Dutchman—British Supremacy of Parliament after Factortame' (1993) 41 American Journal of Comparative Law 551.

Drinóczi, Tímea and Bień-Kacała, Agnieszka, 'Illiberal Constitutionalism: The Case of Hungary and Poland' (2019) 20 German Law Journal 1140.

Drinóczi, Tímea and Bień-Kacała, Agnieszka, *Illiberal Constitutionalism in Poland and Hungary. The Deterioration of Democracy, Misuse of Human Rights and Abuse of the Rule of Law* (Routledge 2022).

Drinóczi, Tímea and Faraguna, Pietro, 'The Constitutional Identity of the EU as a Counterbalance for Unconstitutional Constitutional Identities of the Member States' in Jurgen de Poorter, Gerhard van der Schyff, Maarten Stremler, Maartje De Visser, Ingrid Leijten, and Charlotte van Oirsouw, *European Yearbook of Constitutional Law 2022. A Constitutional Identity for the EU?* (Springer 2023) 57.

Edwards, Liam, 'Allister and Others v Secretary of State for Northern Ireland: A Summary of the "NI Protocol" Case' (10 May 2023) <https://www.diritticomparati.it/allister-and-others-v-secretary-of-state-for-northern-ireland-a-summary-of-the-ni-protocol-case/>.

Ekins, Richard, 'Restoring Parliamentary Democracy' (2018) 39 Cardozo Law Review 997, 1017.

Ekins, Richard, *Protecting the Constitution* (Policy Exchange 2019).

Ekins, Richard, 'The Constitutional Dynamics of Brexit' (2022) 12 Notre Dame Journal of International & Comparative Law 46.

Ekins, Richard and Gee, Graham, 'How Not to Dismiss Human Rights Law Reform' (Policy Exchange, Judicial Power Project, 11 May 2016) <https://judicialpowerproject.org.uk/richard-ekins-and-graham-gee-how-not-to-dismiss-human-rights-law-reform/>.

Ekins, Richard and Gee, Graham, 'Written Evidence from Policy Exchange's Judicial Power Project (HRA0033)' UK Parliament, Joint Committee on Human Rights, Twenty Years of the Human Rights Act Inquiry para 2 <https://data.parliament.uk/writtenevidence/committeeevidence.svc/evidencedocument/human-rights-committee/20-years-of-the-human-rights-act/written/90593.html>.

Elliott, Mark, 'Parliamentary Sovereignty and the New Constitutional Order: Legislative Freedom, Political Reality and Convention' (2002) 22 Legal Studies 340.

Elster, Jon, 'Constitution-making and Violence' (2012) 41 Journal of Legal Analysis 7.

Ewing, Keith D, 'The Human Rights Act and Parliamentary Democracy' (1999) 62 The Modern Law Review 79.

Fabbrini, Sergio, *Manuale di autodifesa europeista. Come rispondere alla sfida del sovranismo* (LUISS University Press 2019).

Fabbrini, Federico and Sajó, András, 'The Dangers of Constitutional Identity' (2019) 25 European Law Journal 457.

Fabbrini, Sergio and Zgaga, Tiziano, 'Right-Wing Sovereignism in the European Union: Definition, Features and Implications' (2024) 62 Journal of Common Market Studies 341.

Faraguna, Pietro, 'Unamendability and Constitutional Identity in the Italian Constitutional Experience' (2019) 21 European Journal of Law Reform 329.

Faraguna, Pietro, 'Populism and Constitutional Amendment' in Giacomo Delledonne, Giuseppe Martinico, Matteo Monti and Fabio Pacini (eds), *Italian Populism and Constitutional Law. Strategies, Conflicts and Dilemmas* (Palgrave 2020) 97.

Fella, Stefano, 'Poland: The Law and Justice Government and Relations with the EU, 2015–2023' Commons Library Research Briefing (13 February 2024) <https://researchbriefings.files.parliament.uk/documents/CBP-9868/CBP-9868.pdf>.

Feltri, Stefano, 'Why Is the ESM so Controversial (only) in Italy? A Conversation with Klaus Regling' (Bocconi Institute for European Policymaking 15 January 2024) <https://iep.

unibocconi.eu/publications/why-esm-so-controversial-only-italy-conversation-klaus-regling-0>.
Ferrajoli, Luigi, 'L'alleanza perversa fra sovranismi e liberismo' (2019) 2 costituzionalismo.it 1.
Ferrajoli, Luigi, and Paria, Iura. *Los Fundamentos de La Democracia Constitucional* (Trotta 2020) 19–51.
Ferrarese, Alberto, 'Casapound alle europee senza programma per uscire dall'Ue' (16 May 2019) <https://www.policymakermag.it/fact-checking/casapound-europee-senza-programma-uscire-ue/>.
Finnis, John, 'Brexit and the Balance of Our Constitution', Judicial Power Project (2016) <https://judicialpowerproject.org.uk/wp-content/uploads/2016/12/Finnis-2016-Brexit-and-the-Balance-of-Our-Constitution2.pdf>.
Finnis, John, 'Terminating Treaty-Based UK Rights' (26 October 2016) <https://ukconstitutionallaw.org/2016/10/26/john-finnis-terminating-treaty-based-uk-rights/>.
Follesdal, Andreas and Hix, Simon, 'Why There Is a Democratic Deficit in the EU: A Response to Majone and Moravcsik' (2006) 44 Journal of Common Market Studies 533.
Folvarčný, Adam and Kopeček, Lubomír, 'Which Conservatism? The Identity of the Polish Law and Justice Party' (2020) 16 Politics in Central Europe 159.
Francis, Claire, 'Factortame Ltd. v. Secretary of State for Transport' (1990) 84 American Journal of International Law 269.
Frankenberg, Günter, *Comparative Constitutional Studies: Between Magic and Deceit* (Edward Elgar 2018).
Fukuyama, Francis, *Identity: The Demand for Dignity and the Politics of Resentment* (Deusto 2019).
Galligan, Denis J, 'The Paradox of Constitutionalism or the Potential of Constitutional Theory?' (2008) 28 Oxford Journal of Legal Studies 343.
Gallo, Daniele, 'Challenging EU Constitutional Law: The Italian Constitutional Court's New Stance on Direct Effect and the Preliminary Reference Procedure' (2019) 25 European Law Journal 434.
García Andrade, Paula, 'La ciudadanía europea y la sucesión de Estados: a vueltas con las implicaciones de una separación territorial en el seno de la UE' (2014) 49 Revista de Derecho Comunitario Europeo 997.
Gardiner, James A, 'In Search of Sub-National Constitutionalism' (2008) 4 European Constitutional Law Review 325.
Gardiner, Patrick, 'Conflating the Powers of the Commissarial and the Sovereign Dictator in Tunisia' (29 November 2022) <https://verfassungsblog.de/conflating-the-powers-of-the-commissarial-and-the-sovereign-dictator-in-tunisia/>.
Garbowski, Christopher, 'Catholicism in the New Poland: A Religion and Society in Transition' (2020) 40 Occasional Papers on Religion in Eastern Europe 35.
Garner, Oliver, 'Referring Brexit to the Court of Justice of the European Union: Why Revoking an Article 50 Notice Should be Left to the United Kingdom' (14 November 2016) <https://www.europeanlawblog.eu/pub/referring-brexit-to-the-court-of-justice-of-the-european-union-why-revoking-an-article-50-notice-should-be-left-to-the-united-kingdom/release/1>.
Garner, Oliver, 'Can the United Kingdom Unilaterally Revoke Its Article 50 Notification to Withdraw from the EU? Wightman v Secretary of State for DexEU CSIH 62' (24 September 2018) <https://www.europeanlawblog.eu/pub/can-the-united-kingdom-unilaterally-revoke-its-article-50-notification-to-withdraw-from-the-eu-wightman-v-secretary-of-state-for-dexeu-2018-csih-62/release/1>.

Garner, Oliver, 'The Brexit Sovereignty Problem' (17 April 2024) Review of Democracy <https://revdem.ceu.edu/2024/04/17/the-brexit-sovereignty-problem/>.

Garner, Oliver, 'Bridging Brexit and the Values Crisis: From Constitutional Resistance to Deliberation?' re:constitution Working Paper 33/2024 <https:// reconstitution.eu/fileadmin/bilder/re_constitution/33-2024_WP_reconstitution_Garner_finalDOI.pdf>.

Garner, Oliver, *Constitutional Disintegration and Disruption: Withdrawal and Opt-Outs from the European Union* (Oxford University Press 2025).

Gerards, Janneke, 'The Irrelevance of the Netherlands Constitution, and the Impossibility of Changing It' (2016) 77 Revue interdisciplinaire d'études juridiques 207.

Ghiglione, Giorgio, 'How an Obscure General Became the Star of Italy's Far Right' Foreign Policy (10 May 2024) <https://foreignpolicy.com/2024/05/10/italy-roberto-vannacci-far-right-meloni-eu-election/>.

Gifford, Chris, 'The UK and the European Union: Dimensions of Sovereignty and the Problem of Eurosceptic Britishness' (2010) 63 Parliamentary Affairs 321.

Ginsburg, Tom, 'The Global Spread of Constitutional Review' in Keith E. Whittington, R. Daniel Kelemen, and Gregory A. Caldeira (eds), *Oxford Handbook of Law and Politics* (Oxford University Press 2008) 81.

Ginsburg, Tom and Simpser, Alberto (eds), *Constitutions in Authoritarian Regimes* (Cambridge University Press 2014).

Ginsburg, Tom and Versteeg, Mila, 'Why Do Countries Adopt Constitutional Review?' (2014) 30 The Journal of Law, Economics, and Organization 587.

Giusti, Serena, *The Fall and Rise of National Interest: A Contemporary Approach* (Palgrave 2022).

Gliszczyńska-Grabias, Aleksandra and Sadurski, Wojciech, 'Is It Polexit Yet? Comment on Case K 3/21 of 7 October 2021 by the Constitutional Tribunal of Poland' (2023) 19 European Constitutional Law Review 163.

Gordon, Michael, 'The European Union Act 2011' (12 January 2012) <https://ukconstitutionallaw.org/2012/01/12/mike-gordon-the-european-union-act-2011/>.

Gordon, Michael, 'Brexit: A Challenge for the UK Constitution, of the UK Constitution?' (2016) 12 European Constitutional Law Review 409.

Granat, Miroslaw and Granat, Katarzyna, *The Constitution of Poland. A Contextual Analysis* (Hart Publishing 2019).

Griffith, John A, 'The Political Constitution' (1979) 42 Modern Law Review 1.

Grimm, Dieter, 'Does Europe Need a Constitution?' (1995) 1 European Law Journal 282.

Grimm, Dieter, *Sovereignty: The Origin and Future of a Political and Legal Concept* (Columbia University Press 2015).

Grimm, Dieter, 'Constituent Power and Limits of Constitutional Amendments' (2016) 2 Nomos 1.

Group of Twelve, 'Sailing on High Seas: Reforming and Enlarging the EU for the 21st Century' (2023) <https://www.diplomatie.gouv.fr/IMG/pdf/20230919_group_of_twelve_report_updated14.12.2023_cle88fb88.pdf>.

Grossi, Paolo, *A History of European Law* (Blackwell 2010) 154.

Guarino, Giuseppe, 'The "Truth" about Europe and the euro. A Second Essay' (2014) 26 Nomos. Le attualità del diritto, 25.

Guastaferro, Barbara, 'Beyond the Exceptionalism of Constitutional Conflict: The Ordinary Functions of the Identity Clause' (2012) 31 Yearbook of European Law 263.

Guazzarotti, Andrea, 'Sovranità e integrazione europea' (2017) 7 Rivista AIC 1.

Häberle, Peter, 'Die verfassunggebende Gewalt des Volkes im Verfassungsstaat – eine vergleichende Textstufenanalyse' (1987) 112 Archiv des öffentlichen Rechts 54.

Halikiopoulou, Daphne, Nanou, Kyriaki, and Vasilopoulou, Sofia, 'The Paradox of Nationalism: The Common Denominator of Radical Right and Radical Left Euroscepticism' (2012) 51 European Journal of Political Research 504.

Halmai, Gábor, 'Can the Rule of Law Be Restored by Violating Its Principles? The Current Polish Debate' (3 January 2025) <https://verfassungsblog.de/can-the-rule-of-law-be-restored-by-violating-its-principles/>.

Hammarlund, Karl G, 'Between the Mirror and the Wall: Boundary and Identity in Peter Weiss' Novel Die Ästhetik des Widerstands' in Karl G Hammarlund (ed), *Borders as Experience* (Forskning i Halmstad 2009) 117.

Harmsen, Robert, 'Concluding Comment: On Understanding the Relationship between Populism and Euroscepticism' (2010) 11 Perspectives on European Politics and Society 333.

Havlík, Vratislav and Hloušek, Vít, 'Where Have All the "Exiters" Gone? Contextualising the Concept of Hard Euroscepticism' (2025) 63 Journal of Common Market Studies 351.

Hein, Michael, 'Do Constitutional Entrenchment Clauses Matter? Constitutional Review of Constitutional Amendments in Europe' (2020) 18 International Journal of Constitutional Law 88.

Henry, Patrick, 'We the People? or We the States?' (1788) <https://www.redhill.org/speech/we-people-or-we-states>.

Hernández Delgado, Pau, 'La nueva derecha española. Una experiencia intelectual entre el tardofranquismo y la globalización' (2024) 9 Tiempo devorado: revista de historia actual 4.

Herrero de Miñón, Miguel, 'Constitución Española y Unión Europea: Comentarios al Artículo 93 de La Constitución Española' (1992) 26 Revista de las Cortes Generales 7.

Herrero y Rodríguez de Miñón, Miguel, Gómez-Ferrer, José María Jover, Martín, Áurea Roldán, and Alonso, José Amérigo, 'La Respuesta Constitucional a la Integración Europea' (2005) 25 Revista Española de Derecho Constitucional 239.

Hloušek, Vít and Havlík, Vratislav, 'Eurosceptic Narratives in the Age of COVID-19: The Central European States in Focus' (2024) 40 East European Politics 154.

House of Lords EU Select Committee, 'The Treaty of Lisbon: An Impact Assessment' (13 March 2008) <https://publications.parliament.uk/pa/ld200708/ldselect/ldeucom/62/62.pdf>.

Howe, Geoffrey, 'The European Communities Act 1972' (1973) 49 International Affairs 1.

Itzcovich, Giulio, *Teorie e ideologie del diritto comunitario* (Giappichelli 2006).

Jacobsohn, Gary Jeffrey, *Constitutional Identity* (Harvard University Press 2010).

Jakab, András and Kirchmair, Lando, *Saving the European Union from Its Illiberal Member States* (Oxford University Press 2025).

Jaraczewski, Jakub, 'Gazing into the Abyss. The K 3/21 Decision of the Polish Constitutional Tribunal' (12 October 2021) <https://verfassungsblog.de/gazing-into-the-abyss/>.

Jay, Zoë, 'Keeping Rights at Home: British Conceptions of Rights and Compliance with the European Court of Human Rights' (2017) 19 The British Journal of Politics and International Relations 842.

Kaidatzis, Akritas, Kalampakou, Eleni, Kamtsidou, Ifigeneia, Papastylianos, Christos, and Stratilatis, Costas (eds), *The People's Constitution: The Populist Transformation of Constitutional Law?* (Springer 2024).

Kavanagh, Aileen, 'What's so Weak about "Weak-Form Review"? The Case of the UK Human Rights Act 1998' (2015) 13 International Journal of Constitutional Law 1008.

Kelemen, R Daniel, 'Europe's Other Democratic Deficit: National Authoritarianism in Europe's Democratic Union' (2017) 52 Government and Opposition 211.

Kelemen, R Daniel and Pech, Laurent, 'Why Autocrats Love Constitutional Identity and Constitutional Pluralism. Lessons from Hungary and Poland', Reconnect Working Paper no 2 (2018), <http://icedd.luiss.it/files/2019/02/Why-autocrats-love-constitutional.pdf>.

Kelemen, R Daniel and Pech, Laurent, 'The Uses and Abuses of Constitutional Pluralism: Undermining the Rule of Law in the Name of Constitutional Identity in Hungary and Poland' (2019) 21 Cambridge Yearbook of European Legal Studies 59.

Kelsen, Hans, *Vom Wesen und Wert der Demokratie* (JBC Mohr 1929) 61.

Kelsen, Hans, 'Judicial Review of Legislation: A Comparative Study of the Austrian and the American Constitution' (1942) 4 The Journal of Politics 183.

Kelsen, Hans, *The Guardian of the Constitution: Hans Kelsen and Carl Schmitt on the Limits of Constitutional Law* (Lars Vinx ed and tr, Cambridge University Press 2015).

Kocemba, Karolina and Stambulski, Michał, 'Populism, Non-State Actors and Right-Wing Legal Mobilization in Europe' (2024) 20 International Journal of Law in Context 297.

Koncewicz, Tomasz Tadeusz, 'Unconstitutional Capture and Constitutional Recapture. Of the Rule of Law, Separation of Powers and Judicial Promises' Jean Monnet Working Paper No 3/2017 <https://jeanmonnetprogram.org/paper/unconstitutional-capture-and-constitutional-recapture-of-the-rule-of-law-separation-of-powers-and-judicial-promises/>.

Koncewicz, Tomasz Tadeusz, 'When Legal Fundamentalism Meets Political Justice: The Case of Poland' (2022) 55 Israel Law Review 302.

Kopecký, Petr and Mudde, Cas, 'The Two Sides of Euroscepticism: Party Positions on European Integration in East Central Europe' (2002) 3 European Union Politics 297.

Kościerzyński, Jakub (ed), Justice under Pressure—Repressions as a Means of Attempting to Take Control over the Judiciary and the Prosecution in Poland. Years 2015–2019 (2020) <https://ruleoflaw.pl/wp-content/uploads/2020/02/Raport_EN.pdf>.

Kotwas, Marta and Kubik, Jan, 'Symbolic Thickening of Public Culture and the Rise of Right-Wing Populism in Poland' (2019) 33 East European Politics and Societies and Cultures 435.

Kovács, Kriszta and Scheppele, Kim Lane, 'The Fragility of an Independent Judiciary: Lessons from Hungary and Poland—and the European Union' (2018) 51 Communist and Post-Communist Studies 189.

Kowalik-Bańczyk, Krystyna, 'Should We Polish It Up? The Polish Constitutional Tribunal and the Idea of Supremacy of EU Law' (2005) 6 German Law Journal 1355.

Kowalik-Bańczyk, Krystyna, 'Report on Poland' in Giuseppe Martinico and Oreste Pollicino (eds), *The National Judicial Treatment of the ECHR and EU Laws* (Europa Law Publishing 2010) 327.

Kosař, David and Šipulová, Katarína, 'Comparative Court-Packing' (2023) 21 International Journal of Constitutional Law 80.

Krzyżanowska, Katarzyna, 'Legal Mobilisation within the Populist Supreme Court in Poland' (2024) 20 International Journal of Law in Context 324.

Kühn, Zdeněk, 'The Application of European Law in the New Member States: Several (Early) Predictions' (2005) 6 German Law Journal 563.

Kumm, Mattias and Ferres Comella, Victor, 'The Primacy Clause of the Constitutional Treaty and the Future of Constitutional Conflict in the European Union' (2005) 3 International Journal of Constitutional Law 473.

Laneri, Calogero, 'Il Pci di Enrico Berlinguer e le elezioni europee attraverso la lettura della stampa comunista (1979–1984)' (2017) 32 Diacronie [Online] 1.

Larsen, Signe Rehling, 'Varieties of Constitutionalism in the European Union' (2021) 84 Modern Law Review 477.

Legutko, Ryszard, 'What's Wrong with Liberalism?' (2008) 50 Modern Age 7.

Legutko, Ryszard, 'Why I Am Not a Liberal' (1 March 2020) <https://firstthings.com/why-i-am-not-a-liberal>.

Legutko, Ryszard, *The Demon in Democracy: Totalitarian Temptations in Free Societies* (Encounter Books 2016).

Lollini, Andrea and Palermo, Francesco, 'Comparative Law and the "Proceduralization" of Constitution-Building Processes' in Julia Raue and Patrick Sutter (eds), *Facets and Practices of State-Building* (Brill/Martinus Nijhoff, 2009) 301.

López Castillo, Antonio, *Constitución e integración. El fundamento constitucional de la integración supranacional europea en España y en la RFA* (Centro de Estudios Políticos y Constitucionales 1996).

López Castillo, Antonio, 'La Unión Europea «en constitución» y la Constitución estatal en (espera de) reformas. A propósito de la DTC 1/2004 de 13 diciembre' in Antonio López Castillo, Alejandro Saiz Arnaiz and Víctor Ferreres Comella (eds), *Constitución española y constitución europea* (Centro de Estudios Políticos y Constitucionales 2005) 13.

Lorimer, Marta, *Europe as Ideological Resource European Integration and Far Right Legitimation in France and Italy* (Oxford University Press 2024).

Luciani, Massimo, 'Il brusco risveglio. I controlimiti e la fine mancata della storia costituzionale' (2016) 6 Rivista AIC 1.

Lynch, Philip and Whitaker, Richard, 'Rivalry on the Right: The Conservatives, the UK Independence Party (UKIP) and the EU Issue' (2013) 8 British Politics 285.

Lynch, Philip, Whitaker, Richard, and Loomes, Gemma, 'The UK Independence Party: Understanding a Niche Party's Strategy, Candidates and Supporters' (2012) 65 Parliamentary Affairs 733.

MacCormick, Neil, 'The Maastricht-Urteil: Sovereignty Now' (1995) 1 European Law Journal 259.

MacCormick, Neil, 'Democracy, Subsidiarity, and Citizenship in the "European Commonwealth"' (1997) 16 Law and Philosophy 331.

MacMillan, Catherine, 'Reversing the Myth? Dystopian Narratives of the EU in UKIP and Front National Discourse' (2018) 26 Journal of Contemporary European Studies 117.

Magone, José M, 'Divided Europe? Euroscepticism in Central, Eastern and Southern Europe' in Kyriakos N Demetriou (ed), *The European Union in Crisis: Explorations in Representation and Democratic Legitimacy* (Springer International Publishing 2015) 33.

Mangas Martín, Araceli A, 'La secesión de territorios en un Estado miembro: efectos en el Derecho de la Unión Europea' (2013) 25 Revista de Derecho de la Unión Europea 47–68.

Martín y Pérez de Nanclares, José, 'Hacia Una Nueva Concepcion Del Articulo 93 de La Constitucion: Comentario a La Declaracion 1/2004 Del Tribunal Constitucional' (2005) 57 Revista Española de Derecho Internacional 799.

Martinico, Giuseppe, *Lo spirito polemico del diritto europeo: studio sulle ambizioni costituzionali dell'Unione* (Aracne 2011).

Martinico, Giuseppe, 'The "Polemical" Spirit of European Constitutional Law: On the Importance of Conflicts in EU Law' (2015) 16 German Law Journal 1343.

Martinico, Giuseppe, 'National Courts and Judicial Disobedience to the ECHR: A Comparative Overview' in Oddný Mjöll Arnardóttir and Antoine Buyse (eds), *Shifting Centres of Gravity in Human Rights Protection. Rethinking Relations between the ECHR, EU, and National Legal Orders* (Routledge 2016) 59.

Martinico, Giuseppe, 'Functional Disobedience, National Courts and the ECtHR' in András Sajó and Renáta Uitz (eds), *Critical Essays on Human Rights Criticism* (Eleven 2020) 247.

Martinico, Giuseppe, *Filtering Populist Claims to Fight Populism: The Italian Case in a Comparative Perspective* (Cambridge University Press 2021).
Martinico, Giuseppe, *The Tangled Complexity of the EU Constitutional Process: The Frustrating Knot of Europe* (Routledge 2022).
Martinico, Giuseppe, 'Populists in Power and Constitutional Counternarratives' (2024) 45 Cardozo Law Review 1527.
Marzi, Paolo, 'Euroscepticism: A Meta-Analysis' (2025) 60 Acta Politica 704 <https://doi.org/10.1057/s41269-024-00351-9>.
Mastroianni, Roberto, 'La Corte costituzionale si rivolge alla Corte di giustizia in tema di "controlimiti" costituzionali: è un vero dialogo?' (2017) 14 Federalismi.it. Rivista di diritto pubblico italiano, comparato, europeo 1.
McCrudden, Christopher, 'Transnational Culture Wars' (2015) 13 International Journal of Constitutional Law 434.
McHarg, Aileen, 'Navigating without Maps: Constitutional Silence and the Management of the Brexit Crisis' (2018) 16 International Journal of Constitutional Law 952.
Mirkine-Guetzévitch, Boris, *Les Nouvelles tendances du droit constitutionnel* (Giard 1931).
Mitchell, John DB, 'What Happened to the Constitution on 1st January 1973?' (1980) 11 Cambrian Law Review 6.
Modrzejewski, Arkadiusz, 'Catholic and Nationalist Populism in the Current Poland' (2017) 10 Perspective Politice 21.
Molina, Ignacio, 'Independentismo e integración europea (I): la imposible adhesión automática a la UE de un territorio secesionado' (2012) <https://www.files.ethz.ch/isn/155537/ARI80-Molina_UE_Escocia_Catalunya.pdf>.
Morgan, Edmund S, *Inventing the People: The Rise of Popular Sovereignty in England and America* (W W Norton & Company 1989).
Moroska-Bonkiewicz, Aleksandra, 'Political Responses to the Extreme Right in Poland. Motivations and Constraints for Collaboration in the Executive Arena' (2019) 47 Studia Polityczne 65.
Mortati, Costantino, *Lezioni sulle forme di governo* (CEDAM 1973).
Mudde, Cas, *Are Populists Friends or Foes of Constitutionalism?* (The Foundation for Law, Justice and Society 2013).
Mudde, Cas, 'Three Decades of Populist Radical Right Parties in Western Europe: So What?' (2013) 52 European Journal of Political Research 1.
Murphy, Cian, 'Report on the UK and Ireland' in Giuseppe Martinico and Oreste Pollicino (eds), *The National Judicial Treatment of the ECHR and EU Laws: A Comparative Constitutional Perspective* (Europa Law Publishing 2010) 479.
Nicotina, Alberto, 'Measuring the Impact of Populism in the Face of EU Multi-Level Governance: Politics and Constitutional Change' in Akritas Kaidatzis, Eleni Kalampakou, Ifigeneia Kamtsidou, Christos Papastylianos, and Costas Stratilatis (eds), *The People's Constitution: The Populist Transformation of Constitutional Law?* (Springer 2024) 205.
Ochoa Espejo, Paulina, 'Populism and the Idea of The People' in Cristóbal Rovira Kaltwasser, Paul A. Taggart, Paulina Ochoa Espejo, and Pierre Ostiguy (eds), *The Oxford Handbook of Populism* (Oxford University Press 2017) 607.
Öner, Selcen, 'Growing Fusion of Populism and Euroscepticism in Italy: A Comparative Analysis of the League and The Five Star Movement' (2020) 24 Tripodos 13.
Oomen, Barbara, 'Strengthening Constitutional Identity Where There Is None: The Case of the Netherlands' (2016) 77 Revue interdisciplinaire d'études juridiques 235.

Pajno, Alessandro, 'Il rispetto dei vincoli derivanti dall'ordinamento comunitario come limite alla potestà legislativa nel nuovo Titolo V della Costituzione' (2003) 23 Le Istituzioni del federalismo 814.

Palm, Anja and Barana, Luca, 'Italy's Migration Policy: A Self-Defeating Approach Spells Marginalisation in Europe' (Istituto Affari Internazionali 2019) <https://www.iai.it/en/pubblicazioni/italys-migration-policy-self-defeating-approach-spells-marginalisation-europe>.

Pasquinucci, Daniele, 'From Narrative to Counter-Narrative: The European Constraint and the Rise of Italian Populist Euroscepticism' (2020) 30 Journal of Contemporary European Studies 39.

Pasquinucci, Daniele, *Il frutto avvelenato. Il vincolo europeo e la critica all'Europa* (Mondadori 2022).

Paterniti, Francesco, 'La riforma dell'art. 117, 1° co. della Costituzione e le nuove prospettive dei rapporti tra ordinamento giuridico nazionale e Unione Europea' (2004) 49 Giurisprudenza costituzionale 2101.

Peers, Steve, 'Article 50 TEU: The Uses and Abuses of the Process of Withdrawing from the EU' (8 December 2014) <http://eulawanalysis.blogspot.com/2014/12/article-50-teu-uses-and-abuses-of.html>.

Peers, Steve, 'The End—or a New Beginning? The EU/UK Withdrawal Agreement' (2020) 39 Yearbook of European Law 122.

Pech, Laurent and Scheppele, Kim Lane, 'Illiberalism within: Rule of Law Backsliding in the EU' (2017) 19 Cambridge Yearbook of European Legal Studies 3.

Penasa, Simone, 'The Italian Way to Migration: Was It "True" Populism? Populist Policies as Constitutional Antigens' in Giacomo Delledonne, Giuseppe Martinico, Matteo Monti, and Fabio Pacini (eds), *Italian Populism and Constitutional Law. Strategies, Conflicts and Dilemmas* (Palgrave 2020) 255.

Pérez Tremps, Pablo, *Constitución Española y Comunidad Europea* (Civitas 1993).

Peters, Anne, 'Compensatory Constitutionalism: The Function and Potential of Fundamental International Norms and Structures' (2006) 19 Leiden Journal of International Law 579.

Pető, Andrea, 'Current Comment: The Illiberal Academic Authority. An Oxymoron?' (2021) 44 Berichte zur Wissenschaftsgeschichte 461.

Pierdominici, Leonardo, Constitutional Change through Euro Crisis Law: Italy (2014) European University Institute <https://eurocrisislaw.eui.eu/wp-content/uploads/sites/55/2019/05/Italy.pdf>.

Pierdominici, Leonardo, 'Teoria e ideologia del vincolo esterno: è predicabile un suo significato costituzionale?' in Giuseppe Martinico and Leonardo Pierdominici (eds), *Miserie del sovranismo giuridico. Il valore aggiunto del costituzionalismo europeo* (Castelvecchi 2023) 109.

Pinelli, Cesare, 'I limiti generali alla potestà legislativa statale e regionale e i rapporti con l'ordinamento comunitario' (2001) 125 Foro italiano 194.

Pinelli, Cesare, 'The Formation of a Constitutional Tradition in Continental Europe since World War II' (2016) 22 European Public Law 257.

Pirro, Andrea LP and van Kessel, Stijn, 'United in Opposition? The Populist Radical Right's EU-Pessimism in Times of Crisis' (2017) 4 Journal of European Integration 405.

Poiares Maduro, Miguel, 'Interpreting European Law: Judicial Adjudication in a Context of Constitutional Pluralism' (2007) 1 European Journal of Legal Studies 137.

Poiares Maduro, Miguel, 'Passion and Reason in European Integration' (2010) <https://papers.ssrn.com/sol3/papers.cfm?abstract_id=1709950>.

Poli, Eleonora and Valentiner, Mark, 'From Albertini to Anti-Europeanism: Shades of Euroscepticism in Italy' (2014) 54 L'Europe en Formation Revue d'études sur la construction européenne et le fédéralisme 66.
Pollicino, Oreste, L'allargamento ad est dell'Europa e rapporti tra Corti costituzionali e Corti europee. *Verso una teoria generale dell'impatto interordinamentale del diritto sovranazionale?* (Giuffrè 2010).
Ragin, Charles, *The Comparative Method. Moving Beyond Qualitative and Quantitative Strategies* (University of California Press 1987).
Ramiro, Luis and Gomez, Raul, 'Radical-Left Populism during the Great Recession: Podemos and Its Competition with the Established Radical Left' (2017) 65 Political Studies 108.
Rawls, John, *Political Liberalism* (Columbia University Press 2005).
Real-Dato, José and Sojka, Aleksandra, 'The Rise of (Faulty) Euroscepticism? The Impact of a Decade of Crises in Spain'(2024) 29 South European Society and Politics 457.
Reform UK, 'Our Contract with You' (2024).
Remotti, Francesco, *Contro l'identità* (Laterza 1996).
Revelli, Marco, *Populismo 2.0* (Einaudi 2017).
Ridaura Martinez, Maria Josefa, 'La Reforma Del Articulo 135 de La Constitución Española: ¿Pueden Los Mercados Quebrar El Consenso Constitucional?' (2012) 29 Teoría y Realidad Constitucional 237.
Rihoux, Benoît and De Meur, Gisèle, 'Crisp-Set Qualitative Comparative Analysis (csQCA)' in Benoît Rihoux and Charles Ragin (eds), *Configurational Comparative Methods* (Sage 2009) 59.
Rihoux, Benoît and Ragin, Charles C. (eds), *Configurational Comparative Methods. Qualitative Comparative Analysis (QCA) and Related Techniques* (Sage 2009) xviii.
Rizzo, Marco, *Il golpe europeo. I comunisti contro l'Unione* (Baldini Castoldi Dalai 2012).
Rodin, Siniša, 'Discourse and Authority in European and Post-Communist Legal Culture' (2008) 1 Croatian Yearbook of European Law and Policy 1.
Rodríguez Iglesias, Gil Carlos, 'No Existe Contradicción Entre La Constitución Española y La Constitución Europea: La Declaración Del Tribunal Constitucional' (2005) 9 Revista de Derecho Comunitario Europeo 5.
Rosenfeld, Michel, *The Identity of the Constitutional Subject: Selfhood, Citizenship, Culture, and Community* (Routledge 1994).
Ross, Andrew S and Bhatia, Aditi, '"Ruled Britannia": Metaphorical Construction of the EU as Enemy in UKIP Campaign Posters' (2021) 26 The International Journal of Press/Politics 188.
Roux, Christophe and Verzichelli, Luca, 'Italy: Still a Pro-European, but Not a Fully Europeanised Elite?' (2010) 15 South European Society and Politics 11.
Roznai, Yaniv, 'Unconstitutional Constitutional Amendments—The Migration and Success of a Constitutional Idea' (2013) 61 The American Journal of Comparative Law 657.
Roznai, Yaniv, 'Negotiating the Eternal: The Paradox of Entrenching Secularism in Constitutions' (2017) 86 Michigan State Law Review 253.
Roznai, Yaniv, *Unconstitutional Constitutional Amendments. The Limits of Amendment Powers* (Oxford University Press 2019).
Roznai, Yaniv and Brandes, Tamar Hostovsky, 'Democratic Erosion, Populist Constitutionalism, and the Unconstitutional Constitutional Amendments Doctrine' (2020) 14 Law & Ethics of Human Rights 19.
Rubinelli, Lucia, *Constituent Power. A History* (Oxford University Press 2020).

Ruggeri, Antonio, 'Dimensione europea della tutela dei diritti fondamentali e tecniche interpretative' (2009) 6 Federalismi.it. Rivista di diritto pubblico italiano, comunitario e comparato 1.

Ruiz Almendral, Violeta, 'Estabilidad Presupuestaria y Reforma Constitucional' (2012) 41 Revista Española de Derecho Europeo 33.

Rylatt, Jake, 'The Irrevocability of an Article 50 Notification: Lex Specialis and the Irrelevance of the Purported Customary Right to Unilaterally Revoke' (27 July 2016) <https://ukconstitutionallaw.org/2016/07/27/jake-rylatt-the-irrevocability-of-an-article-50-notification-lex-specialis-and-the-irrelevance-of-the-purported-customary-right-to-unilaterally-revoke/>.

Sadurski, Wojciech, *Poland's Constitutional Breakdown* (Oxford University Press 2019).

Sadurski, Wojciech, 'Polish Constitutional Tribunal Under PiS: From an Activist Court, to a Paralysed Tribunal, to a Governmental Enabler' (2019) 11 Hague Journal on the Rule of Law 63.

Saiz Arnaiz, Alejandro, *La apertura constitucional al derecho internacional y europeo de los derechos humanos. El artículo 10.2 de la Constitución Española* (Centro de Estudios Políticos y Constitucionales 1999).

Saiz Arnaiz, Alejandro, 'De primacía, supremacía y derechos fundamentales en la Europa integrada: la Declaración del Tribunal Constitucional de 13 diciembre de 2004 y el Tratado por el que establece una Constitución para Europa' in Antonio López Castillo, Alejandro Saiz Arnaiz and Víctor Ferreres Comella (eds), *Constitución española y constitución europea* (Centro de Estudios Políticos y Constitucionales 2005) 51.

Sajó, András, 'Emotions in Constitutional Design' (2010) 8 International Journal of Constitutional Law 354.

Sajó, András and Uitz, Renáta, *The Constitution of Freedom: An Introduction to Legal Constitutionalism* (Oxford University Press 2017).

Sajó, András, Uitz, Renata, and Holmes, Stephen (eds), *The Routledge Handbook of Illiberalism* (Routledge 2022).

Sales, Philip and Ekins, Richard, 'Rights-Consistent Interpretation and the Human Rights Act 1998' (2011) 127 Law Quarterly Review 217.

Sandro, Paolo, *The Making of Constitutional Democracy. From Creation to Application of Law* (Hart Publishing 2022).

Sarmiento, Daniel, 'Adults in the (Deliberation) Room. A comment on M.A.S.' (2018) 37 Quaderni costituzionali 228.

Sartori, Giovanni, 'Constitutionalism: A Preliminary Discussion' (1962) 56 The American Political Science Review 853.

Sassoon, Donald, 'Eurocommunism, the Labour Party and the EEC' (1979) 50 The Political Quarterly 86.

Sawicki, Jan, 'La collisione insanabile tra diritto europeo primario e diritto costituzionale interno come prodotto della manomissione ermeneutica di quest'ultimo' (2021) 11 DPCE Online 3601.

Scheppele, Kim Lane, 'Autocratic Legalism' (2018) 85 The University of Chicago Law Review 545.

Scheppele, Kim Lane, 'Blinded by Legality' (23 December 2024) <https://verfassungsblog.de/blinded-by-legality/>.

Scheppele, Kim Lane, 'The Opportunism of Populists and the Defense of Constitutional Liberalism' (2019) 20 German Law Journal 314.

Scheppele, Kim Lane, 'The Treaties without a Guardian: The European Commission and the Rule of Law' (2023) 29 Columbia Journal of European Law 93.

Schill, Stephan W and Bogdandy, Armin von, 'Overcoming Absolute Primacy: Respect for National Identity under the Lisbon Treaty' (2011) 48 Common Market Law Review 1417.

Schmitt, Carl, *Constitutional Theory* (Duke University Press 2008).

Schneider, Carsten Q and Wagemann, Claudius, *Set-Theoretic Methods for the Social Sciences. A Guide to Qualitative Comparative Analysis* (Cambridge University Press 2013) 24.

Scholtes, Julian, *The Abuse of Constitutional Identity in the European Union* (Oxford University Press 2023).

Schriewer, Berenike, *Zur Theorie der internationalen Offenheit und der Völkerrechtsfreundlichkeit einer Rechtsordnung und ihrer Erprobung am Beispiel der EU-Rechtsordnung* (Duncker & Humblot 2017).

Schultz, Andrzej and Sawicki, Jakub, 'Polish(ing) Broken Tribunal. The New Polish Coalition Government's Package to Restore the Constitutional Tribunal—A Wobbly Constitutional Reset?' (22 March 2024) <https://verfassungsblog.de/polishing-broken-tribunal/>.

Schutte, Camilo B, 'Spain Tribunal Constitucional on the European Constitution. Declaration of 13 December 2004' (2005) 1 European Constitutional Law Review 281.

Schütze, Robert, 'Constitutionalism(s)' in Roger Masterman and Robert Schütze (eds), *Cambridge Companion to Comparative Constitutional Law* (Cambridge University Press 2019) 40.

Schütze, Robert, '"Integration-through-Law": Grand Theory, Revisionist History' (2025) 4 European Law Open 162.

Sieyès, Emmanuel-Joseph, Qu'est-ce que le Tiers état? (1789) <http://www.leboucher.com/pdf/sieyes/tiers.pdf>.

Sitter, Nick, 'The Politics of Opposition and European Integration in Scandinavia: Is Euro-Scepticism a Government-Opposition Dynamic?' (2001) 24 West European Politics 22.

Solanes Mullor, Joan and Torres Pérez, Aida, 'The Constitution of Spain: The Challenges for the Constitutional Order under European and Global Governance' in Anneli Albi and Samo Bardutzky (eds), *National Constitutions in European and Global Governance: Democracy, Rights, the Rule of Law: National Reports* (TMC Asser Press 2019) 547.

Somma, Alessandro, 'Un sovranismo democratico per un nuovo europeismo' (2018) MicroMega <https://www.micromega.net/>.

Somma, Alessandro, 'Europa, sovranità e ordine economico nel prisma delle teorie federaliste' (2020) 10 DPCE online 427.

Somma, Alessandro, *Quando l'Europa tradì sé stessa. E come continua a tradirsi nonostante la pandemia* (Laterza 2021).

Sorgonà, Gregorio, 'The Italian Right-Wing and the European Integration Process: The Case of the Italian Social Movement' (2022) 27 Journal of Modern Italian Studies 383.

Spiegeleire, Stephan De, Skinner, Clarissa, and Sweijs, Tim, 'The Rise of Populist Sovereignism: What It Is, Where It Comes from and What It Means for International Security and Defense' (The Hague Centre for Strategic Studies 2017) ii.

Spieker, Luke Dimitrios, *EU Values before the Court of Justice: Foundations, Potential, Risks* (Oxford 2023).

Stambulski, Michał, 'Schrödinger's Judges. Challenges to the Rule of Law Restoration in Poland' (19 December 2024) <https://verfassungsblog.de/schrodingers-judges/>.

Stein, Eric, 'International Law in Internal Law: Toward Internationalization of Central-Eastern European Constitutions?' (1994) 88 American Journal of International Law 427.

Stoeckl, Kristina, 'Traditional Values, Family, Homeschooling: The Role of Russia and the Russian Orthodox Church in Transnational Moral Conservative Networks and Their Efforts at Reshaping Human Rights' (2023) 21 International Journal of Constitutional Law 224.

Stolfi, Melissa, 'The "Revival" of PiS: The Transformation of Campaign Strategies from the Kaczyński Twins to Andrzej Duda' (2024) 10 Journal of Liberty and International Affairs 14.

Stone Sweet, Alec, 'Constitutional Courts and Parliamentary Democracy' (2002) 25 West European Politics 77.

Stone Sweet, Alec, 'Why Europe Rejected American Judicial Review: And Why It May Not Matter' (2003) 101 Michigan Law Review 2744.

Streeten, Charles, 'Putting the Toothpaste Back in the Tube: Can an Article 50 Notification Be Revoked?' (13 July 2016) <https://ukconstitutionallaw.org/2016/07/13/charles-streeten-putting-the-toothpaste-back-in-the-tube-can-an-article-50-notification-be-revoked/>.

Styczyńska, Natasza, 'Contesting European Union from the "Heart of Europe": A Peculiar Case of Polish Populist Euroscepticism after 2015' (2023) 0 Political Studies Review 1.

Styczyńska, Natasza and Meijer, Jan, 'Populist Euroscepticism in Poland: Towards a Framework for Analysis' in Haris Dajč and Natasza Styczyńska (eds), *Faces of Populism in Central and South-Eastern Europe* (Jagiellonian University Press 2023) 177.

Surkov, Vladislav I, 'Nationalization of the Future: Paragraphs pro Sovereign Democracy' (2009) 47 Russian Studies in Philosophy 8.

Suteu, Silvia, *Eternity Clauses in Democratic Constitutionalism* (Oxford University Press 2021).

Szelewa, Dorota, 'Populism, Religion and Catholic Civil Society in Poland: The Case of Primary Education' (2021) 20 Social Policy and Society 310.

Taggart, Paul, 'A Touchstone of Dissent: Euroscepticism in Contemporary Western European Party Systems' (1998) 33 European Journal of Political Research 363.

Taggart, Paul and Pirro, Andrea LP, 'European Populism before the Pandemic: Ideology, Euroscepticism, Electoral Performance, and Government Participation of 63 Parties in 30 Countries' (2021) 51 Italian Political Science Review/Rivista Italiana di Scienza Politica 281.

Taggart, Paul and Szczerbiak, Aleks, 'Contemporary Euroscepticism in the Party Systems of the European Union Candidate States of Central and Eastern Europe' (2004) 43 European Journal of Political Research 1.

Taggart, Paul and Szczerbiak, Aleks, 'The Party Politics of Euroscepticism in EU Member and Candidate States' Sussex European Institute Working Paper 51 (2002).

Taggart, Paul and Szczerbiak, Aleks, 'Theorising Party-Based Euroscepticism: Problems of Definition, Measurement and Causality' (2023) SEI Working Paper No 69 <https://aei.pitt.edu/6562/>.

Tarchi, Marco and Carioti, Antonio, *Le tre età della fiamma* (Solferino 2024).

Theiler, Tobias, 'The Origins of Euroscepticism in German-Speaking Switzerland' (2004) 43 European Journal of Political Research 635.

Thiele, Alexander, 'Whoever Equates Karlsruhe to Warsaw Is Wildly Mistaken' (10 October 2021) <https://verfassungsblog.de/whoever-equals-karlsruhe-to-warsaw-is-wildly-mistaken/>.

Thornhill, Chris, 'Constitutionalism and Populism: National Political Integration and Global Legal Integration' (2020) 12 International Theory 1.

Tomuschat, Christian, 'Staatsrechtliche Entscheidung für die internationale Offenheit' in Josef Isensee and Paul Kirchhof (eds), *Handbuch des Staatsrechts*, vol XI (CF Müller 2013) 226.

Tonge, Jonathan, Wilks-Heeg, Stuart, and Thompson, Louise, 'Conclusion: The BBC and the Election: Boris, Brexit and Corbyn' (2020) 73 Parliamentary Affairs 288.

Torres Pérez, Aida, 'Melloni in Three Acts: From Dialogue to Monologue' (2014) 10(2) European Constitutional Law Review 308.

Tournier-Sol, Karine, 'From UKIP to the Brexit Party: The Politicization of European Integration and Disruptive Impact on National and European Arenas' (2021) 29 Journal of Contemporary European Studies 380.

Trindade, Francis A, 'Parliamentary Sovereignty and the Primacy of European Community Law' (1972) 35 Modern Law Review 375.

Tushnet, Mark, 'Alternative Forms of Judicial Review' (2003) 101 Michigan Law Review 2781.

Tyrrell, Helene and Young, Alison, 'Written Evidence from Dr Hélène Tyrrell and Professor Alison Young (HRR0001)' (2022) UK Parliament, Joint Committee on Human Rights, Human Rights Act Reform Inquiry, paras 34–36 <https://committees.parliament.uk/writtenevidence/106528/pdf/>.

Urbinati, Nadia, 'Democracy and Populism' (1998) 5 Constellations 110.

Valditara, Giuseppe, Sovranismo. *Una speranza per la democrazia* (Book Time 2017).

Vampa, Davide, *Brothers of Italy. A New Populist Wave in an Unstable Party System* (Springer 2023).

Vanhala, Lisa, *Making Rights a Reality? Disability Rights Activists and Legal Mobilization* (Cambridge University Press 2010).

Varsori, Antonio, *La Cenerentola d'Europa? L'Italia e l'integrazione europea dal 1947 ad oggi* (Rubbettino 2010) 313.

Vasilopoulou, Sofia, 'Varieties of Euroscepticism: The Case of the European Extreme Right' (2009) 5 Journal of Contemporary European Research 3.

Vasilopoulou, Sofia, 'Continuity and Change in the Study of Euroscepticism: Plus Ça Change?' (2013) 51 Journal of Common Market Studies 153.

Vasilopoulou, Sofia, 'The Party Politics of Euroscepticism in Times of Crisis: The Case of Greece' (2018) 38 Politics 311.

Vázquez García, Rafael, Delgado Fernández, Santiago, and Jerez Mir, Miguel, 'Spanish Political Parties and the European Union: Analysis of Euromanifestos (1987–2004)' (2010) 11 Perspectives on European Politics and Society 201.

Verdugo, Sergio, 'Is It Time to Abandon the Theory of Constituent Power?' (2023) 21 International Journal of Constitutional Law 14.

Vidal Prado, Carlos, *El impacto del nuevo derecho europeo en los Tribunales Constitucionales* (Editorial Colex 2004).

Volkens, Andrea, Burst, Tobias, Krause, Werner, Lehmann, Pola, Matthieß, Theres, Regel, Sven, Weßels, Bernhard, and Zehnter, Lisa, 'The Manifesto Data Collection. Manifesto Project (MRG/CMP/MARPOR). Version 2021a' (2021) Wissenschaftszentrum Berlin Für Sozialforschung (WZB) <https://doi.org/10.25522/manifesto.mpds.2021a>.

Voßkuhle, Andreas, 'Multilevel Cooperation of the European Constitutional Courts: Der Europäische Verfassungsgerichtsverbund' (2010) 6 European Constitutional Law Review 175.

Wade, Henry WR, 'Sovereignty and the European Communities' (1972) 88 Law Quarterly Review 1.

Wade, Henry WR, 'Sovereignty: Revolution or Evolution?' (1996) 112 Law Quarterly Review 568.

Wadowski, Dariusz, 'Religion and Religiosity in Contemporary Poland' (2020) 1 Central European Journal for Contemporary Religion 35.

Walker, Neil, 'Illiberalism and National Sovereignty' in András Sajó, Renata Uitz, and Stephen Holmes (eds), *The Routledge Handbook of Illiberalism* (Routledge 2022) 250.

Wellings, Ben, 'Losing the Peace: Euroscepticism and the Foundations of Contemporary English Nationalism' (2010) 16 Nations and Nationalism 488.

Wendel, Mattias, 'Lisbon Before the Courts: Comparative Perspectives' (2011) 7 European Constitutional Law Review 96.

Wendel, Mattias, 'The Fog of Identity and Judicial Contestation: Preventive and Defensive Constitutional Identity Review in Germany' (2021) 27 European Public Law 474.

Wendel, Mattias, 'Constructive Misunderstandings—How the PSPP Conflict was Eventually Settled and How it Reflects Constitutional Pluralism' in Matej Avbelj (ed), *The Future of EU Constitutionalism* (Hart 2023) 53.

Wilkinson, Michael, 'Authoritarian Liberalism as Authoritarian Constitutionalism' in Helena Alviar Garcia and Günter Frankenberg (eds), *Authoritarian Constitutionalism: Comparative Analysis and Critique* (Edward Elgar 2019) 317.

Williams, Robert F and Tarr, G Alan, 'Subnational Constitutional Space: A View from the States, Provinces, Regions, Lander, and Cantons' in G Alan Tarr, Robert F Williams, and Joseph Marko (eds), *Federalism, Subnational Constitutions, and Minority Rights* (Praeger 2004) 3.

Wind, Marlene, 'The Backlash to European Constitutionalism: Why We Should Not Embrace the Identitarian Counter Wave' (2021) 2(3) Revue Européenne du Droit 48.

Wolff, Elisabetta Cassina, 'CasaPound Italia: "Back to Believing. The Struggle Continues"' (2019) 8 Fascism 61.

Young, Alison, *Unchecked Power?* (Bristol University Press 2024).

Zemans, Frances Kahn, 'Legal Mobilization: The Neglected Role of the Law in the Political System' (1983) 77 American Political Science Review 690.

Ziółkothiel, Michał, 'Heavy Clouds, No Rain. Unmasking the Polish Constitutional Tribunal Challenging the Primacy of the EU Law and the Court of Justice in case K 3/212' (2024) 16 Krytyka Prawa. Niezależne Studia nad Prawem 421.

Ziółkowski, Michał and Grabowska-Moroz, Barbara, 'Enforcement of EU Values and the Tyranny of National Identity—Polish Examples and Excuses' (26 November 2019) <https://verfassungsblog.de/enforcement-of-eu-values-and-the-tyranny-of-national-identity-polish-examples-and-excuses/>.

Zoll, Fryderyk, Południak-Gierz, Katarzyna, and Bańczyk, Wojciech, 'Primacy of EU Law and Jurisprudence of Polish Constitutional Tribunal' Policy Department for Citizens' Rights and Constitutional Affairs Directorate-General for Internal Policies PE 732.475 (2022) <https://www.europarl.europa.eu/RegData/etudes/STUD/2022/732475/IPOL_STU(2022)732475_EN.pdf>.

Index

For the benefit of digital users, indexed terms that span two pages (e.g., 52–53) may, on occasion, appear on only one of those pages.

The manufacturer's authorised representative in the EU for product safety is Oxford University Press España S.A. of el Parque Empresarial San Fernando de Henares, Avenida de Castilla, 2 – 28830 Madrid (www.oup.es/en or product.safety@oup.com). OUP España S.A. also acts as importer into Spain of products made by the manufacturer.

www.ingramcontent.com/pod-product-compliance
Ingram Content Group UK Ltd.
Pitfield, Milton Keynes, MK11 3LW, UK
UKHW021459220926
475862UK00003B/34
9780198959175